MW00709888

Souvenir –

29. December 1914

May God bless you
dear Irene and be
with you through
all the coming years

I.M. Bertrand

Cabra

ST. MARY'S DOMINICAN CONVENT, CABRA, DUBLIN.

THE
Dominican Manual:

A SELECTION
OF
PRAYERS AND DEVOTIONS,

AUTHORISED BY THE CHURCH, AND ENRICHED WITH
NUMEROUS INDULGENCES.

Pie Pater Dominice,
Tuorum memor operum;
Sta coram summo Judice,
Pro **tuo** cœtu pauperum.

Dublín :
BROWNE AND NOLAN, LTD., NASSAU STREET.

ALL RIGHTS RESERVED.

Nihil Obstat :

THOMAS O'DONNELL,

Censor Theol. Deput.

Imprimatur :

✠ GULIELMUS,

Archiep. Dublinen.,

Hiberniæ Primas.

Die 16ᵃ Junii, 1913.

CONTENTS.

———

CONTENTS.

CONTENTS.

FEASTS OF OBLIGATION

IN IRELAND.

All Sundays in the year.
Nativity and Circumcision of our Lord.
Epiphany and Ascension of our Lord.

Assumption of B.V.M.
Feast of St. Patrick.
Feast of SS. Peter and Paul.
Solemnity of All Saints.

FASTING DAYS ON ONE MEAL.

Wednesdays and Fridays in Advent.
Quarter Tense or Ember Days.
Days of Lent, Sundays excepted.

Vigils of Nativity of our Lord and of Pentecost.
Vigil of SS. Peter and Paul.
Vigil of Assumption of B.V.M.
Vigil of All Saints.

DAYS OF ABSTINENCE FROM FLESH MEAT.

All Fridays throughout the year, except the Friday on which in any year Christmas Day may fall. The whole time of Lent, unless otherwise allowed by the Bishop.

The time for complying with the Paschal Precept in Ireland begins on Ash Wednesday and ends on Ascension Day in some dioceses; in others it is extended to the Octave Day of the Feast of SS. Peter and Paul, July 6th.

INDULGENCES.

By an Indulgence is meant a relaxation or remission of the temporal punishment due to sins which are already forgiven, both as to their guilt and the eternal punishment they deserved. Some Indulgences are called *Plenary*; others are called *Partial*. A *Plenary* Indulgence is so called because when its full effect is gained, it remits the *entire* of the debt of temporal punishment due on account of sin. A *Partial* Indulgence is so called, because by it a penitent is released, in part only, from the debt of temporal punishment. For example, a Partial Indulgence of ten years remits as much of the temporal punishment due to sin as would have been remitted by ten years of the Canonical Penances formerly imposed on penitents.

To Indulgences of a certain number of years, the Holy Father frequently adds a similar number of *Quarantines*. These Quarantines have reference to the Lental Fast. Thus, an Indulgence of seven years and as many Quarantines means the remission of as much temporal punishment as would be remitted by the performance of seven years of Canonical Penances, joined to the special austerities of seven Lents observed in all their strictness.

A *Jubilee* is a Plenary Indulgence granted in the most solemn manner, and accompanied with special privileges.

In order to gain an Indulgence, whether Plenary or Partial, it is necessary :—

1. To perform faithfully all the works prescribed;

2. To have the intention of gaining the Indulgence;

3. To be in the state of grace, at least when the last of the prescribed works is performed, for it is then that the fruit of the Indulgence is applied.

For a Plenary Indulgence it is necessary besides, to be free from wilful venial sin, and all affection to venial sin.

Confession and Communion, as also some prayers for the intention of the Pope, are usually among the works prescribed for the gaining of a Plenary Indulgence. As to Confession—those who are in the habit of going to Confession *at least once a week*, may gain all the Plenary Indulgences occurring in the interval between one Confession and another, without being obliged to confess each time specially for each Indulgence.

By one Communion several Indulgences occurring on the same day, for each of which Communion may be prescribed, can be gained. The other works, however, which are enjoined must be performed as often as there are Indulgences to be gained.

When no *particular* prayers are prescribed for the Pope's intention, then one is free to say any prayers for that purpose, as for instance, the Our Father and Hail Mary five times. These prayers should be said in the Church, if this condition be required.

A Plenary Indulgence may be gained by the faithful of Ireland on the first Sunday of each month, and

On the Feasts of
{
Circumcision and Epiphany of our Lord;
Purification, of B. V. M., or on the following Sunday
St. Patrick, or on any of the seven following days;
Annunciation and Assumption of B. V. M.;
Resurrection and Ascension of our Lord;
Pentecost;
Corpus Christi;
Trinity Sunday, or on any of the seven following days;
SS. Peter and Paul, or on any day within the Octave;
Immaculate Conception and Nativity of B. V. M., or on Sunday after;
All Saints;
Nativity of Our Lord;
Patron Saint of the Church or Oratory.
}

CALENDAR.

January.

1	CIRCUMCISION OF OUR LORD. [Limerick.
2	St. Munchin. Bp., Patron of
3	St. Fintan. C.
4	St. Fiadhnat. V.
5	St. Telesphorus. P. M.
6	EPIPHANY OF OUR LORD
7	St. Donnan of Inis-Aingin, C
8	St. Albert. Bp., Patron of Cashel.
9	St. Finan of Lindisfarne.
10	B. Gundisalvus. O.P.
11	St. Suibhne. Ab.
12	St. Cummian of Bobbio. Bp.
13	St. Ailell. Bp. of Armagh
14	St. Hilary, Bp.
15	St. Ita, V.
16	St. Fursey, Ab. [V., O.P. B. Stephana de Quinzanis.
17	St. Anthony, Ab.
18	Chair of St. Peter at Rome.
19	B. Andrew de Pescheria, O.P.
20	St. Fechin. Ab.
21	St. Agnes, V. M. [MM.
22	SS. Vincent and Anastasius.
23	The Espousal of B.V.M. St. Raymund de Pennafort, O.P.
24	B. Marcolinus of Forli, O.P.
25	Conversion of St. Paul
26	B. Margaret of Hungary, V., O.P. [of the Church
27	St. John Chrysostom, Doctor
28	Translation of the body of St. Thomas Aquinas, O.P.
29	St. Francis de Sales, Doctor of the Church.
30	St. Martina, V. M. [Ferns.
31	St. Aidan, Bp., Patron of

Sunday within the Oct. of Epiphany—*The finding of our Lord in the Temple.*
Second Sunday after Epiphany—Feast of the Most Holy Name of Jesus.

February.

1	St. Brigid, V., Patroness of Ireland.
2	Purification B.V.M.
3	St. Colman, Bp., Patron of Kilmacduagh.
4	St. Cuanna, Ab.
5	St. Agatha, V. M.
6	St. Mel, Bp., Patron of Ardagh.
7	St. Aedh, Bp. of Sletty.
8	St. John of Matha, C.
9	B. Bernard Scammacca, C.
10	St. Scholastica, V.
11	St. Theodora, Empress.
12	B. Reginald of Orleans, O.P.
13	St. Catherine de Ricci. V., O.P.
14	B. Nicholas de Palea, C., O.P.
15	B. Jordan of Saxony. C., O.P
16	St. Taucho, Bp. of Verdan in Saxony.
17	St. Fintan, Ab. of Clonenagh.
18	B. Laurence of Ripafratta. O.P.
19	B. Alvarez of Cordova, O.P.
20	St. Colga the Wise, C.
21	B. Aimo Taparellus, O.P.
22	The Chair of St. Peter at Antioch.
23	St. Fiugar, M. in Cornwall
24	St. Mathias, Ap.
25	B. Constantius a Fabriano, O.P.
26	St. Maonna, Bp.
27	St. Comidhan of Glenussen.
28	B. Vilana de Bottis, Widow. O.P.

March.

1 B. Christopher. O.P.
2 B. Henry Suso. O.P.
3 St. Celechrist. Bp.
4 St. Cassimir of Poland.
5 St. Kieran. Bp., Patron of Ossory.
6 B. Jordan of Pisa. O.P.
7 St. Thomas Aquinas, O.P., Doctor of the Church.
8 St. Cathaldus. Bp.
9 St. Frances of Rome. W.
10 B. Peter de Jeremia, O.P.
11 St. Aengus, Ab.
12 St. Gregory the Great. P., and Doctor of the Church.
13 St. Gerald. Bp. of Mayo.
14 St. Talmach. C.
15 The Three Sons of Nessan.
16 St. Finan. the Leper.
17 ST. PATRICK. Bp., Apostle of Ireland.
18 St. Gabriel. Archangel. B. Sibbylina, V., O.P.
19 St. Joseph, Spouse of the B.V.M.
20 St. Cuthbert. Bp.
21 St. Benedict, Ab. St. Enda, Ab.
22 B. Ambrose Sansedonius, O.P.
23 St. Boedan, C.
24 St. Macartan. Bp., Patron of Clogher.
25 THE ANNUNCIATION of the B. V. M.
26 St. Sinchell. Bp.
27 St. Rupert. Bp., Apostle o. Bavaria.
28 St. Conall. Bp.
29 SS. Ethnea & Sodelbhia, VV.
30 St. Mochua, Ab.
31 St. Machabeus, Ab. of Armagh.

April.

1 St. Gobban, C.
2 St. Francis de Paula. C.
3 The S. Stigmias of St. Catherine of Sienna, V., O.P.
4 St. Tighernach, Bp. of Clones.
5 St. Vincent Ferrer. O.P. St. Patrick enters on his Apostolate in Ireland.
6 St. Celsus. Bishop of Armagh.
7 St. Fiuan Cam. C.
8 St. Cennfaeladh. Ab.
9 B. Anthony Pavonius. O.P.
10 B. Anthony Nevrot. O.P.
11 St. Leo the Great. P.
12 St. Conda. Ab.
13 B. Margaret de Castelio. O.P.
14 B. Peter Gonzales. O.P.
15 St. Ruadhan. Ab.
16 St. Tetghal. C.
17 B. Clara Gambacurta. O.P.
18 St. Laserian. Bp., Patron of Leighlin.
19 St. Cillen. C.
20 St. Agnes of Monte Pulciano. V. O.P.
21 B. Bartholemew de Cerveriis. M., O.P.
22 St. Cuillean. Bp.
23 St. George. M.
24 St. Diarmait. Bp.
25 St. Mark. Evangelist.
26 St. Conain. C. BB. Dominic & Gregory. O.P.
27 St. Asicus. Bp. Patron of Elphin.
28 St. Cronan, Bp., Patron of Roscrea.
29 St. Peter, M., O.P.
30 St. Catherine of Sienna. V., O.P.

Third Sunday after Easter—Feast of the Patronage of St. Joseph.

May.

1 SS. Philip and James, Ap.
2 St. Athanasius. Bp.
3 The Finding of the Holy Cross.
   St. Conlaeth, Bp., Patron of Kildare.
4 St. Monica, Widow.
5 *St. Pius V., Pope, O.P.*
6 St. John at the Latin Gate.
7 St. Lassar, V.
8 St. Odhran. Bp.
9 St. Gregory, Nazianzen. Bp.
10 *St. Antoninus, Bp., O.P.*
11 St. Criotan. C.
12 *B. Jane of Portugal, O.P*
13 *B. Albert of Bergamo. O.P.*
14 *B. Giles of Portugal. O.P.*
15 Conversion of St. Augustin.
    St. Dympna, V.
16 St. Brendan, Bp., Patron of Kerry and of Clonfert.
17 St. Siollan. Bp.
18 St. Momaedhog, Bp.
19 St. Richeall. V.
20 *B. Columba of Rieti. O.P.*
21 St. Barrfinn. Bp.
22 *St. Servatius. Bp.*
23 St. Goban of Tescoffin.
24 Our Lady help of Christians.
    Translation of the relics of St. Dominic.
25 St. Gregory VII.. P.
26 St. Philip Neri. C.
27 St. M. Magdalene de Pazzi.
28 *B. Mary Bartholomæa, O.P.*
29 *BB. William & Companions, O.P.*
30 St. Ernine. C.
31 *B. James Salomonius, O.P.*

June.

1 *BB. Alphonsus Navarete and Companions, O.P.*
2 *BB. Sadoc and Companions, Martyrs, O.P.*
3 St. Kevin. Ab., Patron of Glendalough.
4 B. Cornelius, Bp. of Armagh.
5 St. Boniface. Bp., M.
6 St. Norbert. Bp., C.
7 *B. Stephen Bandelli, O.P.*
8 St. Luaithren. V.
9 St. Columbkille. Ab., Patron of Ireland.
10 *B. John Dominic. Bp., O.P.*
11 St. Barnabas, Ap.
12 St. Torannan. Bp.
13 St. Anthony of Padua. C.
14 St. Basil. Bp., Doctor of the Church.
15 St. Sinell. C.
16 St. J. Francis Regis, C.
17 St. Moling. Bp.
18 *B. Osanna of Mantua, O.P.*
19 St. Juliana Falconieri, V.
20 St. Faolan. C.
21 St. Aloysius Gonzaga, C.
22 St. Paulinus. Bp.
23 St. Mochaoi. Ab.
24 The Nativity of St. John the Baptist.
25 St. Moluog, C.
26 SS. John and Paul, MM.
27 St. Dioman, C.
28 St. Crummine. Bp.
29 SS. PETER AND PAUL. App.
30 St. Failbhe, C.

First Sunday after the Octave of Trinity—Feast of the Most Pure Heart of Mary.

July.	August.
1 St. Rumold. Bp. of Dublin. M.	1 St. Peter's Chains.
2 Visitation B.V.M.	2 *B. Jane d'Aza, O.P. (Mother of St. Dominic).*
3 *B. Mark of Modena. O.P.*	3 St. Fethilim, Bp., Patron of Kilmore.
4 St. Bolcan. C.	4 *St. Dominic. Founder of the Order of Preachers.*
5 St. Fergus. C.	
6 St. Moninna.	5 Dedication of the Ch. of B. V. M. ad Nives.
7 *B. Benedict XI., Pope, O.P.*	
8 St. Kilian and Companions.	6 Transfiguration of Our Lord.
9 *St. John and Companions, Martyrs, of Gorcum, O.P.*	7 St. Cajetan, C.
10 St. Etto, C.	8 *B. Augustine, Bp., O.P.*
11 St. Berran, C.	9 *B. John of Salerno. O.P.*
12 St. John Gualbert. Anniversary of those interred in the Dominican Cemeteries.	10 St. Laurence, M.
	11 St. Attracta, V.
	12 St. Clare, V.
	St. Muiredhech, Bp., Patron of Killala.
13 *B. James A. Voragina, Bp., O.P.*	13 St. Moloca, C.
14 St. Bonaventure, Bp., Doct. of the Church.	14 St. Fachanan, Bp., Patron of Ross and Kilfenora.
15 St. Henry II. of Germany.	15 ASSUMPTION OF THE B. V. M.
16 Commemoration of the B. V. M. of Mount Carmel.	
17 St. Alexins. C.	16 *St. Hyacinth. O P.*
18 *B. Ceslas, C. O.P.*	17 *B. Emily Bicchievi. O.P.*
19 St. Vincent de Paul, C.	18 St. Daigh, the Artificer.
20 St. Jerome Emilian, C.	19 St. Mochta, Bp.
21 St. Praxedes, V.	20 St. Bernard. Ab., Doctor of the Church.
22 *St. Mary Magdalen. Protectress of the Dominican Order.*	21 St. J. Frances de Chantal, W.
23 *B. Jane of Orvieto, O.P.*	22 St. Sincha. V.
24 St. Declan. Bp.	23 *B. James of Mevania. O.P.*
25 St. James. Ap.	24 St. Bartholomew, Ap.
26 St. Anne, Mother of the B. V. M.	25 St. Michen. C.
	26 St. Aireid. C.
27 *B. Augustin of Begella. O.P.*	27 St. Auxilius. Bp.
	28 St. Augustin, Bp. & Doctor of the Church.
28 *B. Anthony ab Ecclesia. O.P.*	29 Martyrdom of St. John the Baptist.
29 St. Martha. V.	30 *St. Rose of Lima. V., O.P.* St. Fiacre, C.
30 *B. Mannes (Brother of St. Dominic).*	
31 St. Ignatius of Loyola, C.	31 St. Raymund Nonnatus, C.

September.

1 St. Giles, Ab.
2 St. Geinten, C.
3 St. Macnisius, Bp., Patron of Connor.
  B. Guala, Bp., O.P.
4 St. Ultan of Ardbraccan,Bp.
5 B. Catherine of Raconigi, V., O.P.
6 St. Bega, V.
7 St. Grimonia, V. M.
8 The Nativity of the B.V.M.
9 St. Kieran, Patron of Clonmacnoise.
10 St. Finnian of Moville, Bp.
11 St. Loarn, Bp.
12 St. Ailbhe, Bp., Patron of Emly.
13 St. Dagan, Bp.   [Cross.
14 The Exaltation of the Holy
15 Commemoration of St. Dominic in Suriano.
16 B. Imelda, V., O.P.
17 St. Feme, V.
18 St. Gemma, V.
19 SS Januarius and Companions, MM.
20 B. Francis Possadas, C., O.P.
21 St. Matthew, Ap.
22 St. Aedh, C.   [Raphoe.
23 St. Eunan, Bp., Patron of
24 B. Dalmatius Monerius, O.P.
25 St. Finbar, Bp., Patron of Cork.
26 St. Colmanela, Ab.
27 SS. Cosmas and Damian, MM.
28 St. Fiachra, Bp.
29 Dedic. of the Church of St. Michael the Archangel.
30 St. Jerome, Doct. of the Ch.

Sunday after the Nativity of B.V.M.
  —Feast of the Name of Mary.
Third Sunday of September—
  Feast of the Seven Dolours of
  the B.V.M.

October.

1 St. Wasnulph, C. [Angels.
2 Feast of the Guardian
3 B. John Massias, O.P.
4 St. Francis of Assisi. C.
5 SS. Placidus & Companions, MM.
6 St. Bruno, C.
7 B. Matthew Carrieri, O.P.
8 St. Bridget of Sweden.
9 St. Fintan, Ab.
10 St. Lewis Bertrand, O.P.
11 St. Canice, Ab., Patron of Kilkenny.
12 B. James of Ulm, C., O.P.
13 St. Edward, Kg., C.
14 B. Magdalen de Panateriis. V., O.P.
15 St. Teresa, V.
16 St. Gall, Ab.
17 St. Maenach, C.
18 St. Luke, Evangelist.
19 St. Peter of Alcantara.
20 St. Maeleoin, Bp.
21 SS. Ursula and Companions, VV., MM.
22 B. Peter of Tiferno, O.P.
23 B. Bartholomew of Braganza, Bp., O.P.
24 St. Raphael, Archangel.
25 St. Duthract, V.
26 B. Damian a Finario, O.P.
   B. Margaret M. Alacoque.
27 St. Abban, Ab.
28 SS Simon and Jude, App.
29 B. Benvenuta Bojani. O.S.D.
30 The Holy Martyrs and other Saints whose relics are kept in the Dominican Churches.
31 St. Failan. Bp., M.

First Sunday of October—Feast of
  the Holy Rosary.
Second Sunday—The Anniversary
  of the Dedication of the Churches
  of Ireland.

November.

1 FEAST OF ALL SAINTS.
2 Commemoration of the Faithful Departed.
3 St. Malachy, Bp., Patron of Armagh.
   B. Simon Ballachi, O.P.
4 St. Charles Borromeo, Bp.
5 B. Martin de Porres, O.P.
6 St. Cronan, Ab.   [O.P.
7 B. Stephen de Ruffia, Martyr.
8 St. Fionnchan, C. [Dominic.
9 All Saints of the Order of St.
10 St. Osnat, V.
11 St. Martin of Tours, Bp.
12 St. Livinus, Bp. and M., Patron of Ghent.
13 St. Stanislaus Kostka, C.
14 St. Lawrence O'Toole, B., Patron of Dublin.
15 B. Albert the Great, O.P.
16 B. Lucy of Narni, O.P.
17 St. Gregory Thaumaturgus, Bp.   [of Lucca.
18 St. Frigidian, Bp., Patron
19 St. Elizabeth of Hungary, Widow.
20 St. Felix of Valois, C.
21 Presentation of the B.V.M.
22 St. Cecilia, V.M.
23 St. Clement, P., M.
24 St. Columban, Ab., Patron of Bobbio; St. Colman, Bp., Patron of Cloyne.
25 St. Catherine, V.M., Protectress of the Dominican Order.
26 St. John of the Cross, C.
27 St. Seachnall, Bp.: B. Margaret of Savoy, O.S.D. [O.P.
28 B. James de Benefactis, Bp.,
29 St. Brendan of Birr, Ab.
30 St. Andrew, Ap.

Second Sunday of November—Feast of the Patronage of the B.V.M.

December.

1 St. Nessan, C.
2 St. Bibiana, V.M.
3 St. Francis Xavier, C.
4 St. Peter Chrysologus, Bp.
5 St. Sabbas, Ab.
6 St. Nicholas, Bp., Patron of Galway.
7 St. Ambrose, Bp., Doctor of the Church.
8 The Immaculate Conception of the B.V.M.
9 SS. Fiedhlim and Mughain, VV.
10 St. Modiomog, Bp.
11 St. Damasus, P.
12 St. Finian of Clonard, Ab.
13 St. Lucy, V.M.
14 St. Dallan, Bp.
15 St. Flann, Ab.
16 St. Beanus, Bp.
17 St. Crunmael, Ab.
18 St. Flannan, Bp., Patron of Killaloe.
19 B. Sebastian, O.P.
20 St. Diarmait, Bp.
21 St. Thomas, Ap.
22 B. Mary Mancini, O.P.
23 St. Luchair, C.
24 St. Mochúa, C.
25 NATIVITY OF OUR LORD.
26 St. Stephen, Protomartyr.
   St. Jarlath, Bp., Patron of Tuam.
27 St. John, Ap., Ev.
28 The Holy Innocents, MM.
29 St. Thomas of Canterbury, Bp., M.
30 St. Connla, Bp.
31 St. Sylvester, Pope.

DOMINICAN MANUAL.

~~~~~~

On Prayer.

———

"Thou, O Lord, art sweet and mild, and plenteous in mercy to all who call upon thee."—*Ps.* lxxxv. 5.

PRAYER is an elevation of the soul to God; it is a conversation with God; it is the continual occupation of the blessed in heaven; their food—their rest—their whole felicity. It is the key of paradise, by means of which we can obtain all graces; it is a remedy for all our sins, the most speedy and efficacious consolation in time of trouble. When we pray to the Lord, he opens his hands, and gives us more than we ask. He reproaches us not with our sins; he appears, on the contrary, to forget them.

"We ought always to pray."—*Luke* xviii. 1.

I will open to you, says our Lord, but you must knock and seek, and then you shall find.

Our infirmities and miseries, the dangers to which we are continually exposed, the temptations we have to encounter; our weaknesses, our inability to do the least good without the grace of God; all are convincing proofs of the necessity we have for prayer. Let us then pray for "Prayer is the strength which saves, the courage which perseveres, the mystic bridge cast over the abyss which joins the soul to God."—*Ravignan*. Let us pray, for we are as the frail ship exposed to stormy winds and tempests. By prayer, we obtain the help of God's saving arm, which alone can rescue us from shipwreck. We must

LET US PRAY.

WE give thee thanks, Almighty God, for thy care and preservation of us in the night past; for having brought us in safety to the beginning of another day; and for all the manifold blessings which thou hast bestowed upon us. Grant that we may pass the remainder of our lives in worthy acts of praise and thanksgiving.

R. We give thee thanks, O Lord, for all thy mercies.

V. Unto thee, O Lord, have we lifted up our voice:

R. And early in the morning our prayer shall come before thee.

V. Vouchsafe, O Lord, this day,

R. To keep us without sin.

V. Have mercy upon us, O Lord.

R. Have mercy upon us.

V. Our help is in the name of the Lord;

R. Who hath made heaven and earth.

LET US PRAY.

LORD God Almighty, who hast brought us to the beginning of this day, let thy powerful grace so conduct us through it, that we may not fall into any sin, but that all our thoughts, words, and works may be guided by the rules of thy heavenly justice, and tend to the observance of thy holy law, through our Lord Jesus Christ thy Son, who liveth and reigneth with thee in the unity of the Holy Ghost, one God for ever and ever. Amen.

O God, the Creator and Governor of all men, in whom we live, and move, and have our being, and without whom we can do nothing: we consecrate all our thoughts, words, deeds, and sufferings of this day, to the glory of thy name, and of our Lord Jesus Christ.

O holy Lord, Father Almighty, Eternal God, vouchsafe this day to direct and sanctify our hearts and bodies in thy law, and in the works of thy commandments, that here and hereafter by thy assistance we may deserve to be saved, through Christ our Lord. Amen.

THE LORD'S PRAYER.

OUR Father, who art in heaven, hallowed be thy name; thy kingdom come; thy will be done on earth, as it is in heaven. Give us this day our daily bread; and forgive us our trespasses, as we forgive them who trespass against us. And lead us not into temptation; but deliver us from evil. Amen.

THE ANGELICAL SALUTATION.

HAIL, Mary, full of grace, the Lord is with thee; blessed art thou amongst women, and blessed is the fruit of thy womb, Jesus. Holy Mary, Mother of God, pray for us sinners, now and at the hour of our death. Amen.

THE APOSTLES' CREED.

I BELIEVE in God, the Father Almighty, Creator of heaven and earth; and in Jesus Christ, his only Son, our Lord; who was conceived by the Holy

Ghost: born of the Virgin Mary; suffered under Pontius Pilate; was crucified, dead, and buried; he descended into hell; the third day he arose again from the dead; he ascended into heaven, and sitteth at the right hand of God the Father Almighty; from thence he shall come to judge the living and the dead, I believe in the Holy Ghost; the Holy Catholic Church; the communion of saints; the forgiveness of sins; the resurrection of the body; and life everlasting. Amen.

O Sacred Heart of Jesus, I implore,
That I may ever love thee more and more. Amen.

THE CONFITEOR.

I CONFESS to Almighty God, to blessed Mary, ever Virgin, to blessed Michael the Archangel, to blessed John the Baptist, to the holy Apostles Peter and Paul, and to all the saints, that I have sinned exceedingly in thought, word, and deed, *through my fault, through my fault, through my most grievous fault.* Therefore I beseech the blessed Mary, ever Virgin, blessed Michael the Archangel, blessed John the Baptist, the holy Apostles Peter and Paul, and all the saints, to pray to the Lord our God for me. Amen.

May the Almighty God have mercy on me, forgive me my sins, and bring me to life everlasting. Amen.

May the Almighty and merciful Lord grant me ✠ pardon, absolution and remission of my sins. Amen.

ACT OF CONTRITION.

O MY God! I am heartily sorry for having offended thee, and I detest my sins most sincerely, because they displease thee, my God, who art so deserving of all my love for thy infinite goodness and most amiable perfections; and I firmly purpose, by thy holy grace, never more to offend thee, and to amend my life. Amen.

ACT OF FAITH.

O MY God, I firmly believe in thee and in all that thou hast revealed to thy Holy Catholic Church, because thou art Truth itself, who neither canst deceive nor be deceived.

ACT OF HOPE.

O MY God, who hast graciously promised every blessing, even heaven itself, through Jesus Christ, to those who keep thy commandments; relying on thy infinite power, goodness and mercy, and on thy sacred promises to which thou art always faithful, I confidently hope to obtain the pardon of all my sins, grace to serve thee faithfully in this life, by doing the good works thou hast commanded, and which, with thy assistance, I will perform, and eternal happiness in the next, through my Lord and Saviour Jesus Christ. Amen.

ACT OF CHARITY.

O MY God, I love thee with my whole heart and soul, and above all things, because thou art

infinitely good and perfect, and most worthy of all
my love; and for thy sake, I love my neighbour as
myself. Mercifully grant, O my God, that having
loved thee on earth, I may love and enjoy thee for
ever in heaven. Amen.

HAIL, holy Queen, Mother of Mercy! hail, our life,
our sweetness, and our hope. To thee do we
cry, poor banished children of Eve; to thee do we
send up our sighs, mourning and weeping in this
valley of tears. Turn then, most gracious Advocate,
thine eyes of mercy towards us, and, after this
our exile, show unto us the blessed fruit of thy
womb, Jesus. O clement! O loving! O sweet Virgin
Mary!

V. Pray for us. O holy Mother of God.

R. That we may be made worthy of the promises
of Christ.

> Angel of God, dear Angel mine,
> Whose care I am, by Power divine:
> Rule me, and guide and guard my ways,
> And teach me how my God to praise. Amen.

O great saint whose name I bear, St. Dominic,
and you my holy patrons, protect me, pray for me,
that like you, I may serve God faithfully on earth,
and glorify him eternally with you in heaven.
Amen.

ANGELUS.

V. The Angel of the Lord declared unto Mary.

R. And she conceived of the Holy Ghost.

 Hail Mary, &c.

V. Behold the handmaid of the Lord.

R. May it be done unto me according to thy word.

 Hail Mary, &c.

V. And the Word was made Flesh.

R. And dwelt amongst us.

 Hail Mary, &c.

V. Pray for us, O holy Mother of God,

R. That we may be made worthy of the promises of Christ.

LET US PRAY.

POUR forth, we beseech thee, O Lord, thy grace into our hearts, that we, to whom the Incarnation of Christ thy Son was made known by the message of an angel, may by his passion and cross be brought to the glory of his resurrection. Through the same Christ our Lord. Amen.

V. May the divine assistance remain always with us.

R. Amen.

V. And may the souls of the faithful departed, through the mercy of God, rest in peace.

R. Amen.

Instead of the *Angelus,* the *Regina Cœli, Triumph, O Queen of Heaven,* is said *standing,* from Easter to Trinity Sunday.

 Triumph, O Queen of Heaven, to see, Alleluia,

 The Sacred Infant born of thee, Alleluia;

Spring up in glory from the tomb, Alleluia;
Oh, by thy prayers prevent our doom, Alleluia.
V. Rejoice and be glad, O Virgin Mary, Alleluia.
R. Because our Lord is truly risen, Alleluia.

LET US PRAY.

O GOD, who, by the resurrection of thy Son our Lord Jesus Christ, hast vouchsafed to gladden the world, grant, we beseech thee, that, by the intercession of the Virgin Mary, his Mother, we may receive the joys of eternal life. Through the same Jesus Christ our Lord. *R.* Amen.

Through thy Sacred Virginity and thine Immaculate Conception, O most chaste Virgin Mary, Mother of God and Queen of Angels, obtain for us purity of soul and body. Amen.

May the Lord bless us, and protect us from all evil, and bring us to everlasting life. And may the souls of the faithful departed, through the mercy of God, rest in peace. Amen.

LITANY OF
The Most Holy Name of Jesus.

LORD have mercy on us.
Christ, have mercy on us.
Lord have mercy on us.
Jesus, hear us.
Jesus, graciously hear us.

God, the Father of heaven.
God the Son, Redeemer of the world,
God, the Holy Ghost.
Holy Trinity, One God,
Jesus, son of the living God,
Jesus, splendour of the Father,
Jesus, brightness of Eternal Light,
Jesus, king of Glory,
Jesus, sun of Justice.
Jesus, son of the Virgin Mary,
Jesus, most amiable,
Jesus, most admirable,
Jesus, mighty God,
Jesus, Father of the world to come,
Jesus, Angel of great counsel,
Jesus, most powerful,
Jesus, most patient,
Jesus, most obedient,
Jesus, meek and humble of heart,
Jesus, lover of chastity,
Jesus, lover of us,
Jesus, God of peace,
Jesus, author of life,
Jesus, example of virtues,
Jesus, zealous lover of souls,
Jesus, our God,
Jesus, our refuge,
Jesus, Father of the poor,
Jesus, treasure of the faithful,
Jesus, good shepherd,

Have mercy on us.

Jesus, true light,
Jesus, eternal wisdom,
Jesus, infinite goodness,
Jesus, our way and our life,
Jesus, joy of Angels,
Jesus, king of Patriarchs,
Jesus, master of the Apostles,
Jesus, teacher of the Evangelists,
Jesus, strength of Martyrs,
Jesus, light of Confessors,
Jesus, spouse of Virgins,
Jesus, crown of all Saints,

Be merciful unto us,
    Spare us, O Lord Jesus.
Be merciful unto us,
    Graciously hear us, O Lord Jesus.

From all evil,
From all sin,
From thy wrath,
From the snares of the devil,
From the spirit of fornication,
From everlasting death,
From the neglect of thy inspirations,
Through the mystery of thy holy incarnation,
Through thy nativity,
Through thy infancy,
Through thy most divine life,
Through thy labours,
Through thy agony and passion,
Through thy cross and dereliction,

Have mercy on us.

Lord Jesus, deliver us.

Through thy pains and torments,
Through thy death and burial,
Through thy glorious resurrection,
Through thy ascension,
Through thy institution of the most holy
    Eucharist,
Through thy joys and glory,
In the day of Judgment,

Lord Jesus, deliver us.

Lamb of God, who takest away the sins of the world,
*   Spare us, O Lord Jesus.*
Lamb of God, who takest away the sins of the world,
*   Graciously hear us, O Lord Jesus.*
Lamb of God, who takest away the sins of the world,
*   Have mercy upon us, O Lord Jesus.*
Lord Jesus, hear us.
*   Lord Jesus, graciously hear us.*

LET US PRAY.

O LORD Jesus Christ, who hast said: Ask, and ye
shall receive; seek, and ye shall find; knock,
and it shall be opened unto you; grant, we beseech
thee, to our most humble supplications, the gift of
thy divine charity, that we may ever love thee with
our whole hearts, and never cease from praising and
glorifying thy name.

O Divine Redeemer, give us a perpetual fear and
love of thy holy name, for thou never ceasest to
direct and govern by thy grace, those whom thou
instructest in the solidity of thy love, who livest and
reignest, world without end. Amen.

PRAYER OF ST. ALOYSIUS.

TO thee, O holy Mary, my sovereign Mistress, to thy blessed trust and special charge, and to the bosom of thy mercy, this day and every day, and at the hour of my death, I commend myself, my soul and my body ; to thee I commit all my hope and all my consolation, my distresses and my miseries, my life and the end thereof ; that through thy most holy intercession, and through thy merits, all my works may be directed and disposed, according to thy will and the will of thy Son.   Amen.

BLESSING.

THE peace of our Lord Jesus Christ, the virtue of his sacred passion, the sign of his holy cross, the purity and humility of the Blessed Virgin Mary, the protection of the Angels and the intercession of all the Saints and Elect of God, be with me and defend me, now, and at the hour of my death, sweet Jesus. Amen.

A PRAYER BEFORE MEAT.

BLESS us, O Lord, and these thy gifts, which of thy bounty we are to receive ; through Jesus Christ our Lord.   Amen.

A PRAYER AFTER MEAT.

WE give thee thanks, Almighty God, for all thy benefits, who livest and reignest for ever. Amen.

May the souls of the faithful departed, through the mercy of God, rest in peace.   Amen.

how to Spend the Day in a holy Manner.

Wherever you go, whatever you do, walk in the presence of God.

Perform all your actions from a pure motive of pleasing God.

In all temptations say: "Jesus and Mary help me!" Repeat the Hail Mary or some other short prayer, until you shall have conquered the enemy and recovered your wonted peace of mind.

"My God is my helper, and in him will I put my trust."—*Ps.* xvii. 3.

The Meditation.

THE invaluable fruits of Meditation should induce every Christian to practise it with ardour and perseverance.

Prayer is justly styled the food of the soul, but food in order to promote vigour and maintain life, must be digested. It is by meditation and reflection that the soul digests and draws nutriment from the truths of eternity. By meditation, we learn to know God and to adore him. In meditation, we "taste and see how sweet is the Lord." We find that " He is the Father of mercies, and the God of all consolation." St. Liguori asserts, that the person who meditates cannot be lost; she will either cease to meditate or she will save her soul.

The morning is the best time for meditation, before the duties of the day press on the mind.

What then should we do *before* prayer, *during* prayer, *after* prayer ?

"*Before* prayer, prepare thy soul; and be not as a man that tempteth God."—*Eccli.* xviii. 23.

Make lively acts of faith in the presence of God, acts of humility and of sorrow, and beg earnestly the assistance of divine grace in the following or any other form of words :—

O my God, I firmly believe that thou art here present, and I adore thee from the depths of my nothingness. Too often have I offended thee, my God; I am sorry for all my sins, pardon me in thy infinite mercy. Eternal Father, for the love of Jesus and of Mary, enlighten me in this meditation and enable me to profit by it. Hail Mary, Glory be to the Father, and to the Son, and to the Holy Ghost. As it was in the beginning, is now and ever shall be, God, world without end. Amen.

What should be done *during* prayer? Prayer is the work of the understanding and of the will. The understanding studies the truths proposed by meditation, and when it has done its duty, the will produces affections and acts of virtue suitable to the subject and to the disposition of the soul; they must all tend to the ruin of sin, to sorrow for faults, to petitions for pardon; to acts of faith, hope, charity, humility, patience, &c. The will ought always to form a resolution to correct a particular fault or to practise some particular virtue on the very first occasion of doing so. Then we should have recourse to the powerful intercession of the Holy Mother of God, and end with a vocal prayer, as the *Anima Christi*, making supplication for the souls in purgatory, for the prelates of the Church, for sinners, and for all our relations, friends, and benefactors. Prayer should never be discontinued in time of spiritual dryness. Let us go to meditation to wait on our God and to please him; let us thank him when he, vouchsafes us consolation—and if he seems not to heed us, let us still remain peaceably in his divine presence, adoring him and exposing to him our wants; for, "if he seems far off," says Habacuc, "he will appear in the end and will not lie; if he make any delay, wait for him; for, coming, he will come and will not be slack."—*Hab.* ii. 3.

What should be done *after* Prayer ?

After Prayer, we should be faithful to our resolutions,

and by guard of the senses and sweetness of manner, prove
to all that we have held converse with God, the source of
all sanctity.

O Thou by whom we come to God,
The Life, the Truth, the Way;
The path of prayer Thyself hast trod,
Lord! teach us how to pray.

Prayers of St. Ignatius.

DEAREST Jesus, teach me to be generous; teach
me to serve thee as thou deservest: to give,
and not to count the cost; to fight, and not to heed
the wounds; to toil, and not to ask for rest; to
labour, and not to seek for any reward, save to feel
that I do thy holy will, O my God.   Amen.

RECEIVE, O Lord, my memory, my will, my
understanding, my entire liberty. Thou hast
given me all that I possess. I surrender all to thy
Divine will, that thou mayest dispose of me as it
shall please thee. Give me only thy love and thy
grace, and I shall be happy, and shall have no more
to ask.

Night Prayer.

Say your night prayers with great fervour—never omit your examination of conscience—read over your meditation for next morning. Offer your sleep to God, in union with that which our divine Lord took upon earth. If you awake during the night, take holy water, and raise your heart to God by some short aspiration of love.

IN the name of the Father, and of the Son, and of the Holy Ghost. Amen.

Blessed be the holy and undivided Trinity, now and for evermore. Amen.

Our Father, &c.

Hail Mary, &c.

I believe in God, &c.

O ETERNAL, Infinite, and Almighty God, whose glory the heaven of heavens cannot contain, look down on thy unworthy servant, prostrate at the feet of thy mercy, and humbly confessing to thee, in the sight of all thy holy angels and blessed saints, the sinfulness and vanity of her life, and especially the transgressions of this day.

I CONFESS to Almighty God, to blessed Mary, ever Virgin, to blessed Michael the Archangel, to blessed John the Baptist, to the holy Apostles, Peter and Paul, and to all the saints, that I have sinned exceedingly in thought, word and deed, *through my fault, through my fault, through my most grievous fault.*

Here examine diligently the sins you may have fallen into this day,
by thought, word, deed, or omission:

Against God.—By omission or negligence in the
discharge of religious duties; irreverence,
wilful distractions or inattention at prayer;
resistance to the divine grace; want of confidence and resignation.

Against our Neighbour.—By rash judgments,
hatred, jealousy, desire of revenge, quarrelling,
passion, detraction, false reports, damaging,
either in goods or in reputation; bad example,
want of obedience or charity.

Against Ourselves.—By vanity, human respect,
lies; thoughts, desires, words or actions
contrary to purity; intemperance, sloth.

Therefore I beseech the blessed Mary, ever Virgin,
blessed Michael the Archangel, blessed John the
Baptist, the holy Apostles Peter and Paul, and all the
saints, to pray to the Lord our God for me. Amen.

May the Almighty God have mercy on me, forgive
me my sins, and bring me to life everlasting. Amen.

May the Almighty and merciful Lord grant me ✠
pardon, absolution, and remission of my sins.
Amen.

ACT OF CONTRITION.

O MY God, I am sorry, and beg pardon for all my
sins, and detest them above all things, because
they deserve thy dreadful punishments, because they
have crucified my loving Saviour, Jesus Christ, and,
most of all, because they offend thine infinite good-

ness, and I firmly resolve. by the help of thy grace, never to offend thee again, and carefully to avoid the occasions of sin.

HYMN.

Now with the fast-departing light,
    Maker of all! we ask of thee,
Of thy great mercy, thro' the night
    Our guardian and defence to be.
Far off let idle visions fly :
    No phantom of the night molest ;
Curb thou our raging enemy,
    That we in chaste repose may rest.
Father of mercies, hear our cry ;
    Hear us, O sole-begotten Son :
Who with the Holy Ghost most high,
    Reignest while endless ages run.

Antiph. Save us, O Lord, whilst awake, and keep us whilst asleep, that we may watch with Christ and rest in peace.

Preserve us, O Lord, as the apple of thine eye ; and under the shadow of thy wings protect us.

Vouchsafe, O Lord, to keep us this **night** without sin.

    V. Have mercy on us, O Lord.
    R. Have mercy on us.
    V. Let thy mercy, O Lord, be upon **us**.
    R. As we have hoped in thee.
    V. O Lord, hear my prayer.
    R. And let my cry come **unto** thee.

LET US PRAY.

VISIT, we beseech thee, O Lord, this habitation, and drive far from it all the snares of the enemy. Let thy holy Angels dwell herein to preserve us in peace, and may thy blessing be always upon us, through Christ our Lord. Amen.

May the Almighty and merciful Lord, Father, Son, and Holy Ghost, bless us and keep us, and deliver us from all evil. Amen.

We fly to thy patronage, O holy Mother of God, despise not our petitions in our necessities, but deliver us from all dangers, O ever glorious and Blessed Virgin.

Angels, Archangels, Thrones and Dominations, Principalities and Powers, Virtues of Heaven, praise the Lord from heaven and pray for us.

O Great Father, holy Dominic, in the hour of death take us to thee, and always lovingly look down upon us here below.

All ye saints of God, vouchsafe to intercede for us.

V. Stay with us, O Lord.

R. Because the evening of our life approaches.

V. Vouchsafe that I praise thee, O Sacred Virgin.

R. And give me strength against thine enemies.

V. He hath given his angels charge over thee.

R. That they keep thee in all thy ways.

V. Loving Father Dominic, be mindful of thy works.

R. Stand before the Judge and plead for thy poor children.

V. O Lord, hear my prayer.

R. And let my supplication come unto thee.

LET US PRAY.

PROTECT, O Lord, thy servants with the rampart of peace; and trusting in the patronage of the Blessed Mary ever Virgin, strengthen us against all our enemies.

O God, who with unspeakable Providence hast vouchsafed to appoint thy holy angels to be our guardians, grant to thy humble supplicants that we may be always defended by their protection, and enjoy their everlasting society.

Grant, we beseech thee, O Almighty God, that we who are pressed down by the weight of our sins, may be comforted by the protection of our Blessed Father Dominic, thy Confessor, who livest and reignest, God, world without end. Amen.

Let us pray for the faithful departed.

Eternal light shine upon them with thy saints for ever, for thou art merciful.

LET US PRAY.

O GOD, the Creator and Redeemer of all the faithful, grant to the souls of thy servants departed the full remission of all their sins, that by means of pious supplications, they may obtain that pardon of which they have ever been desirous through Christ our Lord. Amen.

Eternal rest grant to them, O Lord,
And let perpetual light shine upon them.
May they rest in peace. Amen.

LITANY OF
Our Blessed Lady of Loretto.

WE fly to thy patronage, O holy mother of God, despise not our prayers in our necessities, but deliver us from all dangers, O ever glorious and blessed Virgin.

Lord, have mercy on us.

Christ, have mercy on us.

Lord, have mercy on us.

Christ, hear us.

Christ, graciously hear us.

God, the Father of heaven, *Have mercy on us.*

God, the Son, Redeemer of the world, *Have mercy on us.*

God, the Holy Ghost, *Have mercy on us*

Holy Trinity, one God, *Have mercy on us.*

Holy Mary,

Holy Mother of God,

Holy Virgin of virgins,

Mother of Christ,

Mother of Divine grace,

Mother most pure,

Mother most chaste,

Mother inviolate,

Pray for us.

Mother undefiled.
Mother most amiable,
Mother most admirable,
Mother of Good Counsel,
Mother of our Creator,
Mother of our Redeemer,
Virgin most prudent,
Virgin most venerable,
Virgin most renowned,
Virgin most powerful,
Virgin most merciful,
Virgin most faithful,
Mirror of justice,
Seat of wisdom,
Cause of our joy,
Spiritual Vessel,
Vessel of honour,
Singular Vessel of devotion,
Mystical Rose,
Tower of David,
Tower of ivory,
House of gold,
Ark of the covenant,
Gate of heaven,
Morning Star,
Health of the weak,
Refuge of sinners,
Comforter of the afflicted,
Help of Christians,
Queen of Angels,
Queen of Patriarchs,

Pray for us.

Queen of Prophets,
Queen of Apostles,
Queen of Martyrs,
Queen of Confessors,
Queen of Virgins,
Queen of all Saints,
Queen conceived without original sin,
Queen of the most holy Rosary.

I pray for us.

Lamb of God, who takest away the sins of the world,
Spare us, O Lord,

Lamb of God, who takest away the sins of the world.
Graciously hear us, O Lord.

Lamb of God, who takest away the sins of the world.
Have mercy on us.

V. Pray for us, O holy Mother of God,

R. That we may be made worthy of the promises of Christ.

LET US PRAY.

GRANT, we beseech thee, O Lord God, that we thy servants may enjoy perpetual health of mind and body ; and by the glorious intercession of the Blessed Mary ever Virgin, we may be freed from present sorrow, and come to possess eternal joy. Through Christ our Lord. Amen.

V. May the divine assistance remain always with us.

R. Amen.

V. And may the souls of the faithful departed, through the mercy of God, rest in peace.

R. Amen.

THE MEMORARE.

REMEMBER, O most pious and tender Virgin
Mary, that it has never been heard of in any
age that those who implored thy powerful protection
were ever abandoned by thee. I, therefore, O sacred
Virgin, animated with the most lively confidence,
cast myself at thy sacred feet, most earnestly beseeching thee to adopt me for ever as thy child, to
take care of my eternal salvation, and to watch over
me now and at the hour of my death. Oh, do not,
Mother of the Word Incarnate! despise my prayer,
but graciously hear and obtain the grant of my
petitions. Amen.

Prayer to the Sacred Heart of Jesus.
Which may be said before retiring to rest.

O SACRED Heart of Jesus, how indulgent is thy
goodness! thou wouldst have me sleep and
thou wouldst watch over me. Thy affections burn
whilst mine are buried in sleep. Nevertheless, I
desire, as often as my heart shall beat this night, to
unite it to thine and to whatever shall be done in thy
honour by the Immaculate heart of Mary, by my
good Angel, by holy St. Joseph, by St. Dominic,
and by all the Blessed. Divine Jesus, I offer thee
the rest I am about to take, beseeching thee to open
to me thy Sacred Heart, and to allow me to repose
therein this night and for ever.

Holy Mother of God, and all ye blessed Angels and Saints, pray for me, and vouchsafe to supply my place in adoring, loving, honouring, blessing, and praising Jesus in the most holy and august Sacrament of the Altar, for all eternity. Amen.

✠ God the Father, bless me; Jesus Christ, defend and keep me; the virtue of the Holy Ghost enlighten and sanctify me, this night and for ever. Amen.

Into thy hands, O Lord, I commend my spirit. Lord Jesus receive my soul. Amen.

Act of Divine Love and Oblation.

O MY God and my All! I most ardently desire, by every breath I draw, by every thought, word and action, by every movement of body and soul, to tell thee a thousand and a thousand times that I love thee more than my life, or anything in the world, and that I consecrate myself to thee, renewing my baptismal vows, together with the promises and resolutions of my life past. I offer thee, also, all the homage, love, joy, praise, thanks, and adoration of the Church militant, triumphant, and suffering; all that it has offered, or will offer, thee to the end of time; all the love, complacency, and delights thou possessest in thy divine essence, one God in three Persons; all the homage my beloved Jesus renders thee in the Adorable Sacrament of the Altar; and all the masses that are now celebrating, that I may be a victim immolated with each, to thy honour and glory, without will, wish, or desire, but those solely of pleasing thee, loving thee, living for thee, and dying for thee. I am thine, O my God, make me so entirely and eternally. Above all, take my heart, fill it with thy love, extirpate from it all other affections, and make of it a burning furnace of pure flames of thy most ardent love for ever and ever. Amen.

May the most just, the most high, and the most amiable will of God be done, praised, and eternally exalted in all things. Amen.

PRAYER FOR THE CHOICE OF A STATE OF LIFE.

O ETERNAL God, light of the world, for whose glory the whole creation is ordained, to thee I submit my whole being ; I beseech thy mercy to direct me in the choice of a state of life ; that guided by thee I may walk in the path most pleasing to thee and most proper for working out my salvation.

O Queen of heaven, and Mother of Jesus, be a Mother to me, obtain for me of thy Divine Son that I may hear his call and faithfully accomplish his holy will. Amen.

ACT OF OBLATION TO THE WILL OF GOD.

LORD Jesus Christ, do with us, in us, and by us, in all that concerns us, in all that belongs to us, and in all things for time and eternity, whatsoever thou pleasest. Grant that we may have no desire but that of pleasing thee, and no pursuit but that of possessing thee eternally. Amen.

Occasional Prayers.

FOR THE HOLY CATHOLIC CHURCH.

DEFEND, O Lord, thy servants, we beseech thee, from all dangers both of soul and body; and, by the intercession of the blessed and glorious Virgin Mary, Mother of God, of the blessed Apostles Peter and Paul, of blessed *N.*, and of all thy saints, mercifully grant us the blessings of peace and safety; that all adversities and errors being removed, thy Church may freely and securely serve thee; through our Lord, &c.

FOR THE POPE.

O GOD, the Pastor and Ruler of all the faithful, mercifully look upon thy servant *N.*, whom thou hast been pleased to appoint the pastor of thy Church; grant, we beseech thee, that both by word and example he may edify those over whom he is set; and, together with the flock committed to his care, may attain everlasting life; through, &c.

FOR THE BISHOPS AND THE PEOPLE COMMITTED TO THEM.

ALMIGHTY and Everlasting God, who alone workest great marvels, send down upon thy servants, the Bishops of thy Church [*especially N. our Bishop*], and all the congregations committed unto them, the spirit of thy saving grace; and that they may truly please thee, pour upon them the continual dew of thy blessing; through, &c.

FOR A CONGREGATION OR FAMILY.

DEFEND, we beseech thee, O Lord, by the intercession of the blessed Mary, ever Virgin, this thy family from all adversity; and mercifully protect us, now prostrate before thee with our whole hearts, from all the snares of our enemies; through, &c.

FOR PRESERVATION OF CONCORD IN A CONGREGATION.

O GOD, who art the giver of peace and lover of charity, grant to thy servants true concord and union with thy holy will, that we may be delivered from all temptations which assault us; through, &c.

IN ANY NECESSITY.

O GOD, our refuge and our strength, the author of all godliness, give ear to the fervent prayers of thy Church: that what we ask in faith we may effectually obtain; through, &c.

IN ANY TRIBULATION.

O ALMIGHTY God, despise not thy people who cry unto thee in their affliction: but for the glory of thy name, turn away thine anger, and help us in our tribulations; through, &c.

IN TIME OF FAMINE AND PESTILENCE.

GRANT, we beseech thee, O Lord, an answer to our hearty supplications; and, thy wrath being appeased, turn away from us this famine (or pestilence); that the hearts of men may know that these scourges proceed from thine anger, and cease by thy mercy; through, &c.

FOR RAIN.

O GOD, in whom we live, move, and have our being, send us, we beseech thee, seasonable rain; that enjoying a sufficiency of the necessaries of this life, we may aspire with more confidence after those blessings which are eternal; through, &c.

FOR FAIR WEATHER.

HEAR us, O Lord, crying out to thee, and grant our humble request of a dry season; that we who are justly afflicted for our sins, may experience thy clemency and mercy; through, &c.

AGAINST STORMS.

DEFEND, we beseech thee, O Lord, this house against the assaults of our spiritual enemies; and cause the present dreadful disorder of the air to cease.

O Almighty and Eternal God, who both healest us by chastisement, and preservest us by the grant of thy pardon, hear our humble prayers: that we may rejoice in the ceasing of this storm; and always make a good use of the grant of thy favours; through, &c.

FOR THE FORGIVENESS OF SINS.

O GOD, who rejectest none that come unto thee, but in pity art appeased even with the greatest sinners who repent, mercifully regard our prayers in our humiliation, and lighten our hearts, that we may be able to fulfil thy commandments: through, &c.

FOR THE TEMPTED AND AFFLICTED.

O GOD, who justifiest the ungodly that repent, and willest not the death of the sinner, we humbly entreat thy Majesty to protect thy servants with thy heavenly assistance, who trust in thy mercy, and preserve them by thy continual protection, that they may constantly serve thee, and by no temptation be separated from thee: through, &c.

A PRAYER FOR PERSEVERANCE IN GOODNESS.

GRANT, O Lord Jesus Christ, that I may persevere in good purposes, and in thy holy service, to my death; and that I may this day perfectly begin, for all I have hitherto done is nothing. Amen.

FOR OUR FRIENDS.

O GOD, who, by the grace of the Holy Spirit, hast poured into the hearts of thy faithful the gifts of charity, grant to thy servants, for whom we implore thy mercy, health both of body and soul, that they may love thee with all their strength, and cheerfully perform those things which are pleasing unto thee; through, &c.

FOR A FRIEND IN DISTRESS.

VOUCHSAFE, O merciful Lord, to afford the sweetnes of thy comfort to thy afflicted servant, (N.) and to remove according to thy accustomed mercy, the heavy burden of her calamities. Give her, we humbly beseech thee, patience in her sufferings, resignation to thy good pleasure, perseverance in thy service, and a happy translation from this suffering life to thy eternal felicity. Amen.

FOR ANOTHER'S CONVERSION.

O DIVINE and adorable Saviour, thou who art the way, the truth, and the life, I beseech thee to have mercy upon (*N.*) and bring him to the knowledge and love of thy truth. Thou, O Lord, knowest all his darkness, his weakness, and his doubts; have pity upon him, O merciful Saviour; let the bright beams of thy eternal truth shine upon his mind; clear away the cloud of error and of prejudice from his eyes, and may he himself submit to the teaching of thy Church. Oh, let not the soul for whom I pray, be shut out from thy blessed fold! Unite him to thyself in the sacraments of thy love, and grant that partaking of the blessings of thy grace in this life, he may come at last to the possession of those eternal rewards which thou hast promised to all who believe in thee, and who do thy will. Hear this my petition, O merciful Jesus, who, with the Father and the Holy Ghost, livest and reignest for ever and ever. Amen.

FOR THE SICK.

V. Heal thy servants, O Lord, who are sick, and who put their trust in thee.

R. Send them help, O Lord, and comfort them from thy holy place.

O ALMIGHTY and Everlasting God, the eternal salvation of them that believe in thee, hear us on behalf of thy servants who are sick; for whom we humbly crave the help of thy mercy ; that, their health being restored to them, they may render thanks to thee in thy Church ; through, &c.

A PRAYER BEFORE STUDY OR INSTRUCTIONS.

O Incomprehensible Creator, the true Fountain of light, and only Author of all knowledge, vouchsafe, we beseech thee, to enlighten our understandings, and to remove from us all darkness of sin and ignorance. Thou, who makest eloquent the tongues of those that want utterance, direct our tongues, and pour on our lips the grace of thy blessing. Give us a diligent and obedient spirit, quickness of apprehension, capacity of retaining, and the powerful assistance of thy holy grace; that what we hear or learn, we may apply to thy honour and the eternal salvation of our own souls, through Jesus Christ our Lord. Amen.

PRAYER IN TIME OF CALAMITY.

O JESUS, divine Redeemer, be merciful unto us and to the whole world. Amen.

O powerful God, O holy God, O immortal God, have pity on us and on all that are in the world. Amen.

Pardon and mercy, O my Jesus, during these present dangers, pour on us thy most Precious Blood. Amen.

O Eternal Father, be merciful to us. By the Blood of Jesus Christ, thy only Son, be merciful unto us, we beseech thee. Amen.

PRAYER TO JESUS CRUCIFIED,

To obtain the Grace of a Happy Death.

MY Lord Jesus Christ, through that bitterness which thou didst suffer on the cross, when thy blessed soul was separated from thy sacred body have pity on my sinful soul, when it shall depart from my miserable body, and shall enter into eternity. Amen.

O Mary, watch the hour when my departing soul shall lose its hold on earthly things, and shall stand unveiled in the presence of its great Creator. Oh, be then to me a powerful advocate and a tender Mother, and place the sacred merits of thy Son Jesus, in the scales of justice in my behalf. Amen.

PRAYER TO THE MOTHER OF GOOD COUNSEL.

WE fly to thy protection, O Holy Mother of God, thou art the defence of all good Christians, the Seat of Wisdom, the Mother of Good Counsel. Oh! mayest thou shed upon us the light of thy countenance, and direct and sanctify all our undertakings.

Thou knowest, Most Holy Virgin, how much we require thy all-powerful aid; put an end, then, Sweet Mother, to the evils that afflict us; heal our wounds; relieve our wants and miseries; and obtain for us strength and courage to struggle against the assaults of the enemy, and to detect his snares; and, through thy intercession. to persevere until death in the holy fear and love of God. Amen.

ON THE

Holy Sacrifice of the Mass.

"From the rising of the sun even to the going down, my name is great among the Gentiles, and in every place there is Sacrifice, and there is offered to my name a clean oblation : for my name is great among the Gentiles, saith the Lord of hosts."—*Malac.* i, 11.

THE Sacrifice of the Mass is essentially the same as the Sacrifice of the Cross. It is the most pleasing offering we could make to God during an entire eternity. It is, of all things here below, that which procures most joy to the Church Triumphant—most help to the Church Suffering—most profit to the Church Militant.

The Sacrifice of the Mass is a holocaust most perfect, since we render to God an infinite honour in offering to him our Divine Lord.

It is a sacrifice of propitiation, since it is the same as that offered on the Cross, which has effaced all the sins of men by the Blood of Jesus Christ shed thereon ; which has paid with superabundance, all that was due for them to the Divine Justice. We ought then to use with great care this means of obtaining pardon of our sins, and of averting from us the vengeance of God.

The Sacrifice of the Mass is eucharistic ; by it we offer to God thanksgiving worthy of the benefits he bestows upon us. *What shall I render to the Lord for all he has done for me?* asks holy David. What can we render for all his benefits? Alas! we have nothing . . . . . But, our dear Lord, touched with compassion at the sight of our poverty, has enriched us with all his treasures, has instituted the Sacrifice of the Mass in which he gives himself to us, that we may take him and offer him to God his Father, in gratitude for all he has given to us.

Finally, the Sacrifice of the Mass is impetratory to obtain all goods of body and soul of which we have need ; for our Lord is of infinitely greater value than anything we can ask of God. Holy Mass has the power of obtaining what we ask : 1. Because Jesus Christ offers to his Father in our favour all the merits of his life and death. 2. Because our Lord actually prays in heaven for those who offer the Mass or for whom it is offered. 3. Because of the prayers of the Church which are made at Mass. 4. Because of our own prayers which are then more efficacious than they are at any other time.

The Sacrifice of the Mass obtains for the sinner the grace of repentance : that is, it presses the divine mercy to have pity on him. It obtains for the just, pardon of venial sins, because of the interior acts of virtue it makes him practise, and which acts of themselves efface these sins. It obtains for the just an increase of habitual grace, charity, and all virtues ; it obtains great actual graces, particular succours to perform good works, to live in charity and to persevere till death. Finally, we obtain by this Sacrifice all necessary temporal things, as far as God finds it expedient to bestow them for his glory and our own salvation.

Let us then always bring to this august Sacrifice the most earnest devotion ; let us make an offering of ourselves with Christ to his Eternal Father, let our hearts, thoughts and imaginations be buried in God from the beginning to the end of the Mass ; for there is no other act of religion so holy, so divine, so rich in graces and in heavenly blessings.

Ordinary of the Mass.

THE ASPERGES.

Ant. Asperges me, Domine, hyssopo, et mundabor: lavabis me, et super nivem dealbabor.

Ps. Miserere mei Deus, secundum magnam misericordiam tuam.

V. Gloria Patri, &c.
Ant. Asperges me.

Ant. Thou shalt sprinkle me with hyssop, O Lord, and I shall be cleansed; thou shalt wash me, and I shall be made whiter than snow.

Ps. Have mercy on me, O God, according to thy great mercy.

V. Glory be, &c.
Ant. Thou shalt sprinkle me.

The Priest, being returned to the foot of the Altar, says:

V. Ostende nobis, Domine, misericordiam tuam.
R. Et salutare tuum da nobis.
V. Domine, exaudi orationem meam.
R. Et clamor meus ad te veniat.
V. Dominus vobiscum
R. Et cum spiritu tuo.

V. Show us, O Lord, thy mercy.
R. And grant us thy salvation.
V. O Lord, hear my prayer.
R. And let my cry come unto thee.
V. The Lord be with you.
R. And with thy spirit.

Let us Pray.

Exaudi nos, Domine sancte, Pater omnipotens, æterne Deus; et mittere digneris sanctum angelum tuum de cœlis, qui custodiat, foveat, protegat, visitet, atque defendat omnes habitantes in hoc habitaculo. Per Christum Dominum nostrum. Amen.

Hear us, O holy Lord, Almighty Father, Eternal God; and vouchsafe to send thy holy angel from heaven, to guard, cherish, protect, visit, and defend all that are assembled in this house. Through Christ our Lord, Amen.

From Easter to Whit Sunday inclusively, instead of the foregoing Anthem, the following is sung, and Alleluia is added to the V. (Ostende nobis, and also to its R. (Et salutare).

Ant. Vidi aquam egredientem de templo a latere dextro. Alleluia;

Ant. I saw water flowing from the right side of the temple,

Devotions at Mass.

RECEIVE, O holy Trinity, one God, the holy sacrifice of the body and blood of our Lord Jesus Christ, which I, thy unworthy servant, desire now to offer unto thy divine Majesty by the hands of this thy minister, with all the sacrifices which have ever been or are to be offered unto thee, in union with that most holy sacrifice offered by our Lord himself at the last supper, and on the altar of the cross. I offer it unto thee with the utmost affection of devotion, out of pure love for thine infinite goodness, and according to the intention of our holy mother Church :

1. To the great and eternal glory and love of thy divine Majesty.

2. In acknowledgment of thy sovereign excellence and supreme dominion over us, and our subjection to thee, and dependence upon thee.

3. In perpetual commemoration of the passion and death of the same Christ our Lord.

4. For the honour and greater glory of the Blessed Virgin, and of all the saints triumphant.

5. In eternal thanksgiving for all thy benefits conferred upon the most sacred humanity of our Lord, upon the Blessed Virgin his Mother, upon the saints my patrons; and for all the benefits hitherto

et omnes ad quos pervenit aqua ista salvi facti sunt, et dicent. Alleluia.

Ps. Confitemini Domino, quoniam bonus: quoniam in sæculum misericordia ejus. Gloria, &c.

Alleluia: and all to whom that water came were saved, and they shall say. Alleluia.

Ps. Praise the Lord, for he is good: for his mercy endureth for ever. Glory, &c.

ORDINARY OF THE MASS.

The Priest begins at the foot of the Altar.

In nomine Patris, et Filii, et Spiritus Sancti. Amen.

In the name of the Father, and of the Son, and of the Holy Ghost. Amen.

Introibo ad altare Dei.

R. Ad Deum, qui lætificat juventutem meam.

I will go unto the altar of God.

R. To God, who giveth joy to my youth.

* *Psalm* xlii.

S. Judica me, Deus, et discerne causam meam de gente non sancta: ab homine iniquo et doloso erue me.

P. Judge me, O God, and distinguish my cause from the nation that is not holy; deliver me from the unjust and deceitful man.

M. Quia tu es, Deus, fortitudo mea quare me repulisti? et quare tristis incedo dum affligit me inimicus?

R. For thou, O God, art my strength, why hast thou cast me off? and why do I go sorrowful whilst the enemy afflicteth me?

S. Emitte lucem tuam et veritatem tuam: ipse me deduxerunt et adduxerunt in montem sanctum tuum, et in tabernacula tua.

P. Send forth thy light and thy truth; they have conducted me and brought me unto thy holy mount, and unto thy tabernacles.

M. Et introibo ad altare Dei: ad Deum qui lætificat juventutem meam.

R. And I will go unto the altar of God: to God, who giveth joy to my youth.

S. Confitebor tibi in cithara, Deus, Deus meus: quare tristis es, anima mea? et quare conturbas me?

P. I will praise thee on the harp, O God, my God: why art thou sorrowful, O my soul? and why dost thou disquiet me?

M. Spera in Deo, quoniam adhuc confitebor illi: salutare vultus mei, et Deus meus.

R. Hope in God, for I will still give praise to him; who is the salvation of my countenance, and my God.

S. Gloria Patri, et Filio, et Spiritui Sancto.

P. Glory be to the Father, and to the Son, and to the Holy Ghost.

M. Sicut erat in principio, et nunc, et semper, et in sæcula sæculorum. Amen.

R. As it was in the beginning, is now, and ever shall be, world without end. Amen.

* The above Psalm is not said in Passion time, when the Mass peculiar to the time is said, nor in Masses for the Dead.

or yet to be conferred upon all the blessed and pre-destinated, and upon me, the most unworthy of all.

6. In satisfaction for my sins, and for the sins of all the faithful, living or dead.

7. In particular, I offer it for the attainment of these (*N. N.*) graces or blessings, for these (*N. N.*) persons particularly recommended to me, and for all for whom I am accustomed or bound to pray; that thou wouldst grant to the departed rest, and to the living grace to know, and love, and glorify thee perfectly now in this life, and hereafter blissfully in heaven. Accept and perfect this my desire, and vouchsafe thy abundant grace and blessing for its accomplishment.

AT THE CONFITEOR.

O BLESSED Trinity, one God, Father, Son, and Holy Ghost, prostrate in spirit before thee I here confess in the sight of the whole court of heaven, and of all the faithful, my innumerable treasons against thy divine Majesty. I have sinned, O Lord, I have sinned: I have grievously offended through the whole course of my life, in thought, word, and deed; and therefore am unworthy to lift my eyes to heaven, or so much as to name thy sacred name: how much more am I unworthy to appear here in thy sanctuary, and to assist among thy angels at these heavenly mysteries, which require so much purity, because Jesus Christ himself is here in person, both Priest and Victim! But, O my God, thy

V. Introibo ad altare Dei.

R. Ad Deum, qui lætificat juventutem meam.
V. Adjutorium nostrum in
nomine Domini.
R. Qui fecit cœlum et terram.

V. I will go unto the altar of
God.
R. To God, who giveth joy to
my youth.
V. Our help is in the name of
the Lord.
R. Who hath made heaven and
earth.

Then, joining his hands and humb'y bowing down, h · says the Confession.

S. Confiteor Deo omnipotenti,
&c.
M. Misereatur tui omnipotens
Deus, et dimissis peccatis tuis,
perducat te ad vitam æternam.

S. Amen.
M. Confiteor Deo omnipotenti,
beatæ Mariæ semper Virgini,
beato Michaeli Archangelo, beato
Joanni Baptistæ, sanctis Apostolis Petro et Paulo, omnibus
sanctis, et tibi pater, quia peccavi
nimis cogitatione, verbo, et opere,
mea culpa, mea culpa, mea maxi-
ma culpa. Ideo precor beatam
Mariam semper Virginem, beatum Michaelem Archangelum,
beatum Joannem Baptistam,
sanctos Apostolos Petrum et
Paulum, omnes Sanctos, et te
pater, orare pro me ad Dominum
Deum nostrum.

P. I confess to Almighty God,
&c.
R. May Almighty God have
mercy upon thee, forgive thee thy
sins, and bring thee to life everlasting.
P. Amen.
R. I confess to Almighty God,
to blessed Mary ever Virgin, to
blessed Michael the Archangel, to
blessed John Baptist, to the holy
Apostles Peter and Paul, to all
the Saints, and to you father,
that I have sinned exceedingly in
thought, word, and deed [*here
strike the breast thrice*], through
my fault, through my fault,
through my most grievous fault.
Therefore I beseech blessed Mary
ever Virgin, blessed Michael the
Archangel, blessed John Baptist,
the holy Apostles Peter and Paul,
and all the Saints, and you,
father, to pray to the Lord our
God for me.

Then the Priest, with his hands joined, gives the Absolution, saying :

S. Misereatur vestri omnipotens Deus, et dimissis peccatis
vestris, perducat vos ad vitam
æternam.
M. Amen.

P. May Almighty God have
mercy upon you, forgive you your
sins, and bring you to life everlasting.
R. Amen.

Signing himself with the sign of the Cross, he says:

S. ✠ Indulgentiam, absolutionem, et remissionem peccatorum
nostrorum tribuat nobis omnipotens et misericors Dominus.
M. Amen.

P. ✠ May the Almighty and
Merciful Lord grant us pardon,
absolution and remission of our
sins.
R. Amen.

mercies are above all thy works, and thou wilt not despise a contrite and humble heart; and therefore I here venture to come into thy temple, and with the poor publican, strike my breast and say, God be merciful to me a sinner. Amen.

ANOTHER PRAYER AT THE CONFITEOR.

O DIVINE Jesus, thou art the victim charged with all the iniquities of the world; thou didst weep for them bitter tears; thou didst expiate them by the most dreadful torments and by the most cruel of deaths. I come to mingle my tears with thine; I confess to thee, in the presence of Mary ever Virgin and of all the Saints, that I have sinned exceedingly: that it is my ingratitude that pierced thy heart, and put thee to a cruel death. O God, my Saviour, through thy tears, through thy agony in the Garden, and through thy precious blood and the wound in thy Sacred Heart, I beseech thee to accept this my confession, and mercifully pardon all my deficiencies, that, according to the greatness of thy mercy, I may be fully and perfectly absolved in heaven; who livest and reignest, &c.

WHEN THE PRIEST GOES TO THE ALTAR.

L ET us adore the Heart of Jesus, which has loved us so much; let us prostrate ourselves before him, and bewail the sins of which we have been guilty. Grant us, O Lord, a contrite and humble heart; let the homage of our adorations be as acceptable to thee as if we offered thee thousands of victims.

Then, bowing down, he proceeds:

V. Deus, tu conversus, vivificabis nos.
R. Et plebs tua lætabitur in te.

V. Ostende nobis, Domine, misericordiam tuam.
R. Et salutare tuum da nobis.
V. Domine, exaudi orationem meam.
R. Et clamor meus ad te veniat.

V. Dominus vobiscum.
R. Et cum spiritu tuo.

V. Thou being turned again, O God, wilt quicken us.
R. And thy people shall rejoice in thee.

V. Show us, O Lord, thy mercy.
R. And grant us thy salvation.
V. O Lord, hear my prayer.

R. And let my cry come unto thee.
V. The Lord be with you.
R. And with thy spirit.

Ascending to the Altar, he says secretly:

Aufer a nobis, quæsumus, Domine, iniquitates nostras; ut ad Sancta sanctorum puris mereamur mentibus introire. Per Christum Dominum nostrum. Amen.

Take away from us our iniquities, we beseech thee, O Lord: that we may be worthy to enter with pure minds into the holy of holies. Through Christ our Lord Amen.

Bowing down over the Altar, he says:

Oramus te Domine, per merita sanctorum tuorum quorum reliquiæ hic sunt, et omnium sanctorum, ut indulgere digneris omnia peccata mea. Amen.

We beseech thee, O Lord, by the merits of thy saints whose relics are here, and of all the saints, that thou wouldst vouchsafe to forgive me all my sins. Amen.

[At High Mass the Altar is here incensed.] Then the Priest, signing himself with the sign of the Cross, reads the Introit.*

The Kyrie eleison *is then said:*

Kyrie eleison (*three times*).   *Lord have mercy upon us.*
Christe eleison (*three times*).   *Christ have mercy upon us.*
Kyrie eleison (*three times*).   *Lord have mercy upon us.*

Afterwards, standing at the middle of the Altar, extending, and then joining his hands, he says the Gloria in excelsis.†

Gloria in excelsis. Deo et in terra pax hominibus bonæ voluntatis. Laudamus te; benedicimus

Glory be to God on high, and on earth peace to men of good will. We praise thee; we bless thee; we

---

* These, as well as the Collects, Epistle, Gradual, Gospel, Offertory, Secreta, Communion, and Post-Communions, are variable, and may be found in the Missal.
† The *Gloria* is omitted during Lent and Advent, when the Mass peculiar to the time is said, and in Masses for the Dead.

AT THE INTROIT.

THE Lord hath opened the gates of heaven; he hath rained down manna to feed us; he hath given us the bread of angels. Thy goodness, O my God, hath prepared it for the poor and humble heart; blessed art thou, O God of Israel, thou only canst work such wonders for me. I will offer to thee, in the presence of all thy people, the homage of my love and gratitude.

AT THE KYRIE.

O FATHER of infinite mercy, have pity on thy children; O Jesus, sacrificed for us, apply to us the merits of thy precious blood; O Holy Ghost, the Sanctifier, descend into our hearts, and inflame them with thy love.

Or,

HAVE mercy on me, O Lord, and forgive me all my sins; and though I have nothing of my own to move thy goodness, yet let my importunity prevail: have mercy, O Lord, have mercy on me.

AT THE GLORIA IN EXCELSIS.

WHAT happiness for us that the Son of the Most High should have been pleased to dwell amongst us, and have vouchsafed to offer us a dwelling in his Divine Heart! Suffer us, O Lord, to mingle our voices with those of the angelic choir, to thank thee for so great a favour; and let us say with them, " Glory to God in the highest heavens."

te; adoramus te; glorificamus te. Gratias agimus tibi propter magnam gloriam tuam, Domine Deus, Rex cœlestis, Deus Pater omnipotens. Domine Fili unigenite Jesu Christe; Domine Deus, Agnus Dei, Filius Patris, qui tollis peccata mundi, miserere nobis; qui tollis peccata mundi, suscipe deprecationem nostram: qui sedes ad dexteram Patris, miserere nobis. Quoniam tu solus sanctus; tu solus Dominus: tu solus altissimus, Jesu Christe, cum Sancto Spiritu, in gloria Dei Patris. Amen.

adore thee; we glorify thee. We give thee thanks for thy great glory, O Lord God, heavenly King, God the Father Almighty. O Lord Jesus Christ, the only-begotten Son: O Lord God, Lamb of God, Son of the Father, who takest away the sins of the world, have mercy on us: thou who takest away the sins of the world, receive our prayers: thou who sittest at the right hand of the Father, have mercy on us. For thou only art holy: thou only art the Lord: thou only, O Jesus Christ, with the Holy Ghost, art most high in the glory of God the Father. Amen.

The Priest kisses the Altar, and turning to the people, says

V. Dominus vobiscum.

R. Et cum spiritu tuo.

V. The Lord be with you.

R. And with thy spirit.

Then follow the Collects, *which may be found in the* Missal, *or the following may be used instead:*

Defend us, O Lord, we beseech thee, from all dangers of soul and body; and by the intercession of the glorious and blessed Mary ever Virgin, Mother of God, St. Joseph, the blessed Apostles Peter and Paul, the blessed .N., and all thy Saints, grant us, in thy mercy, health and peace; that all adversities and errors being done away, thy Church may serve thee with a pure and undisturbed devotion. Through, &c.

O Almighty and Everlasting God, by whose Spirit the whole body of the Church is sanctified and governed; hear our humble supplications for all degrees and orders thereof, that by the assistance of thy grace, they may faithfully serve thee. Through our Lord Jesus Christ thy Son, who liveth and reigneth with thee in the unity of the same Holy Ghost, God, world without end. Amen.

Then is read the Epistle, *or the following may be read instead:*

Rejoice in the Lord always; again I say, rejoice. Let your modesty be known to all men: the Lord is nigh. Be nothing solicitous, but in everything, by prayer and supplication with thanksgiving, let your petitions be made known to God. And the peace of God, which surpasseth all understanding, keep your hearts and minds in Christ Jesus. For the rest, brethren, whatsoever things are holy, whatsoever things are amiable, whatsoever things

O Almighty Father, we praise thee, we bless thee, we adore thee; we give thee thanks for all the benefits which thou hast lavished upon us without ceasing. O Jesus, Lamb without spot, who takest away the sins of the world, have mercy on us; thou only art holy, thou only art the Lord, who reignest with the Father and the Holy Ghost in glory, and meritest all our homage on earth.

AT THE COLLECTS.

O LORD, vouchsafe favourably to hear the prayers which thy priest offers to thee for the Church and for me.

I earnestly beseech thee to grant me those graces and virtues of which I have need, in order to deserve thy love. Fill my heart with eternal gratitude for all the blessings which thou hast conferred upon me, with a lively horror of sin, and with perfect charity towards my neighbour. Make my whole life worthy of one who is thy child. I deserve not to be heard for my own sake, O my God, but I beseech thy mercy through the infinite merits of thy divine Son.

O divine Jesus, inexhaustible Fountain of good things, open to us, we beseech thee, the interior of thy Heart; that having entered, by pious meditation, into this august sanctuary of divine love, we may fix for ever our hearts there, as the place wherein are found the treasure, the repose, and the happiness of holy souls.

are of good repute, if there be any virtue, if there be any praise of discipline, think on these things. The things which you have both learned, and received, and heard, and seen in me, these do ye; and the God of peace shall be with you. (*Phil.* iv. 4–9).

After which:

Deo gratias.   Thanks be to God.

Then the Gradual. Tract. Alleluia, *or* Sequence.

Before the Gospel.

Munda cor meum ac labia mea, omnipotens Deus. qui labia Isaiæ prophetæ calculo mundasti ignito; ita me tua grata miseratione dignare mundare, ut sanctum Evangelium tuum digne valeam nuntiare. Per Christum Dominum nostrum. Amen.

Cleanse my heart and my lips, O Almighty God, who didst cleanse the lips of the prophet Isaias with a burning coal ; and vouchsafe, through thy gracious mercy, so to purify me, that I may worthily proclaim thy holy Gospel. Through Christ our Lord. Amen.

* Jube Domine benedicere ; Dominus sit in corde meo et in labiis meis. ut digne. et competenter annuntiem Evangelium suum. Amen.

The Lord be in my heart and on my lips, that I may worthily, and in a becoming manner, announce his holy Gospel.

V. Dominus vobiscum.

V. The Lord be with you.

R. Et cum spiritu tuo.

R. And with thy spirit.

V. Sequentia (*vel* initium) sancti Evangelii secundum *N.*

V. The continuation (*or* beginning) of the holy Gospel according to *N.*

R. Gloria tibi, Domine.

R. Glory be to thee, O Lord.

Then is read the Gospel, *or the following may be used instead:*

If ye love me. keep my commandments. And I will ask the Father, and he will give you another Paraclete. that he may abide with you for ever. the Spirit of truth, whom the world cannot receive. because it seeth him not, nor knoweth him ; but you shall know him. because he shall abide with you, and shall be in you. I will not leave you orphans ; I will come to you. Yet a little while, and the world seeth me no more. But ye see me. because I live, and you shall live. In that day ye shall know that I am in my Father, and you in me. and I in you. He that hath my commandments, and keepeth them. he it is that loveth me. And he that

* This is omitted in Masses for the Dead.

AT THE EPISTLE.

THOU hast vouchsafed, O Lord, to teach us thy sacred truths by the prophets and apostles : oh, grant that we may so improve by their doctrine and examples in the love of thy holy name and of thy holy law, that we may show forth by our lives whose disciples we are ; that we may no longer follow the corrupt inclinations of flesh and blood, but master all our passions; that we may be ever directed by thy light and strengthened by thy grace, to walk in the way of thy commandments, and to serve thee with clean hearts. Through our Lord Jesus Christ.

AT THE GOSPEL.

O GOD, the Father of light, blessed for ever be thy mercy, whereby thou hast called the nations of the earth from the darkness of ignorance and the shades of death into the marvellous light of thy Faith; grant that all mankind, being delivered by thee from the slavery of Satan and of sin, may take upon them the light burden and sweet yoke of thy holy law ; that thy name may be known and praised through all the earth, so that we may become one family of saints, through Christ our Lord.

PRAYER BEFORE THE SERMON.

I WILL hear what the Lord will say unto me. O Jesus, light of the world, enlighten my understanding, that I may comprehend thy word ; and cleanse my heart, that it may bring forth fruit. Amen.

loveth me shall be loved by my Father; and I will love him, and I will manifest myself to him.

R. Laus tibi, Christe.

*Per evangelica dicta deleantur nostra delicta.

R. Praise be to thee. O Christ.

By the words of the Gospel may our sins be blotted out.

* Omitted in Masses for the Dead.

Nicene Creed.

Credo in unum Deum, Patrem omnipotentem, Factorem cœli et terræ, visibilium omnium et invisibilium.

Et in unum Dominum Jesum Christum, Filium Dei unigenitum, et ex Patre natum ante omnia sæcula. Deum de Deo; Lumen de Lumine; Deum verum de Deo vero; genitum non factum: consubstantialem Patri, per quem omnia facta sunt. Qui propter nos homines et propter nostram salutem, descendit de cœlis, et incarnatus est de Spiritu Sancto, ex Maria Virgine; ET HOMO FACTUS EST. [*Hic genuflectitur.*] Crucifixus etiam pro nobis: sub Pontio Pilato passus, et sepultus est. Et resurrexit tertia die secundum Scripturas; et ascendit in cœlum, sedet ad dexteram Patris: et iterum venturus est cum gloria judicare vivos et mortuos: cujus regni non erit finis.

Et in Spiritum Sanctum, Dominum et vivificantem, qui ex Patre Filioque procedit; qui cum Patre et Filio simul adoratur et conglorificatur; qui locutus est per prophetas. Et unam sanctam Catholicam et Apostolicam Ecclesiam. Confiteor unum baptisma in remissionem peccatorum. Et expecto resurrectionem mortuorum, et vitam venturi sæculi. Amen.

I believe in one God, the Father almighty, maker of heaven and earth, and of all things visible and invisible.

And in one Lord Jesus Christ, the only-begotten Son of God, born of the Father before all ages God of God; Light of Light; true God of true God; begotten not made; consubstantial with the Father, by whom all things were made. Who for us men, and for our salvation, came down from heaven, and was incarnate by the Holy Ghost of the Virgin Mary: AND WAS MADE MAN. He was crucified also for us, suffered under Pontius Pilate, and was buried. The third day he rose again according to the scriptures; and ascended into heaven and sitteth at the right hand of the Father; and he shall come again with glory to judge both the living and the dead: of whose kingdom there shall be no end.

And I believe in the Holy Ghost, the Lord and life-giver, who proceedeth from the Father and the Son; who together with the Father and the Son is adored and glorified: who spake by the prophets. And one holy Catholic and Apostolic Church. I confess one baptism for the remission of sins. And I look for the resurrection of the dead, and the life of the world to come. Amen.

V. Dominus vobiscum.

R. Et cum spiritu tuo.

V. The Lord be with you.

R. And with thy spirit.

The Credo is always said on Sundays, and on most of the greater festivals. It is omitted in Masses for the Dead.

AT THE CREED.

I FIRMLY believe—because God who is Infallible Truth hath so revealed it to the Holy Catholic Church, and through the Church to us—I firmly believe that there is only one God, in Three Divine Persons, equal and distinct, whose names are Father, Son, and Holy Ghost ; that the Son became man, and through the operation of the Holy Spirit took flesh and a human soul in the womb of the most pure Virgin Mary, that he died for us upon the cross, rose again, ascended into heaven, and that he will come from thence at the end of the world to judge all the living and dead, to give paradise to the good, and hell to the wicked, for ever ; and furthermore, upon the same motive, I believe everything that the Holy Church believes and teaches. In this faith and for this faith I desire to live and die. Grant, O Lord, that my life may be comfortable with my faith, that my faith may be animated by good works, that I may never be ashamed to declare myself a Catholic, and may constantly maintain the interests of thy holy religion. Draw closer to me, Lord, the bonds that bind me to thy Holy Church ; put into my heart a spirit of perfect obedience to its lawful pastors. In its bosom I became thy child, and in its bosom I desire to live and die. Amen.

DURING THE OFFERTORY.

I ADORE thee. O my God ; and, in union with the priest, offer thee this sacrifice, for thy honour and

Then the Priest reads the Offertory, and taking the paten with the Host, says :

Suscipe, sancte Pater, omnipotens, æterne Deus, hanc immaculatam Hostiam, quam ego indignus famulus tuus offero tibi, Deo meo vivo et vero, pro innumerabilibus peccatis, et offensionibus, et negligentiis meis, et pro omnibus circumstantibus: sed et pro omnibus fidelibus Christianis, vivis atque defunctis: ut mihi et illis proficiat ad salutem in vitam æternam. Amen.

Accept, O holy Father, Almighty, Eternal God, this immaculate Host, which I, thy unworthy servant, offer unto thee, my living and true God, for my innumerable sins, offences, and negligences, and for all here present; as also for all faithful Christians, both living and dead, that it may be profitable for my own and for their salvation unto eternal life. Amen.

Pouring wine and water into the chalice, he says :

Deus, ✠ qui humanæ substantiæ dignitatem mirabiliter condidisti, et mirabilius reformasti: da nobis per hujus aquæ et vini mysterium, ejus divinitatis esse consortes, qui humanitatis nostræ fieri dignatus est particeps, Jesus Christus, Filius tuus, Dominus noster; qui tecum vivit et regnat in unitate Spiritus Sancti Deus, per omnia sæcula sæculorum. Amen.

O God ✠ who in creating human nature, didst wonderfully dignify it, and hast still more wonderfully renewed it; grant that, by the mystery of this water and wine, we may be made partakers of his divinity who vouchsafed to become partaker of our humanity, Jesus Christ, thy Son, our Lord; who liveth and reigneth with thee in the unity of, &c.

Offering up the chalice, he says :

Offerimus tibi, Domine, calicem salutaris, tuam deprecantes clementiam, ut in conspectu divinæ Majestatis tuæ, pro nostra et totius mundi salute cum odore suavitatis ascendat. Amen.

We offer unto thee, O Lord, the chalice of salvation, beseeching thy clemency, that, in the sight of thy divine Majesty, it may ascend with the odour of sweetness, for our salvation, and for that of the whole world. Amen.

Bowing down, he says:

In spiritu humilitatis, et in animo contrito, suscipiamur a te, Domine, et sic fiat sacrificium nostrum in conspectu tuo hodie, ut placeat tibi, Domine Deus

In the spirit of humility, and with a contrite heart, let us be received by thee, O Lord: and grant that the sacrifice we offer in thy sight this day may be pleasing to thee, O Lord God.

glory, in thanksgiving for all the benefits conferred upon myself and upon the whole world; and in satisfaction for my many sins, and the sins of other men. Accept, O Lord, of this holocaust, which is no other than thy divine Son at once made priest and victim, offering and offerer, and apply his saving merits to my needy soul. Be comforted, O my heart, Jesus sacrifices himself for thee.

O my Lord Jesus Christ, in remembrance and praise of the boundless love, with which thou didst give thyself wholly to us upon the altar of the cross, behold I offer unto thee this day this present sacrifice of the Mass, together with all the Masses which are celebrated throughout the world, by the hands of thy priests, to be presented to thy Eternal Father in union with, and in virtue of, that oblation in which thou thyself, dying on the cross, didst offer thy sacred body and blood for the salvation of the world.

Grant that the oblation of the same, thy body and blood, which here is renewed in mystery, and is made under the form of bread and wine, may effectually obtain its proper fruit; that thereby the living may receive grace, and the faithful departed, everlasting rest.

Accept, also, O Lord, this same sacrifice, which contains in itself the fruit of thy passion and death, as an act of thanksgiving for the innumerable benefits thou has conferred upon us, and a propitiation and satisfaction for the countless sins we have committed, the good we have omitted to do, and the punishments we have deserved. Who livest, &c.

Elevating his eyes and stretching out his hands, he says:

Veni, sanctificator, omnipotens æterne Deus, et bene✠dic hoc sacrificium, tuo sancto nomini præparatum.

Come, O sanctifier, almighty, eternal God, and bless✠this sacrifice, prepared to thy holy name.

At High Mass, he blesses the incense:

Per intercessionem beati Michælis archangeli, stantis a dextris altaris incensi, et omnium electorum suorum, incensum istud dignetur Dominus benedicere, et in odorem suavitatis accipere. Per Christum Dominum nostrum. Amen.

May the Lord, by the intercession of blessed Michael the archangel, standing at the right hand of the altar of incense, and of all his elect, vouchsafe to bless this incense, and receive it as an odour of sweetness. Through, &c. Amen.

He incenses the bread and wine, saying:

Incensum istud a te benedictum ascendat ad te, Domine, et descendat super nos misericordia tua.

May this incense which thou hast blessed, O Lord, ascend to thee, and may thy mercy descend upon us.

Then he incenses the Altar, saying:

Dirigatur, Domine, oratio mea sicut incensum in conspectu tuo: elevatio manuum mearum sacrificium vespertinum. Pone, Domine, custodiam ori meo, et ostium circumstantiæ labiis meis, ut non declinet cor meum in verba malitiæ, ad excusandas excusationes in peccatis.

Let my prayer, O Lord, be directed as incense in thy sight: the lifting up of my hands as evening sacrifice. Set a watch, O Lord, before my mouth, and a door round about my lips, that my heart may not incline to evil words, to make excuses in sins.

Giving the censer to the Deacon, he says:

Accendat in nobis Dominus ignem sui amoris, et flammam æternæ caritatis. Amen.

May the Lord enkindle in us the fire of his love, and the flame of everlasting charity. Amen.

Washing his fingers, he recites the following:

Lavabo inter innocentes manus meas: et circumdabo altare tuum, Domine. Ut audiam vocem laudis, et enarrem universa mirabilia tua. Domine, dilexi decorem domus tuæ, et locum habitationis gloriæ tuæ. Ne perdas cum impiis, Deus, animam meam: et cum

I will wash my hands among the innocent: and will encompass thy altar, O Lord. That I may hear the voice of praise, and tell of all thy marvellous works. I have loved, O Lord, the beauty of thy house, and the place where thy glory dwelleth. Take not

Or,

O ETERNAL Father, who wast pleased that by this most holy sacrifice of the New Law, thy only-begotten Son be offered to thee ; I offer the same to thy divine Majesty, and in union therewith I offer myself, and all that of thy bounty thou hast bestowed upon me. Look upon me, and have mercy upon me. Amen.

O my soul, how Jesus Christ hath loved us! At what a price he hath redeemed us! Not with gold, nor with riches, but by the voluntary shedding of his blood. He hath sacrificed himself for us : let us, then, live only for him, let us sacrifice ourselves together with him.

Thou willest, O Jesus, that I should be a victim of love, wholly consecrated to thy Divine Heart : it is my most ardent desire. Thy benefits are numberless ; thou hast broken the bonds of my servitude; thou hast adopted me for thy child ; thou hast admitted me to thy table ; thou hast given me a place in thy Divine Heart ; and even yet, for all my continual prevarications, thou preparest me an everlasting blessedness : how could I ever forget so many benefits ! I will publish thy mercies, and will never cease to love thee with all the fervour of my heart. But, O my God, my heart is not full enough of love and fervour to be an offering worthy of thee. What, then, shall I give thee? I will give thee thy Son. That Son, the most worthy object of thy complacency, will supply my inability. O Lord, look not on me, but on this divine offering.

viris sanguinum vitam meam. In quorum manibus iniquitates sunt: dextera eorum repleta est muneribus. Ego autem in innocentia mea ingressus sum: redime me, et miserere mei. Pes meus stetit in directo: in ecclesiis benedicam te, Domine. *Gloria, etc.

away my soul, O God, with the wicked, nor my life with bloody men. In whose hands are iniquities: their right hand is filled with gifts. As for me, I have walked in my innocence; redeem me, and have mercy upon me. My foot hath stood in the right path: in the churches I will bless thee, O Lord. Glory, &c.

Bowing before the Altar, he says:

Suscipe, sancta Trinitas, hanc oblationem quam tibi offerimus ob memoriam Passionis Resurrectionis, et Ascensionis Jesu Christi Domini nostri: et in honorem beatæ Mariæ semper Virginis, et beati Joannis Baptistæ, et sanctorum Apostolorum Petri et Pauli, et istorum et omnium Sanctorum: ut illis proficiat ad honorem, nobis autem ad salutem: et illi pro nobis intercedere dignentur in coelis, quorum memoriam agimus in terris. Per eundem.

Receive, O Holy Trinity, this oblation, which we make to thee, in memory of the Passion, Resurrection, and Ascension of our Lord Jesus Christ, and in honour of the blessed Mary ever Virgin, of blessed John Baptist, the holy Apostles Peter and Paul, of these and of all the Saints: that it may be available to their honour and our salvation: and may they vouchsafe to intercede for us in heaven, whose memory we celebrate on earth. Through, &c.

Turning to the people, he says:

Orate, fratres, ut meum ac vestrum sacrificium acceptabile fiat apud Deum Patrem omnipotentem.

R. Suscipiat Dominus sacrificium de manibus tuis, ad laudem et gloriam nominis sui, ad utilitatem quoque nostram, totiusque Ecclesiæ suæ sanctæ. Amen.

Brethren, pray that my sacrifice and yours may be acceptable to God the Father Almighty.

R. May the Lord receive the sacrifice from thy hands, to the praise and glory of his name, to our benefit, and to that of all his holy Church. Amen.

He then recites the Secret Prayers,

Which, being finished, he says in an audible voice:

V. Per omnia sæcula sæculorum.

R. Amen.
V. Dominus vobiscum.
R. Et cum spiritu tuo.
V. Sursum corda.

V. World without end.

R. Amen.
V. The Lord be with you.
R. And with thy spirit.
V. Lift up your hearts.

* The Gloria is omitted in Passion-time, when the Mass peculiar to the time is said; and in Masses for the Dead.

AT THE LAVABO.

O MY Jesus, would that I could take thee to witness of the holiness of my life and the innocence of my heart! But it is in thy mercy only that I place my hope; my consolation is in meditating on thy promises to the penitent heart, and thy faithfulness in performing them : confounded at all the sins that I have committed to this day, and encouraged by the favours which thou hast bestowed upon me, I can but promise to correspond better with thy graces than I have hitherto done. I will purify myself more and more with tears of penitence ; I will bless thee as I do this day ; and I will sing of the wonders of thy power and of thy mercy.

AT THE SUSCIPE.

O MOST holy and adorable Trinity, vouchsafe to receive this our sacrifice in remembrance of our Saviour's Passion, Resurrection, and glorious Ascension : and grant that we may die with him to our sins, rise with him to a new life, and ascend with him to thee. Let those saints, whose memory we celebrate on earth, remember us before thy throne in heaven, and obtain mercy for us, through the same Jesus Christ our Lord. Amen.

AT THE ORATE FRATRES.

THE creature can offer nothing to the Creator that can be worthy of his acceptance ; I unite myself. therefore. to the sacrifice of Jesus Christ, which can alone merit anything in my behalf. I desire nothing

R. Habemus ad Dominum.

V. Gratias agamus Domino Deo nostro.

R. Dignum et justum est.

Vere dignum et justum est, æquum et salutare, nos tibi semper et ubique, gratias agere, Domine sancte, Pater omnipotens, æterne Deus. Per Christum Dominum nostrum; per quem Majestatem tuam laudant angeli, adorant dominationes, tremunt potestates, cœli cœlorumque virtutes, ac beata seraphim, socia exultatione concelebrant. Cum quibus et nostras voces, ut admitti jubeas deprecamur, supplici confessione dicentes: Sanctus, sanctus, sanctus, Dominus Deus Sabaoth. Pleni sunt cœli et terra gloria tua. Hosanna in excelsis. Benedictus qui venit in nomine Domini. Hosanna in excelsis.

R. We have them lifted up unto the Lord.

V. Let us give thanks to the Lord our God.

R. It is meet and just.

It is truly meet and just, right and salutary, that we should always, and in all places, give thanks to thee, O holy Lord, Father Almighty, Eternal God. Through Christ our Lord; through whom the angels praise thy Majesty, the dominations adore, the powers do hold in awe, the heavens, and the virtues of the heavens, and the blessed seraphim, do celebrate with united joy. In union with whom, we beseech thee, that thou wouldst command our voices also to be admitted with suppliant confession, saying; Holy, holy, holy, Lord God of Sabaoth. Heaven and earth are full of thy glory. Hosanna in the highest. Blessed is he that cometh in the name of the Lord. Hosanna in the highest.

CANON OF THE MASS.

Te igitur, clementissime Pater, per Jesum Christum Filium tuum Dominum nostrum, supplices rogamus ac petimus uti accepta habeas et benedicas hæc ✠ dona, hæc ✠ munera, hæc ✠ sancta sacrificia illibata, in primis, quæ tibi offerimus pro Ecclesia tua sancta Catholica: quam pacificare, custodire, adunare, et regere digneris toto orbe terrarum, una cum famulo tuo Papa nostro N., et Antistite nostro N., et omnibus orthodoxis, atque Catholicæ et Apostolicæ Fidei cultoribus.

We therefore humbly pray and beseech thee, most merciful Father, through Jesus Christ thy Son, our Lord *[he kisses the Altar]*, that thou wouldst vouchsafe to accept and bless these ✠ gifts, these ✠ presents, these ✠ holy unspotted sacrifices, which in the first place, we offer thee for thy holy Catholic Church, to which vouchsafe to grant peace: as also to protect, unite, and govern it throughout the world, together with thy servant N. our Pope, N. our Bishop, as also all orthodox believers and professors of the Catholic and Apostolic Faith.

but through him and with him. I have no wish beyond him. O God of mercy, I seek nothing but thy love. Graciously accept of the sacrifice of my heart and of my whole self, and may it, like the sacrifice of Jesus, be pleasing to thee and unite us to him.

AT THE SECRETA.

MERCIFULLY hear our prayers, O Lord, and graciously accept this oblation which we thy servants make to thee; and as we offer it to the honour of thy name, so may it be to us here a means of obtaining thy grace, and life everlasting hereafter. Through Jesus Christ. Amen.

AT THE PREFACE.

LIFT up, O Lord, do thou thyself lift up my heart to thee. Take from it all unholy thoughts, all earthly affections. Lift it wholly up to heaven, where thou art worthily adored, and to the altar, where thou art about to manifest thyself to me. My life is but one continual succession of thy mercies; let it be one continual succession of thanksgivings: and as thou art now about to renew the greatest of all sacrifices, is it not meet that I should burst forth in expressions of heartfelt gratitude? Suffer me, then, to join my feeble voice with the voices of all the heavenly spirits, and in union with them to say, in a transport of joy and admiration:

HOLY, HOLY, HOLY, LORD GOD OF SABAOTH. HEAVEN AND EARTH ARE FULL OF THY GLORY. HOSANNA IN THE HIGHEST.

BLESSED IS HE THAT COMETH IN THE NAME OF THE LORD. HOSANNA IN THE HIGHEST.

COMMEMORATION OF THE LIVING.

Memento, Domine, famulorum famularumque tuarum. N. et N.	Be mindful, O Lord, of thy servants, men and women, N. and N.

He pauses, and prays silently for those he intends to pray for, and proceeds:

Et omnium circumstantium, quorum tibi fides cognita est, et nota devotio: pro quibus tibi offerimus, vel qui tibi offerunt hoc sacrificium laudis, pro se, suisque omnibus, pro redemptione animarum suarum, pro spe salutis et incolumitatis suæ: tibique reddunt vota sua, æterno Deo, vivo et vero.

Communicantes, et memoriam venerantes, in primis gloriosæ semper Virginis Mariæ Genitricis Dei et Domini nostri Jesu Christi: sed et beatorum Apostolorum ac Martyrum tuorum, Petri et Pauli, Andreæ, Jacobi, Joannis, Thomæ, Jacobi, Philippi, Bartholomæi, Matthæi, Simonis et Thaddæi; Lini, Cleti, Clementis, Xysti, Cornelii, Cypriani, Laurentii, Chrysogoni, Joannis et Pauli, Cosmæ et Damiani, et omnium Sanctorum tuorum: quorum meritis precibusque concedas, ut in omnibus protectionis tuæ muniamur auxilio. Per eundem Christum Dominum nostrum. Amen.

And of all here present, whose faith and devotion are known unto thee; for whom we offer or who offer up to thee, this sacrifice of praise for themselves, their families and friends, for the redemption of their souls, for the hope of their safety and salvation, and who pay their vows to thee, the eternal, living, and true God.

Communicating with, and honouring in the first place the memory of the glorious and ever Virgin Mary, Mother of God and our Lord Jesus Christ; as also of the blessed Apostles and Martyrs, Peter and Paul, Andrew, James, John, Thomas, James, Philip, Bartholomew, Matthew, Simon and Thaddeus, Linus, Cletus, Clement, Xystus, Cornelius, Cyprian, Lawrence, Chrysogonus, John and Paul, Cosmas and Damian, and of all thy Saints; by whose merits and prayers grant that we may be always defended by the help of thy protection. Through the same Christ our Lord. Amen.

Spreading his hands over the oblation, he says:

Hanc igitur oblationem servitutis nostræ, sed et cunctæ familiæ tuæ, quæsumus, Domine, ut placatus accipias; diesque nostros in tua pace disponas, atque ab æterna damnatione nos eripi, et in electorum tuorum jubeas grege numerari. Per Christum Dominum nostrum. Amen.

Quam oblationem, tu Deus, in omnibus, quæsumus benedic-✠

We therefore beseech thee, O Lord, graciously to accept this oblation of our service, as also of thy whole family; dispose our days in thy peace, command us to be delivered from eternal damnation, and to be numbered in the flock of thy elect. Through Christ our Lord. Amen.

Which oblation do thou, O God, vouchsafe in all things to make

AT THE CANON.

O ETERNAL and most merciful Father, behold, we come to offer thee our homage this day; we desire to adore, praise, and glorify thee, and to give thee thanks for thy great glory, joining our hearts and voices with all thy blessed in heaven, and with thy whole Church upon earth. But acknowledging our great unworthiness and innumerable sins, for which we are heartily sorry and humbly beg thy pardon, we dare not venture to approach thee otherwise than in company of thy Son, our Advocate and Mediator, Jesus Christ, whom thou hast given us to be both our High Priest and Sacrifice. With him, therefore, and through him we venture to offer thee this sacrifice; to his most sacred intentions we desire to unite ours; and with this offering which he makes of himself, we desire to make an offering of our whole being to thee. With him, and through him, we beseech thee to exalt thy holy Catholic Church, throughout the whole world; to maintain her in peace, unity, holiness, and truth; to have mercy on thy servant *N.* our chief bishop, *N.* our prelate, and on all that truly fear thee; on our pastor [*parents, children*], friends and benefactors, &c.; on all those whom we have in any way scandalised, injured or offended, or for whom we are on any other account bound to pray; on all that are in their agony, or under violent temptations, or other necessities, corporal or spiritual; on all our enemies; and, in a word, on all poor sinners; that we may all be converted to thee, and find mercy, through Jesus

tain. adscrip✠tam. ra✠tam. rationabilem. acceptabilemque facere digneris; ut nobis cor✠pus et san✠guis fiat dilectissimi Filii tui Domini nostri Jesu Christi.

Qui pridie quam pateretur. accepit panem in sanctas ac venerabiles manus suas. et elevatis oculis in coelum, ad te Deum Patrem suum omnipotentem: tibi gratias agens, bene✠dixit. fregit deditque discipulis suis, dicens: Accipite, et manducate ex hoc omnes; HOC EST ENIM CORPUS MEUM.

blessed, approved. ratified. reasonable, and accepta'le. that it may become to us the body ✠ and ✠ blood of thy most beloved Son Jesus Christ our Lord.

Who the day before he suffered took bread *he takes the Host*] into his holy and venerable hands *he raises his eyes to heaven*]. and with his eyes lifted up towards heaven, to thee God. his almighty Father, giving thanks to thee. did bless, break, and give to his disciples. saying: Take, and eat ye all of this; FOR THIS IS MY BODY.

After pronouncing the words of consecration, the Priest. kneeling, adores the Sacred Host, and rising, he elevates it.

(At the Elevation, the bell is rung thrice.)

Simili modo postquam coenatum est. accipiens et hunc praeclarum calicem in sanctas ac venerabiles manus suas, item tibi gratias agens. bene✠dixit, deditque discipulis suis, dicens: Accipite et bibite ex eo omnes: HIC EST ENIM CALIX SANGUINIS MEI NOVI ET ÆTERNI TESTAMENTI; MYSTERIUM FIDEI; QUI PRO VOBIS ET PRO MULTIS EFFUNDETUR IN REMISSIONEM PECCATORUM.

Hæc quotiescumque feceritis, in mei memoriam facietis.

In like manner. after he had supped [*he takes the chalice in both his hands*], taking also this excellent chalice into his holy and venerable hands. and giving thee thanks, he bless✠ed. and gave to his disciples. saying: Take, and drink ye all of this; FOR THIS IS THE CHALICE OF MY BLOOD, OF THE NEW AND ETERNAL TESTAMENT; THE MYSTERY OF FAITH; WHICH SHALL BE SHED FOR YOU, AND FOR MANY, TO THE REMISSION OF SINS.

As often as ye do these things, ye shall do them in remembrance of me.

Kneeling. he adores. and rising, elevates the Chalice.

Unde et memores, Domine, nos servi tui. sed et plebs tua sancta, ejusdem Christi Filii tui Domini nostri, tam beatæ passionis, necnon et ab inferis resurrectionis, sed et in coelos gloriosæ ascensionis, offerimus præclaræ Majestati tuæ, de tuis donis ac datis,

Wherefore, O Lord, we thy servants, as also thy holy people. calling to mind the blessed passion of the same Christ thy Son our Lord. his resurrection from hell. and glorious ascension into heaven, offer unto thy most excellent Majesty, of thy gifts and grants, a

Christ thy Son; through whom we hope one day to be admitted into the company of all thy saints and elect, whose memory we here celebrate, whose prayers we desire, and with whom we communicate in these holy mysteries Amen.

AT THE CONSECRATION.

[Bow down your body and soul in solemn adoration; make an act of faith in the real presence of your Saviour's body and blood, soul and divinity, under the sacramental veils. Offer your whole self to him, and through him to his Father: beg that your heart and soul may be happily changed into him.]

AT THE ELEVATION OF THE HOST.

(Here the bell is rung thrice.)

HAIL, true Body, born of the Virgin Mary, which didst truly suffer and wast immolated on the cross for man, whose side was pierced, and flowed with water and with blood: may we have a foretaste of thee in the last agony of death. O kind, O loving one, Jesus, Son of Mary, have mercy on me! Amen.

Or,

HAIL, saving Victim, incarnate Word, sacrificed for me and all mankind! Hail precious Body of the Son of God! Hail sacred Flesh, torn with nails, pierced with a lance, and bleeding on a cross for us sinners! O amazing goodness! O infinite love! Oh, let that tender love plead now in my behalf; let all my iniquities be here effaced, let my soul be cleansed from all its defilements. Lord, i believe in thee; I hope in thee; I love thee. To thee be honour, praise, and glory, from all creatures, for ever and ever. Amen.

Hostiam ✠ puram, Hostiam ✠ sanctam, Hostiam ✠ immaculatam, panem ✠ sanctum vitæ æternæ, et calicem ✠ salutis perpetuæ.

pure ✠ Host, a holy ✠ Host, an immaculate ✠ Host, the holy ✠ bread of eternal life, and the chalice ✠ of everlasting salvation.

Extending his hands, he proceeds:

Supra quæ propitio ac sereno vultu respicere digneris, et accepta habere, sicuti accepta habere dignatus es munera pueri tui justi Abel, et sacrificium Patriarchæ nostri Abrahæ; et quod tibi obtulit summus sacerdos tuus Melchisedech, sanctum sacrificium, immaculatam hostiam.

Upon which vouchsafe to look with a propitious and serene countenance, and to accept them, as thou wert graciously pleased to accept the gifts of thy just servant Abel, and the sacrifice of our Patriarch Abraham, and that which thy high-priest Melchisedech offered to thee, a holy sacrifice, an immaculate host.

Bowing down, he says:

Supplices te rogamus, omnipotens Deus, jube hæc perferri per manus sancti angeli tui in sublime altare tuum, in conspectu divinæ Majestatis tuæ, ut quotquot ex hac altaris participatione, sacrosanctum Filii tui corpus ✠ et ✠ sanguinem sumpserimus, omni benedictione cœlesti et gratia repleamur. Per eundem Christum Dominum nostrum. Amen.

We most humbly beseech thee, almighty God, command these things to be carried by the hands of thy holy angel to thy altar on high, in the sight of thy divine Majesty, that as many of us [*he kisses the Altar*] as, by participation at this Altar, shall receive the most sacred body ✠ and ✠ blood of thy Son, may be filled with all heavenly benediction and grace. Through the same Christ, &c. Amen.

Memento etiam, Domine, famulorum famularumque tuarum N. et N., qui nos præcesserunt cum signo fidei, et dormiunt in somno pacis.

Be mindful also, O Lord, of thy servants and handmaids N. and N., who are gone before us, with the sign of faith, and repose in the sleep of peace.

He prays for such of the Dead as he intends to pray for.

Ipsis, Domine, et omnibus in Christo quiescentibus, locum refrigerii, lucis et pacis, ut indulgeas, deprecamur. Per eundem Christum, &c. Amen.

To these, O Lord, and to all that rest in Christ, grant, we beseech thee, a place of refreshment, light, and peace. Through the same Christ our Lord. Amen.

Here, striking his breast and slightly raising his voice, he says:

Nobis quoque peccatoribus famulis tuis, de multitudine mise

And to us sinners, thy servants, hoping in the multitude of thy

AT THE ELEVATION OF THE CHALICE.
(Here also the bell is rung thrice.)

SAVIOUR of the world, save us ; for by thy cross and by thy blood thou hast redeemed us ; help us, we beseech thee, O our God. Amen.

Have mercy on me, dear Jesus, and grant that thy blood may not be shed in vain for me, I most humbly beseech thee. Amen.

Or,

HAIL, sacred Blood, flowing from the wounds of Jesus Christ, and washing away the sins of the world! O cleanse, sanctify, and preserve my soul, that nothing in future may ever separate me from thee. Behold, O Eternal Father, thy holy Jesus, and look upon the face of thy Christ, in whom thou art well pleased. Hear the voice of his blood crying out to thee, not for vengeance, but for mercy and pardon. Accept this divine oblation, and through the infinite merits of all the sufferings that Jesus endured on the cross for our salvation, be pleased to look upon us, and upon all thy people, with an eye of mercy.

AT THE MEMENTO FOR THE DEAD.

I OFFER thee again, O Lord, this holy sacrifice of the body and blood of thy only Son, in behalf of the faithful departed, and in particular for the souls of [*here name whom you chiefly propose to pray for*] my parents [*if dead*], relatives, benefactors, neighbours, &c. Likewise of such as I have any ways injured, or been the occasion of their sins ; of such as have injured me, and been my enemies ; of such as die in

rationum tuarum sperantibus, partem aliquam et societatem donare digneris, cum tuis sanctis apostolis et martyribus: cum Joanne. Stephano. Matthia, Barnaba, Ignatio, Alexandro, Marcellino, Petro, Felicitate, Perpetua, Agatha. Lucia. Agnete, Cæcilia, Anastasia, et omnibus sanctis tuis : intra quorum nos consortium, non æstimator meriti, sed veniæ, quæsumus, largitor admitte. Per Christum Dominum nostrum.

Per quem hæc omnia, Domine, semper bona creas, sancti ✠ ficas vivi ✠ ficas, bene ✠ dicis, et præstas nobis. Per ip ✠ sum, et cum ip ✠ so, et in ip ✠ so, est tibi Deo Patri ✠ omnipotenti, in unitate Spiritus ✠ Sancti, omnis honor et gloria.

V. Per omnia secula saeculorum.

R. Amen.

ORENUS.

Præceptis salutaribus moniti, et divina institutione formati, audemus dicere:

Pater noster, qui es in cœlis, sanctificetur nomen tuum: adveniat regnum tuum; fiat voluntas tua sicut in cœlo et in terra. Panem nostrum quotidianum da nobis hodie; et dimitte nobis debita nostra, sicut et nos dimittimus debitoribus nostris. Et ne nos inducas in tentationem.

R. Sed libera nos a malo.

He then says in a low voice, "Amen," *and continues:*

Libera nos quæsumus, Domine, ab omnibus malis, præteritis, præsentibus, et futuris: et intercedente beata et gloriosa semper Virgine Dei Genitrice Maria, cum beatis Apostolis tuis Petro et Paulo, atque Andrea, et omnibus Sanctis, da propitius pacem in diebus nostris: ut ope miseri-

mercies, vouchsafe to grant some part and fellowship with thy holy apostles and martyrs; with John, Stephen, Matthias, Barnabas, Ignatius, Alexander, Marcellinus, Peter, Felicitas, Perpetua, Agatha, Lucy, Agnes, Cecily, Anastasia, and with all thy Saints: into whose company we beseech thee to admit us, not considering our merit, but freely pardoning our offences. Through Christ our Lord.

By whom, O Lord, thou dost always create, sanctify, ✠ quicken, ✠ bless, ✠ and give us all these good things. Through him ✠ and with him, ✠ and in him, ✠ is to thee, God the Father ✠ Almighty, in the unity of the Holy ✠ Ghost, all honour and glory.

V. For ever and ever.

R. Amen.

Instructed by thy saving precepts, and following thy divine institution, we presume to say:

Our Father, who art in heaven, hallowed be thy name: thy kingdom come : thy will be done on earth as it is in heaven. Give us this day our daily bread; and forgive us our trespasses, as we forgive them that trespass against us. And lead us not into temptation.

R. But deliver us from evil.

Deliver us, we beseech thee, O Lord, from all evils, past, present, and to come; and by the intercession of the blessed and glorious Mary ever Virgin, Mother of God, together with thy blessed Apostles Peter and Paul, and Andrew, and all the Saints [*making the sign of the Cross on*

war, or have none to pray for them. To these, O
Lord, and to all that rest in Christ, grant, we beseech
thee, a place of refreshment, light and peace. Through
the same Christ our Lord. Amen.

AT THE NOBIS QUOQUE PECCATORIBUS.

VOUCHSAFE to grant the same to us, poor and
miserable sinners; judge us not according to our
demerits; but through the infinite multitude of thy
mercies, in which we hope, liberally extend to us thy
grace and pardon.

We ask it of thee in the name of thy dear Son,
who liveth and reigneth eternally with thee, and in
that form of prayer which he himself hath taught us.

AT THE PATER NOSTER.

OUR Father, who reignest in heaven, come and
reign in my soul, come and sanctify it by thy
presence; come and subject it to thy holy will, and
render it obedient to the inspirations of thy grace.
Extinguish in my heart every feeling of hatred and
revenge; forgive me as I forgive. Grant to me such
wisdom and such strength that I may triumph over
all temptations. Deliver me from all those evils
which oppress me, and under which I groan, being
burdened. I come to thee, as a child to his father, to
be fed; as a subject to his prince, to be protected; as
one afflicted, to his only succour, to be consoled and
comforted.

Or,

THOU, O ineffable God, art our Father. Our
Father, because thou hast created us with so much

cordiæ tuæ adjuti. et a peccato simus semper liberi. et ab omni perturbatione securi. Per eundem Dominum nostrum Jesum Christum Filium tuum. Qui tecum vivit et regnat in unitate Spiritus Sancti Deus.

himself with the paten. he kisses it, and says], mercifully grant peace in our days; that by the assistance of thy mercy we may be always free from sin, and secure from all disturbance. Through the same Jesus Christ thy Son our Lord. Who with thee in the unity of the Holy Ghost liveth and reigneth God.

Then he says aloud:

V. Per omnia sæcula sæculorum.

R. Amen.

V. Pax ✠ Domini sit ✠ semper vobis ✠ cum.

R. Et cum spiritu tuo.

V. World without end.

R. Amen.

V. May the peace of the ✠ Lord be ✠ always with ✠ you.

R. And with thy spirit.

In a low voice:

Hæc commixtio et consecratio corporis et sanguinis Domini nostri Jesu Christi fiat accipientibus nobis in vitam æternam. Amen.

May this mingling and consecration of the body and blood of our Lord Jesus Christ be to us that receive it effectual to eternal life. Amen.

Striking his breast three times, he says

*Agnus Dei, qui tollis peccata mundi, miserere nobis (twice); or Dona eis requiem (twice).

Agnus Dei, qui tollis peccata mundi, dona nobis pacem: or Dona eis requiem sempiternam.

Domine Jesu Christe, qui dixisti Apostolis tuis, Pacem relinquo vobis, pacem meam do vobis; ne respicias peccata mea, sed fidem Ecclesiæ tuæ; eamque secundum voluntatem tuam pacificare et coadunare digneris; qui vivis et regnas Deus, per omnia sæcula sæculorum. Amen.

Domine Jesu Christe, Fili Dei vivi, qui ex voluntate Patris, cooperante Spiritu Sancto, per mortem tuam mundum vivificasti; libera me per hoc sacrosanctum corpus et sanguinem tuum ab omnibus iniquitatibus meis, et uni-

Lamb of God, who takest away the sins of the world, have mercy upon us (twice).

Lamb of God, who takest away the sins of the world, grant us thy peace.

Lord Jesus Christ, who saidst to thy Apostles: Peace I leave with you. my peace I give unto you; regard not my sins, but the faith of thy Church; and vouchsafe to it that peace and unity which is agreeable to thy will; who livest and reignest God for ever and ever. Amen.

Lord Jesus Christ, Son of the living God, who, according to the will of the Father, through the co-operation of the Holy Ghost. hast by thy death given life to the world; deliver me by this. thy most sacred body and blood,

* In Masses for the Dead, the priest does not strike his breast at the "Agnus," and he omits the first of the three following prayers.

love. Our Father, because thou hast redeemed us with so much blood. Our Father because thou dost preserve us by thy omnipotence. Deal with us, O Lord, as thy children; and grant that we may truly reverence thee as our Father. Endow us, we beseech thee, with grace to seek only thy glory, as becomes the children of so good a Parent. We were created by thee, we are governed by thee. O grant that we may live only for thee.

AT THE LIBERA NOS.

DELIVER us, we beseech thee, O Lord, from all evils, past, present, and to come; and by the intercession of Blessed Mary ever Virgin, and of all the saints, mercifully grant peace in our days, that by the assistance of thy holy grace we may be always free from sin and secure from all disturbance.

AT THE PAX DOMINI.

THY body was broken, and thy blood shed for us. Grant that the commemoration of this holy mystery may obtain for us peace; and that those who receive it may find everlasting rest.

O Lamb of God, pure and spotless victim who alone canst satisfy the justice of an offended God, vouchsafe to make me partaker of the merits of thy sacrifice. What lessons of humility, meekness, charity and patience dost thou not give! Impress these virtues upon my heart, that it may be to thee a pleasant habitation, wherein thou mayest repose as in an abode of peace.

versis malis, et fac me tuis semper inhærere mandatis. et a te nunqu. m separari permittas: qui eum eodem Deo Patre et Spiritu Sancto vivis et regnas Deus in sæcula sæculorum. Amen.

from all my iniquities and from all evils: and make me always adhere to thy commandments, and never suffer me to be separated from thee; who with the same God the Father and Holy Ghost livest and reignest God for ever and ever. Amen.

Perceptio corporis tui, Domine Jesu Christe, quod ego indignus sumere præsumo, non mihi proveniat in judicium et condemnationem; sed pro tua pietate prosit mihi ad tutamentum mentis et corporis, et ad medelam percipiendam. Qui vivis et regnas cum Deo Patre, in unitate Spiritus Sancti, Deus per omnia sæcula sæculorum. Amen.

Let not the participation of thy body, O Lord Jesus Christ, which I, unworthy, presume to receive, turn to my judgment and condemnation: but through thy goodness may it be to me a safeguard and remedy, both of soul and body. Who with God the Father, in the unity of the Holy Ghost. livest and reignest God for ever and ever. Amen.

Having made a genuflection. the Priest rises and says:

Panem cœlestem accipiam, et nomen Domini invocabo.

I will take the bread of heaven, and call upon the name of the Lord.

Then striking his breast, and raising his voice a little. he says three times:

Domine. non sum dignus ut intres sub tectum meum; sed tantum dic verbo, et sanabitur anima mea.

Lord. I am not worthy that thou shouldst enter under my roof; say but the word, and my soul shall be healed.

After which he says:

Corpus Domini nostri Jesu Christi custodiat animam meam in vitam æternam. Amen.

May the body of our Lord Jesus Christ preserve my soul to life everlasting. Amen.

He then receives the sacred Host. and after a short pause, says:

Quid retribuam Domino pro omnibus quæ retribuit mihi? Calicem salutaris accipiam. et nomen Domini invocabo. Laudans invocabo Dominum, et ab inimicis meis salvus ero.

What shall I render to the Lord for all he hath rendered unto me? I will take the chalice of salvation, and call upon the name of the Lord. Praising I will call upon the Lord, and I shall be saved from my enemies.

AFTER THE AGNUS DEI.

IN saying to thy Apostles, Peace I leave with you, my peace I give unto you, thou hast promised, O Lord, to all thy Church, that peace which the world cannot give—peace with thee, and peace with ourselves.

Let nothing, O Lord, ever interrupt this holy peace; let nothing separate us from thee, to whom we heartily desire to be united, through the blessed sacrament of peace and reconciliation. Let this food of angels strengthen us in every Christian duty, so as never more to yield under temptations, or fall into our common weaknesses.

———

O my good God, and sweet Saviour Jesus, who art present here for my sake, and givest thyself to me for daily food, and for the supply of all my necessities: since without thee, who art the true food of my soul, I cannot live, I humbly beseech thee to refresh me spiritually, and make me partaker of that grace which they experience who devoutly receive thee. O good Jesus, despise me not, but vouchsafe to visit thy servant, and by thy grace to work and perfect all the effects and virtues of thy holy sacrament in me, to thy honour, O my God, and the eternal salvation of my soul. Amen.

Soul of Christ, sanctify me; body of Christ, save me; Blood of Christ, inebriate me; Water issuing from the side of Christ, wash me; Passion of Christ, strengthen me. O good Jesus, hear me, hide me within thy wounds; never suffer me to be separated from thee; from the

Receiving the Chalice he says:

Sanguis Domini nostri Jesu Christi custodiat animam meam in vitam æternam. Amen.

May the blood of our Lord Jesus Christ preserve my soul to everlasting life. Amen.

Those who are to communicate go up to the Sanctuary at the Domine, non sum dignus, *when the bell rings: the Acolyte spreads a cloth before them, and says the* Confiteor.

Then the Priest, turning to the Communicants, pronounces the Absolution.

Misereatur vestri, &c. Indulgentiam, absolutionem, &c.

May Almighty God have mercy, &c. May the almighty and merciful Lord, &c.

Elevating one of the sacred Particles, and turning towards the people, he says:

Ecce Agnus Dei, ecce qui tollit peccata mundi.

Behold the Lamb of God, behold him who taketh away the sins of the world.

And then repeats three times, Domine, non sum dignus, &c.

He then administers the Holy Communion, saying to each:

Corpus Domini nostri Jesu Christi custodiat animam tuam in vitam æternam. Amen.

May the body of our Lord Jesus Christ preserve thy soul to life everlasting. Amen.

Taking the first ablution, he says:

Quod ore sumpsimus, Domine, pura mente capiamus: et de munere temporali fiat nobis remedium sempiternum.

Grant, O Lord, that what we have taken with our mouth we may receive with a pure mind; and of a temporal gift may it become to us an eternal remedy.

Taking the second ablution, he says:

Corpus tuum, Domine, quod sumpsi, et sanguis quem potavi, adhæreat visceribus meis: et præsta, ut in me non remaneat scelerum macula, quem pura et

May thy body, O Lord, which I have received, and thy blood which I have drunk, cleave to my bowels; and grant that no stain of sin may remain in me, who have

malignant enemy defend me; at the hour of my death call me, and bid me come unto thee, that with thy saints I may praise thee for all eternity. Amen.

AT THE DOMINE NON SUM DIGNUS.

GOD only can be worthy of receiving God; how, then, can a soul so sinful as mine merit so great a happiness! But thou, O Lord, regardest not thy greatness but thy mercy. Thou willest that I come to thee, as one sick to the physician who can heal him, as one poor to the rich lord who can assist him. O God of love, behold at thy feet the poorest, the most infirm, of thy creatures. Unite me to thyself, and I shall become rich and whole in thy sight. Work, I beseech thee, this miracle, worthy of thy omnipotence and charity.

WHILE THE PRIEST COMMUNICATES.

O SACRED banquet, in which Christ is received, the memory of his passion is renewed, the mind is filled with grace, and a pledge of future glory is given to us!

Grant, O Lord Jesus, that we may so reverence the sacred mysteries of thy body and blood, that we may ever find in ourselves the fruits of thy redemption. Amen.

ACT OF SPIRITUAL COMMUNION FOR THOSE WHO DO NOT INTEND TO COMMUNICATE.

O MY most loving Saviour, since I cannot have the happiness of receiving thee this day, suffer

sancta refecerunt sacramenta. Qui vivis et regnas in sæcula sæculorum. Amen.

been refreshed with pure and holy sacraments. Who livest, &c. Amen.

V. Dominus vobiscum.
R. Et cum spiritu tuo.

V. The Lord be with you.
R. And with thy spirit.

Then he reads the Post-Communions.

Afterwards he turns again towards the people, and says:

V. Dominus vobiscum.
R. Et cum spiritu tuo.
* Ite, missa est.
R. Deo gratias.

V. The Lord be with you.
R. And with thy spirit.
Go, the Mass is ended.
R. Thanks be to God.

* In place of "Ite, missa est," the priest sometimes says, turned towards the altar, "Benedicamus Domino," and in Masses for the Dead, "Requiescant in Pace." R. Amen.

Bowing down before the Altar, he says:

Placeat tibi, sancta Trinitas, obsequium servitutis meæ; et præsta nt sacrificium quod oculis tuæ Majestatis indignus obtuli, tibi sit acceptabile, mihique, et omnibus pro quibus illud obtuli, sit, te miserante, propitiabile. Per Christum Dominum nostrum. Amen.

O holy Trinity, let the performance of my homage be pleasing to thee; and grant that the sacrifice which I, unworthy, have offered up in the sight of thy Majesty, may be acceptable to thee, and through thy mercy be a propitiation for me, and all those for whom I have offered it. Through Christ our Lord. Amen.

Then he kisses the Altar, and raising his eyes, extending, raising, and joining his hands, he bows his head to the Crucifix, and says:

Benedicat vos omnipotens Deus, Pater, et Filius ✠ et Spiritus Sanctus. Amen.

May Almighty God, the Father, and the Son, ✠ and the Holy Ghost, bless you. Amen.

At the word "Deus," he turns towards the people, and makes the sign of the Cross on them. Then turning to the Gospel side of the Altar he says:

V. Dominus vobiscum.
R. Et cum spiritu tuo

V. The Lord be with you.
R. And with thy spirit.

(The Blessing is omitted in Masses for the Dead.)

me to gather up the precious crumbs that fall from thy table, and to unite myself to thy divine heart by faith, hope, and charity. I confess I do not deserve the children's bread ; but I venture humbly to declare that, away from thee, my soul is dried up with thirst, and my heart cast down with faintness. Come, then, into me, O my divine Jesus ; come into my mind, to illuminate it with thy light ; come into my heart, to enkindle in it the fire of thy love, and to unite it so intimately with thy own, that it may be no more I that live, but thou that livest in me, and reignest in me for ever.

PRAYER DURING THE ABLUTIONS.

GRANT us, O Lord, a part in the fruits of thy death and passion, which we have this day commemorated. I adore thy goodness, O gracious Lord, for thy inestimable favour in admitting me to be present again at that holy sacrifice where thou art both priest and victim. Oh, make me always sensible of so great a blessing, and let not my unworthiness put a bar to thy mercy and goodness.

AT THE COMMUNION.

LET it be now, O Lord, the effect of thy mercy, that we, who have been present at this holy mystery, may find the benefit of it in our souls.

Oh, how sweet, Lord, is thy spirit; who, to show thy sweetness towards thy children, givest them the most delicious bread from heaven, and sendest the proud away empty.

He then begins the Gospel according to St. John, saying:

V. Initium sancti Evangelii secundum Joannem.

R. Gloria tibi. Domine.

In principio erat Verbum, et Verbum erat apud Deum, et Deus erat Verbum: hoc erat in principio apud Deum. Omnia per ipsum facta sunt, et sine ipso factum est nihil quod factum est; in ipso vita erat, et vita erat lux hominum; et lux in tenebris lucet, et tenebrae eam non comprehenderunt.

Fuit homo missus a Deo, cui nomen erat Joannes. Hic venit in testimonium, ut testimonium perhiberet de lumine, ut omnes crederent per illum. Non erat ille lux; sed ut testimonium perhiberet de lumine. Erat lux vera quae illuminat omnem hominem venientem in hunc mundum.

In mundo erat, et mundus per ipsum factus est, et mundus eum non cognovit. In propria venit, et sui eum non receperunt. Quotquot autem receperunt eum, dedit eis potestatem filios Dei fieri: his qui credunt in nomine ejus, qui non ex sanguinibus, neque ex voluntate carnis, neque ex voluntate viri, sed ex Deo nati sunt. ET VERBUM CARO FACTUM EST [*hic genuflectitur*], et habitavit in nobis; et vidimus gloriam ejus, gloriam quasi Unigeniti a Patre, plenum gratiae et veritatis.

R. Deo gratias.

V. The beginning of the holy Gospel according to St. John.

R. Glory be to thee, O Lord.

In the beginning was the Word, and the Word was with God, and the Word was God; the same was in the beginning with God. All things were made by him, and without him was made nothing that was made: in him was life, and the life was the light of men: and the light shineth in darkness, and the darkness did not comprehend it.

There was a man sent from God, whose name was John. This man came for a witness to bear witness of the light, that all men might believe through him. He was not the light, but was to bear witness of the light. That was the true light which enlighteneth every man that cometh into this world.

He was in the world, and the world was made by him, and the world knew him not. He came unto his own, and his own received him not. But as many as received him, to them he gave power to be made the sons of God, to them that believe in his name, who are born not of blood, nor of the will of the flesh, nor of the will of man, but of God. AND THE WORD WAS MADE FLESH [*here the people kneel down*], and dwelt among us, and we saw his glory, as it were the glory of the Only-begotten of the Father, full of grace and truth.

R. Thanks be to God.

When a Feast falls on a Sunday, or other day which has a proper Gospel of its own, the Gospel of the day is read instead of the Gospel of St. John.

AT THE POST-COMMUNIONS.

POUR forth upon us, O Lord, the Spirit of thy love, that, by thy mercy, thou mayest make those of one mind whom thou hast fed with one celestial food. Through our Lord Jesus Christ, who liveth and reigneth with thee in the unity of the same Holy Spirit, &c.

AT THE LAST GOSPEL.

O ETERNAL Word, speak to my soul, which adores thee in profound silence: thou who art the great Creator of all things, abandon not, I beseech thee, thy own creature: be thou my life, my light, and my all.

LET US PRAY.

WE give thee thanks, almighty and gracious Father, that thou hast permitted us this day to offer our homage to thy divine Majesty. Of thine infinite mercy grant us pardon of our sins, and all things necessary for the welfare of our souls and bodies. Amen.

PRAYERS ORDERED BY OUR HOLY FATHER POPE LEO XIII. TO BE SAID KNEELING AFTER THE CELEBRATION OF LOW MASS IN ALL CHURCHES OF THE WORLD.

Hail Mary, &c., *to be said thrice by the Priest and People.*

Hail, holy Queen, Mother of Mercy, hail; our life,

our sweetness, and our hope! To thee do we cry, poor banished children of Eve. To thee do we send up our sighs, mourning and weeping in this valley of tears. Turn then, most gracious Advocate, thine eyes of mercy towards us; and after this our exile, show unto us the blessed fruit of thy womb, Jesus. O clement, O loving, O Sweet Virgin Mary.

V. Pray for us, O holy Mother of God.

R. That we may be made worthy of the promises of Christ.

LET US PRAY.

O GOD our refuge and our strength, look down with favour on thy people who cry to thee; and through the intercession of the glorious and Immaculate Virgin Mary, Mother of God, of St. Joseph, her Spouse, of thy blessed Apostles, Peter and Paul, and of all the Saints, in mercy and goodness hear our prayers for the conversion of sinners, and for the liberty and exaltation of our Holy Mother the Church. Through the same Christ our Lord. Amen.

Blessed Michael, Archangel, defend us in the hour of conflict; be our safeguard against the wickedness and snares of the devil. May God restrain him we humbly pray. And do thou, O Prince of the heavenly host, by the power of God thrust, down to hell, Satan, and with him the other wicked spirits who wander through the world for the ruin of souls. Amen.

(300 *days' Indulgence.*)

The Manner of Serving Mass,

ACCORDING TO THE DOMINICAN RITE.*

The Clerk gives wine and water before the beginning of the Mass. In presenting the water (except in Masses for the Dead), he says. "Benedicite;" and after the blessing answers, "Amen."

P. In nomine Patris, et Filii, et Spiritus Sancti. Amen. Confitemini Domino quoniam bonus.

C. Quoniam in sæculum misericordia ejus.

P. Confiteor Deo omnipotenti, et Beatæ Mariæ semper Virgini, et Beato Dominico Patri nostro, et omnibus Sanctis, et vobis, Fratres, quia peccavi nimis cogitatione, locutione, opere et omissione, mea culpa, precor vos orare pro me.

C. Misereatur tui omnipotens Deus, et dimittat tibi omnia peccata tua, liberet te ab omni malo, salvet et confirmet in omni opere bono, et perducat te ad vitam æternam.

P. Amen.

C. Confiteor Deo omnipotenti, et Beatæ Mariæ semper Virgini, et Beato Dominico Patri nostro, et omnibus Sanctis, et tibi, Pater, quia peccavi nimis cogitatione, locutione, opere et omissione, mea culpa, precor te orare pro me.

* The Dominican Rite, though substantially the same, differs in a few particulars from that of the Seculars. It is of the highest antiquity, being the Romano-Gallican, introduced from Rome into France in the reign of Charlemagne.

P. Misereatur vestri Omnipotens Deus et dimittat vobis omnia peccata vestra, liberet vos ab omni malo, salvet et confirmet in omni opere bono, et perducat vos ad vitam æternam.

C. Amen.

P. Absolutionem et remissionem omnium peccatorum vestrorum tribuat vobis omnipotens et misericors Dominus.

C. Amen.

P. Adjutorium nostrum in nomine Domini.

C. Qui fecit cœlum et terram.

The Clerk is *not* to say *Deo gratias* after the Epistle, nor *Laus tibi Christe* after the Gospel. No answer is returned when the Priest says the *Orate Fratres*. The *Domine non sum dignus* is not said.

A METHOD OF HEARING MASS FOR
The Souls of the Faithful Departed.

MAKE YOUR INTENTION.

O GOD of all mercy, I come to offer thee the blood of the Lamb without spot for the souls which thou lovest, and which sigh only after the blessedness of seeing thee and glorifying thee. Just as are the punishments which thou inflictest, open to them this day the boundless treasures of the satisfactions of thy divine Son ; and bestow upon them in this holy sacrifice wherewithal to discharge the debt which they still owe to thy sovereign justice.

[If you intend to communicate, and wish to offer your Communion for particular Souls, say :

I beseech thee, O Lord, to apply to the souls of *N.N.* the indulgences which I shall be able to obtain by the communion I am about to make.]

WHILST THE PRIEST IS AT THE FOOT OF THE ALTAR.

WE confess our sins, O God; and we acknowledge that if thou hadst regard only to our iniquities, no one could be justified in thy sight, and endure the severity of thy countenance. Woe to us if thou judgest us without mercy! To appease thy justice, we have recourse, after the example of thy saints, to the unbloody sacrifice of him who was pleased to be nailed to the cross for us, and who never ceaseth to make intercession with thee on our behalf. Forgive us our sins; forgive also our brethren departed the sins which they committed against thee whilst they abode in this land of exile. Let thy mercy prevail over thy justice, since thou hast promised graciously to hear those who show mercy, and be thou faithful to thy promises.

THE INTROIT.

REQUIEM æternam dona eis, Domine; et lux perpetua luceat eis. *Ps.* 64. Te decet hymnus Deus, in Sion; et tibi reddetur votum in Jerusalem. Exaudi orationem meam: ad te omnis caro veniet. Requiem, &c.

ETERNAL rest give unto them, O Lord; and let perpetual light shine upon them. *Ps.* 64. A hymn, O God, becometh thee in Sion; and a vow shall be paid to thee in Jerusalem. Oh, hear my prayer: to thee shall all flesh come. Eternal, &c.

AT THE KYRIE.

O JESUS, show thyself a God of mercy; have pity on the souls that groan in the place of suffering and expiation.

7

THE COLLECT.

FIDELIUM Deus omnium Conditor et Redemptor, animabus famulorum famularumque tuarum remissionem cunctorum tribue peccatorum; ut indulgentiam, quam semper optaverunt, piis supplicationibus consequantur. Qui vivis et regnas, etc.

O GOD, the Creator and Redeemer of all the faithful, give to the souls of thy servants departed the remission of all their sins ; that. through pious supplications. they may obtain the pardon which they have always desired. Who livest and reignest, &c.

Or say.

O MOST gracious God, who art always ready to have mercy and to spare, forget not, I beseech thee. the souls of thy servants whom thou hast summoned to thy judgment ; let thy holy angels conduct them into the heavenly country : they have believed and hoped in thee, let them not be disappointed in their hope. but enter speedily into possession of that throne of glory which thou hast prepared for thy elect.

AT THE EPISTLE.

" BRETHREN, we will not have you ignorant concerning them that are asleep, that you be not sorrowful, even as others who have no hope. For if we believe that Jesus died and rose again, even so them who have slept through Jesus, will God bring with him. For this we say unto you in the word of the Lord, that we who are alive, who remain unto the coming of the Lord, shall not

prevent them who have slept. For the Lord himself
shall come down from heaven with commandment,
and with the voice of an Archangel, and with the
trumpet of God ; and the dead who are in Christ
shall rise first. Then we who are alive, who are left,
shall be taken up together with them in the clouds
to meet Christ, into the air, and so shall we be always
with the Lord. Wherefore, comfort ye one another
with these words." (1 *Thess.* iv. 12–17.)

Or say:

O LORD, I believe that the souls of those who at
their departure out of this world, have still to
satisfy thy sovereign justice, are relieved by the
oblation of the holy sacrifice. What consolation is
there in this most blessed doctrine ! I see therein
the accomplishment of that declaration of thy word,
that thou wilt never forget the souls of thy servants ;
therefore also wouldst thou have us come to the
succour of the faithful departed by prayers, and alms,
and sacrifices. O Lord, I enter, with all my heart,
into thy merciful designs ; and I come this day to
unite myself with the pious intentions of the Church,
by praying for those whom thou didst adopt at the
baptismal font, and hast given to us for brethren.

THE GRADUAL.

REQUIEM æternam
dona eis, Domine ; et
lux perpetua luceat eis.
V. Ps. cxi. In memoria
æterna erit justus : ab

ETERNAL rest give
unto them. O Lord ;
and let perpetual light
shine upon them. *V.*
The just shall be in ever

auditione mala non time-
bit.

lasting remembrance : he
shall not be afraid for evil
report.

THE TRACT.

ABSOLVE, Domine, animas omnium fidelium defunctorum ab omni vinculo delictorum. *V.* Et gratia tua illis succurrente, mereantur evadere judicium ultionis. *V.* Et lucis æternæ beatitudine perfrui.

RELEASE, O Lord, the souls of all the faithful departed from the bonds of their sins. *V.* And, by the assistance of thy grace, may they merit to escape the sentence of condemnation. *V.* And enjoy the bliss of eternal light.

SEQUENCE.

Dies iræ, dies illa
Solvet sæclum in favilla
Teste David cum Sibylla.

Nigher still, and still more nigh
Draws the day of prophecy,
Doom'd to melt the earth and sky.

Quantus tremor est futurus,
Quando Judex est venturus,

Cuncta stricte discussurus!

Oh, what trembling there shall be
When the world its Judge shall see,
Coming in dread majesty !

Tuba mirum spargens sonum

Per sepulchra regionum,
Coget omnes ante thronum.

Hark ! the trump, with thrilling tone,
From sepulchral regions lone,
Summons all before the throne,

Mors stupebit et natura,
Cum resurget creatura,
Judicanti responsura.

Time and death it doth appal,
To see the buried ages all
Rise to answer at the call.

Liber scriptus proferetur,
In quo totum continetur,
Unde mundus judicetur.

Now the books are open spread;
Now the writing must be read,
Which doth judge the quick and dead.

Judex ergo cum sedebit,
Quidquid latet, apparebit
Nil inultum remanebit.

Now, before the Judge severe,
Hidden things must all appear ;
Nought can pass unpunish'd here.

Quid sum miser tunc dicturus?
Quem patronum rogaturus?
Cum vix justus sit securus.

What shall guilty I then plead?
Who for me will intercede,
When e'en saints shall comfort need?

Rex tremendæ majestatis.
Qui salvandos salvas gratis,
Salva me, fons pietatis!

King of dreadful majesty,
Who dost freely justify,
Fount of pity save thou me!

Recordare Jesu pie,
Quod sum causa tuæ viæ,
Ne me perdas illa die.

Recollect, O Love divine,
'Twas for this lost sheep of thine
Thou thy glory didst resign:

Quærens me sedisti lassus,
Redemisti crucem passus:
Tantus labor non sit cassus.

Satest wearied seeking me;
Sufferedst upon the tree;
Let not vain thy labour be.

Juste Judex ultionis,
Donum fac remissionis
Ante diem rationis.

Judge of justice, hear my prayer;
Spare me, Lord, in mercy spare;
Ere the reckoning-day appear.

Ingemisco tanquam reus,
Culpa rubet vultus meus.

Lo, thy gracious face I seek;
Shame and grief are on my cheek:

Supplicanti parce Deus.

Sighs and tears my sorrow speak.

Qui Mariam absolvisti,
Et latronem exaudisti.
Mihi quoque spem dedisti.

Thou didst Mary's guilt forgive;
Didst the dying thief receive;
Hence doth hope within me live.

Preces meæ non sunt dignæ.

Worthless are my prayers, I know;

Sed tu bonus fac benigne,
Ne perenni cremer igne.

Yet, oh, cause me not to go
Into everlasting woe.

Inter oves locum præsta,
Et ab bœdis me sequestra.
Statuens in parte dextra,

Sever'd from the guilty band,
Make me with thy sheep to stand,
Placing me on thy right hand.

Confutatis maledictis,

When the cursed in anguish flee
Into flames of misery;

Flammis acribus addictis,
Voca me cum benedictis.

With the blest then call thou me.

Oro supplex et acclinis,
Cor contritum quasi cinis:

Suppliant in the dust I lie;
My heart a cinder, crush'd and dry;

Gere curam mei finis.

Help me, Lord, when death is nigh.

Lacrymosa dies illa,	Full of tears, and full of dread,
Qua resurget ex favilla	Is the day that wakes the dead,
Judicandus homo reus.	Calling all with solemn blast,
Huic ergo parce Deus;	From the ashes of the past.
Pie Jesu Domine,	Lord of mercy, Jesu blest.
Dona eis requiem.	Grant the faithful light and rest.
Amen.	Amen.

AT THE GOSPEL.

" AT that time, Martha said to Jesus : Lord, if thou hadst been here, my brother had not died. But now, also, I know that whatsoever thou wilt ask of God, God will give it thee. Jesus saith to her : Thy brother shall rise again. Martha saith to him ; I know that he shall rise again in the resurrection at the last day. Jesus said to her : I am the resurrection and the life ; he that believeth in me, although he be dead, shall live. And everyone that liveth, and believeth in me, shall not die for ever. Believest thou this ? She saith to him : Yea, Lord, I have believed that thou art Christ, the Son of the living God, who art come into this world." *St. John* xi. 21-27.

Or say :

ENLIGHTEN me, O Lord, and teach me what I must do, that I may not be confounded with those who have shut their eyes to the light of thy Gospel. Look down compassionately upon me, and vouchsafe, O most merciful Jesus, to pronounce that sentence in my behalf: *Thy sins are forgiven thee.* And let the faithful departed, for whom I pray, hear those words of joy which thou utteredst on the cross to the penitent thief : *this day thou shalt be with me in paradise.* I know that I am not worthy that thou shouldst hear me. We must pay that which we owe to thy justice. We must return to the dust from whence we came. We must be purified by fire before we can enjoy thy presence. But, Lord, thy mercies are greater than our sins; we shall say to thee with the Psalmist: My lot is in thy hands; deliver me out of the hands of my enemies, and from them that persecute me. Make thy face to shine upon thy servant; save me in thy mercy. Let me not be confounded, O Lord, for I have called upon thee.

THE OFFERTORY.

DOMINE Jesu Christe, Rex gloriæ, libera animas omnium fidelium defunctorum de pœnis inferni, et de profundo lacu: libera eas de ore leonis, ne absorbeat eas tartarus, ne cadant in obscurum: sed signifer sanctus Michael repræsentet eas in lucem sanctam: * quam olim Abrahæ promisisti, et semini ejus. *V.* Hostias et preces tibi, Domine, laudis offerimus: tu suscipe pro animabus illis, quarum hodie memoriam facimus: fac eas, Domine, de morte

LORD Jesus Christ, King of Glory, deliver the souls of all the faithful departed from the pains of hell, and from the deep pit: deliver them from the lion's mouth, lest hell swallow them up, lest they fall into darkness: and let the standard-bearer, St. Michael, bring them into the holy light:* as thou didst promise of old to Abraham and to his seed. *V.* We offer thee, O Lord, a sacrifice of praise and prayers; accept them on behalf of the souls

transire ad vitam. *Quam, | we commemorate this day;
etc. | and make them pass, O
Lord, from death to life.
* As, &c.

AT THE SECRETA.

I WILL go down, O just Judge of the living and the
dead, I will go down in spirit to that dread place
where thy hand is heavy on thy children, the heirs
of thy glory. There I will sigh and lament, I will
unite my prayers to the sacrifice of thy dear Son, that
thou mayest shorten their pains, and change their
sufferings into consolation, their humiliation into
glory. Lord, in the grief that oppresses them, their
souls cry unto thee. Have mercy on me, for I
acknowledge that I have sinned in thy sight. One
thing I have asked of thee, this shall I seek after ;
that I may dwell in thy house for ever, to behold the
fair beauty of thy temple. I believe verily to see
thy face in the land of the living.

DURING THE PREFACE.

IT is just and reasonable, right and salutary, to give
thee thanks at all times and in all places. Father
Almighty, Eternal God, through Jesus Christ, our
Lord ; through whom thou hast given us the hope
of a blessed resurrection, to the end that, if the
recollection of the sentence of death passed upon all
men comes to sadden us, the promise of immortality
may encourage and console our faith ; for to those
who are faithful to thee, O Lord, to die is to lose a
mortal life to pass into a better, and when this their

earthly tabernacle is dissolved, they obtain one in the heavens, which shall endure eternally. And therefore, with all the heavenly host, we sing a hymn to thy glory, saying without ceasing: Holy, holy, holy, Lord God of Sabaoth ; heaven and earth are full of thy glory. Blessed is he that cometh in the name of the Lord ; his blood cries aloud for pardon, and its voice reacheth even to the throne of mercy.

DURING THE CANON.

O ALMIGHTY God, whose providence extendeth over all thy creatures, for thou art their Father, cast an eye of pity on the souls that love thee, and whose bitterest pain it is to be separated from thee. Remember, O my God, that they are the work of thy hands, and the price of the sufferings, the death, and the infinite merits of thy divine Son Jesus. Wilt thou not relent towards them for his name's sake ? We offer thee, on their behalf, the precious blood which was shed for them on the cross ; the powerful intercession of the blessed Virgin Mary, of St. Joseph, St. Peter, and St. Paul, and all the Saints ; the humble supplications of thy Church, and the prayers and meritorious works of all the faithful. Having this confidence, we hope all from thy mercy, O my God, for the souls which were dear unto us, and which thou hast made it our duty to love and succour. Let thy paternal tenderness disarm at length thy justice. Open to them thy heart ; manifest to them thy glory ; show thyself to them as thou art, and let flow into their souls that torrent of delights of which thou art the everlasting source.

AT THE ELEVATION.

O HOLY Victim, immolated for the salvation of the world, listen favourably to our prayers. O precious Blood of our Saviour, shed to take away our sins, sanctify us, and cry for mercy on the souls of the faithful departed.

CONTINUANCE OF THE CANON.

O JESUS, who didst go down into Limbo to deliver thence the souls of the patriarchs and prophets who awaited thy coming, visit the souls of thy servants in their place of suffering. Moderate, with the dew of thy grace, the heat of the furnace in which they are tried. Thou hast said that thou wilt consider as done unto thyself, the least good which we shall do unto our brethren : I may hope then, that the relief which I shall procure for the souls of the faithful will be as acceptable to thee as if I had procured it for thyself. Cease from thy anger, O my God, through the intercession of Her who is the comfortress of the afflicted, and through the prayers of all the heavenly host, who plead for the blessedness of the souls in purgatory. Grant, I beseech thee, eternal rest to these our brethren on whose behalf we prostrate ourselves before thee.

AT THE PATER.

O JESUS, O thou at whose name every knee doth bow in heaven, on earth, and under the earth; O thou who art the sovereign Judge of the living and the dead, let thy name be hallowed by the deliverance of the souls for whom we pray. Let the gate of thy tabernacles be opened to them, and thy will to save them be done this day. Grant that, after having eaten the bread of affliction, they may be nourished with the living bread, which is the fruition of thyself. We beseech thee in thy mercy to forgive the sins of *our parents, friends, and benefactors*, ——, and the sins which we have caused them to commit, that thou mayest not impute the guilt to them in the rigour of thy justice. Preserve us from those avenging flames, which, alas! we have too justly merited by the abuse of thy graces, our tepidity in thy service, and our unfaithfulness in resisting temptation. Deliver us from sin, the greatest of all evils. We know that it is a fearful thing to fall into the hands of the living God.

AT THE AGNUS DEI.

O JESUS, how great is the love which led thee to offer thyself, as a lamb to the sacrifice, for the expiation of the sins of the world! What tongue can worthily extol that charity which leads thee to become surety for our debts, even after our death! What ought not our gratitude to be for so great a benefit!

Lamb of God, who, by thy death, didst overcome the roaring lion that goeth about seeking whom he may devour, have mercy on the faithful departed.

Lamb without spot, who wast immolated to the justice of thy divine Father, to the end that he might forgive us our sins, have mercy on those who have died united by love to thy Sacred Heart.

Lamb of God, who wast offered in sacrifice, that thou mightest lead us out of this land of perdition to the true land of promise ; thou who hast said : *I am the resurrection and the life ; he that believeth in me, although he be dead, shall live*—give to the souls of the faithful departed that life, the principle of which was imparted to them by the grace of the holy sacraments ; bestow upon them the happiness of which they have so often received the precious pledge in thy heavenly banquet. I desire to have part therein (*spiritually*), that I may obtain for them, as much as in me lies, the society of thine elect for ever ; I offer to thee on their behalf, and especially for *N.*, all the devotions and good works which I may be enabled to perform. Despise not my humble prayer ; but be thou thyself my consolation in my loss, and grant relief to those souls which were so dear to me, and especially *N.*

COMMUNION.

LET shine upon them, O Lord, thy eternal light, that they may dwell for ever with thy saints : grant this favour to them, I beseech thee, O God of mercy.

POST-COMMUNION.

O MY God, who hast constituted prayer for the souls in purgatory one of the most essential of our duties, grant that I may find, in thy infinite merits and charity, the pardon of all my past tepidity and sloth. Let the remembrance of thy justice, which keeps them fast bound in prison for faults

which I myself so commonly commit, excite in me a
firm resolution of entering on the way of penance to
expiate my sins, and cause me to walk with more
circumspection, that I may not relapse into my
former errors.   I will no longer delay to do penance.
Henceforth I will labour thereat whilst there is yet
time.   I will pray most humbly for the souls of the
faithful departed ; I will deprive myself even of
allowable pleasures and enjoyments, to quench the
flames in which they suffer ; I will pour my alms into
the lap of the poor, to make interest on their behalf.
Bless these resolutions, O my God, and grant me
grace to fulfil them.

THE LAST GOSPEL.

"I KNOW that my Redeemer liveth, and in the
last day I shall rise out of the earth, and I shall
be clothed again with my skin, and in my flesh I
shall see my God, my Saviour ; my eyes shall behold
him ; this my hope is laid up in my bosom." (*Job*
xix. 25-27.)

"I will look towards the Lord, I will wait for God
my Saviour ; my God will hear my voice.   I shall
arise when I sit in darkness, the Lord is my light. . . .
He will bring me forth into the light, I shall behold
his justice." (*Mich.* vii. 7-9.)

OFFERING OF THE PASSION OF CHRIST FOR THE FAITHFUL DEPARTED.
(St Gertrude.)

LOOK down, O Father of compassion, from thy high
and holy seat upon the hapless souls detained

in purgatory.   Look upon all the pains and torments wherewith they are so piteously chastised: regard now the plaintive groans and tears which they pour forth unto thee; hear the prayers and the supplications wherewith they entreat thy mercy, and be merciful unto their sins.   Remember, O most compassionate Father, all the sufferings which thy Son hath endured for them ; remember his precious Blood, shed in such abundance for them ; call to mind the most bitter death which he suffered for them, and have mercy on them.   For all the sins they have ever committed against thee I offer thee the most holy life and conversation of thy most beloved Son ; for all their negligences I offer thee his most fervent desires towards thee ; for all their omissions I offer thee the great abundance of his merits ; for their every insult and wrong to thee I offer thee the sweet submission with which he honoured thee.   Finally, for all the chastisements which they have ever incurred I offer thee all the mortifications, fastings, watchings, the labours and afflictions, wounds and stripes, passion and death, which he endured in such spotless innocence and with such loving eagerness ; beseeching thee now to suffer thy anger to be appeased towards them, and to lead them forth into everlasting joy.   Amen.

A Devout Method of Hearing Mass,

Commemorating the Mysteries of the Passion.

A PRAYER BEFORE MASS.

O DIVINE Jesus! sacred Victim, immolated for the redemption of mankind! I earnestly beseech thee that I may assist at this adorable sacrifice with the most lively faith, animated hope, unbounded gratitude, and tender love. Permit me to follow thee in spirit through the different stages of thy sacred passion, and give me an abundant share of that infinite charity which induced thee to suffer such excessive torments for my sake.

With the daughters of Sion, who met thee carrying thy cross, and thy blessed Mother, who saw thee expire for our salvation, I desire to compassionate thy sufferings, and to detest sin, as the only sovereign evil. I offer this divine sacrifice to commemorate in a special manner thy dolorous passion, and to obtain through its efficacious merits the grace of true and sincere devotion towards thy life-giving sufferings and death.

AT THE BEGINNING OF THE MASS.

The priest going from the sacristy to the altar, represents Jesus Christ retiring from the Cenacle to the Garden of Gethsemani. Unite your sentiments with the divine disposition of the Son of God, and dispose yourself by sincere repentance to assist worthily at the great sacrifice about to be offered.

O DIVINE Lord! in the multitude of thy mercies I will enter thy house, and adore thee in thy holy temple. Though my sins are multiplied beyond number, yet I will appeal to thy unbounded mercies, which far exceed my malice, or the extent of my ingratitude. I will confide in the sufferings of my Redeemer, and hope, through his infinite merits, to find grace and salvation. O dear Jesus : thou who hast washed me heretofore in the laver of baptism, wash me yet more from my iniquity, and cleanse me from my sin : sprinkle me with thy blood, and I shall be cleansed ; wash me, and I shall be made whiter than snow.

AT THE INTROIT.

When the priest bows and kisses the altar, contemplate our divine Lord prostrate before his heavenly Father, loaded with the sins of mankind, and bathed in blood through excess of sorrow. Reflect on the anguish which the treacherous kiss of Judas caused our divine Redeemer.

O GOOD Jesus! I fervently bless thee, for all thou hast done and suffered for my salvation. Give me grace to weep over those sins which drew streams of blood from thy sacred veins. I desire to commemorate with the most lively and humble contrition, thy agony in the garden, and I firmly resolve to detest my sins to the latest moment of my life. Pierce my soul with grief, for having repaid thy goodness with ingratitude, and let me frequently cry out with the humble publican : O God! be merciful to me a sinner. May those bonds which confined thy sacred hands, burst the fetters of my sins, and restore me to the sweet liberty of thy children. I cast myself at thy sacred feet, and conjure thee to strengthen me by thy all-powerful grace, that under every trial and affliction I may submit cheerfully to the decrees of thy adorable Providence, and never cease to bless thy holy name.

AT THE KYRIE ELEISON AND GLORIA IN EXCELSIS.

The *Kyrie eleison* is repeated three times to honour the adorable Trinity; it may also serve to remind you of the denials of St. Peter, and excite the deepest regret for your much more frequent denials of so good a Master. At the *Gloria in excelsis*, reflect on the miraculous conversions which signalised the public life of Jesus Christ, and beg that one benign glance may convert and penetrate your soul, as it did that of St. Peter.

O MY God! have mercy on me, according to thy great mercy; pardon me, who have so often had the misfortune of denying thee, by a life altogether opposite to thy sacred maxims. Look on me, divine Jesus, with that compassion and tenderness which the sight of misery always excited in thy most amiable heart. Purify me, as thou didst thy penitent apostle, that I may worthily unite with thy Church in celebrating the wonderful work of man's redemption. O how fervently should I join in thy praises, most amiable Jesus! How ardently should I sing, Glory be to God on high, glory be to that adorable Being, who, forgetful of his own glory, underwent for my sake such prodigious humiliations! O my sovereign King! my divine and adorable Model! since thou wert pleased to descend so low as my frail nature, grant that I may place all my glory, honour, and happiness, in sharing thy humiliations, and carrying thy cross.

AT THE EPISTLE AND GOSPEL.

When the Priest goes from the middle of the altar to the *Epistle* side, and thence to the *Gospel* side, represent to yourself the eternal Son of God, dragged about to the different tribunals of Annas, Caiphas, Pilate, and Herod; and when you stand to hear the Gospel, remember that it is the word of Him, who alone has the words of eternal life; of Him, who came from heaven to instruct you, and who, for your sake, confirmed his doctrine by shedding his precious blood.

O ETERNAL God! unerring Truth! whose sacred word I am so happy as to hear, penetrate my heart by the influence of thy grace, that I may not hear it to my eternal reprobation, like the Jews who so long and so fruitlessly listened to thy sacred maxims. O spotless Lamb of God! while thy judges proclaim thee an impostor, I rise without fear or shame to declare in the face of heaven and earth, that I believe thee to be Christ, the Son of the living God, and that I most unreservedly assent to all and every article proposed by thy holy Church to my belief. But, O divine Lord! give me grace to profess my faith by my actions as well as by my words. Have mercy on all who are involved in the dreadful night of infidelity; may the light of thy grace shine upon them, and so penetrate their hearts, that they may embrace the truth, and be united to the communion of the holy Church.

AT THE OFFERTORY.

When the priest unveils the chalice, and offers the bread and wine, contemplate your merciful Redeemer, stripped of his garments, bound to a pillar, and cruelly scourged; offer yourself, in union with the sacrifice he then offered of his precious blood, and which he renews on the altar.

A DORABLE Jesus! when I reflect on the torments thou didst endure when fastened to the pillar, I begin to conceive the enormity of sin, and the immense extent of thy eternal love. I behold in thy wounds the greatness of my ingratitude, and the depth of the misery to which I am reduced. But, O Lord! how happy am I, in being able to present thee, at this moment, a victim of thanksgiving and atonement, fully proportioned to, or rather far exceeding, the magnitude of my obligation, and the multitude of my crimes. I offer thee the streams of blood that flowed from thy sacred body during thy ignominious scourging, and also the bread and wine which is now presented to thy divine Majesty. Accept, in union with this precious oblation, my body and soul, my thoughts, words, desires, affections, and sufferings; in fine, my whole being, that henceforward I may be entirely thine by the bonds of ardent charity.

AT THE LAVABO AND ORATE FRATRES.

When the priest washes his hands, call to mind the testimony which Pilate gave to the innocence of Jesus Christ; and at the *Orate fratres* adore your Saviour, exhibited to the people as a mock king. Prostrate yourself in spirit before your Sovereign Lord, and pour out at his sacred feet the grateful effusions of your compassion and love.

O MOST adorable Blood! which flowed as a remedy for all human woes, I beseech thee to wash, purify, and sanctify my sinful soul, that I may, with a pure and upright conscience, assist at these awful mysteries. I cannot, O my God! presume to wash my hands among the innocent, for alas! I have been long since excluded from the happy few who never offended thee; but, at least, I can claim a privilege not reserved to the innocent alone, but

mercifully granted even to the most guilty. I can
wash my hands, my heart, my soul, in thy precious
blood. I can cast myself on thy divine mercy, with
a firm resolution, rather to die, than to offend thee
during the remainder of my life. O King of my
soul! I acknowledge thee for my sole and sovereign
Lord. O Jesus! I implore, by the sorrow and agony
of heart thou didst endure when Barabbas was preferred to thee, that thou wouldst preserve me from
ever preferring any created object to thy friendship
and favour. By thy ignominious clothing with a purple
garment, I entreat thee to give me a garment of
justice, when I shall appear before thy dread tribunal,
and I fervently conjure thee, that through thy infinite
mercy and the merits of thy thorny crown I may
hereafter obtain a crown of immortal glory.

AT THE PREFACE.

The priest praying some time in secret before the *Preface*, represents and commemorates the admirable silence observed by Jesus
Christ in the course of his sacred passion. Do you now address
your divine Lord in the secret of your heart; represent to him all
your spiritual necessities; implore an application of his infinite
merits to the wounds of your soul, and when the priest raises his
voice to recite the Preface, do you redouble your fervour, and join
in spirit with the Church militant, triumphant, and suffering, in
praising and magnifying that divine Lamb who was slain for the
health and life of his own creatures.

O DIVINE Searcher of hearts! from whom nothing is hidden, since thou desirest so ardently
to establish thy reign in my soul, permit me to represent to thee its miseries, and all the obstacles
which unfortunately oppose the sweet empire of
thy love in my heart. O Lord, thou needest not

my representations to discern my wants. I am too insensible to feel my miseries as I ought—too weak to call loudly on thy mercy—too guilty to deserve being heard. Let my silence then speak, O most merciful saviour! let my multiplied miseries plead on my behalf. Thou wilt not be deaf to their eloquent supplications: and surely, my God! thou needest but consult thy own sacred heart, and that infinite love which brings thee daily on our altars, to find motives for granting pardon and mercy to the most unworthy of thy creatures. O blessed spirits of heaven! holy and happy saints of God! who, in the mirror of his adorable sanctity, behold the enormity of sin, supply for me, who am un-worthy to join with the Church in celebrating his praise and magnifying his goodness.

AT THE CANON.

Let the low voice in which the *Canon* is read, remind you of that mourning and consternation which amazed and silenced all nature at the sufferings of Jesus Christ; and when the priest spreads his hands over the oblation, making the sign of the cross, call to mind the torments our divine Redeemer endured when fastened to the cross.

O MY God, when I reflect on the number and enormity of my sins, I am sensible that I have no claim to a share in those precious graces which thou hast died to purchase for thy creatures; but when I contemplate that cross on which thou didst agonise—when I turn my eyes on this altar, this new Calvary, on which thou art about to descend, and again offer thyself for my salvation, I feel convinced that thou wilt always be to me a Jesus, a Saviour. Accept, therefore, of my whole being, in union with the sacred oblation I am about to offer. Purify my sinful soul in those streams of blood which gushed from thy adorable wounds, and which will soon flow on this altar. Grant to us all, through its efficacious merits, the grace to practise what thy holy law commands, and to avoid what it prohibits. Extend the blessings of peace and unity to thy Church; repentance and pardon to all sinners; comfort to the sick, the dying, and the afflicted; in a word, mercy and eternal happiness to all, since for all, O divine Victim! thou didst shed thy adorable and saving blood. I particularly implore thy precious graces, O my God, for those for whom I am bound to pray—those who have recommended themselves to my prayers—who pray for me, or who, at this moment, may specially want thy divine assistance. O may this adorable and august sacrifice be received by thy Divine Majesty as was the victim which Christ offered in his own person on the altar of the cross.

AT THE ELEVATION.

At the *Elevation* of the sacred host and chalice, reflect on the pangs which Jesus endured, when, lifted up between heaven and earth, his precious blood flowed abundantly for the remission of your sins, for the conversion of the world, and of his greatest enemies. Let the first-fruit of his cross and passion, applied to the penitent thief on the cross, encourage you to recur confidently to his mercies, and to hope that his infinite love will one day assign you likewise a place in Paradise.

HAIL, O King of Glory! Prince of Peace! and Saviour of the World! Hail, O immaculate

Victim! sacrificed for me and all mankind on the altar of the cross. I bless thee, I adore thee, I love thee, O divine Jesus! and I ardently invite the whole universe to join in praising and blessing thy holy name. O bleeding and adorable Victim of my sins! why have I not the faith, the love, the anguish which penetrated the hearts of those who beheld thy sacred blood flow from thy precious wounds? Hear, O eternal God! the voice of this blood, which cries loudly, not for vengeance, but for pardon and mercy. O! let it plead powerfully on my behalf; let it blot out my sins, cleanse every stain from my soul, and render me pure and pleasing in thy sight.

AFTER THE ELEVATION.

BEHOLD, O Almighty and all-gracious God! thy Son Jesus, in whom thou art well pleased. Look upon the face of thy Christ and my Saviour, here present; look upon this spotless Lamb, this adorable victim, this pure holocaust of obedience, humbled to the ignominious death of the cross. Behold in him what may move thee to look upon us with an eye of mercy and compassion. He is our High Priest, sprinkled with his own blood. Receive the sacrifice he has offered for us, in consideration of the honour and homage that are due to thy sovereign goodness from me and all creatures. Extend, O compassionate Creator! its efficacious virtue to the souls of the faithful departed, and grant them rest and life everlasting, particularly to *N. N.* : deign to mitigate their punishment, and translate them to that place of glory for which they are destined. Thou didst once promise that, looking on the rainbow, thou wouldst remember the covenant made between thee and the Patriarch Noe (*Gen.* ix.): canst thou then look on the blood of thy beloved Son Jesus, offered to thee in sacrifice, without remembering the great covenant of the New Law, sealed and confirmed with the effusion of his sacred blood?

O dearest Jesus! why cannot I love thee as thy goodness deserves? The more thou hast humbled thyself for my sake, the more I am bound to love thee, and spend my life in thy service. Remember thou hast purchased my soul at a dear rate; O let not thy blood be lost or shed in vain, but receive me into the number of thy elect. I detest my sins, which were the cause of thy sufferings; alas! they were the nails that pierced thy hands and feet, and fastened thee to an ignominious cross. O who will give sorrow to my heart, and a fountain of tears to my eyes, that I may bewail them in the bitterness of my soul all the days of my life, and thus, at the hour of death, be entitled to hear those consolatory words addressed to the penitent thief: *This day shalt thou be with me in Paradise.* I acknowledge, that I do not deserve to be ranked among the number of thy children; yet, in obedience to thy precept, and with profound veneration for thy sacred words, I will presume to say that heavenly prayer which thou hast taught me: *Our Father, &c.*

AT THE AGNUS DEI.

When the priest says the *Agnus Dei*, reflect on the miraculous change of heart wrought in the Centurion and other witnesses of the death of Jesus Christ, and be careful, as far as it depends on you, not to depart from this new Calvary without participating in their holy dispositions.

O INNOCENT Lamb of God! who takest away the sins of the world, have mercy on me, for thy peculiar and distinguishing property is infinite mercy. Give to my heart the sorrow and repentance of those who mourned thy cruel death, and teach me, like them, to place all my hopes in thee, and to love and seek thee as my only sovereign Good. I most humbly beseech thee, by all the anguish thou didst endure during the course of thy passion, especially at the separation of thy sacred soul from thy body, that thou wouldst have mercy and compassion on me, when I shall be on the point of appearing before thy dread tribunal. Let thy passion and death then interpose between my soul and the rigours of thy justice. Ah! while I yet sojourn in this valley of tears, let the remembrance of thy bitter draught of vinegar and gall preserve me from delighting in the false pleasures of this world, and let thy burning thirst upon the cross make me thirst only after the enjoyment of thy presence. May the recollection of thy saving death penetrate my soul with such lively gratitude, that from this moment I may place all my happiness in loving and serving thee, my only joy and sovereign felicity.

AT THE COMMUNION.

The *Priest's Communion* represents the burial of Jesus Christ's sacred body when it was taken from the cross; and the covering of the chalice is a figure of the sepulchre shut up, and covered with a stone. This is the time peculiarly adapted to invite our Lord by a spiritual communion to repose in your heart, and to honour it frequently by his sacramental presence, or habitually by the influence of his holy grace.

O MY God! how can I reflect on the happiness of those who approach worthily to the holy Eucharist, without ardently desiring to enjoy the like blessing? how can I assist at this adorable sacrifice, without regretting the sins and miseries which justly deter me from receiving thee sacramentally. I am not worthy, O infinite purity! to lodge thee in my heart; I am not worthy to share in the happiness of those who now enjoy thy sacramental presence. But, Lord! though I cannot unite myself to thee really, yet I am not forbidden to do so in spirit and desire. I believe most firmly that thou art present in this sacred host; I hope in that infinite mercy which detains thee therein; and I ardently love and desire to receive thee, notwithstanding my unworthiness. I unite in the adoration, love, humility, and fervour of all who this day received thee throughout the universe, with the most perfect dispositions; and I earnestly beg of thee, by that tender love which induces thee to give thyself to thy creatures, to accept of every thought, word, and action, from this to my next communion, as so many acts of love, desire, and preparation to receive thee; and I earnestly conjure thee to crown all thy blessings by the inestimable grace of a worthy communion at the hour of my death.

AT THE LAST COLLECTS.

The last Collects represent the apparitions and instructions of Jesus Christ to his Apostles and Disciples after his resurrection: and the *Priest's Blessing* denotes that parting benediction given by our divine Lord, when ascending into heaven. Remember, when the last Gospel is being read at the left side of the altar, that Jesus Christ did not come to call the just but sinners to repentance, and that his infinite mercy in thus daily renewing on our altars the Sacrifice of the Cross, should animate even the most guilty to recur with confidence to his infinite goodness and abundant merits.

O BLESSED Redeemer! who coming forth from the grave didst rise triumphant over death, I praise and glorify thee for all thy mercies, and in particular for having conversed so long with thy apostles, and confirmed them in that saving faith, which they were destined to transmit to succeeding ages. O! how shall I thank thee for the inestimable advantage of having beheld thee sacrificed on this altar, and for having thereby participated in the abundant merits of thy passion and death. Let me not depart from this sanctuary without those sentiments of piety, and that spiritual strength for the amendment of my life, which may be always drawn from this adorable sacrifice. Pardon, O Lord! my distractions and irreverences. Engrave on my heart the remembrance of thy sufferings, that I may henceforward glory only in Jesus Christ, and in him crucified. Teach me to follow thy divine example, that rising with thee to a new life, I may, through thy powerful grace, advance daily and hourly in virtue, and at length attain to the unlimited and eternal enjoyment of thee, my God and my All! in the kingdom of thy glory. Amen

Indulgenced Devotions for Mass.

FIRST PART.

From the beginning of Mass to the Gospel.

In the name of the ✠ Father, and of the Son, and of the Holy Ghost. Amen.

MY God, I am now about to assist at the most holy sacrifice of the Mass. With my whole heart and soul, I beg of thee the proper dispositions to perform well this sacred duty.

Holy Mary, pray for me.

St. Joseph, St. Dominic, all ye holy saints and angels, intercede for me.

Eternal Father, I offer to thee the sacrifice which thy beloved Son Jesus made of himself upon the cross, and which he now renews upon this altar; I offer it to thee in the name of all creatures, together with the masses which have been celebrated, and which shall be celebrated in the whole world, in order to adore thee, and to give thee the honour which thou dost deserve: to render to thee due thanks for thy innumerable benefits, to appease thy anger for our sins, and to give thee due satisfaction for them; to entreat thee also for myself, for the Church, for the whole world, and for the blessed souls in purgatory. Amen.

THREE DEVOUT ACTS OF OBLATION TO THE MOST AUGUST TRINITY.

I. We offer to the most holy Trinity, the merits

of Jesus Christ, in thanksgiving for the most precious blood, which Jesus shed in the garden for us ; and through his merits we implore of the divine Majesty the pardon of our sins.

Our Father, Hail Mary, *and* Glory be to the Father.

II. We offer to the most holy Trinity, the merits of Jesus Christ, in thanksgiving for his most precious death, suffered for us upon the Cross ; and through his merits we implore of the divine Majesty the remission of the punishment due to our sins.

Our Father, Hail Mary, *and* Glory be to the Father.

III. We offer to the most holy Trinity, the merits of Jesus Christ, in thanksgiving for his ineffable charity in coming down from heaven to take human flesh on earth, and to suffer and die for us upon the Cross, and through his merits to implore the divine Majesty to conduct our souls after death to celestial glory.

Our Father, Hail Mary, *and* Glory be to the Father.

O Father, O Son, O Holy Ghost! O most sacred Trinity! O Jesus! O Mary! ye blessed angels, all ye saints of heaven, obtain for me the graces which I ask through the most precious blood of Jesus Christ.

1. To do always the will of God. 2. To be always with God. 3. To think of no other but God. 4. To love God alone. 5. To do all for God. 6. To seek only the glory of God. 7. To become holy only for God. 8. To know well my own nothingness. 9. To know more and more the will of my God. 10. And to——[*here mention some particular pious petition.*]

Most holy Mary, offer to the Eternal Father the most precious blood of Jesus Christ for my soul, for the holy souls in purgatory, for the wants of the holy Catholic Church, for the conversion of sinners, and for the whole world.

Then recite Glory be to the Father, &c., *three times to the most precious blood of Jesus Christ, the* Hail Mary *once to the dolorous Virgin Mary, and the versicle,*

Eternal rest grant them. O Lord, and let perpetual light shine unto them, *for the suffering souls in purgatory.*

A DEVOUT PRAYER TO ALMIGHTY GOD FOR HIS MERCY AND DIVINE PROTECTION.

DELIVER us, we beseech thee, O Lord! in thy clemency, from the chains of our sins, and protect us thy servants, and our dwellings in all holiness, by the intercession of the Blessed Virgin Mary, Mother of God, of thy Blessed Apostles, Peter and Paul, and of all the saints; cleanse from iniquity all our relations and friends, and adorn them with virtues : grant us peace and health, and preserve us from our enemies, visible and invisible ; drive away carnal desires, give healthful temperature to the air we breathe, grant us charity towards both friends and enemies.   Protect thy city ; preserve our chief Pontiff [*name him*] ; defend from every adversity all prelates and princes, and the whole Christian people.   May thy blessing be always upon us, and grant eternal rest to all the faithful departed, through Christ our Lord.   Amen.

SECOND PART.

From the Gospel to the Elevation.

AN ACT OF CONSECRATION TO JESUS, TO BE MADE BEFORE A PICTURE OF HIS SACRED HEART.

I, *N. N.,* desirous to make the best return in my power for thy benefits, and the most ample atonement for my transgressions, give thee my heart, and consecrate my whole being to thee, O amiable Jesus! and I purpose, with the assistance of thy grace, never more to offend thee.

AN OFFERING OF OURSELVES TO THE PROTECTION OF THE BLESSED VIRGIN MARY.

O MOST holy Virgin, Mother of the Word Incarnate, depository of graces, and refuge of us miserable sinners! we have recourse to thy maternal love with a lively faith, and we ask the grace to do always the will of God and thine. We resign ourselves into thy most sacred hands, and beg of thee to save us soul and body. We confidently hope that thou, O most loving Mother! wilt graciously hear us, and therefore with a lively faith we say:

Hail Mary, *three times.*

LET US PRAY.

PROTECT, we beseech thee, O Lord! thy servants from every frailty, by the intercession of the Blessed Virgin Mary; and while we prostrate ourselves before thee with our whole hearts, mercifully preserve us from the snares of our enemies, through Christ, our Lord. Amen.

Sweet heart of Mary, be my salvation.

A DEVOUT PRAYER AND FIVE PATERS AND AVES, IN
MEMORY OF THE PASSION AND DEATH OF JESUS
CHRIST.

O LORD Jesus Christ! who, to redeem the world
from the slavery of hell, wouldst be born amongst
us passible and mortal, didst suffer thyself to be
circumcised, to be reproved and persecuted by the
Jews, to be betrayed by Judas, thy disciple, with a
sacrilegious kiss, and, as a meek and innocent Lamb,
to be bound with cords, and inhumanly dragged to
the tribunals of Annas, Caiphas, Pilate, and Herod:
didst submit to be accused by false witnesses, torn
with scourges, crowned with thorns, struck on the
face, defiled with spittle, blindfolded through derision,
insulted in a thousand ways, outraged, saturated with
reproaches and ignominy ; and, finally, being stripped
of thy garments, nailed to and elevated on a cross
between two thieves, presented with gall and vinegar
to drink, and pierced with the lance, wouldst con-
summate the great work of our redemption. Oh,
my most merciful Redeemer! by these so many and
so atrocious pains, suffered for love of me, which I,
though unworthy, commemorate, and by thy holy
cross and bitter death, preserve me from the pains of
hell, and vouchsafe to bring me to Paradise, where thou
hast conducted the penitent thief, crucified with thee,
my Jesus : who, with the Father and the Holy Ghost,
livest and reignest, God, world without end.   Amen
Then say : Our Father, Hail Mary, *and* Glory be to
the Father, *five times.*

ASPIRATIONS OF DIVINE PRAISE.

BLESSED be God. Blessed be his Holy Name.
Blessed be Jesus Christ, true God and true man.
Blessed be the Name of Jesus. Blessed be his most
Sacred Heart. Blessed be Jesus in the most Holy
Sacrament of the Altar. Blessed be the great Mother
of God, Mary most holy. Blessed be her holy and
Immaculate Conception. Blessed be the name of
Mary, Virgin and Mother. Blessed be God in his
Angels and in his Saints.

Holy, holy, holy, Lord God of Hosts ; all the
earth is full of thy glory. Glory be to the Father,
glory be to the Son, glory be to the Holy Ghost.

THIRD PART.
From the Elevation to the Communion.

At the Elevation of both sacred species, adore **Jesus Christ**
in the Blessed Sacrament, and say :

O Sacrament most holy !
O Sacrament divine !
All praise and all thanksgiving
Be every moment thine ! Amen.

A SHORT ACT OF OBLATION OF THE MOST SACRED BLOOD OF JESUS.

ETERNAL Father, I offer thee the most precious
Blood of Jesus Christ, in satisfaction for my
sins, and for the wants of the holy Catholic Church.

Dearest Jesus, be not thou my Judge, but my
Saviour !

My Jesus ! mercy.
Mary ! help.
Jesus, my God, I love thee above all things.
Jesus, Jesus, Jesus.

OFFERINGS OF THE PRECIOUS BLOOD OF JESUS.

1. O ETERNAL Father! I offer thee the merits of the most precious Blood of Jesus, thy beloved Son, and my divine Redeemer, for the propagation and exaltation of my dear mother the Holy Church, for the safety and prosperity of her visible head, the holy Roman Pontiff, for the cardinals, bishops, and pastors of souls, and for all the ministers of the sanctuary.

V. Glory be to the Father, and to the Son, and to the Holy Ghost.

R. As it was in the beginning, is now, and ever shall be, world without end.   Amen.

Blessed and praised for evermore be Jesus, who hath saved us with his blood.

2. Eternal Father! I offer thee the merits of the most precious Blood of Jesus, thy beloved Son and my divine Redeemer, for the peace and concord of kings and catholic princes, for the humiliation of the enemies of the holy faith, and for the happiness of all christian people.

Glory be to the Father, &c.   Blessed and praised, &c.

3. Eternal Father! I offer thee the merits of the most precious Blood of Jesus, thy beloved Son and my divine Redeemer, for the repentance of unbelievers, the extirpation of all heresies, and the conversion of sinners.

Glory be to the Father, &c.   Blessed and praised, &c.

4. Eternal Father! I offer thee the merits of the most precious Blood of Jesus, thy beloved Son and my divine Redeemer, for all my relations. friends, and enemies for the poor, the sick, and those in tribulation, and for all those for whom thou willest I should pray, or knowest that I ought to pray.

Glory be to the Father, &c.   Blessed and praised, &c.

6. Eternal Father! I offer thee the merits of the most precious Blood of Jesus, thy beloved Son and my divine Redeemer, for all those who shall this day pass to another life, that thou mayest deliver them from the pains of hell, and admit them speedily to the possession of thy glory.

Glory be to the Father, &c.   Blessed and praised, &c.

6. Eternal Father, I offer thee the merits of the most precious blood of Jesus, thy beloved Son, and my divine Redeemer, for all those who esteem this great treasure of his sacred Blood, for those who are united with me in adoring and honouring it, and finally, for those who endeavour to promote this holy devotion.

Glory be to the Father, &c.   Blessed and praised, &c.

7. Eternal Father, I offer thee the merits of the most precious Blood of Jesus, thy beloved Son, and my divine Redeemer, for all my spiritual and temporal wants. for the relief of the holy souls suffering in purgatory, and especially for those who have been

most devoted to this price of our redemption, and to the dolours and sufferings of the Blessed Virgin Mary, our beloved Mother.

Glory be to the Father, &c.   Blessed and praised, &c.

Blessed and exalted be the Blood of Jesus, now and always, and through all eternity.   Amen.

FOURTH PART.

From the Communion to the End of the Mass.

SPIRITUAL COMMUNION.

O MY God, I am heartily sorry for having offended thee, because by my sins I have offended thy infinite goodness.   I will never offend thee any more.

My God, I believe in thee, because thou art Truth itself, who neither canst deceive nor be deceived.

My God, I hope in thee for grace and for glory, because thou art infinitely powerful and infinitely merciful.

My God, I love thee with all my heart, because thou art infinitely good, and for thy sake I love my neighbour as myself.

O divine Jesus, I am not worthy to receive thee sacramentally, but I beseech thee come at least spiritually into my heart and unite it so intimately with thy own, that it may be no more I that live, but thou that livest in me and reignest in me for ever.   Amen.

A PRAYER TO THE MOST BLESSED SACRAMENT, AND TO THE SACRED HEART OF JESUS.

BEHOLD, O most loving Jesus! the wonderful extent of thy excessive charity. Thou hast prepared for me of thy sacred flesh and most precious blood, a divine banquet, where thou givest me thyself without reserve. Who has urged thee to this excess of love? Assuredly no other than thy own most loving Heart. O adorable Heart of my Jesus, most ardent furnace of divine love! receive my soul into thy most sacred wound, in order that in this school of charity I may learn to make a return of love to that God who has given me such admirable proofs of his love.

OFFERING OF THE MOST PRECIOUS BLOOD OF JESUS CHRIST TO HIS ETERNAL FATHER, IN ORDER TO OBTAIN HIS DIVINE BENEDICTION.

ETERNAL Father, I offer thee the precious blood of Jesus, shed for us through exceeding love, and with exceeding pain from the wound of his right hand. Through the merits and virtue of which, we beseech thy divine Majesty to bestow on us thy sacred benediction, that by its efficacy we may be protected from our enemies, and delivered from every evil. For this purpose we say: May the blessing of Almighty God, Father, Son, and Holy Ghost, descend upon us, and remain always with us. Amen.

Then say: Our Father, Hail Mary, *and* Glory be to the Father, *once, to the most adorable Trinity, in thanksgiving for all its blessings and benefits.*

THREE PRAYERS TO THE B.V.M.

I. MOST holy Virgin, I venerate thee with my whole heart above all angels and saints in paradise, as the Daughter of the Eternal Father, and I consecrate to thee my soul with all its powers.

Hail Mary.

II. MOST holy Virgin, I venerate thee with my whole heart above all angels and saints in paradise, as the Mother of the Only-begotten Son, and I consecrate to thee my body with all its senses.

Hail Mary.

III. MOST holy Virgin, I venerate thee with my whole heart above all angels and saints in paradise, as the Spouse of the Holy Ghost, and I consecrate to thee my heart and all its affections, praying thee to obtain for me from the ever-blessed Trinity all that is necessary for my salvation.

Hail Mary.

THE PSALM DE PROFUNDIS.

Psalm cxxix.

OUT of the depths I have cried to thee, O Lord! Lord, hear my voice.

Let thine ears be attentive to the voice of my supplication.

If thou. O Lord! wilt mark iniquities: Lord, who shall stand it?

For with thee there is merciful forgiveness: and by reason of thy law, I have waited for thee. O Lord.

My soul hath relied on his word; my soul hath hoped in the Lord.

From the morning watch even until night, let Israel hope in the Lord.

Because with the Lord there is mercy. and with him plentiful redemption.

And he shall redeem Israel from all his iniquities.

V. Give them. O Lord. eternal rest.

R. And let perpetual light shine upon them.

V. May they rest in peace.

R. Amen.

LET US PRAY.

O GOD, the Creator and Redeemer of all the faithful, give to the souls of thy servants departed the full remission of all their sins, that by means of pious supplications they may obtain that pardon of which they have ever been desirous, through Jesus Christ our Lord. Amen.

V. Give them, O Lord, eternal rest.

R. And let perpetual light shine upon them.

V. May they rest in peace.

R. Amen.

Method of Assisting at Mass.

BY ST. LEONARD OF PORT MAURICE.

FIRST PART.

In the first part, from the Confiteor to the end of the Gospel, you must discharge your first obligation. which consists in honouring the Divine Majesty. to whom you undoubtedly owe a tribute of honour and praise. You must, therefore, humble yourself exceedingly at the thought of your own unworthiness, acknowledging yourself to be nothing in comparison with the infinite Majesty whom you are come to adore, and being careful to let your exterior correspond with the sentiments of your heart, pray as follows :—

MY God! I adore thee and acknowledge thee for the Lord and Master of my soul. I confess that all that I have, and all that I am, come solely from the hand of thy bounty. But, since thy sovereign Majesty deserves and demands infinite honour and homage, and on my part, my extreme poverty and misery are such, that I cannot of myself discharge the debt which I owe thee, I offer thee the humiliation and the homage which thou receivest from Jesus upon this altar. I prostrate and humble myself, together with Jesus, before thy supreme Majesty. I adore thee with the same humiliations and the same sentiments as my Jesus does, and I rejoice at seeing thee thus infinitely honoured for me by thy most blessed Son.

Here close your book, and continue to form repeated interior acts of joy at the infinite honour which Jesus Christ gives to his Eternal Father. Repeat also at intervals these or similar words.

YES, my God, I feel the greatest satisfaction in considering the honour which thy Divine Majesty receives from this holy sacrifice. My joy and happiness are such as cannot be expressed.

Do not, however, confine yourself to a scrupulous repetition of the same words; but give free scope to the sentiments which your devotion may suggest, whilst you are united in a spirit of recollection with your God.

SECOND PART.

The second part is from the conclusion of the Gospel to the Elevation. You are indebted to God for many great and innumerable benefits which he has bestowed upon you. Offer him, then, in thanksgiving this gift of infinite value, the adorable Body and the precious Blood of Jesus Christ. Invite all the angels and saints of heaven to join you, and for this end pray in the following manner.

O MY God! who lovest me so tenderly, and whom I shall never love as much as thou deservest, thou seest me here before thee laden with numberless benefits, which thou hast been pleased to bestow upon me in time, to say nothing of those which thou hast in store for me in eternity. I acknowledge and confess that thy mercies towards me have been, and are still infinite. Nevertheless I am ready to discharge the debt, which I owe thee, with the rigour of strict justice. Receive in payment of what I owe, in thanksgiving, and as a testimony of my gratitude, this Divine Blood, this adorable Body, this pure, holy, and spotless Victim, which I present to thee by the hands of thy minister. This offering is certainly more than sufficient to repay thee for all the benefits thou hast ever bestowed upon me. This offering alone, being of infinite value, is equivalent to all thou hast ever done for me, or which thou wilt do for me through all eternity. O all you angels of the Lord, and all you blessed citizens of the heavenly Sion, return for me to our God immortal thanks; and, in gratitude for so many favours, offer him not only this Mass, but all the Masses which are now being celebrated in every part of the world, that the tenderness and mercy, which induce him to load me with his benefits, may receive a just return, and that he may be repaid for the graces which he has ever bestowed upon me, which he still grants at every instant, and which he wishes to continue for endless ages.

Oh, with what sweet complacency will not God receive this testimony of affectionate gratitude, and this offering of infinite value! In order to impress these pious and tender sentiments still more deeply upon your heart, invite again the whole court of heaven to thank God for you, and say within yourself.

O YOU, my holy patrons, and all you celestial spirits, who stand before the throne of the Most High! return for me a thousand acts of thanksgiving to the ineffable goodness of my God, that I may not live and die under the guilt of the blackest ingratitude. Beseech him to accept my good will, and the sincere desires of my heart; but especially conjure him to regard the most loving thanks which Jesus Christ offers him in my behalf in this holy sacrifice.

During the consecration (wherein the essence of this holy sacrifice principally consists) contemplate with the eyes of your soul Jesus Christ elevated upon the cross: bow yourself down to adore your Saviour, who now becomes present on the altar, first under the appearance of bread, and then under the appearance of wine. Make a lively act of faith in this great truth, together with an act of sincere gratitude to Jesus Christ for all his mercies, and of sorrow for your sins, begging that your heart, and the hearts of all his creatures, may be inseparably united to him.

THIRD PART.

In the third part of the Mass, from the Elevation to the Communion, you must endeavour to discharge the debt which you have contracted with the Divine Justice, by your numberless and grievous sins. With this view say with a contrite heart

BEHOLD, O my God! a traitor and a perfidious wretch, who has so repeatedly rebelled against thee. Alas! filled with confusion, and penetrated with the most heartfelt grief. I detest and abominate my numberless sins, and in atonement for them, I offer thee Jesus Christ thy Divine Son. He has undertaken to make satisfaction for me by immolating himself upon this altar. I offer thee, therefore, all his merits, by presenting to thee the Blood of this same Jesus, God and man, who has here vouchsafed to renew, in my behalf, the sacrifice which he heretofore offered upon the altar of the cross. And because this divine Jesus, who has descended for me upon this altar, wishes to become my mediator and my advocate, and his precious Blood is soliciting my pardon at thy equitable tribunal, I unite my voice to that of the Blood which love has caused to flow from his veins, and I implore with confidence thy generous mercy, hoping that it will cover and efface the multitude and enormity of my crimes. The Blood of my Jesus is calling aloud to thee for mercy, and my contrite and humble heart unites its feeble voice with it. Ah, my God, and Master of my heart! if my tears are incapable of moving thee to mercy, canst thou resist the voice of the sighs and groans of my Jesus? Cannot that mercy, which upon the cross and with his Blood has signed the redemption of all mankind, obtain forgiveness for me upon this altar? Yes, I hope it can: through the virtue of this adorable Blood. thou wilt pardon me all, even the most heinous of my crimes; and, on my part, I will daily strive to wash them away with penitential tears.

Here close your book, and make in your heart repeated acts of the most lively and sincere contrition; and, from the interior of your soul, without articulating the words with your lips, say to your Divine Jesus.

AMIABLE Jesus! give to my eyes the tears of Peter, to my heart the contrition of Magdalen, and to my soul the grief of all the saints, who from sinners have been converted into true penitents, that by assisting at this mass, I may obtain the entire pardon of all my sins.

Repeat these acts several times: and thus. through the mediation of Jesus Christ. you will abundantly repay the debt which you have contracted with the Divine Justice by your sins.

At the communion of the priest, you must make a spiritual communion. unless you have the happiness of communicating sacramentally. For this purpose you may recite the following prayer.

O MY God! my heart is truly afflicted at having so often offended and insulted thee, who art my only and my sovereign good, goodness itself, infinite goodness, and worthy of all the affections of my soul. My amiable and adorable Jesus! I believe that thou art present upon this altar. Yes, I believe that the Sacred Host and the Chalice really contain thy immaculate Body, thy most precious Blood, thy Soul, and thy Divinity. Thou art the tenderest of fathers, and I love thee above all things. Come, then, dear Jesus, and enter into my heart; come, and satisfy my desires; come, and sanctify my soul. O my sweetest Jesus! come without delay.

To augment your devotion, figure to your mind, that the Blessed Virgin, or your angel guardian, or your holy patron, comes to present you with the Sacred Host, and, tenderly embracing Jesus in your heart, make interiorly and at intervals this short act of love.

M Y dear Jesus! I love thee; yes, I love thee above all things, and with all the ardour of my soul. My only hope is in thee. Never suffer me to have the misfortune to forsake thee.

This spiritual communion is of infinite advantage to the soul. Oh, how many, by the frequent repetition of this salutary practice have arrived at the most eminent degree of sanctity!

FOURTH PART.

In the fourth part, from the communion to the conclusion, you must pray for the graces and blessings which you want either for yourself or others; but pray with confidence, under the conviction that, in offering to the Eternal Father his beloved Son, he will

refuse you nothing that he sees expedient for you.   For this
purpose say with humility:

MY God, I acknowledge myself unworthy of any
favour from thee.   I confess, with all sincerity,
my extreme perfidiousness, and that in consequence
of the multitude and enormity of my sins, I do not
deserve to be heard.   Canst thou resist the prayer
which thy adorable Son presents in my behalf upon
this altar, where he offers thee his life and his Blood?
O God of my heart! hear the supplication of Him
who is pleading for me to thy Divine Majesty: and
in consideration of his merits, grant me all the
graces which thou seest necessary for me to succeed
in the great affair of my salvation.   Jesus inspires
me with confidence to beg for the general pardon of
my sins, the grace of loving thee, and of final perseverance.   Moreover, confiding in the intercession of
my Saviour, I presume to ask for every virtue in the
most heroic degree, and the most efficacious help to
become a true saint.   I ask, also, for the conversion
of all unbelievers and sinners, and especially of such
as are united to me by the ties of kindred.   I conjure thee to grant the deliverance, not only of one
but of all those poor souls who are now suffering in
purgatory.   Convert, O Lord! all those souls whom
thou hast created after thy own image, and who are
spread over the face of the earth, that this miserable
and sinful world may be changed into a paradise of
delights for thy Divine Majesty; that all our hearts
may be so many temples in which thou mayst be

loved, praised and adored, till the happy period arrives when we shall praise and glorify thee together for all eternity. Amen.

You may continue to pray on behalf of yourself, your relations, and friends for whatever you please.

Pray especially with fervour and confidence for the peace and welfare of the Holy Catholic Church, being assured that your prayers joined with those of your Divine Saviour will be favourably received.

OFFERING TO THE DIVINE INCARNATE WORD OF HIS OWN MOST PRECIOUS BLOOD, FOR PERSONS OF ALL CONDITIONS.

O MOST Holy Word! I offer thee thy priests, and in their behalf I offer thee whatever is most dear to thee in heaven and on earth, in union with all thy most precious Blood; and I pray thee to enable them fitly to comprehend the high degree to which they are exalted, and to hold in extreme abhorrence whatever can dishonour their dignity or contaminate their lives.

O Most Loving Word! I offer thee the virgins consecrated to thee, and in their behalf I offer thee the most precious Blood which thou didst sweat in thine agony in the garden. I place these doves in their own nest, and these lilies in their garden, thy most amiable Heart; and I pray thee to make them know the height of the vocation to which thou hast called them, and faithfully correspond to thy love.

O Eternal Word! I offer thee all the faithful sons of Holy Church, thy Spouse, the members of that body of which thou art the head; and I offer thee

in their behalf the most precious Blood which thou
didst shed in thy scourging. I pray thee that
they may remember the solemn renunciation of the
world, the flesh, and the devil, which they made in
Baptism; and that they may lead such lives as will
not bring discredit on the faith which they profess.

O Divine Word! I offer thee all poor sinners, and
in their behalf I offer thee the most precious
Blood and Water which issued from thy sacred side
when pierced by the lance. I pray thee to wash
the stains from their souls in this Blood and Water,
and to grant that, with a timely repentance, they
may, by returning love for love, make up for the
sins they have committed against thee.

O Eternal Word! I offer thee all heretics, and in
their behalf I offer thee that most precious Blood
which thou didst shed from thy body, all wounded
as it was, when thou wast stripped to be crucified.
I entreat thee to have compassion on these poor
sheep, which, separated from thy fold, are in danger
of losing themselves in the paths of error and
obstinacy; and place them in the bosom of thy
Church, where alone are found truth and safety.

O Divine Word! I offer thee all infidels, and in
their behalf I offer thee the most precious Blood
which thou didst shed from thy most sacred head
when crowned with thorns. I beseech thee to
remember that these souls also are the works of thy
hand. Enlighten them, that they may know their
true and only God, and their Saviour; that they,

too, may be made partakers of the grace of the Sacraments, and of our common redemption.

Eternal Father! I offer thee the intense pains which thy only-begotten Son suffered during the three hours that he was nailed to the cross for love of us; particularly when, in the intensity of his grief and abandonment, he exclaimed, " My God! My God! why hast thou forsaken Me?" I offer them to thee in behalf of all those in their agony, together with the Blood that flowed from his five wounds; that, by the power of his Blood they may be fortified and defended against all temptations, and may reach the port of eternal bliss.

O Most Merciful Word! I offer to thee all the holy souls in Purgatory, and in their behalf I offer thee thy most precious Blood. I beseech thee to grant that this sacred fount of comfort may incessantly flow, to mitigate their pains and to hasten their release, that so they may quickly come to be united with thee in that glory to which they are destined. Amen. Amen.

O Eternal Father! I offer thee the love which Jesus Christ, thy Son, testified towards the human race during the whole course of his Passion, and especially in the pain which he endured in the hiding of the beatific vision from the lower part of his nature. I pray thee that thy complacency in this love may so delight thee, that thou mayest mercifully vouchsafe to overlook the many offences committed against thee in the world at this time.

[Seven *Glorias* in honour of the most precious Blood.]

Preparation for Confession.

Without me, says Christ, you can do nothing.—St. John xv. 5.

When, therefore, we desire to go to confession, we must first implore God to give us his powerful grace. We must ask him, with all the fervour of our soul, light to know all our sins, and courage and strength to confess them to his minister. We are next to examine our consciences, to discover all the mortal sins we may have committed, and the number of times we have fallen into each distinct kind and species of mortal sin.

Then, we must excite ourselves to sorrow by the consideration of hell, which we have deserved; of heaven, whose gates by sin, we have closed against our poor souls, and by the consideration of the sufferings of our Blessed Lord, who shed every drop of his precious blood to redeem us. Finally, we must be determined, with God's grace, never to commit mortal sin again, and to adopt the means necessary to preserve us from falling back into our former grievous transgressions.

PRAYER TO OBTAIN GOD'S GRACE TO MAKE A GOOD CONFESSION.

O GREAT, Almighty and Merciful Lord God! I confess to thee my sins and iniquities; like a deluge they overwhelm me, and as an intolerable burden they oppress me. O Lord, rebuke me not in thy indignation, nor chastise me in thy wrath. O merciful and gracious God, hear my prayer, and let my cry come unto thee. I cast myself down before thee, and humbly supplicate thy mercy. Oh, for the sake of Jesus Christ thy Son, and my Redeemer, take pity upon an unhappy sinner, and pardon the evil I have committed. I acknowledge my transgressions, and my sin is always before me. Cast me not away from thy face, and take not thy Holy Spirit from me. Send forth thy light into my soul, and discover to me all those sins by which I have offended thee.

Assist me by thy grace. that I may be able to declare them to the priest. thy vicar, fully. humbly, and with a contrite heart! that so I may obtain perfect remission of them, through thine infinite goodness. Amen.

O Mary, Virgin Mother of Perpetual Succour, assist me and protect me. O my dear guardian angel, St. Dominic, and all ye saints of God, come now to my assistance, that I may make a good confession, and obtain for me true and real contrition. Amen.

[Here examine the sins you have committed since your last confession, by thought. word, deed or omission, against God, your neighbour, or yourself.]

1st. *Against God.*—Have you confessed or communicated without sufficient preparation ?

Have you omitted your morning or night prayers, or discharged any spiritual duty with wilful distraction ? Have you behaved disrespectfully in the chapel ?

2nd. *Against your Neighbour.*—Have you been disobedient to your parents or superiors ? Have you given way to anger. hatred, jealousy, or desire of revenge ? Have you, by bad example, led others into sin ? Have you been guilty of intemperance, rash judgment, detraction, or lies ? Have you been guilty of theft ? Have you spoken of the faults of others without necessity ?

3rd. *Against Yourself.* — Have you sinned by thoughts, words, looks, actions, or desires contrary to purity? Have you entertained unjust desires of your neighbour's goods? Have you been guilty of pride or vanity in thoughts, words, or actions? Have you given way to envy or sloth?

PRAYER TO BEG THE GRACE OF CONTRITION.

DIVINE Jesus, I desire with my whole heart to bewail my sins as they deserve. But the grace of contrition must be thy gift. Oh, give it me in thy mercy. I beg it through the merits of thy most precious blood, and since thou willest not the death of the sinner, but that he be converted and live, convert me, O God, and hear me in thy mercy.

All my sins displease me exceedingly; I will never more commit them; I am sorry for them; forgive me, O my God, forgive me. Save my poor soul which thou hast redeemed with thy precious blood, I commit myself to thy mercy; I resign myself into thy hands; deal with me according to thy goodness, not according to my iniquity.

Mary, help me! Thou art the refuge of sinners. I place all my hopes in thee.

CONSIDERATIONS AND MOTIVES TO EXCITE US TO TRUE SORROW FOR OUR SINS.

1. There are many souls now burning in hell for one mortal sin! . . . Look into hell, and see what the sinner has gained by his crimes.

"Day and night he shall be tortured." Bound down to his bed of fire, in the rage of his agony he will violently strive to tear himself from it, but he is fastened by the eternal chains of hell. . . . O my God! O infinite and holy God! I confess that I have given the death-blow to my immortal soul.

My sins are more numerous than the grains of sand on the sea-shore.

And yet, only one **of** them was sufficient for my ruin. Hell opened under my feet when I committed my first sin; others followed—until now, like a mountain, they lie heavy upon my soul. O my most merciful Lord, I sincerely repent of all my sins. I hate and detest them from the bottom of my heart. Forgive me this once, and rather will I lose my life itself than ever again separate from thy grace.

2. Mortal sin deprives the soul of all right to heaven, that blessed country, that paradise of delights, where for all eternity the saints enjoy the clear vision of Almighty God. Hear, miserable sinner, the voice of God thy Father and Benefactor, who complains thus of thy ingratitude.—What could I do for thee that I have not done? I created thee to my own image; I redeemed thee with the blood of mine only Son; I made thee a Christian, a Catholic, when millions were left in the darkness of infidelity. I have borne patiently with thy sins and vices; I have given thee many and easy means of salvation. And on thy side what hast thou done? For all, thou hast returned base ingratitude! Oh wretched sinner that I am! O most merciful Lord, have pity on me! The sins of my youth and of my

ignorance remember not ; wash them away in the
sweet streams of thy precious blood; may that precious
blood now bring forth the fruit of a sincere repentance, and open to me a path of life everlasting.

3. Look upon your loving Saviour on the cross
of Calvary! His sacred hands and feet are pierced
through and through with rude nails, hammered
deep into the wood ; his kingly head is crowned with
thorns ; his sacred body is covered with marks of the
cruel scourges; and his unspeakable agony appears
in his dying eyes and in the convulsions of his
suffering limbs. Ah! sinner, it is your transgressions
that have brought your Saviour to this sad extremity.
O Lamb of God, sacrificed, lifeless on the cross,
remember that I am a soul redeemed by thy blood ;
pardon me my sins, for I detest them from the
bottom of my heart.   I have wandered like a sheep
that is gone astray ; but I hear thy sweet voice
crying after me : *Come, dear soul, thou hast gone
after many lovers, but return to me and I will receive
thee yet again.* (*Jer.* iii.)

O my God ! thou art merciful and gracious !
slow to anger and plenteous in mercy ! and as the
heaven is high above the earth, so is thy goodness
great towards them that fear thee and return to
thee from their heart.   As a father pitieth his child,
so thou, O Lord, dost pity them that fear thee ; and
thy mercy is from everlasting to everlasting !

And when again, I cast a look on thy beloved Son,
Jesus Christ, crucified for me, and I contemplate a

God-man pouring out his blood, even to the very last drop, to appease thy wrath against me, to expiate my sins, I am filled with confidence that thou wilt have mercy upon me and receive me again to thy favour. O Jesus, my dear Redeemer! be thou my defence; screen me from the justice and the wrath of thy Eternal Father, and from thy own justice injured by my sins.

ACT OF CONTRITION.

O MY God, I am sorry, and beg pardon for all my sins, and detest them above all things, because they deserve thy dreadful punishments, because they have crucified my loving Saviour, Jesus Christ, and, most of all, because they offend thine infinite goodness; and I firmly resolve, by the help of thy grace, never to offend thee again, and carefully to avoid the occasions of sin.

ACT OF CONTRITION.

O MY GOD, I love thee above all things. I hope, by the merits and passion of Jesus Christ, to obtain pardon of my sins. I grieve from the bottom of my heart for having by them offended thy infinite goodness. I detest them more than all imaginable evils. I unite my grief for them to that by which Jesus Christ was oppressed in the Garden of Olives. I firmly resolve, by the assistance of thy grace, never more to offend thee.

ACT OF CONTRITION.

FORGIVE my sins, O Lord, forgive my sins—the sins of my youth—the sins of maturer years—

the sins of my soul, and the sins of my treacherous body; the sins which by frailty I have committed; my presumptive and crying sins; the sins I have committed to please others; the sins I have committed to please myself. Forgive serious, deliberate. voluntary sins; the sins I know and the sins I know not; the sins I have laboured so long to conceal from others, and which now, alas! are hidden from my own recollection. Let me then, O Lord, be absolved from all my offences, and delivered from the bonds of all their evils, through the life, passion, and death of my dear Lord and Saviour Jesus Christ. Amen.

ANOTHER ACT OF CONTRITION.

O MY God! see me prostrate at the foot of thy cross, sprinkled with thy adorable blood. Ah! that blood pleads for me and implores mercy and forgiveness. O Father of mercies! in the name of thy beloved Son, by the merits of his sacred passion, by his scourging and crowning with thorns, by his blood, his agony, his death, look upon my sinful soul with an eye of pity and compassion. I repent of my sins, O Lord, I am sorry for them from the bottom of my heart, because they have offended thee, the sovereign good, who art infinitely perfect, and worthy of being adored, loved, obeyed, served, and honoured. I firmly resolve, with the assistance of thy holy grace, never to offend thee again. I desire to abandon every occasion of sin, to commence a new life, to love thee with my whole heart and soul, and to die rather than offend thee. Amen.

PRAYER IMMEDIATELY BEFORE CONFESSION.

TO thee, O merciful Jesus, in the bitterness of my soul, I come, beseeching thee to have compassion on me, and to deliver me from my sins. Enable me, O God, by thy grace, to make a full and sincere confession of all my sins to thy minister. Animate and enlighten him with thy divine spirit of wisdom and charity, that he may discern the true state of my heart, and apply to my guilty soul the merits of the passion and blood of thy Son Jesus Christ. To supply for my want of contrition, I offer thee all the sorrow which thy divine heart felt for my sins in the Garden of Olives, begging, through the merits of that Sacred Heart, that thou wilt cleanse me from them, and grant me the grace to avoid them in future. Amen.

Holy Mary, pray for me.

My good angel, and all ye saints of God, intercede for me.

PRAYER AFTER RECEIVING ABSOLUTION.

O MERCIFUL God! as, at the words of thy angel, St. Peter was immediately restored to liberty by the chains falling off from his feet, so grant, dear Lord, that by the words of this holy sacrament, pronounced by the priest, the chains of my sins may be loosed, and all my offences be pardoned.   Amen.

Jesus, Son of David, have mercy on me! O God, be merciful to me a sinner!   O thou, who sufferedst for me, have mercy on me! Sprinkle me with thy blood, O Jesus, and I shall be made whiter than snow!

PRAYER AFTER CONFESSION.

O MOST sweet Jesus! graciously vouchsafe to remember all those holy thoughts that have passed in thy divine mind, from the beginning of the world to this very moment, and particularly thy tender design to become man for the redemption of the world; pardon, through the merits of these, not only all the evil thoughts and vain imaginations I have ever conceived of myself, but those also which I might have excited in the minds of others. Amen.

O most amiable Jesus! look on all the good works thou hast performed for our salvation ; and be pleased now to pardon whatever I have committed against thee. Mercifully direct all my thoughts, words, and actions, to thy greater glory, and regulate them by the model of thine own blessed life.   Amen.

O God of mercy and pity! having now, through thy gracious goodness, disburdened my conscience of the guilt wherewith it was oppressed, and in the humblest manner I was able, discovered all the sins I could possibly think of to thy minister, my ghostly father, I most humbly beseech thee to accept this confession, and forgive me my trespasses, as well such as I forget as those I remember.

Grant me grace, O Lord, to live more carefully and diligently hereafter, and to abstain from my former follies, which I utterly detest, firmly purposing, through thy grace, never more to offend in them especially. O my merciful and most bountiful Saviour! give me grace to withstand those temptations wherewith I am most grievously attacked—*here they are to be mentioned*]—as also to avoid all occasions of offending thee for the future.

O Blessed Virgin Mary! my holy Patron! [*name him or her*], and all ye saints and angels! praise and extol our Lord for his boundless goodness towards me, a most miserable sinner. Beseech him to accept of this my humble confession, and to supply. through his infinite mercies, all its deficiencies. Beg of him to ratify in heaven the sentence of absolution which his minister, the priest, hath pronounced in my favour at the tribunal of confession. Amen.

O sweet Saviour, for thy bitter passion's sake, and for thy tender mercy's sake, forgive and forget what I have been; pity, oh, pity what I am; satisfy for what I deserve, and supply what I desire. Thou didst pardon me when I fled from thee; oh! wilt thou reject me, now that I seek thee?

A METHOD OF OFFERING THE PENANCE ENJOINED
IN CONFESSION.

PRAYER.

O MY God and my Creator, I offer thee the Penance I am about to perform; thou didst impose it on me by the ministry of my confessor, and I desire to perform it with the utmost contrition, devotion, and humility. But, Lord, since thou well knowest that it is inadequate to my sins. and that anything I could do would be incapable of blotting out the least of my offences, permit me to unite this penance. as well as all the actions, pains, and sufferings of my life, to the bitter sufferings of my Redeemer; to the great sacrifice of expiation which Jesus offered on Mount Calvary for my sins: also to the merits of the Blessed Virgin, to the penance and sufferings of all the saints, and all the just, that thereby the deficiencies of my imperfect satisfaction may be abundantly supplied. Amen.

Examination of Conscience for a General Confession.

FIRST COMMANDMENT.

" I am the Lord thy God, thou shalt have no strange Gods before me."

Did I ever wilfully deny an article of my holy faith? How often?

Did I ever join Protestants in their worship ; *for example,* assist at family morning or evening prayer? enter their churches during service. read their books, assist at their marriages, baptisms, funerals, &c. How often?

Did I ever consult fortune-tellers, or make use of charms or the like ; or induce others to commit any such sins? How often?

Was I ever a whole year from confession through my own fault? How many years?

Did I ever neglect my Easter Communion? How often?

Did I ever neglect a large penance imposed on me at confession? How often?

Did I ever wilfully conceal a mortal sin in confession? How often?

SECOND COMMANDMENT.

" Thou shalt not take the name of the Lord thy God in vain."

Did I ever take the name of God in vain? How long was I in this bad habit?

Did I ever swear rashly? How often in the week, month, or year?

Did I ever take a false oath? How often?

Did I ever curse any one from my heart? How often? (*As cursing and swearing frequently proceed from drunkenness, it will be useful here to examine on sins of intemperance.*) How often was I drunk? If this sin was habitual, I am to mention how often in the week, month, or year it occurred.

THIRD COMMANDMENT.

" *Remember to keep holy the Sabbath Day.*"

Did I ever lose Mass on Sundays or Holidays of obligation through my own fault? How often altogether? or, if I had the habit, **how often in the** year?

Was I ever late for Mass through my own fault? How often? How far was Mass advanced?

Did I ever work for two or three hours on Sundays or Holidays of obligation without cause? How often?

Did I ever wilfully eat flesh meat on Fridays or fast days? How often?

FOURTH COMMANDMENT.

" *Honour thy father and thy mother.*"

Did I ever disobey my parents or superiors in any serious matter? How often?

Did I ever curse my parents, call them very bad names, or the like? How often?

Did I ever strike them, or make use of any threatening language towards them? How often? Did I ever wish them any great evil—such as their death—or treat them harshly? How often? Did I ever steal from my parents, and how much?

[*Parents should examine themselves if they allowed their children to go to Protestant schools, or to keep bad company, or to neglect the sacraments, or if they themselves gave them bad example by cursing, swearing, or the like.* How often?]

FIFTH COMMANDMENT.

" Thou shalt not kill."

Was I ever guilty of fighting with my neighbour? How often?

Did I ever wish him any great injury, such as his death, or any other great misfortune? How often?

Did I ever return great spite, malice or hatred to my neighbour? How long did this spite and malice continue?

SIXTH AND NINTH COMMANDMENTS.

" Thou shalt not commit adultery."

" Thou shalt not covet thy neighbour's wife."

Did I ever wilfully indulge in immodest thoughts or desires, and dwell upon them with pleasure, and for how long a time? [*If this sin was habitual, mention for how long a time this bad habit continued.*]

Did I ever make use of immodest words, or sing unbecoming songs? How often?

Did I ever read immodest books, or listen to the reading of them, or lend them to others? How often?

Did I ever look at immodest pictures, statues, or the like? How often?

Did I ever join in immodest and forbidden dances? or encourage them? How often?

Did I ever commit immodest actions with myself or others? How often?

SEVENTH AND TENTH COMMANDMENTS.

" Thou shalt not steal."

" Thou shalt not covet thy neighbour's goods."

Was I ever guilty of dishonesty in buying or selling? How often?

Did I ever take or keep what belonged to another? [*here mention the amount.*]

Did I ever buy or receive stolen goods? How often?

Did I ever neglect to pay my debts, or to make restitution when it was in my power? How often?

EIGHTH COMMANDMENT.

" Thou shalt not bear false witness against thy neighbour."

Did I ever mention to others the grievous sins of my neighbour, except when generally known? How often?

Did I ever tell a great lie to injure my neighbour's character. How often?

The Capital or Deadly Sins.

Pride. Have I been guilty of pride, vain-glory, or contempt of others? How often?

Covetousness. Have I been guilty of covetousness by desiring the goods of others? How often?

Lust. This sin has been examined with the Sixth Commandment.

Anger. This sin has been examined with the Fifth Commandment.

Gluttony. Have I been guilty of gluttony by eating or drinking to excess, so as to endanger or injure my health or reason? How often? and with what scandal?

Envy. Have I rejoiced at the misfortune of my neighbours or yielded to jealousy? How often?

Sloth. Have I squandered away my time in idle or useless occupation?

On Holy Communion.

"I am the bread of life: he that cometh to me shall not hunger; and he that believeth in me shall not thirst."—*St. John* vi. 35.

THE most sublime and holy action a Christian can perform is to receive worthily the sacrament of the Holy Eucharist, which contains God himself.

Oh, sacrament of loving kindness! exclaims St. Augustine. Oh! sign of union! Oh! bond of perfect charity! whereby we become closely united in body and soul to our loving Redeemer. According to the angelic Doctor, this sacrament produces within us four salutary effects :

1. It supports our spiritual life; "He who eats me, the same shall live by me." The sacrament of the Eucharist keeps the soul free from the death of grievous sin; it preserves us from lesser offences, which are the immediate disposition to this most lamentable death.

2. The blessed Eucharist fortifies the soul against all that might prove hurtful and tend to its destruction.

3. It gives growth and increase to our spiritual life; and

4. It fills the soul with delight, imparting to it a certain peace, an inclination to good, a readiness for the practice of virtue.

We should desire nothing more ardently than to receive our divine Lord in Holy Communion. Our only trouble, our only sorrow, says St. Chrysostom, should be to see ourselves deprived of this food of our souls!

To kindle within us before the time of communion holy desires, we may contemplate our divine Saviour under divers aspects, each of which is suitable to his immense loving kindness. We may consider him as a trusty friend, who comes to comfort our hearts, as a loving Father who awaits us with open arms to press us to his bosom ; as a compassionate physician who comes with the balm of his grace to heal the wounds of our soul : as a tender shepherd, who comes to feed us, his poor flock, with his own flesh, and to quench our thirst with his blood. Above all, we must behold in him, our highest and only good, who comes to fill us with all manner of heavenly gifts and blessings.

With these and similar devout reflections, let us approach and receive the God who, for our sakes, died upon the cross.

ASPIRATIONS FOR THE EVE OF COMMUNION.

O SACRAMENT most holy, O Sacrament divine, All praise and all thanksgiving be every moment thine. Amen.

Lord, I am not worthy that thou shouldst enter under my roof, but say only the word, and my soul shall be healed. Amen.

Lord increase my faith. I believe, Lord, help thou my unbelief.

In thee, O Lord, I have hoped, let me never be confounded.

Jesus, my God, I love thee above all things.

God be merciful to me a sinner.

Eucharistic Heart of Jesus, have mercy on us.

Sacred Heart of Jesus, I trust in thee. Amen.

O holy Virgin Mary, prepare my soul for Holy Communion.

Mary, our hope, have pity on me.

COMMEMORATE THE PASSION OF CHRIST.

O LORD Jesus Christ, I desire, in these holy mysteries, to commemorate as thou hast commanded, all thy sufferings; thy agony and bloody sweat; thy being betrayed and apprehended; all the reproaches and calumnies, all the scoffs and affronts, all the blows and buffets, thou hast endured for me; thy being scourged, crowned with thorns, and loaded with a heavy cross for my sins, and for those of the whole world; thy crucifixion and death, together with thy glorious resurrection, and triumphant ascension. I adore thee, and give thee thanks for all that thou hast done and suffered for us; and for giving us, in this Blessed Sacrament, this pledge of our redemption, this victim of our ransom, this body and blood which were offered for us.

ACT OF FAITH.

I MOST firmly believe that in this Holy Sacrament thou art present verily and indeed; that here are thy body and blood, thy soul and thy divinity. I believe that thou, my Saviour, true God and true Man, art really here, with all thy treasures; that here thou communicatest thyself to us, makest us partakers of the fruit of thy passion, and givest us a pledge of eternal life. I believe that there cannot be a greater happiness than to receive thee worthily, nor a greater misery than to receive thee unworthily, All this I must steadfastly believe, because it is taught us by thy Church.

ACT OF CONTRITION.

O LORD, I detest, with my whole heart. all the sins by which I have ever offended thy divine Majesty, from the first moment that I was capable of sinning to this very hour. I desire to lay them all at thy feet, to be cancelled by thy precious blood. Hear me, O Lord, by that infinite love which induced thee to shed thy blood for me. Oh, let not that blood be shed in vain! I detest my sins, because they have offended thy infinite goodness. By thy grace I will never commit them any more: I am sorry for them, and I will be sorry for them as long as I live; and, according to the best of my power. I will do penance for them. Forgive me, dear Lord, for thy mercy's sake; pardon me all that is past; and be thou my keeper for the time to come, that I may never more offend thee.

ACT OF DIVINE LOVE.

O LORD JESUS, God of my heart and life of my soul, as the hart pants after the fountains of water, so does my soul pant after thee, the fountain of life, and the ocean of all good. I am overjoyed at the happy tidings, that I am to go into the house of the Lord; or rather, that our Lord is to come into my house, and take up his abode within me. O happy moments, when I shall be admitted to the embraces of the living God, for whom my poor soul languishes for love! Oh, come, dear Jesus, and take full possession of my heart for ever! I offer it to thee without reserve; I desire to consecrate it eternally to thee. I love thee with my whole soul above all things ; at least. I desire so to love thee. It is nothing less than infinite love that brings thee to me ; oh, teach me to make a suitable return of love!

HUMBLY BEG GOD'S GRACE.

BUT, O my God. thou knowest my great poverty and misery, and that of myself I can do nothing : thou knowest how unworthy I am of this infinite favour; thou alone canst make me worthy. Since thou art so good as to invite me to come to thee, add this one bounty more to all the rest, prepare me for thyself. Cleanse my soul from all its stains, clothe it with the nuptial garment of charity, adorn it with all virtues, and make it a fit abode for thee. Drive sin and the devil far from this dwelling, which thou art pleased to choose for thyself. Oh, rather let me die ten thousand deaths than ever commit one mortal sin.

DEVOUT PRAYER.

O JESUS, thou true and only life of my soul! I earnestly desire to receive thee in this divine mystery ; for without thee. how could I support the labours and fatigues of this miserable life. Whilst thou art with me I cannot fear. I will adhere to thee, my faithful safeguard and sure guide ; I will follow thee, for thou art truly *the way, the truth, and the life.* Oh ! leave me not to the guidance of my own ignorance and blindness ; illuminate my soul with thy brightness ; dispel those gloomy mists wherewith I am surrounded, and shine upon me in a clear, bright day, that I may happily discern my way to thee.

Oh, thou true life and happiness of my soul! thou callest, thou invitest me to come to thee. In thee I shall possess all grace and all blessings. What can I desire in heaven or on earth but thee, my God? What return can I make to thee for all thy favours? Thou requirest no other return but my love. I will love thee then, my Lord and my God. Too late have I known thee, too late have I given myself to thee. I only regret now that there was a moment of my life in which I did not love thee. I am sorry and will be sorry for it whilst I live. I will love, thee, my God, at all times; I will love thee during life; I will love thee in death, that I may love thee for the endless ages of eternity. Amen.

IMPLORE THE PRAYERS OF THE BLESSED VIRGIN AND OF THE SAINTS.

O ALL ye blessed angels and saints of God, who see face to face Him whom I am about to receive under these humble veils: and thou most especially, ever blessed Virgin, Mother of Perpetual Succour, I most humbly beg the assistance of your prayers and intercession. Obtain for me that nuptial robe with which being adorned, I may be admitted to the celestial banquet of the heavenly king. Amen.

A METHOD OF
Hearing Mass before Communion.

To hear Mass with fruit, and to obtain from that adorable Sacrifice
abundant treasures of grace, there is no method more efficacious
than to unite ourselves with Jesus Christ, who is at once our
Priest, Mediator, and Victim. Separated from him, we are nothing;
but even in the eyes of God himself we are truly great by and with
his beloved Son. United thus with Jesus Christ, sharing as it were
in his merits, present yourself before the throne of mercy, saying:

DIVINE Jesus! Mediator of the New Testament!
who didst ascend *into heaven, to appear in the
presence of God for us* (Heb. ix. 24), yet descendest
on our altars, to renew that sacrifice by which we
were all redeemed, mercifully penetrate my heart
with a just sense of the happiness and the advantage
of assisting at a sacrifice, by which I can abundantly
satisfy the justice of God, honour his divine Majesty,
acknowledge his infinite mercies, and obtain the
graces necessary for serving him on earth and
enjoying him in heaven. Permit me, O divine
Jesus! to ascend this new Calvary with thee, that
my whole soul may do homage to the greatness of
thy majesty; that my heart, with all its affections,
may acknowledge thy infinite love; that my memory
may dwell on the admirable mysteries here renewed;
and that the sacrifice of my whole being may accompany that which thou art about to offer. Alas! I am
unworthy to join with thy minister in adoring thee;

I can neither feel the extent of thy blessings nor acknowledge them as I ardently desire to do: but, O Lord! be thou with me, that by thee, and with thee, I may worthily assist at these tremendous mysteries.

FROM THE GLORIA IN EXCELSIS TO THE EPISTLE.

At the *Gloria in excelsis* you may devoutly join in the prayer of the Church, and at the *Dominus vobiscum* and following prayers. imagine you behold Jesus Christ himself turning, as he did to Magdalen, with the consolatory assurance of your sins having been remitted.

O SAVIOUR of my soul! how sweet is the hope that thou hast absolved me from my transgressions ; that thy sacred blood has washed them away : and that thou art about to seal my pardon by the most precious gift thou canst possibly bestow. O divine Lord! let this encouraging hope be realised ; say to my soul, that thou art her salvation. With the fervent penitent of the Gospel, I cast myself at thy sacred feet ; let me hear with her, from thy own adorable lips, the consolatory sentence of peace and mercy ; let me experience with her, the conviction that thou hast accepted my repentance, and granted me pardon. Alas! I well know that I have neither her humility nor her contrition, her fervour, nor her love to offer ; but, O my God! I venture to say, that my hopes are established on still surer grounds than would be those virtues, were I happy enough to possess them. If many sins were pardoned her. because *she* loved thee much, still greater crimes will be remitted to me, because *thou* hast infinitely loved

me, a wretched creature. O adorable Jesus! in thy
love and mercy I firmly trust ; deign then to do for
me what is altogether above my strength and capacity ; purify my soul, and prepare it for the reception
of thy life-giving sacrament.

AT THE EPISTLE AND GOSPEL.

I BELIEVE, O my God! every article proposed
by the Holy Catholic Church to my belief ; and
through thy grace I am disposed to die, rather than
relinquish the precious gift of faith, which elevates
me to the adoption of the sons of God, and
makes me heir and joint-heir with Jesus Christ
(*Rom.* viii. 15. 17.) I believe ; O divine Lord! penetrate my heart and soul with the entire import of
these short but comprehensive words, and let them
produce one of those prodigies of grace and conversion, which so often followed from similar
confessions. I believe all thou hast revealed, without
exception or reserve ; for *thou hast the words of
eternal life*, and thou art likewise *the way* and *the
truth.* (*St. John* xiv. 6.) On thy unerring word I
also most firmly believe that thou art really present
in the august sacrament of which I am about to
participate. O what miracles are contained in this
sacred and ever adorable mystery! Incomprehensible as they are, I believe them all ; I adore thy
omnipotence, which is a sufficient pledge of their
possibility ; and thy boundless love proves to me.
in an endearing manner, that they are real. Were

my faith as animated as I hope it is sincere, my heart would be inflamed at the near approach of its heavenly guest, and every movement of my body and soul would be a transport of gratitude and ardent love. Come, then, O Lord! thou art the God in whom I firmly believe. Come, for thou art the support and term of my hope, and thou art, by excellence, the adorable object of my most fervent love. Come, enliven and increase in my soul the divine virtues infused therein on my admission into the bosom of thy Church. Come, and purify my baptismal robe, that I may present myself before thee with a nuptial garment, and may not deserve to be excluded from the marriage feast.

AT THE OFFERTORY.

While the minister of God disposes the bread and wine for the sacrifice, dispose your heart for participating in its abundant fruits.

RECEIVE, O Lord, this spotless host, which thy minister offers thee in the name of thy Church. Receive, eternal Majesty! this oblation of bread and wine, which will soon become the body and blood of Jesus Christ, who, to render thee in the name of weak mortals the adoration thou meritest, vouchsafed to clothe himself with our miseries — to become susceptible of death, and to immolate himself daily on our altars as the precious victim of our salvation. O omnipotent Lord! behold me at thy feet loaded with miseries, and charged with innumerable debts, which would overwhelm me, were I not provided by

thyself with a treasure of infinite value to acknowledge thy mercies, to satisfy thy justice, and to obtain
for myself and others the graces thou desirest to
bestow.   Animated with the most lively confidence
in the merits of my Redeemer, I offer thee once
more his sufferings and death; and I make this
offering for the great ends for which he instituted
this adorable mystery.   I offer thee this sacred
Victim to adore thee as my God, to testify my love
for thee, my sovereign Benefactor! to thank thee
for the blessings thou hast bestowed on all mankind ;
to implore thy mercy on behalf of all those in the
dreadful state of mortal sin, and to obtain the
deliverance of the suffering souls in purgatory.   To
this offering I unite an unreserved oblation of my
whole being, and I desire to do so with the most
generous and ardent love.   I conjure thee, O my
God ! by the perfect oblation of my divine Saviour,
on the altar of the cross, to pardon my past ingratitude, and to grant me the inestimable grace of
preservation from all mortal sin.   But, O my
sovereign Benefactor! how shall I thank thee for the
precious gift of thy body and blood, which thus
enables me to satisfy my obligation!   This gift,
which the homage of angels and men would be
insufficient to acknowledge, can only be repaid by
itself.   I then offer thee my Redeemer himself,
as a sacrifice of praise, and *pay my vows to thee*
(*Ps.* cxv. 18), in union with him in whom from all
eternity thou wert well pleased.

AT THE PREFACE.

During the prayer which serves as a preliminary to the Canon, or main action of the sacrifice, endeavour to animate your devotion, and prepare with great fervour to adore your Redeemer when he shall have descended on the altar.

PERMIT not, O Lord! that my mind should wander from the consideration of the adorable mysteries now being celebrated on this altar. Enlighten my understanding, inflame and animate every affection of my heart, that I may be attentive to these miracles of mercy and love. O give me to understand *the breadth, and length, and height, and depth* (*Ephes.* iii. 18) of that love which will soon veil thy glories under the humiliating forms of bread and wine! O that my heart were penetrated with ardent love, that I might be enabled to acknowledge less unworthily thy infinite greatness and boundless mercies. Prostrate in spirit before that throne of glory where the cherubim and seraphim, with all the heavenly host, adore thy awful Majesty, I conjure thee to receive my homage, in union with the transports of admiration and love with which they incessantly proclaim that thou art HOLY, HOLY, HOLY, and that *the Lamb which was slain is worthy to receive power, and divinity, and wisdom, and strength, and honour, and glory, and benediction*, for ever and ever. Amen. (*Apoc.* v. 12.)

FROM THE CANON TO THE ELEVATION.

AH! my God, why do I not sigh for thy coming on this altar, with as much ardour as did the ancient patriarchs and prophets; with as much pure desire as thy Blessed Mother, the first and most perfect adorer of thy sacred humanity. I offer thee my heart, soul, mind, strength, desires, and affections, in union with the admirable dispositions of thy saints; but particularly in union with the love and devotion of that incomparable Virgin, in whose pure soul, prepared by thy divine Spirit, and adorned with the treasures of thy grace, thou didst delight to dwell. I offer thee, to atone for my coldness and tepidity, her sacred heart, with all the love with which it ever was, and for all eternity will be, animated. I offer thee her heavenly contemplations, her purity, profound humility, and sufferings at the foot of the cross; beseeching thee, through her intercession, to pardon the iniquities of her unworthy servant.

And thou, O most sacred Virgin! obtain for me a share in the holy dispositions that adorned thy soul from the moment of thy Immaculate Conception; since I am also destined for the residence and sanctuary of a God. O assured refuge of sinners! I address thee with the most lively confidence, beseeching thee to obtain that I may be worthily replenished with him who was born of thee—with him **who is** *the desire and expectation of all nations.*

AT THE CONSECRATION.

The moments which immediately precede the descent of our divine Lord on our altars, and the entrance of the same God into our hearts, are certainly those in which our souls should be penetrated with the most lively sentiments of humility, adoration, love, and gratitude.

Therefore, while all heaven attends in admiration and reverential awe to the adorable mysteries now being celebrated on earth, do you profoundly humble yourself before God, and with lively faith, animated hope, and ardent love, lay all your miseries and sins on the altar; that being washed away by the tide of that precious blood which will soon flow thereon, they may be no obstacle to the grace of a worthy Communion.

O JESUS! *brightness of eternal light, unspotted mirror of God's Majesty!* my sovereign Life, and only Good! thou art he whom I acknowledge for *my Lord and my God,* and who alone art worthy of the homage and adoration of men and angels. O Monarch of heaven and earth! mighty in word and work! *Verily, thou art a hidden God, the God of Israel, the Saviour,* but the shades which conceal thy majesty are those of the tenderest love.

O divine Jesus! thou art now glorified by the homage of numberless angels who invisibly assist at these sacred mysteries. O how should their adoration and love confound and humble me, since it is not for them, but for me, that thou art hidden and degraded on the altar. O holy angels! blessed spirits! love and adore the Almighty for me, and redouble your ardour to supply for my insufficiency.

FROM THE ELEVATION TO THE PATER NOSTER.

Now that your Saviour himself is present on the altar, endeavour to profit of so favourable an opportunity for exposing all your wants and miseries to him, who desires nothing more ardently than to remedy them.

O ADORABLE Jesus! the happy moment is fast approaching, when that sacred body which was immolated on the cross will abide in my heart, and that precious blood, which was shed with so much anguish for my ransom, will be really and truly applied as a sovereign remedy to my soul. My God! is it possible that thou, whom the heavens cannot contain, wilt confine thy greatness within the narrow limits of my heart; that thou, before whom the angels themselves are not pure, wilt unite thyself to a soul like mine, disfigured and defiled with innumerable crimes? O Lord, with the most sincere conviction of my wretchedness, I protest with the centurion, that I am *not worthy thou shouldst enter under my roof.* Shall I then say with St. Peter: *Depart from me, O Lord, for I am a sinful* creature? Shall I depart from this sanctuary, which I am unworthy to enter, and relinquish that happiness for which my soul sighs, but which I shall never merit?

Ah! no, my divine Saviour! I will not leave thee; for to whom should I go but to thee? Hast thou not invited *all that labour and are heavy laden* to approach thee? Therefore, notwithstanding the miseries of my soul, I come, perfectly convinced that *if thou wilt, thou canst make me clean.* I am weak, but thou wilt be my sovereign strength; I am poor, but thou wilt adorn my soul with the riches of thy grace; thou wilt destroy my pride by the force of thy profound humiliations in the centre of my soul! thou wilt warm my tepidity, by the fire which thou camest on earth to enkindle; thou wilt communicate to me thy divinity itself, that I may not live, but that thou mayest live in me. Come, then, O my God! *the desire of the everlasting hills,* the friend of sinners, the comfort of the afflicted, *the hope of all the ends of the earth*, come into my house, and let salvation enter with thee ; come, that my soul, united with thee, may magnify its Lord, and my spirit rejoice in God my Saviour.

FROM THE PATER NOSTER TO THE AGNUS DEI.

At the *Pater Noster* you should devoutly repeat that sacred prayer, in which all others are contained, and rejoice in reflecting that you are authorised by Christ himself to address the Almighty as your Father. Trusting, therefore, in the tenderness of his paternal heart, beg of him to nourish you this day with the true bread of his children.

O FATHER of my soul, who residest in the highest heavens, and yet attendest to the wants of thy children on earth, behold thy prodigal but repentant child, who returns to thee penetrated with regret for having ever sought to shake off that yoke, which thou thyself hast pronounced to be *sweet* and *light*. Pardon me, O my divine Benefactor ! for thou knowest the clay of which I am formed ; thou rememberest that I am but dust. Forget my criminal abuse of thy mercies, for the sake of Him in whose name I dare to address thee, as my Father, my Friend, and only happiness. O give me thy Divine Spirit, that Spirit of love and adoption which will cause me to have recourse to thee in all my necessities. Give me a docile, obedient, and submissive heart, that thy supremely just and adorable will may be the rule of all my actions. But above all, O divine Lord ! give me *the bread of life*, the food of immortality ; give me thy Divine Son ! give me him in whom thou wert always well pleased, that being instructed by *thy wisdom* and *thy word*, I may never deviate from the respect and love due from a child to the best and most indulgent of Fathers.

FROM THE AGNUS DEI TO THE COMMUNION.

The interval between the *Agnus Dei* and the time for communicating, should be spent in fervent acts of confidence and love, to enliven your hope in Him who comes to take away your offences.

LAMB of God, who takest away the sins of the world! let me not be excluded from a share in thy universal mercies. Cleanse and purify my soul; adorn it, I entreat thee, with those virtues which will render me less unworthy of participating in the food of angels.

O adorable Jesus! I am, it is true, wretched and unworthy; but hast thou not denominated thyself the *Father of the poor*; and shall not that endearing title encourage me to recur to thee, as to my Father, and the best of friends? Yes, my God, I will go to thee, for thou well knowest, that had I the heavens and the earth at my disposal, I would sacrifice all, rather than forego the happiness that I am now going to enjoy. *What have I in heaven, and besides thee what do I desire upon earth? Thou art the God of my heart, and the God that is my portion for ever.* (*Ps.* lxxii. 25, 26.)

O amiable Virgin! thou art styled by excellence *Blessed among women;* show thyself now my tender mother and advocate; obtain for me the grace to receive with faith, purity, fervour, and humility, the divine object of thy ardent love.

Blessed spirits! you who unceasingly attend, love, and adore the Almighty Being I am about to receive, intercede for me at this awful moment, and supply by your ardent charity for the tender devotion with which I would wish to receive my Redeemer under my roof.

AT THE CONFITEOR.

Reflect for some moments, in the bitterness of your soul, on the offences which render you unworthy of receiving the God of all holiness. Humbly acknowledging and sincerely detesting them, join in the *Confiteor*, and endeavour, in the spirit of humility and repentance, to cleanse your soul still more from every stain of sin or imperfection.

O DIVINE Redeemer of my soul! into thy sacred heart I cast all my offences : they are not more numerous than thy mercies, nor can they equal the tenderness of that love which invites me to receive thee.

O Jesus! veiled as thou art, I acknowledge thee for *my Lord and my God :* I adore thee with all the powers of my soul, and I fervently love thee with my whole heart.

AFTER COMMUNION.

After having become the living temple of the Divinity, you should remain for some moments prostrate as it were at the sacred feet of your divine Lord. Penetrated with the profound adoration and respect which should result from the presence of the Almighty, produce occasional short acts of faith, hope, gratitude, and principally of love. This may be done in any terms your devotion may suggest, or else by the following prayers :—

O DIVINE Lord! thou hast at length satisfied the earnest desires of my heart. I possess thee, I embrace thee : oh, make me entirely thine.

O Jesus! thou who constitutest the happiness of

the blessed! is it possible that thou art at this moment present in my heart! Yes. I firmly believe that I possess thee, with all the treasure of thy merits.

O most sacred Virgin! who so long bore and so fervently loved the God I now possess, praise and magnify his goodness. Offer him for me those joys which filled thy pure soul at the moment of his incarnation in thy sacred womb, and assist me to make some return for his unbounded mercies.

Remember, O divine Lord! that one visit from thee would suffice to sanctify the greatest sinner; pern it not then that I should receive thee in vain: let not thy precious blood fall on my heart without producing therein the fruits of virtue thou hast so long expected. Oh, take me out of life this moment rather than permit me to relapse into sin.

Adorable Lord of heaven and earth! thou beholdest in my heart thy beloved Son; he is all mine; his abundant merits belong to me at this moment. I offer them to thee, O my God! and in return I ask for the most ardent love, sincere humility, and above all, the grace never to offend thee by any mortal sin.

Prayers after Communion.

O MY God and my all! thou hast at length satisfied the desires of my heart. I possess thee, I cling to thee : O make me thine, eternally thine. Eternal wisdom! teach me the value of these precious moments of thy actual presence in my heart. Oh! assist me thyself to profit by thy stay; let not thy precious blood fall on the barren soil of my heart without softening it and producing the fruits of virtue thou hast so long expected. Stay with me, O beloved Lord, stay with me, for the day is far spent, and the evening of my life approaches. Stay with me, for I have yet a thousand woes to expose to thee, my adorable Saviour—to thee who art my Lord and the only sincere friend of my soul.

O my Jesus, God of mercy and of love! in the depths of my heart, and with all the powers of my soul, I adore, reverence and thank thee. I most ardently welcome thee. Embrace me, O God, and make me all thine own. Thou art our heavenly Physician, who healest all our infirmities by thy precious blood; oh, heal *my* soul, for I have sinned against thee. Thou art the good Shepherd who hast laid down thy life for thy flock; I am that sheep that was lost, and yet thou vouchsafest to feed me with thy body and blood; take me now upon thy shoulders and carry me home. What canst thou

deny me, having given me thyself? O king of
heaven and of earth. rich in mercy, behold I am poor
and needy. thou knowest my wants, and thou alone
canst assist me. O good Jesus, grant me henceforward in all things to know and do thy holy will.
May I delight to feed on thee ; may my soul ever
thirst after thee ; may it ever desire thee, seek thee.
till it happily arrives in thy presence.

May my thoughts be incessantly fixed on thee: of
thee may I always speak, and may I perform all my
actions for the praise and glory of thy name with
humility and love, and so may I persevere to the
end. Thus, mayest thou alone be my hope and my
strength ; my refuge, my help, my wisdom.

ACTS OF DEVOTION, PRAISE, AND THANKSGIVING AFTER COMMUNION.

O LORD Jesus Christ, my Creator and my
Redeemer, my God and my All, whence is this
to me. that my Lord, and so great a Lord, whom
heaven and earth cannot contain. should come into
this poor dwelling, this house of clay of my earthly
habitation ! Oh, that I could entertain thee as I
ought ! Thy loving kindness invites me to thy
embraces ; and I would willingly say, with the spouse
in the Canticles, " I have found him whom my soul
loveth ; I have held him. and will never let him go."
But the awe of so great a majesty checks me, and
the sense of my great unworthiness and innumerable
sins keeps me back. Would that I could embrace

thy feet! that like Magdalen, I could wash them with my tears.

Bow down thyself, with all thy powers, O my soul, to adore the sovereign Majesty which hath vouchsafed to visit thee; pay him the best homage thou art able, as thy first beginning and thy last end; and perfectly annihilate thyself in the presence of this eternal, immense, infinite Deity. Then pour thyself forth in his presence in praise and thanksgiving; and invite all heaven and earth to join with thee in magnifying their Lord and thine, for his mercy and bounty to thee.

What return shall I make to thee, O Lord, for all thou hast done for me? Behold, when I had no being at all, thou didst create me; and when I had gone astray, and was lost in my sins, thou didst redeem me, by dying for me. All that I have, all that I am, is thy gift; and now, after all thy other favours, thou hast given me thyself; blessed be thy name for ever! Thou art great, O Lord, and exceedingly to be praised; great are thy works, and of thy wisdom there is no end; but thy tender mercies, thy bounty and goodness to me, are above all thy works: these I desire to confess and extol for ever. Bless, then, the Lord, O my soul, and let all that is within thee praise and magnify his name. Bless the Lord, O my soul, and see thou never forget all that he hath done for thee. O all ye works of the Lord, bless the Lord, praise and glorify him for ever. O all ye angels of the Lord, bless the Lord, praise and glorify his holy name. Bless the Lord all ye saints, and let the whole Church of heaven and earth join in praising and giving him thanks for all his mercies and graces to me; and so, in some measure, supply for what is due from me. But as all this still falls short of what I owe thee for thy infinite love, I offer to thee, O

Eternal Father, the same Son of thine whom thou hast given me and his thanksgiving, which is infinite in value. Look not, then, upon my insensibility and ingratitude, but upon the face of thy Christ, and with him, and through him, receive this offering of my poor self, which I desire to make to thee.

PRAYER OF ST. THOMAS AQUINAS.

I GIVE thee thanks, O holy Lord, Father Almighty, Eternal God, that thou hast vouchsafed, for no merit of my own, but of the mere condescension of thy mercy, to satisfy me a sinner and thine unworthy servant with the precious body and blood of thy Son our Lord Jesus Christ. I implore thee, let not this holy communion be to me an increase of guilt unto my punishment, but an availing plea unto pardon and forgiveness. Let it be to me the armour of faith and the shield of good will. Grant that it may work the extinction of my vices, the rooting out of concupiscence and of lust, and the increase within me of charity and of patience, of humility and of obedience. Let it be my strong defence against the snares of all my enemies, visible and invisible; the stilling and the calm of all my impulses, carnal and spiritual; my indissoluble union with thee the one and true God, and a blessed consummation at my last end. And I beseech thee that thou wouldst vouchsafe to bring me, sinner as I am, to that ineffable banquet where thou, with thy Son and the Holy Ghost, art to thy Saints true and unfailing Light, fulness of content, joy for evermore, gladness without alloy, consum-

mate and everlasting bliss.   Through the same
Jesus Christ our Lord.   Amen.

I humbly implore thine ineffable mercy, O my
Lord Jesus Christ, that this sacrament of thy body
and blood, which I unworthy have now received, may
be to me the cleansing of all my sins, the strengthen-
ing of what is weak within me, and my sure defence
against all the perils of the world.   May it bestow
upon me thy forgiveness and establish me in grace:
may it be to me the medicine of life, the abiding
memory of thy Passion, my stay in weakness, the
Viaticum and sure supply of all my pilgrimage.   May
it lead me as I go, bring me back when I wander,
receive me when I return, uphold me when I stumble,
raise me again when I fall, strengthen me to persevere even unto the end, and bring me to glory.
O most high God, may the blissful presence of thy
body and blood so change the taste of my heart,
that it may find no sweetness in aught besides thee
alone, may love no other beauty, seek no unpermitted
love, desire no consolation, admit no other delight,
care for no honour but thine, stand in fear of no enemy
or suffering.   Who livest and reignest with God the
Father, in the unity of the Holy Ghost, world without
end.   Amen.

PIOUS ASPIRATIONS TO JESUS.

I HAVE found him whom my soul loveth; I hold
him, and will not let him go.   I embrace thee,
O my Jesus, and receive the full joy of my love.   I
possess thee, thou treasure of my heart, in whom I

possess all things.   I implore thee, let my soul feel
the power of thy presence ; let it taste how sweet
thou art, O my Lord, that, led captive by thy love,
it may seek none else besides thee, nor love aught
but for thy sake.   Thou art my King ; forget not
my tribulation and my need.   Thou art my Judge :
spare me, and be merciful to my sins.   Thou art my
Physician ; heal all my infirmities.   Thou art the
Spouse of my soul ; betroth me to thyself for evermore.   Thou art my Leader and my Defender; place
me by thy side, and then I care not who lifteth his
hand against me.   Thou hast offered thyself a Victim
for me, and I will sacrifice to thee a sacrifice of
praise.   Thou art my Redeemer; redeem my soul
from the power of hell, and preserve me.   Thou art
my God and my All ; for what have I in heaven but
thee, and besides thee what do I desire upon earth ?
Thou, O my God, art the God of my heart, and my
portion for ever.   Amen.

O Glorious Virgin Mother of Good Counsel! look
upon me ; speak good things for me to thy dearest
Son, who has sweetly consoled me with his body and
blood, and offer to him thy merits to supply my
insufficiency.   Give him thanks for me, and obtain
that his sacramental presence may not depart without
leaving the greatest blessings for my soul and body.
My holy Guardian Angel, my blessed patrons, and ye
souls who burn with divine love, " come and I will
tell you what good things the Lord hath done to
my soul."   Come, bless and thank my God for

me, and admire the wondrous grace which I have received.

Praised and blessed for ever be the most holy Sacrament of the Altar. and blessed be the holy and Immaculate Conception of the most holy Virgin Mary. Amen.

A PRAYER BEFORE THE CRUCIFIX OR PICTURE OF JESUS CHRIST CRUCIFIED.

Clement VIII. and Benedict XIV. have granted a Plenary Indulgence to those who recite the following prayer before any image or representation of Christ crucified. provided they confess and approach the holy Communion. This Indulgence is confirmed by Pope Pius VII.. by a Decree of the Sacred Congregation of Indulgences, dated the 10th of April, 1823. and is applicable, by way of suffrage, to the suffering souls in Purgatory.

BEHOLD me. O good and amiable Jesus! prostrate in thy divine presence, and beseeching thee, with all the ardour of my soul, to impress upon my heart lively sentiments of faith, hope and charity. and of repentance for my sins, and a most determined resolution of never offending thee again : whilst with all the affection of my heart, and with the sincerest sorrow, I consider and contemplate thy five wounds, meditating chiefly on the words of the Royal Prophet concerning thee, O my Jesus! "They have dug my hands and feet ; they have numbered all my bones." (*Psalm* xxi. 18.)

At an audience of his Holiness, on the 2nd June, 1881, in reply to a petition made on behalf of the Community of St. Mary's Dominican Convent, Cabra, our Most Holy Father Leo XIII., by Divine Providence Pope, was pleased to grant a Plenary Indulgence, to be gained by the children in the aforesaid Monastery, on the occasion of their approaching for the first time. the Holy Table, provided that they pray devoutly according to the intentions of the Sovereign Pontiff.

Petitions after Communion.

ETERNAL Father, living God, and Protector of our souls, cast thy eyes on Jesus Christ, thy most dear Son, and look upon me with the same tenderness as thou lookest upon him, since he is closely united to me. Regard me not as one separated from him; but for his sake show mercy to me. I offer him to thee; and in virtue of the promise he has made to us, that thou wilt grant whatsoever we shall ask in his name, I beg that his divine virtues may be infused into my soul, and that through the merit of his adorable Incarnation, it would please thee to give me a profound humility; through his presentation in the Temple, a perfect obedience unto death; through his holy life, a contempt of self and the world; through his holy conversation, a sweet meekness and compassion for the afflictions of my neighbour, a perseverance in the path of virtue, a perfect love of thee and all thou lovest. I beseech thee, my God, to give me, in virtue of his death and passion, a seraphic charity, an abnegation of self, and a desire to suffer for thy glory; a will prompt in thy service—as ready in prosperity as in adversity, in life as in death. Most holy and eternal Father, I beg thee, in virtue of the glorious resurrection of thy Son, to protect and defend thy Holy Catholic and Apostolic Church; and I beseech thee, by the love thou bearest to my Redeemer, to bless, maintain, and preserve (N.N.), and to banish from them all that displeases thee.

Eternal Father, I beseech thee, in virtue of his triumphant ascension into heaven, to convert all infidels, heretics, and sinners, and to give thy grace to all who are related to me, that they may work out their salvation, and finally attain eternal happiness. I ask of thee grace for the afflicted, that they may be consoled; inspire them with confidence in thy mercy, and strength to bear their sufferings patiently : and for those that are in poverty, patience under their trials, that they may conform themselves to the sufferings of thy Son. I recommend to thee all thy creatures: and, through the holy name of Jesus, shed in our souls the virtues he practised in this world, in order that we may serve him and love thee as thou deservest. I recommend to thy mercy the souls of the faithful departed, especially those for whom I am most bound to pray. Apply to them the merits of the passion and death of my Saviour Jesus Christ, and in virtue of this holy sacrament grant that they may enjoy thy glory for ever. O holy Father, I cast all my necessities, and those of thy poor creatures, into the abyss of thy infinite goodness; and for this end I unite my intentions, and the petitions I have offered up, to those of Jesus my Saviour, the Blessed Virgin, St. Joseph, St. Dominic, and all the Angels and Saints, and to thy whole Church militant and triumphant, which ceases not to pray to thee, through Jesus Christ thy Son, in whom and by whom thou wilt not turn a deaf ear to our prayers. Amen.

A METHOD OF
Hearing Mass after Communion.

AT THE COMMENCEMENT OF THE MASS.

Having received from your divine Redeemer the most convincing proof of love which God could bestow on his creature, endeavour to testify the lively gratitude which should penetrate your soul. For this purpose you could do nothing better, or more acceptable to God, than to assist anew at the adorable sacrifice; thus offering to the Almighty the only victim of thanksgiving proportioned to the benefit you have received.

O DIVINE Jesus! I possess thee now; thou thyself, omnipotent as thou art, canst give me nothing more estimable, more precious. O my God! how canst thou possibly endure thy present habitation, far more wretched than the stable in which thou wert born?—how canst thou remain with a soul so ungrateful, so tepid, and, even at this moment, so little penetrated with a sense of thy divine presence? O God! *how hast thou multiplied thy mercies* in favour of thy least deserving creature! Should not the profusion of thy benefits terrify me, when I consider my poverty, misery, and inability to acknowledge or repay them? Yet, on the other hand, O divine Benefactor of my soul! when was I ever so rich as at present? Convinced, then, of my personal indigence, yet filled with gratitude for the dignity to which I am raised by the union I have contracted with my Redeemer, I will again offer thee, O King of heaven and earth, a victim of thanksgiving proportioned to thy gifts! I will offer thee *a host of praise*, immolated not only on this altar, but in the midst of my heart.

And thou, O Jesus, *sweet and mild, and plenteous in mercy*, give ear to my earnest petition; let me be now so closely united to thee, that I may become one with thee; create within me that humble, meek, and fervent heart, which will make me pleasing and acceptable in thy sight; let thy divine presence fill my soul with consolation and peace, and let thy mercies be now upon me, *according to the hope I have placed in thee.*

AT THE GLORIA IN EXCELSIS.

You may fervently repeat the *Gloria in excelsis*, a prayer most acceptable to the Divinity, inviting both angels and men to give glory to God, not only on high, but also residing within your breast.

O God of my soul! worthy and adorable object of the praise and benediction of all creatures! permit me to *sing to thee a new canticle*, because in my favour thou *hast done wonderful things.* Permit me to bless thy adorable name, because thou art good, and *thy mercy endureth for ever.* In union with him who is *the splendour of thy glory, and the figure of thy substance*, I praise thee, I bless thee, I adore thee, and rejoice in all that glory, that felicity which is essential to thyself, and which the ingratitude of thy creatures can never lessen. Why cannot I extol thy goodness with lips purified as were those of the Prophet? Why cannot I, O Jesus, residing in my heart! burn with the ardour which consumed the heavenly spirits who first sang the praises of thy hidden majesty? More ardent, though infinitely less favoured than I am, they proclaimed with joy the blessings thou wert come to scatter on earth. Oh! that I had the hearts, the voices of men and angels, to thank thee for those gifts with which thy coming this day has enriched me. O King of Peace! reign in my soul, and let thy dominion be absolute over all its powers, affections, desires, and movements. Let my perverse inclinations become submissive to the orders of thy amiable providence, that I may have no will but thine, no pursuit but that of pleasing thee: and no desire but that of enjoying thee eternally.

AT THE GOSPEL.

Imagine you hear the voice of the Eternal Father, saying, *This is my beloved Son: hear ye him. (St. Matt.* xvii. 5.) Listen with docility, not only to the maxims contained in the Gospel, but also to the words of eternal life, which Christ himself will speak to your heart. Not content with instructing you by his prophets and apostles, he has come this day in person to teach and enlighten you.

O ETERNAL Truth! how happy are those who listen to thy divine inspirations, who hide thy words in their hearts, that they may never sin against thee. *O that my ways may be* henceforth *directed to keep thy justifications.* O that I may this day learn from thy own lips, that true life consists in knowing and loving thee alone. Eternal Wisdom, proceeding out of the mouth of the Most High! my heart is at this moment thy throne and thy possession: teach me to practise the virtues of humility, charity, and obedience. But alas! divine Jesus! I deserve not thy heavenly lessons, I am unworthy that thou shouldst speak to my soul; for I have often transgressed thy law, trampled on thy graces, and slighted thy inspirations. I have gone astray from thee like a sheep that was lost; but, O charitable Pastor! seek thy servant, because, amid all my wanderings, I have never forgotten thy commandments; I have never ceased to acknowledge thee for my God, my Redeemer, my heavenly Guide. Oh! had I fled from sin with the horror it is calculated to inspire—had I valued as I ought, the graces which were purchased for me by thy precious blood, how near should I be to thee at this moment; how pleasing would my soul be in thy sight, how dear would it be to thy merciful heart! O my God! the hope and salvation of those who trust in thee! enlighten my darkness, *that I may know thy testimonies, for I have inclined my heart to keep them for ever.*

AT THE OFFERTORY.

Call to mind the transports of gratitude which filled the soul of Zacheus on receiving into his house *the Salvation of Israel*; persuaded that you are much more favoured than he was, endeavour to imitate his spirit of sacrifice, and take care not to be outdone by a publican in gratitude and fervour.

O ADORABLE Jesus! how insensible should I be to my own eternal and temporal welfare, did I refuse my heart to thee, for whom it was created, and who alone canst satisfy its desires! Yet, my God! in offering thee all that I have, what do I present?— A soul, redeemed indeed by thy precious blood, but stained with such sins as should render it hateful in thy sight; an ungrateful heart, which thou hast

repeatedly demanded, but which I have so long
refused. O my God! canst thou accept now a gift
which thy mercy alone could have caused thee to
require? Yes, divine Jesus! thou wilt now accept
my offering, for I present it to thee, not as *my* heart,
but as *thy* sanctuary: not single, but incorporated
with thee by as strict a union as a God can contract
with his creature. O most merciful Lord! do thou
crown all thy mercies, by bestowing on me that
humble, contrite heart which is the only offering
thou desirest to receive from thy creatures. O divine
Lord! assisted by that grace which I have this day
abundantly received, I now make thee a free oblation
of my whole being, which I am determined never
more to reclaim.

AT THE PREFACE.

Enter into the spirit of the Church, and, in union with the
minister of God, offer to the King of Heaven the hymns of praise
which extol his greatness and bless his mercies for all eternity.

O KING of heaven and earth! thou art he, whose
greatness and whose majesty no created intelli-
gence can ever comprehend, and whose amiable
perfections no human heart can ever sufficiently
love! how then shall I presume to appear before
thee? how shall I pronounce that sacred name I am
so unworthy to utter? Yet, my God, permit me,
for the sake of the adorable Victim I have received,
to offer thee my most fervent adoration, in union
with the angels who surround this altar; or rather,
in union with the acceptable adorations of my divine
Redeemer, the Holy of Holies, the Lord of Angels!

By thee, *O great High Priest, who hath penetrated the heavens* (*Heb.* iv. 14), I can join worthily in the praises which resound in the heavenly Jerusalem! Thou art come to me this day in the name of the Lord. Blessed for ever be that infinite mercy, which is come to pardon me; blessed be that love, which is come to inflame me; blessed be that liberality, which is come to enrich me. O Son of David! Son of the Most High God! may never-ending Hosannas celebrate thy mercies heaped on me; and may I, through thy infinite goodness, one day join in the praise which will ascend before thy throne for all eternity!

AT THE CANON.

At this solemn part of the Mass, let the consideration of the love which the Almighty has this day manifested towards you, animate you not only with gratitude towards your divine Benefactor, but also with a lively interest in the temporal and eternal welfare of all your fellow-creatures. Pray fervently for all, whether friends or enemies since, Jesus Christ loves all, and did not refuse to lay down his life for them.

O DIVINE Jesus! the redeemer of all mankind! who art come to save even those who were lost! whose adorable blood was shed for many to the remission of sins! deign to listen to the prayers I now offer, not for myself alone, but for the great family of mankind, whose Creator, Lord, and Sovereign Master thou art; permit me to offer my supplications for the peace and prosperity of that Holy, Catholic, and Apostolic Church, which was founded on thy unerring word, established by thy miracles, enriched by thy merits, and peopled by thy saints; of that Church, whose unworthy child I am.

in whose bosom, through thy grace, I resolve to live and to die ; that Church, which has this day imparted to me her most precious treasure, in giving me the adorable body and blood of her heavenly Spouse.

O my God! bless, sanctify, and protect the Pope, thy representative on earth : have mercy on the Bishops, Priests, and all who labour in thy vineyard : animate them with zeal for the salvation of souls, who are the purchase of thy blood ; give them prudence, perseverance, humility, and patience : inflame their hearts with that ardent zeal which consumed thy holy Apostles. Render their lives as holy as the law they inculcate : make them all according to thy own heart, and let their light so shine before men, that they, seeing their good works, may glorify their Father who is in heaven. O my God! *I seek not that which is profitable to myself, but to many, that they may be saved* (1 *Cor.* x. 33) ; therefore I most earnestly conjure thee to show forth the riches of thy infinite mercy, by pardoning those who are in the dreadful state of mortal sin. Thou art the lamb that *was slain, and hast* thou not *redeemed us to God in thy blood, out of every tribe, and tongue, and people, and nation, and made us to our God a kingdom?* (*Apoc.* v. 9, 10.) Let none then be excluded from that saving faith, which is the only sure road to thee ; let all hear thy voice, O good Pastor of our souls! that all may follow thee, and let there be but one sheepfold and one Shepherd. Permit me, also, adorable Jesus! to implore thy mercy on all who, having received from thee the precious gift of faith, have suffered the light to become darkness in their hearts. O Lord, *forgive them, for they know not what they do*; convert them, and they shall be converted; teach them, before it be too late, that they are created to love and serve thee alone, and let that important truth be so deeply impressed on their hearts, that they may sincerely return to thy love and service.

AT THE ELEVATION.

Implore at this awful moment, that lively faith which will enable you to adore your Saviour with all the powers of your soul not only on this altar, but in the centre of your breast. Choosing with Magdalen the better part, place yourself at the feet of your Redeemer, and disclose to him all the desires and necessities of your soul.

O DIVINE Lord! by what miracle of mercy do I again behold thee on this altar? Ah! my God, when wilt thou set bounds to that love which is so often abused? when wilt thou shield thy too often slighted Majesty from the insults it receives in this ineffable mystery? Oh! that I could repair them all in this moment by the sacrifice of ten thousand lives! O divine Jesus! how true it is, that thy *delight is to be with the children of men* (*Prov.* viii. 31); for though thy eternal throne is surrounded by heavenly spirits, who adore thee as a God of infinite Majesty, and who love thee as the source of infinite goodness itself; yet thou bowest the very heavens to come on this altar, and even into the wretched mansion of my soul. I need not then ascend to heaven to find thee, O Lord; I need not even seek thee on this altar, for in this happy moment I enjoy thy sacramental presence. O Divine Lord! what great things hast thou done in my soul! But, my God! what can be the reason that I am so little sensible of thy adorable presence? How is it possible that I conceal fire in my bosom, and yet do not burn? Why am I so slothful and tepid, when I possess in my soul the principle of life? Alas! how little return of gratitude hast thou ever met in my heart!—but, my God, what can resist thee? Hast thou not often triumphed over hearts equal even in malice to mine? Do, then, I conjure thee, that for which thou art come; transform me into thyself, and let me experience the effect of the petition thou didst deign to make on our behalf, viz., that we should be one with thee, as thou and thy heavenly Father art one. (*St. John* xvii. 21.)

AT THE SECOND MEMENTO.

It is a holy and wholesome thought to pray for the dead, that they may be loosed from their sins (2 *Mac.* xii. 46); therefore endeavour to accelerate the bliss of those who are destined to love and praise God for eternity, and who will abundantly repay, before the throne of the Most High, the charitable interest of their intercessors on earth.

O ALMIGHTY God! the resurrection and the life! he that believeth in thee, even though he were dead, shall certainly live, and enjoy in thy kingdom the true liberty of the children of God. Look, then, I beseech thee, with compassion and mercy on those suffering souls who have always believed and confessed thy name. O Sovereign Lord!

remember that they are *the work of thy own hands* (*Job* x. 3); created in thy power, redeemed in thy mercy, preserved in thy goodness, and formed to thy adorable image. Ah! why then hidest thou thy adorable face from those who have been dear to thy sacred heart, and who long to behold and enjoy thee, their sovereign Beatitude? Accept, O Eternal God! in their favour, the adorable Victim, who now offers himself to thee on this altar, and whom I likewise possess in the centre of my soul. Apply to them also, O Lord, the indulgence which thy Church this day holds forth in thy name to worthy communicants, and let not my imperfect dispositions be an obstacle to the exercise of thy mercy on their behalf. In consideration of thy beloved Son, cease to remember their iniquities, and take no further revenge of their sins. I particularly implore thy mercy, O Lord! for my parents, friends, and benefactors; for all those who are most abandoned; for those to whose sufferings I may have been accessory; for all who, during life, were most devoted to the adorable sacrament of thy love, and also for those who were the fervent clients of thy Blessed Mother. O Almighty Lord! transport them into thy bosom, where they shall be replenished with the goods of thy house; confirm them in thy sight for ever, that they may joyfully sing a hymn to thee in Sion, and pay to thee a vow in Jerusalem. (*Ps.* lxiv. 2.)

AT THE PATER NOSTER.

After repeating with the Priest the Pater noster call to mind the indulgence which the prodigal son experienced from his father on his sincere return, and acknowledge with gratitude, that the tenderness of his good parent has been infinitely surpassed in your favour by your heavenly Father.

ALMIGHTY Lord! how shall I presume to address thee as my Father, since by the abuse of thy mercies I have forfeited the title of thy child? O my God! I acknowledge that I have squandered thy graces, that I have been deaf to thy voice, and have abandoned thee, my only good. I have sinned against heaven and before thee, and were I treated as I deserve, I should be for ever excluded from that kingdom which I was created to enjoy. Yet notwithstanding all, I will not despair, for I possess in my soul the sweet pledge of my forgiveness ;—thou canst not behold me without looking at the same time on the face of that dear Son, whose delight, while on earth, and whose food it was, to do thy will. But, O my God! hast thou not already anticipated my conversion? Didst thou not see me from afar, by facilitating to me the means of return to thy arms? Didst thou not clothe me in the tribunal of thy mercy with the robe of innocence? And this very day hast thou not fed me with the heavenly banquet, which is prepared only for the children of thy kingdom? Why didst thou load me with mercies, often denied to those whom thou hast always with thee, and who have never disobeyed thee in any thing? Ah! it is because I was lost, and thou hast found me, because I was dead, and by thy all-reviving grace I am now re-animated. O complete thy mercies, Infinite Goodness; *restore unto me the joy of thy salvation;* restore unto me that peace and happiness I once enjoyed in thy service. I am not worthy to be called thy child, but I entreat thee once more, in the name of thy beloved Son, to receive me among the last of those who are happy enough to love and serve thee.

AT THE DOMINE NON SUM DIGNUS.

You should have been sincerely persuaded, with the centurion. that you were unworthy to receive under your roof the Lord of Glory, but since, overlooking your misery, he has not disdained to visit you in person, beseech of him, who is meek and humble of heart, to destroy every vice in your soul, particularly that *pride,* which *is the beginning of all sin.* (*Eccli.* x. 15.)

DIVINE Jesus! I was not worthy to receive thee—I am unworthy to possess thee—and I acknowledge myself infinitely undeserving of thy stay in my sinful heart. O may the love and humility of this thy minister, and of all those happy souls who are at this moment about to receive thee in any part of the world, supply for the little preparation thou hast found in my heart; and may their thanksgiving and lively gratitude offer thee such lively homage as thou canst never expect to receive from me. My God! since thou hast condescended to enter under my roof; since thou hast come in person to heal my soul, when one word would have sufficed, leave me not without effecting the cure for which thou art come; depart not, until thou hast planted on the ruins of my pride and vanity the divine virtues

of humility and meekness, so strongly inculcated by
thy divine example. Teach me, I beseech thee, to
walk in thy footsteps ; make choice of my heart, to
model it after thine, and to adorn it with the solid
virtues of charity, patience, compassion for the poor
and afflicted, a lively horror of sin, and of all that
offends thy divine Majesty.

AT THE BLESSING AND LAST GOSPEL.

At the Priest's blessing, most fervently implore the parting
benediction of your divine Guest, that it may remain as a memorial
and a preservative of the graces you have this day received.

MY God, thou shalt never leave me until thou
bless me—until thou givest me that efficacious
benediction which will be the safeguard of thy graces.
That the world may know I sincerely love thee, and
have had the happiness of receiving thee, I will
follow thee, and serve thee faithfully to the last
moment of life ; but yet, my God! with what
diffidence should I make these promises! How often
have I promised to be faithful to thy law, and yet on
occasions of trial, how repeatedly have I transgressed!
Thou hast given me thy precious body and blood,
yet I have ungratefully refused thee the most trifling
sacrifices. Thus have I hitherto acted, and what I
once did, I may and certainly shall do again, if not
supported by thy powerful grace. Yet, notwithstanding my experience of past weakness, I do again
promise to keep thy commandments, to love thee
and serve thee with all my heart and soul. Remain
with me, O Divine Lord, by the influence of thy
all-powerful grace ; take my whole being, and reign

over me so absolutely, that I may never acknowledge any King or Master but thee. May I rather die than forget thy infinite goodness and unspeakable mercies: may these same *mercies give thee glory*, and may they *follow me all the days of my life*. In the strength of the heavenly nourishment I have received, may I walk steadily in the paths of virtue until I come to that happy region where I shall eternally sing *Benediction and glory, and wisdom, and thanksgiving, and honour, and power, and strength to our God, for ever and ever*, Amen. (*Apoc.* v. 12.)

Sacrament of Baptism.

BY the Sacrament of Baptism, we are delivered from the power of Satan, whose slaves we were born by original sin. Being washed, by virtue of the Son of God in Baptism, we receive a new birth; are made children of God by grace; incorporated in Christ: consecrated as temples of the Holy Ghost; and become living members of the Church, with an undoubted right to the kingdom of heaven.

HOW TO ADMINISTER BAPTISM.

Provided an infant is in danger of dying before a priest can be procured, any other person, whether man, woman, or child, may baptize it in the following manner:—

Whilst pouring common water on the head of the infant, pronounce the words, "I baptize thee in the name of the Father, and of the Son, and of the Holy Ghost," at the same time intending to do what the Church does in administering Baptism.

The water must be common and natural water, and must be poured on by the same person who repeats the words; and care must be taken to repeat the words exactly, and to pronounce them at the same time that the water is poured on.

Sacrament of Confirmation.

The principal effect of Confirmation is to *confirm* and *fortify* those who receive it in the profession of the true faith; to arm them against their spiritual enemies, and to complete in them the sanctification which Baptism has begun.

For these purposes the Seven Gifts of the Holy Ghost are conferred on the worthy recipient of Confirmation.

No person confirmed should, upon any account, leave the church until she receives the solemn benediction pronounced by the bishop after the sacrament has been administered.

Confirmation imprints on the soul an indelible character; hence it cannot be received more than once.

PRAYER BEFORE CONFIRMATION.

O HOLY Spirit! whom I ardently desire to receive in the Sacrament of Confirmation, grant to my soul the beauty of an angel, the ardour of a seraph, and the purity of a virgin, that so, it may be pleasing in thine eyes: and then, O Spirit of Wisdom, come to dispel the darkness of my mind, that I may clearly see the nothingness of all that passes with time, and the infinite importance of securing my salvation.

Spirit of Understanding and of Knowledge, come to impress on my heart the lessons of my holy religion, and to teach me the science of the saints. Spirit of Counsel, come to guide me in all my undertakings, and to assist me ever to follow thy inspirations rather than the suggestions of Satan or the promptings of self-love. Spirit of Fortitude, come to strengthen me to conquer my passions, and to resist the evil influence of the world's maxims and example. Spirit of Piety, come to fill my heart with the love of God, with love of all that can lead me to God, and dread and horror of whatever can separate me from him. Spirit of Fear, come to impart to me a lively apprehension of sin, and grant me fidelity in avoiding small faults, as the best security against serious ones. May I think so often and so deeply of my last end, that I may never transgress thy law, but, on the contrary, persevere constantly in thy service, and thus merit eternal union with thee in heaven.

O ever glorious and blessed Virgin Mary! Daughter of the Eternal Father, Mother of the Eternal Son, Spouse of the Most Holy Spirit, enriched with a superabundance of grace reserved for thyself alone, take pity on my poverty, and offer to thy heavenly Spouse, as a supplement for my deficiencies, the dispositions of thy pure soul on the day of Pentecost.

Holy Apostles, pray for me. Dear Angel, guardian of my soul, prepare me. All ye saints of God, intercede for me.

ACTS BEFORE CONFIRMATION.

An Act of Faith.—O Holy Spirit, I firmly believe that I am about to receive thee in the Sacrament of Confirmation. I believe it because thou hast said it, and thou art Truth itself.

An Act of Hope.—Relying on thy infinite goodness, O Holy and Sanctifying Spirit, I confidently hope that, receiving thee in the Sacrament of Confirmation, I shall receive the abundance of thy graces. I trust in thee that thou wilt make me a perfect Christian, and that thou wilt give me strength to confess the faith, even at the peril of my life.

An Act of Charity.—I love thee, O Holy Spirit, with all my heart, and with all my soul, above all things, because thou art infinitely good and worthy to be loved. Kindle in my heart the fire of thy love; and grant that, having received thee in the Sacrament of Confirmation, I may faithfully perform all the duties of my state to the end of my life.

ORDER OF CONFIRMATION.

The Bishop proceeds to the faldstool, before the altar, or other convenient place, and sits thereon, with his face to the people, holding his pastoral staff in his left hand. Rising up, he stands with his face towards the persons to be confirmed, and having his hands joined before his breast, he says:

SPIRITUS Sanctus superveniat in vos, et virtus Altissimi custodiat vos a peccatis.

May the Holy Ghost come down upon you, and may the power of the Most High preserve you from sin.

R. Amen.

R. Amen.

Then signing himself, with his right hand, with the sign of the cross from his forehead to his breast, he says:

V. Adjutorium nostrum in nomine Domini.

V. Our help is in the name of the Lord.

R. Qui fecit coelum et terram.

R. Who hath made heaven and earth.

V. Domine, exaudi orationem meam.

V. O Lord, hear my prayer.

R. Et clamor meus ad te veniat.

R. And let my cry come unto thee.

V. Dominus vobiscum.

V. The Lord be with you.

R. Et cum spiritu tuo.

R. And with thy spirit.

Then, with his hands extended towards the persons to be confirmed, he says:

Oremus.

Let us pray.

Omnipotens sempiterne Deus, qui regenerare dignatus es hos famulos tuos ex aqua et Spiritu Sancto, quique dedisti eis remissionem omnium peccatorum, emitte in eos septiformem Spiritum tuum sanctum Paraclitum de cœlis.

Almighty, Everlasting God, who hast vouchsafed to regenerate these thy servants by water and the Holy Ghost and hast given unto them the remission of all their sins, send forth upon them thy Sevenfold Spirit the Holy Paraclete from heaven.

R. Amen.

R. Amen.

V. Spiritum sapientiae et intellectus.

V. The Spirit of wisdom and of understanding.

R. Amen.

R. Amen.

V. Spiritum consilii et fortitudinis.

V. The Spirit of counsel and of fortitude.

R. Amen.

R. Amen.

V. Spiritum scientiae et pietatis.

V. The Spirit of knowledge and of godliness.

R. Amen.

R. Amen.

Adimple eos Spiritu timoris tui, et consigna eos signo cru✠cis Christi. in vitam propitiatus aeternam. Per eundem Dominum nostrum Jesum Christum Filium tuum, qui tecum vivit et regnat in unitate ejusdem Spiritus Sancti Deus, per omnia saecula saeculorum. Amen.

Replenish them with the spirit of thy fear, and sign them with the sign of the cross ✠ of Christ, in thy mercy, unto life eternal. Through the same Jesus Christ thy Son, our Lord, who liveth and reigneth with thee in the unity of the same Holy Spirit, God, world without end. Amen.

The Bishop inquires separately the name of each person to be confirmed, and having dipped the end of the thumb of his right hand in chrism, he says, making therewith at the word cru ✠ cis the sign of the Cross on the forehead of each:

N., Signo te signo cru ✠ cis, et confirmo te chrismate salutis. In nomine Pa ✠ tris, et Fi ✠ lii, et Spiritus ✠ Sancti. Amen.

N., I sign thee with the sign of the Cross ✠, and I confirm thee with the chrism of salvation. In the name of the Fa ✠ ther and of the Son. ✠ and of the Holy ✠ Ghost. Amen.

Then he strikes gently on the cheek the person confirmed, saying:

Pax tecum.

Peace be with thee.

When all have been confirmed, the Bishop washes his hands, and the following anthem is sung, or read by the priest assisting:

Confirma hoc, Deus, quod operatus es in nobis.

Confirm, O Lord, that which thou hast wrought

a templo sancto tuo quod in us, from thy holy est in Jerusalem. temple, which is in Jerusalem.

R. Gloria Patri.   *R.* Glory be to the Father, &c.

Then the antiphon *Confirma hoc,* is repeated, and the Bishop standing towards the altar, says:

V. Ostende nobis, Do-   *V.* Show us, O Lord, mine, misericordiam tuam. thy mercy.

R. Et salutare tuum da   *R.* And grant us thy nobis.   salvation.

V. Domine, exaudi   *V.* O Lord, hear my orationem meam.   prayer.

R. Et clamor meus ad   *R.* And let my cry te veniat.   come unto thee.

V. Dominus vobiscum.   *V.* The Lord be with thee.

R. Et cum spiritu tuo,   *R.* And with thy spirit.

Then, with his hands still joined before his breast, and all the persons confirmed devoutly kneeling, he says:

God, who didst give to thy Apostles the Holy Spirit, and didst ordain that by them and their successors he should be delivered to the rest of the faithful, look mercifully on the service of our humility: and grant that the hearts of those whose foreheads we have anointed with the sacred chrism, and signed with the sign of the holy cross, may by the same Holy Spirit descending upon them, and vouchsafing to dwell therein, be made the temple of

14

his glory. Who, with the Father and the same Holy Spirit, livest and reignest, God, world without end.

R. Amen.

Then he says:

Ecce. sic benedicetur omnis homo qui timet Dominum.	Behold, thus shall every man be blessed that feareth the Lord.

And turning to the persons confirmed, he makes over them the sign of the cross, saying:

Bene✠dicat vos Dominus ex Sion, ut videatis bona Jerusalem omnibus diebus vitae vestrae, et habeatis vitam aeternam.	May the Lord bless✠ you out of Sion, that you may see the good things of Jerusalem all the days of your life, and have life everlasting.
R. Amen.	*R.* Amen.

On returning to your place after having been confirmed, consecrate some moments to thank God for the graces he has so mercifully bestowed upon you in the Sacrament of Confirmation. Imagine you are among the Apostles after the descent of the Holy Ghost, and join most devoutly in the transports with which they glorified God. Renew your good resolutions; place yourself under the protection of the most holy Virgin, praying the august Spouse of the Holy Ghost to obtain for you grace to remain faithful to the divine inspirations, and to perform all that you have promised, for the glory of God and your own salvation.

PRAYER AFTER CONFIRMATION.

O MY God, accept the praises of thy angels and saints in thanksgiving for thy unbounded mercies to me. May the blessed Mother of thy Divine Son, and the glorious choir of Apostles, thank thee for me. May the cross of Christ, with which my forehead has been signed, defend me from all my enemies, and save me at the last day. May the inward unction of sanctifying grace, figured by the chrism with which I have been anointed, penetrate my soul, soften my heart, strengthen my will, and consecrate my whole being to thy service.

O heavenly Spirit! Third Person of the adorable Trinity! whom I have received, and most fervently adore, deign to take eternal possession of my soul, create and maintain therein the purity and sanctity which becomes thy temple. O Spirit of *Wisdom!* preside over all my thoughts, words, and actions from this hour to the moment of my death. Spirit of *Understanding!* enlighten and teach me. Spirit of *Fortitude!* strengthen my weakness. Spirit of *Counsel!* direct my youth and inexperience. Spirit of *Knowledge!* instruct my ignorance. Spirit of *Piety!* make me fervent in good works. Spirit of *Fear!* restrain me from all evil. Spirit of *Peace!* give me thy peace: I neither desire nor ask the peace which the world gives—the false peace found in pleasure and self-gratification—but the solid, lasting peace, which I know from my own experience is found only

in the service of God.   Teach me in future to place
all my glory, all my happiness and peace in serving
my good God, who has so tenderly loved me—in
combating for Jesus my Saviour, who has chosen
me for his soldier, and in listening to and obeying
thy voice. O Divine Spirit! who hast deigned to
make my soul thy habitation.   Heavenly Spirit!
dwelling within me, let thy sacred presence change
my heart, and influence the whole tenor of my future
life.   Let all my works be fruits of charity; infuse
into my heart the joy of a good conscience, and
teach me to delight in the service of God, and to
despise the false joys of the world.   Give me grace
to preserve peace with God, my neighbour, and myself;—give me patience to bear with all the ills of
this life ; make me persevere in the service of God,
and enable me to act on all occasions with Goodness,
Benignity, Mildness, and Fidelity.   Let the heavenly
virtues of Modesty, Continency, and Chastity, adorn
the temple thou hast chosen for thy abode.   O Spirit
of Purity ! by thy all-powerful grace, preserve from
the misfortune of sin my soul, which for all eternity
will be distinguished by the double title and sacred
character of a Christian by Baptism, and a soldier of
Jesus Christ by the Sacrament of Confirmation.
Amen.

Sacrament of Extreme Unction.

The effect of this Sacrament is to impart to the sick person the grace of resisting, in her last moments, the temptations of the devil, and of supporting with patience the pains under which she labours. This Sacrament should never be deferred until the sick person is in imminent danger of death ; on the contrary, we should be anxious to receive it in any illness that will probably terminate fatally.

When the clergyman is called to attend a sick person everything he requires for the administration of the Sacraments should be furnished as nicely as possible in the room where the sick person lies—viz., a small table, covered with a clean linen cloth ; a crucifix, one or two candles, holy water, asperges, a small vessel of common water, and a napkin for the sick person at the time of communion.

The Holy Communion administered to the sick as preparation for death, is called *Viaticum.* It is the safeguard that must preserve the soul on its journey to eternity—it is the pledge of immortal glory. "He that eateth this bread shall live for ever."—*St. John* vi. 52.)

SHORT ACTS TO BE SUGGESTED TO THE SICK, ESPECIALLY WHEN THEY ARE DRAWING NEAR THEIR END.

O MY God, I accept of this illness with which thou hast been pleased to visit me. I bow down my whole soul to adore thee in all thy appointments. I offer up myself to thee for time and eternity.

Lord, do with me what thou pleasest ; not my will, but thine be done. Thy will be done on earth as it is in heaven.

Lord Jesus, who hast died for me, have mercy on me. Lord, I believe in thee. In thee I put all my trust. Oh ! let me never be confounded.

Oh, hide me, dear Jesus, in thy wounds ; bathe my soul in thy precious blood. Oh, protect me and defend me in this hour.

Into thy hands, O Lord, I commit my spirit: Lord Jesus receive my soul.

O my God and my all, I desire to praise thee, to bless thee, and to glorify thee for all eternity.

Glory be to the Father, and to the Son, and to the Holy Ghost.

O divine love, take thou full possession of my soul; Oh, teach me to love thee for ever.

I give thee thanks, with my whole heart, for all thy graces and benefits; oh, pardon me, I beseech thee, all my ingratitude, together with all the other sins of my whole life.

Have mercy on me, O God, according to thy great mercy : and according to the multitude of thy tender mercies, blot out all my iniquity.

O God, be merciful to me a sinner. Incline unto my aid, O God : O Lord make haste to help me.

Remember, dear Jesus, thou hast purchased me for thyself by thy precious blood; oh, let nothing ever separate me from thee. Forgive us our trespasses, as we forgive them that trespass against us.

Holy Mary, Mother of God, pray for us sinners, now and at the hour of our death. O my good Angel, stand by me in this hour. O all you blessed angels and saints of God, assist me by your prayers ; defend me in the combat, that I perish not in the dreadful judgment.

May our Lord Jesus Christ appear to us with a

mild and cheerful countenance, and give us place amongst those who are to be in his presence for ever. Amen.

Embrace with gratitude the great grace which is prepared for you in the Sacrament of Extreme Unction, and whilst the priest anoints your senses, implore with a contrite and humble heart the mercy of God for the forgiveness of all those sins which through any of those avenues, have made their way into your soul ; beg also his supporting grace in this your illness. that you may continue to the end ever faithful to him.

After Extreme Unction return thanks to your loving Saviour for having favoured you with so many helps in your sickness. Beg of him, that his holy unction may produce all its happy fruits in you, by healing your soul of all its weakness and spiritual maladies, by fortifying you against all the temptations of the enemy, by supporting and comforting you under all your pain and anguish. Keep yourself, henceforth, as much as you can in the company of your Lord: bewail your sins at his feet, and call upon him for mercy. Oh! hide your poor soul in his wounds ; bathe yourself in his precious Blood! resign yourself entirely into his hands; be patient under all you suffer ; and offer up all your pains and uneasiness to him. Implore also the intercession of the Blessed Virgin, and of all the glorious angels and saints, that you may be helped by their prayers in life and in death.

Sacrament of Matrimony.

"THIS is a great Sacrament " (*St. Paul*), a representation of that sacred union which exists between Christ and his spouse the Church.

Those who intend to enter this holy state should implore the divine assistance for the guidance they so much need. They must obtain pardon of their sins in the Sacrament of Penance ; for, to receive Matrimony in the state of mortal sin would be to profane a divine institution, and instead of a blessing to merit an endless train of unspeakable miseries.

The Church, in the General Council of Trent,

ever solicitous for the welfare of her children, exhorts the faithful before their marriage to receive with devotion the Holy Communion.

Devotions to the Blessed Sacrament.

Our Blessed Saviour Jesus Christ, is really present in the consecrated Host. He remains upon our altars as upon a throne of love and mercy, whence he dispenses his graces to us, hears and redresses all our wants, accepts our offerings, and grants all our demands.

It is profitable to honour our Blessed Saviour in the Sacrament of his love, under the different titles he assumes and the different relations he maintains with us. We may sometimes pay him our homage in the Blessed Sacrament as *God*; sometimes as our *King*, as our *Model*, our *Judge*. We should frequently visit him, confidently expose to him our necessities, speak to him of our difficulties ; and solicit grace and strength to conquer the obstacles we encounter on the road to heaven.

"Let him that thirsts come to me" (*St. John* vii.) "You shall draw waters in joy from the fountains of your Saviour." (*Isaias* xii.)

Visits to the Most Holy Sacrament.

AN ACT OF ADORATION OF THE MOST HOLY TRINITY.

I MOST humbly adore thee, O uncreated Father, and thee, O Only-begotten Son, and thee, O Holy Ghost the Paraclete, one almighty, everlasting and unchangeable God, Creator of heaven and earth, and of all things visible and invisible. I acknowledge in thee a true and ineffable Trinity of persons, a true and indivisible Unity of substance. I glorify thee, O ever-serene, effulgent Trinity, one only Deity, my most compassionate Lord, my sweetest hope, my dearest light, my most desired repose, my joy, my life, and all my good. To thy most merciful goodness I commend my soul and body; to thy most sacred Majesty I wholly devote myself, and to thy divine will I resign and yield myself eternally. All honour and glory be to thee for ever and ever. Amen.

O heavenly Father, O most forgiving Father, O Lord God, have mercy upon me a wretched sinner, have mercy upon all men. In fullest reparation, expiation, and satisfaction for all my iniquities and negligences, and for the sins of the whole world, and perfectly to supply the deficiency of my good works and merits, I offer to thee thy beloved Son, Christ Jesus, in union with that sovereign charity with which thou didst send him to us, and didst give him to us as our Saviour. I offer thee his transcendent virtues and all that he did and suffered for us. I offer thee his labours, sorrows, torments, and most precious blood. I offer thee the merits of the most blessed Virgin Mary, and of all thy Saints. Assist me, I beseech thee, O most merciful Father, through the same thy Son, by the power of thy Holy Spirit. Have mercy on all unhappy sinners, and graciously call them back to the way of salvation. Grant to the living, pardon and grace, and to the faithful departed eternal light and rest. Amen.

O Holy Spirit, sweetest Comforter, who proceedest from the Father and the Son in an ineffable manner, come, I beseech thee, into my heart. Purify and cleanse me from all sin; sanctify my soul; wash away its defilements, moisten its dryness, heal its wounds, subdue its stubbornness, melt its coldness, and correct its wanderings. Make me truly humble and resigned, that I may be pleasing to thee, and that thou mayest abide with me for ever. O most blessed light, O most amiable light, enlighten me! O ravishing joy of Paradise, O fount of purest delights, O my God, give thyself to me, and kindle vehemently in my inmost soul the fire of thy love. O my Lord, instruct, direct and defend me. Give me strength against all immoderate fears; bestow upon me a right faith, a firm hope, and a sincere and perfect charity; and grant that I may ever do thy most gracious will. Amen.

O sacred banquet, in which Christ is received: the memory of his passion is renewed; the mind is filled with grace; and a pledge of future glory is given to us. Alleluia.

A Prayer
FOR THE BENEDICTION OF THE MOST HOLY SACRAMENT.

O DIVINE Redeemer of our souls, who of thy great goodness hast been pleased to leave us thy precious body and blood in the blessed Sacrament of the Altar, I adore thee with the most profound reverence. I humbly thank thee for all the favours thou hast bestowed upon us, especially for the institution of this most Holy Sacrament. And as thou art the source of every blessing, I entreat thee to pour down thy benediction this day upon us, and upon all those for whom we offer up our prayers. And that nothing may interrupt the course of thy blessing, I beseech thee to banish from my heart all that displeases thee : pardon me my sins, O my God. since I sincerely detest them for love of thee : purify my heart, sanctify my soul, bestow on me a blessing like that which thou didst grant to thy disciples at thy ascension into heaven ; grant me a blessing that may change, consecrate, and unite me perfectly to thee, and may fill me with thy Spirit, and be to me in this life a foretaste of those blessings which thou reservest for thy elect in heaven. All this I beg in the name of the Father, and of the Son, and of the Holy Ghost. Amen.

PRAYER WHEN ASSISTING AT BENEDICTION.

Oh, Jesus! who art about to give thy Benediction to me, and to all who are assembled here, I humbly beseech thee that it may impart to each and all of us the special grace we need. But more than this I ask. Let thy blessing go forth far and wide. Let it be felt in the souls of the afflicted, who cannot come hither to receive it at thy feet. Let the weak and tempted feel its power wherever they may be. Let the poor sinner feel its influence. arousing him to come to thee. Let it cross the seas and animate and comfort the Missioner, away far from home and brethren, and toiling for the love of souls so dear to thy Sacred Heart. I humbly beg thy blessing for N. and N., &c. And may it effect that salutary purpose for which, O Lord, thou dost so lovingly impart it. Amen.

Litany of the Blessed Sacrament.

Lord, have mercy on us.
Christ have mercy on us.
Lord, have mercy on us.
Living bread, that came down from heaven,
Hidden God and Saviour,
Wheat of the elect, and vine bearing virgins,
Perpetual sacrifice, and clean oblation,
Lamb without spot and immaculate feast,
Food of angels, and hidden manna,
Memorial of the wonders of God,
Word made flesh, dwelling in us,
Sacred Host, and Chalice of Benediction,
Mystery of faith, most excellent and venerable
    sacrament,
Atonement for the living and the dead,
Heavenly antidote against the poison of sin,
Most wonderful of all miracles,
Most holy commemoration of the Passion of Christ,
Plenitude of all gifts,
Special memorial of divine love,
Overflowing fountain of divine goodness,
Most high and holy mystery,
Awful and life-giving sacrifice,
Bread made flesh by the omnipotence of the
    Incarnate Word,
Sacrament of piety, sign of unity, and bond of
    charity,

Have mercy on us.

Priest and Victim,
Viaticum of such as die in the Lord,
Pledge of future glory.

Have mercy.

From an unworthy reception of thy body and
blood,
From every occasion of sin.
Through the desire thou hadst to eat this Passover
with thy disciples,
Through thy precious blood, shed for us on the
cross, and really present on our altars,
Through the five wounds thou didst receive in
thy sacred body,

Deliver us, O Lord.

We sinners, *beseech thee to hear us,*
That thou wouldst preserve and increase our
faith, reverence, and devotion towards this
admirable sacrament,
That by sincere confession we may be disposed
for frequent and worthy communion,
That thou wouldst vouchsafe to deliver us from
all tepidity, coldness, and obduracy,
That thou wouldst vouchsafe to impart to us
the precious and heavenly fruits of this most
holy Sacrament,
That at the hour of death thou wouldst defend
and strengthen us by this heavenly Viaticum,
Son of God,

We beseech thee to hear us.

Lamb of God, who takest away the sins of the world,
Spare us, O Lord.
Lamb of God, who takest away the sins of the
world. *Graciously hear us, O Lord.*

Lamb of God, who takest away the sins of the world, *Have mercy on us.*

V. Thou didst give them Bread from heaven. Alleluia.

R. Containing in itself all sweetness. Alleluia.

LET US PRAY.

O God, who in this wondrous Sacrament hast left unto us a memorial of thy Passion, grant us so to venerate the sacred mysteries of thy Body and Blood, that we may ever continue to feel within ourselves the blessed fruit of thy redemption. Who livest and reignest God, for ever and ever. Amen.

Devotions to the Sacred Heart.

The Heart of our adorable Redeemer is the seat of love—the source of perfect charity! In it we shall find arms against temptation, consolation in trouble, strength in weakness.

The particular object of this devotion is to make reparation for the outrages committed against the Heart of Jesus during his mortal life; outrages which continue to be committed against him in the adorable Eucharist, which is the Sacrament of his love.

AN ACT OF ATONEMENT

To the Sacred Heart of Jesus Christ, which may be made in common or in private.

O ADORABLE Heart of my Saviour and my God, penetrated with a lively sorrow at the sight of the outrages which thou hast received, and which thou daily dost receive in the Sacrament of thy love, behold me prostrate at the foot of thy altar, to make an acceptable atonement. Oh, that I were able, by my homage and veneration, to make satisfaction to thine injured honour, and efface, with my tears and with my blood, so many irreverences, profanations, and sacrileges, which outrage thine infinite greatness. How well should my life be disposed of, could it be sacrificed for so worthy an object! Pardon, divine Saviour, my ingratitude, and all the infidelities and indignities which I myself have committed against thy Sovereign Majesty. Remember that thy adorable Heart, bearing the weight of my sins in the days of its mortal life, was sorrowful even unto death ; do not suffer thy agony and thy blood to be unprofitable to me. Annihilate within me my criminal heart, and give me one according to thine—a heart contrite and humble, a heart pure and spotless, a heart which may be henceforth a victim consecrated to thy glory, and inflamed with the sacred fire of thy love : O Lord, I deplore in the bitterness of my heart my former irreverences and sacrileges, which I wish in future to repair, by my pious deportment in the churches, my assiduity in visiting, and my devotion and fervour in receiving, the most holy Sacrament of the Altar. But in order to render my respect and my adoration more grateful to thee, I unite them with those which are rendered to thee in our temples, by those blessed spirits who are at the foot of thy sacred tabernacles. Hear their vows, O my God, and accept the homage of a heart which returns to thee with the sole view of loving only thee, that I may merit loving thee eternally. Amen.

AN ACT OF CONSECRATION TO THE SACRED HEART OF JESUS.

TO thee, O Sacred Heart of Jesus, do I devote and offer up my life, my thoughts, words, actions, and sufferings. May my whole being be no longer employed but in loving, serving, and glorifying thee. O Sacred Heart, be thou henceforth the sole object of my love, the protector of my life, the pledge of my salvation, and my refuge at the hour of my death. Justify me, O blessed and adorable Heart, at the bar of divine justice, and screen me from the anger which my sins deserve. Imprint thyself, like a divine seal, on my heart, that I may never be separated from thee. May my name also be ever engraven upon thee, and may I ever be consecrated to thy glory, ever burning with the flames of thy love, and entirely penetrated with it for all eternity. This is all my desire, to live in thee. One thing have I sought of the Lord, and this will I seek, that I may dwell in the Heart of my Lord all the days of my life. Amen.

ACT OF CONSECRATION TO THE SACRED HEART OF JESUS.

(To be made on Passion Sunday, the Anniversary of the Dedication of Ireland to the Sacred Heart, 1873.)

HUMBLY prostrate, O Lord Jesus Christ, before thy altar, on which thou art really present, we dedicate ourselves and everything dear to us to thy Sacred Heart.

We believe, O Lord Jesus, that thou art the only Son of the Eternal Father, the Word made Flesh, true God and true man, uniting two really distinct natures, the human and the divine, in one Divine Person.

We believe, O Lord Jesus, that for our salvation thou didst suffer and die in thy human nature, and that we have been redeemed by the precious blood which issued from thy Sacred Heart.

We believe that the merits of thy Sacred Heart, O Lord Jesus, are applied to us in the sacraments; and that thou hast given to the Catholic priesthood the power of forgiving sins in the Sacrament of Penance, and hast left us in the Blessed Eucharist thy body and blood, with thy soul and divinity, to strengthen us in our pilgrimage through the darkness of this world.

We believe, O Lord Jesus, that thou hast founded the Holy Catholic Church, the depository of thy doctrines and precepts, to be the unerring guide of thy children in this valley of tears; that thou hast committed the supreme government of this Church to thy Vicar on earth, the Roman Pontiff, rendering him, by thy divine assistance, infallible in his decisions addressed to the Church, regarding faith and morals. We believe that thou wilt be always with the pastors of the Church, when united and acting with thy Vicar on earth, and that the powers of darkness can never lead into error or destroy this divinely-instituted Church, or the Rock of Peter on which she is built.

How can we adequately praise thee, O Sacred Heart of Jesus, for so many gifts and graces! How can we ever sufficiently admire and adore that infinite love for us which burns in thee, the source and origin of all blessings! With the thousands of thousands of angels and saints of the Apocalypse, we cry out : " The Lamb that was slain is worthy to receive power, and divinity, and wisdom, and strength, and honour, and glory, and benediction. . . . . To him that sitteth on the throne, and to the Lamb, benediction, and honour, and glory, and power, for ever and ever." (*Apoc.* v. 12.)

Filled with thankfulness and gratitude for all these benefits conferred on us, without any merit on our part, again we consecrate ourselves, our thoughts, words, and actions ; our sorrows and our hopes ; our friends, our families, our parish, our diocese, and our country to thee, O Sacred Heart of Jesus ; we desire to belong entirely to thee, to know nothing but thee, to seek thee before all things, and to despise the pleasures, riches, and honours of this world, if they be an impediment to us in thy service.

Teach us, O Sacred Heart of Jesus, meekness and humility by thy example in the grotto of Bethlehem, and by every act of thy life : teach us patience and resignation to the holy will of God by thy agony and sufferings on the Cross ; teach us also to admire thy power, and wisdom, and love, which shine forth so wonderfully in the mystery of the Holy Eucharist.

We recommend to thee, O Sacred Heart of Jesus, the prosperity of the Holy Catholic Church, outside of which there is no salvation ; the welfare and happiness of our Holy Father the Pope, now abandoned by the powers of earth, and surrounded by great difficulties.

We recommend to thee also the cause of so many bishops, priests, and other faithful Catholics cruelly persecuted in many countries, and doomed to suffer the severest trials, equal to those of the early martyrs, because they will not betray the rights and liberties of the Church, and subject their consciences to the powers of earth. O Sacred Heart of Jesus! grant that we and all our afflicted brethren, clad with the breastplate of faith and the helmet of salvation, may fight a good fight, persevere to the end, and merit an imperishable crown. Above all, grant us true charity, so that, whilst serving our Creator, we may love our neighbours as ourselves ; and, united in the performance of good works, co-operate with each other in upholding religion and promoting God's glory on earth.

We recommend to thee, O Sacred Heart of Jesus, unhappy sinners detained in the bonds of iniquity, and straying in the mazes of indifference, heresy, or infidelity. May they be converted and live ; may they return to the fold of Christ, and to the jurisdiction of the one Shepherd !

We recommend to thee, O Sacred Heart of Jesus ! our own dear country, which, through a long night of persecution, has always faithfully adhered to thy true Church and to the Rock of Peter, upon which thou hast built it. Look upon her wants, heal her many wounds, banish infidelity from her borders, protect her from that wild revolutionary spirit now so widely spread in other countries, guard her against the dark deeds of secret societies, so severely censured by the Church. Grant to her children, rich and poor, the advantages of a good Catholic education; put an end to proselytism, and inspire our rulers with wisdom and mercy, so that we may lead good and holy lives, and, freed from the fear of our enemies, spend our days in sanctity and justice.

May we live altogether for thee, O Sacred Heart of Jesus; may our thoughts be ever directed to thee; may it be our greatest desire always to serve thee and promote thy glory on earth: and, when we are called to another world, may we die with thy sacred name, and with the names of Mary and Joseph, on our lips.

Holy Virgin, and St. Joseph, St. Patrick, St. Brigid, and St. Laurence, our holy patrons, present our petitions at the throne of mercy, and obtain for us the grace that, having served God faithfully on earth, we may hereafter see him face to face, enjoy the happiness of his presence, rejoice with the angels and saints in heaven, and sing the praises of the Lord Jesus and his Sacred Heart, with raptures of delight, for endless ages in the regions of eternal bliss.   Amen.

Act of Reparation

FOR THE INNUMERABLE IRREVERENCES AND GRIEVOUS
OFFENCES BY WHICH WE HAVE INSULTED THE
HEART OF JESUS.

*To be made on the Feast itself or at any other time in presence of
the Blessed Sacrament.*

O MOST amiable and adorable Heart of Jesus,
centre of all hearts, glowing with charity, and
inflamed with zeal for the interest of thy Father, and
for the salvation of mankind! O Heart ever sensible of our misery, and ever ready to redress our
evils! the real victim of love in the holy Eucharist,
and a propitiatory sacrifice for sin on the altar of the
cross; seeing that the generality of Christians make
no other return for thy mercies than contempt for
thy favours, forgetfulness of their own obligation, and
ingratitude to the best of Benefactors, is it not just
that we thy servants, penetrated with the deepest sense
of the indignities offered to thee, should, as far as is
in our power, make a due and satisfactory reparation
of honour to thy most sacred Majesty. Prostrate,
therefore, in body, and with humble and contrite
hearts, we solemnly declare before heaven and earth
our utter detestation and abhorrence of such conduct. Inexpressible was the bitterness which our
manifold sins brought on thy tender Heart; insuffer-
able the weight of our iniquities, which pressed thy
face to the earth in the Garden of Olives; and incon-
ceivable thy anguish when expiring with love, grief,

and agony, on Mount Calvary, yet thou didst, with
thy last breath, pray for sinners, and invite them to
their duty and repentance. This we know, dear
Redeemer, and would most willingly redress thy
sufferings, by our own, or share with thee in thine.

O merciful Jesus! ever present on our Altars,
with a heart open to receive all who labour and are
burthened: O adorable Heart of Jesus, source of
true contrition, give to our hearts the spirit of sincere penance, and to our eyes a fountain of tears,
that we may bewail all our sins and the sins of the
world. Pardon, O Divine Jesus, all the injuries and
outrages done to thee by sinners; forgive all the
impieties, irreverences, and sacrileges which have
been committed against thee in the holy sacrament
of the Eucharist, since its institution. Graciously
receive the small tribute of our sincere repentance,
as an agreeable offering in thy sight, and in requital
for the benefits we daily receive from the Altar,
where thou art a living and continued sacrifice, and
in union with that bloody holocaust thou didst present to thy Eternal Father on the cross.

Sweet Jesus! give thy blessing to the ardent
desire we now entertain, and the holy resolution we
have taken, of ever loving and adoring thee with our
whole mind, and with our whole heart, in the Sacrament of thy love; thus to repair, by a true conversion of heart, and ardent zeal for thy glory, our
past negligences and infidelities. Be thou, O adorable Jesus! who knowest our frailty, be thou our

Mediator with thy heavenly Father, whom we have so grievously offended: strengthen our weakness, confirm our resolutions, and with thy charity, humility, meekness, and patience, cancel the multitude of our iniquities. Be thou our support, our refuge and our strength. that nothing henceforth in life or death may ever separate us from thee. Amen.

Litany of the Sacred Heart of Jesus.

[From Encyclical of His Holiness Pope Leo XIII., on the Consecration of Mankind to the Sacred Heart of Jesus.]

Lord, have mercy on us.
Christ, have mercy on us.
Lord, have mercy on us.
Christ, hear us.
Christ, graciously hear us.
God, the Father of heaven,
God, the Son, Redeemer of the world,
God, the Holy Ghost,
Holy Trinity, one God,
Heart of Jesus, Son of the eternal Father,
Heart of Jesus, formed by the Holy Ghost in the womb of the Virgin Mary,
Heart of Jesus, most intimately united to the Word of God,
Heart of Jesus, of infinite majesty,
Heart of Jesus, holy temple of God,
Heart of Jesus, Tabernacle of the Most High,

Have mercy on us.

Heart of Jesus, house of God and gate of
    heaven.
Heart of Jesus, burning furnace of charity.
Heart of Jesus, sanctuary of justice and love,
Heart of Jesus, full of goodness and love,
Heart of Jesus, abyss of all virtues,
Heart of Jesus, most worthy of all praise,
Heart of Jesus, King and centre of all hearts,
Heart of Jesus, in which are all the treasures of
    wisdom and knowledge.
Heart of Jesus, in which dwells all the fulness
    of the Godhead,
Heart of Jesus, in which the Father is well
    pleased,
Heart of Jesus, of whose fulness we all have
    received,
Heart of Jesus, the desire of the everlasting
    hills,
Heart of Jesus, patient and full of mercy,
Heart of Jesus, rich to all that call on thee,
Heart of Jesus, source of life and holiness,
Heart of Jesus, propitiation for our sins,
Heart of Jesus, filled with reproaches,
Heart of Jesus, bruised for our sins,
Heart of Jesus, obedient even unto death,
Heart of Jesus, pierced with a lance,
Heart of Jesus, source of all consolation,
Heart of Jesus, our life and our resurrection,
Heart of Jesus, our peace and our reconciliation,
Heart of Jesus, victim for sinners,

Have mercy on us.

Heart of Jesus, salvation of them that hope
    in thee,
Heart of Jesus, hope of them that die in thee,
Heart of Jesus, delight of all the saints,
Lamb of God, who takest away the sins of the
    world, *Spare us, O Lord.*
Lamb of God, who takest away the sins of the
    world, *Graciously hear us, O Lord.*
Lamb of God, who takest away the sins of the
    world, *Have mercy on us.*
V. Jesus, meek and humble of heart.
R. Make our hearts like unto thine.

LET US PRAY.

O ALMIGHTY and eternal God, look on the heart
of thy most beloved Son and on the praise and
satisfaction it renders thee in the name of sinners,
and, being appeased, grant pardon to those that
implore thy mercy in the name of the same Jesus
Christ, thy Son, who liveth and reigneth with thee
in the unity of the Holy Ghost, God, world without
end. Amen.

FORM OF CONSECRATION TO THE MOST SACRED HEART OF JESUS.

MOST sweet Jesus, Redeemer of the human race,
look down upon us most humbly prostrate
before thine altar. Thine we are. Thine we desire
ever to remain: and that we may be the more
securely united to thee, behold each one of us here
to-day freely consecrates himself to thy most Sacred

Heart. Many, indeed, have never known thee; many, too, have despised thy commandments and rejected thee. Have mercy on them all, O most merciful Jesus, and draw them all to thy most Sacred Heart! Be thou, O Lord, King, not only of the faithful who have never departed from thee, but also of the prodigal children who have turned their backs upon thee. Grant that they may return to their father's house, lest they perish of wretchedness and hunger. Be thou King of those who have been deceived by error or whom discord keeps estranged. Bring them back to the haven of truth and to the unity of faith, that soon there may be but one fold and one shepherd. Be thou King, moreover, of all those who continue in the ancient superstition of the Gentiles. Refuse not to deliver them out of darkness into the light and the kingdom of God. Grant, O Lord, to thy Church freedom and security; give peace and order to all nations; make the earth resound from pole to pole with one voice: "Praise to the Divine Heart, through which our salvation has been accomplished: to the same be glory and honour for ever. Amen."— 300 *days' Indulg.* (*once a day*).

May the Sacred Heart of Jesus be everywhere loved. 100 *days' Indulg.*—(*Pius IX*, 23 *Sept.*, 1860.)

Heart of Jesus, in Thee I trust. 300 *days' Indulgence.*—(*Pius X.*, 27 *June*, 1906.)

O Lord, preserve in us the faith. 100 *days' Indulgence.*—(*Pius X.*, 20 *March*, 1908.)

DEVOTIONS TO

The Sacred Passion of Our Lord.

"There is nothing more efficacious for curing the wounds of our conscience than continually to meditate on the sorrows and sufferings of our blessed Lord."—St. Bernard.

(Note. —Many Plenary and Partial Indulgences may be gained by going round the Stations of the Cross in the state of grace, meditating on the Passion. The following method is by St. Alphonsus Liguori.)

PRAYER BEFORE THE HIGH ALTAR.

O JESUS CHRIST, my Lord! with what great love thou didst pass over this painful road, which led thee to death: and I, how often I have abandoned thee! But now I love thee with my whole soul, and because I love thee, I am sincerely sorry for having offended thee. My Jesus, pardon me, and permit me to accompany thee in this journey. Thou art going to die for love of me, and it is my wish also, O my dearest Redeemer! to die for love of thee. O yes, my Jesus! in thy love I wish to live, in thy love I wish to die.

FIRST STATION.

JESUS IS CONDEMNED TO DEATH.

V. We adore thee, O Christ! and bless thee.

R. Because by thy holy cross thou hast redeemed the world.

Consider how Jesus, after having been scourged and crowned with thorns, was unjustly condemned by Pilate to die on the cross. *Pause and meditate awhile.*

My adorable Jesus ! it was not Pilate—no, it was my sins—that condemned thee to die. I beseech thee, by the merits of this sorrowful journey, to assist my soul in her journey towards eternity. I love thee, my beloved Jesus ; I love thee more than myself ; I repent with my whole heart of having offended thee. Never permit me to separate myself from thee again. Grant that I may love thee always ; and then do with me what thou wilt.

Our Father. Hail Mary.

Glory be to the Father, &c.

> O Jesus ! who, for love of me,
> Didst bear thy cross to Calvary ;
> In thy sweet mercy grant to me
> To suffer and to die with thee.

SECOND STATION.

JESUS IS MADE TO BEAR HIS CROSS.

V. We adore thee, O Christ ! and bless thee.

R. Because by thy holy cross thou hast redeemed the world.

Consider how Jesus, in making this journey with the cross on his shoulders, thought of us, and offered for us to his Father the death he was about to undergo. *Pause, &c.*

My most beloved Jesus! I embrace all the tribulations thou hast destined for me until death. I beseech thee, by the merits of the pain thou didst suffer in carrying thy cross, to give me the necessary help to carry mine with perfect patience and resignation. I love thee, Jesus, my love! above all things; I repent with my whole heart of having offended thee. Never permit me to separate myself from thee again. Grant that I may love thee always; and then do with me what thou wilt.

Our Father. Hail Mary.

Glory be to the Father, &c.

O Jesus! who, for love of me, &c.

THIRD STATION.

JESUS FALLS THE FIRST TIME UNDER HIS CROSS.

V. We adore thee, O Christ! and bless thee.

R. Because by thy holy cross thou hast redeemed the world.

Consider this first fall of Jesus under his cross, his flesh was torn by the scourges, his head crowned with thorns, and he had lost a great quantity of blood. He was so weakened he could scarcely walk, and yet he had to carry this great load upon his shoulders. The soldiers struck him rudely, and thus he fell several times. *Pause, &c.*

My Jesus, it is not the weight of the cross, but of my sins, which has made thee suffer so much pain. Ah! by the merits of this first fall, deliver me from the misfortune of falling into mortal sin. I love thee, O my Jesus! I repent with my whole heart of having offended thee. Never permit me to separate myself from thee again. Grant that I may love thee always: and then do with me what thou wilt.

Our Father. Hail Mary.

Glory be to the Father, &c.

O Jesus! who, for love of me, &c.

FOURTH STATION

JESUS MEETS HIS AFFLICTED MOTHER

V. We adore thee, O Christ! and bless thee.

R. Because by thy holy cross thou hast redeemed the world.

Consider the meeting of the Son and the Mother, which took place on this journey. Their looks became like so many arrows to wound those hearts which loved each other so tenderly. *Pause, &c.*

My sweet Jesus, by the sorrow thou didst experience in this meeting, grant me the grace of a truly devoted love for thy most holy Mother. And thou, my Queen, who wast overwhelmed with sorrow, obtain for me, by thy intercession, a continual and tender remembrance of the passion of thy Son. I love thee, Jesus, my love! above all things; I repent of ever having offended thee. Never permit me to separate myself from thee again. Grant that I may love thee always; and then do with me what thou wilt.

Our Father. Hail Mary.

Glory be to the Father, &c.

O Jesus! who, for love of me, &c.

FIFTH STATION.

THE CYRENEAN HELPS JESUS TO CARRY HIS CROSS.

V. We adore thee, O Christ! and bless thee.

R. Because by thy holy cross thou hast redeemed the world.

Consider how the Jews, seeing that at each step Jesus was on the point of expiring, and fearing he would die on the way, when they wished him to die the ignominious death of the cross, constrained Simon the Cyrenean to carry the cross behind our Lord *Pause, &c.*

My most beloved Jesus! I will not refuse the cross as the Cyrenean did! I accept it; I embrace it. I accept in particular the death thou hast destined for me, with all its pains; I unite it to thy death; I offer it to thee. Thou hast died for love of me! I will die for love of thee. Help me by thy grace. I love thee, Jesus, my love! above all things: I repent with my whole heart of having offended thee. Never permit me to separate myself from thee again. Grant that I may love thee always: and then do with me what thou wilt.

Our Father. Hail Mary.

Glory be to the Father, &c.

O Jesus! who, for love of me, &c.

SIXTH STATION.

VERONICA WIPES THE FACE OF JESUS.

V. We adore thee, O Christ! and bless thee.

R. Because by thy holy cross thou hast redeemed the world

Consider how the holy woman named Veronica, seeing Jesus so ill used, and his face bathed in sweat and blood, presented him with a towel, with which he wiped his adorable face, leaving on it the impression of his holy countenance. *Pause, &c.*

My most beloved Jesus, thy face was beautiful before, but in this journey it has lost all its beauty, and wounds and blood have disfigured it. Alas! my soul also was once beautiful, when it received thy grace in baptism; but I have disfigured it since by my sins. Thou alone, my redeemer, canst restore it to its former beauty. Do this by thy passion, O Jesus! I repent with my whole heart of having offended thee. Never permit me to separate myself from thee again. Grant that I may love thee always and then do with me what thou wilt.

Our Father. Hail Mary.

Glory be to the Father, &c.

O Jesus! who, for love of me, &c.

SEVENTH STATION.

JESUS FALLS THE SECOND TIME.

V. We adore thee, O Christ! and bless thee.

R. Because by thy holy cross thou hast redeemed the world.

Consider the second fall of Jesus under the cross : a fall which renews the pain of all the wounds of his head and members. *Pause, &c.*

My most sweet Jesus! how many times thou hast pardoned me, and how many times have I fallen again, and begun again to offend thee! Oh! by the merits of this second fall, give me the necessary helps to persevere in thy grace until death. Grant that in all temptations which assail me, I may always commend myself to thee. I love thee, Jesus, my love! above all things; I repent with my whole heart of having offended thee. Never permit me to separate myself from thee again. Grant that I may love thee always; and then do with me what thou wilt.

Our Father. Hail Mary.
Glory be to the Father, &c.

O Jesus! who, for love of me, &c,

EIGHTH STATION.

JESUS SPEAKS TO THE DAUGHTERS OF JERUSALEM.

V. We adore thee, O Christ! and bless thee.
R. Because by thy holy cross thou hast redeemed the world.

Consider how these women wept with compassion at seeing Jesus in such a pitiable state, streaming with blood, as he walked along. "My children," said he, "weep not for me, but for yourselves and your children." *Pause, &c.*

My Jesus! laden with sorrows, I weep for the offences I have committed against thee, because of the pains they have deserved, and still more because of the displeasure they have caused thee, who hast loved me so much. It is thy love, more than the fear of hell, which causes me to weep for my sins. My Jesus! I love thee more than myself. I repent with my whole heart of having offended thee. Never permit me to separate myself from thee again. Grant that I may love thee always; and then do with me what thou wilt.

Our Father, Hail Mary.
Glory be to the Father, &c.

O Jesus! who, for love of me, &c.

NINTH STATION.

JESUS FALLS THE THIRD TIME.

V. We adore thee, O Christ! and bless thee.

R. Because by thy holy cross thou hast redeemed the world.

Consider the third fall of Jesus Christ. His weakness was extreme, and the cruelty of his executioners excessive, who tried to hasten his steps when he could scarcely move. *Pause, &c.*

Ah! my outraged Jesus, by the merits of the weakness thou didst suffer in going to Calvary, give me strength sufficient to conquer all human respect, and all my wicked passions, which have led me to despise thy friendship. I love thee, Jesus, my love! above all things; I repent with my whole heart of having offended thee. Never permit me to separate myself from thee again. Grant that I may love thee always; and then do with me what thou wilt.

Our Father. Hail Mary.
Glory be to the Father, &c.

O Jesus ! who, for love of me, &o.

TENTH STATION.

JESUS STRIPPED OF HIS GARMENTS.

V. We adore thee, O Christ ! and bless thee.
R. Because by thy holy cross thou hast redeemed the world.

Consider the violence with which the executioners stripped Jesus. His inner garments adhered to his torn flesh, and they dragged them off so roughly that the skin came with them. Compassionate your Saviour thus cruelly treated. *Pause, &c.*

My innocent Jesus! by the merits of the torment thou hast felt, help me to strip myself of all affection to things of earth, in order that I may place all my love in thee, who art so worthy of my love. I love thee, O Jesus! above all things; I repent with my whole heart of ever having offended thee. Never permit me to separate myself from thee again. Grant that I may

love thee always; and then do with me what thou
wilt.

Our Father.   Hail Mary.
Glory be to the Father, &c.

O Jesus! who, for love of me, &c.

ELEVENTH STATION.

JESUS IS NAILED TO THE CROSS.

V. We adore thee, O Christ! and bless thee.
R. Because by thy holy cross thou hast redeemed
the world.

Consider how Jesus. after being thrown on the
cross, extended his hands, and offered to his eternal
Father the sacrifice of his life for our salvation.
These barbarians fastened him with nails, and then
securing the cross, allowed him to die with anguish
on this infamous gibbet.   *Pause, &c.*

My Jesus! loaded with contempt, nail my heart
to thy feet, that it may ever remain there to love
thee, and never quit thee again.   I love thee more
than myself.   I repent with my whole heart of having offended thee.   Never permit me to separate myself from thee again. Grant that I may love thee
always; and then do with me what thou wilt.

Our Father.   Hail Mary.
Glory be to the Father, &c.

O Jesus! who, for love of me, &c.

TWELFTH STATION.

JESUS DIES ON THE CROSS.

V. We adore thee, O Christ! and bless thee.

R. Because by thy holy cross thou hast redeemed the world.

Consider how Jesus, after three hours' agony on the cross, consumed with anguish, abandoned himself to the weight of his body, bowed his head, and died. *Pause, &c.*

O my dying Jesus! I kiss devoutly the cross on which thou didst die for love of me. I have merited by my sins to die a miserable death, but thy death is my hope. Ah! by the merits of thy death, give me grace to die embracing thy feet, and burning with love for thee. I commit my soul into thy hands. I love thee, O Jesus! above all things; I repent of ever having offended thee. Permit not that I ever offend thee again. Grant that I may love thee always; and then do with me what thou wilt.

Our Father. Hail Mary,
Glory be to the Father, &c.

O Jesus! who, for love of me, &c.

THIRTEENTH STATION.

JESUS IS TAKEN DOWN FROM THE CROSS.

V. We adore thee, O Christ! and bless thee.

R. Because by thy holy cross thou hast redeemed the world.

Consider how our Lord, having expired, two of his disciples, Joseph and Nicodemus, took him down from the cross, and placed him in the arms of his afflicted Mother, who received him with unutterable tenderness, and pressed him to her bosom. *Pause. &c.*

O Mother of sorrow! for the love of this Son, accept me for thy servant, and pray for me. And thou, my Redeemer, since thou hast died for me, permit me to love thee; for I wish but thee; and nothing more. I love thee, my Jesus! above all things; I repent of ever having offended thee. Never permit me to offend thee again. Grant that I may love thee always; and then do with me what thou wilt.

Our Father. Hail Mary.

Glory be to the Father, &c.

O Jesus! who, for love of me, &c.

FOURTEENTH STATION.
JESUS IS PLACED IN THE SEPULCHRE.

V. We adore thee, O Christ! and bless thee.

R. Because by thy holy cross thou hast redeemed the world.

Consider how the disciples carried the body of Jesus to bury it, accompanied by his holy Mother, who arranged it in the sepulchre with her own hands Then they closed the tomb, and all withdrew. *Pause, &c.*

Ah! my buried Jesus. I kiss the stone that encloses thee. But thou didst rise again the third day. I beseech thee, by thy resurrection, to make me rise glorious with thee at the last day, to be always united with thee in heaven, to praise thee and love thee for ever. O Jesus! I love thee, and I repent of ever having offended thee. Permit not that I ever offend thee again. Grant that I may love thee always; and then do with me what thou wilt.

Our Father. Hail Mary.

Glory be to the Father, &c.

O Jesus! who, for love of me, &c.

The Stations of the Cross, or, the Way of the Cross, is enriched with innumerable indulgences. The following decree of the Sacred Congregation of Indulgences will make this clear :—

In order to gain the indulgences of the fourteen Stations of the Cross, nothing more is necessary than to move from one Station to another, as far as the number of the Faithful making the Stations and the size of the place in which they are erected will allow, and to meditate on the Passion of Jesus Christ, our Divine Saviour.

Therefore other prayers, such as Pater, Ave, Miserere, &c., are only a praiseworthy custom of the faithful.

The indulgences are abundant, and are applicable to the holy souls in purgatory.

The necessary conditions :—(1) state of grace; (2) intention of gaining the indulgences; (3) go round the Stations—canonically erected; (4) Meditate on the sufferings of our blessed Lord.—*Sept.* 22, 1829.

ANIMA CHRISTI.

Soul of Christ, be my sanctification
Body of Christ, be my salvation ;
Blood of Christ, fill all my veins,
Water of Christ's side, wash out my stains
Passion of Christ, my comfort be
O good Jesus! listen to me ;
In thy wounds I fain would hide,
Ne'er to be parted from thy side ;
Guard me should the foe assail me.
Call me when my life shall fail me
Bid me come to thee above.
With thy saints to sing thy love.
World without end.   Amen.

300 days' indulgence each time ; 7 years if said
after Communion.—Pius IX., 1854.

OFFERING OF THE PASSION OF CHRIST FOR OUR SINS.

O MOST loving Father, in atonement and satisfaction for all my sins, I offer thee the passion of thy most beloved Son, from the plaintive wail he uttered when laid upon straw in the manger, through all the helplessness of his infancy, the privations of his boyhood, the adversities of his youth, the sufferings of his manhood, until that hour when he bowed his head upon the cross and with a loud cry gave up the ghost. And in atonement and satisfac-

tion for all my negligences, I offer thee, O most
loving Father, the most holy life and conversation
of thy Son, most perfect in its every thought, and
word and action, from the hour when he came down
from his lofty throne to the Virgin's womb, and
thence came forth into our dreary wilderness, to the
hour when he presented to thy Fatherly regard the
glory of his conquering flesh.   Amen.

The Fifteen Tuesdays in Honour of St. Dominic.

The Devotion of the Fifteen Tuesdays is a course of spiritual
exercises in honour of St. Dominic and of the fifteen mysteries
of the Rosary.   The Convent of Bologna, needing repair, it became
necessary to disturb the tomb of St. Dominic.   This was done on
the 24th of May, twelve years after his death, with permission of
Pope Gregory IX.   As the lid of the coffin was raised in presence
of bishops, prelates, and hundreds of friars preachers, it was found
that the features of the saint had undergone no change.   They
wore the same look of sweetness which had distinguished them
during life.   The whole church was filled with an extraordinary
perfume, and miracles attested the sanctity of the servant of God.
The devotion of the people increased day by day, and as the
opening of the tomb and translation of the relics took place on a
Tuesday, that day was thenceforth consecrated to the honour of the
saint in all churches and convents of the Order.

The Devotion of the Fifteen Tuesdays may be performed before
the Feast of the Saint, the 4th of August; or it may be performed
simultaneously with the Devotion of the Fifteen Saturdays.   On
each Tuesday, *Holy Communion should be received.*

FIRST TUESDAY.

Consideration 1.—Our blessed Lord descends from
heaven and becomes man to redeem a sinful world.

2. St. Dominic is raised up by Divine Providence
to save the Church in her most imminent dangers.

Prayer.

O BLESSED Father St. Dominic, cast upon my poor sinful soul one look of mercy and of protection. Obtain for me the pardon of my sins and the grant of my present petition.

R. Oh, admirable hope, which, in the hour of thy death, thou didst bestow upon thy weeping brethren, promising that after death thou wouldst assist thy children; O Father fulfil thy word and help us by thy prayers.

LITANY OF ST. DOMINIC.

LORD. have mercy on us.
　Christ, have mercy on us.
Lord, have mercy on us.
Who dwellest in light inaccessible, *have mercy on us.*
Splendour of the Father's glory, *have mercy on us.*
Sanctifying Spirit, *have mercy on us.*
Father, Son, and Holy Ghost, *have mercy on us.*
Mary, Mother of holy love,
Holy Father St. Dominic,
Glory of the House of Guzman,
Follower of Jesus Christ,
Eminently endowed with the virtues of his
　　Sacred Heart,
Singularly devoted to our Blessed Lady,
Promoter of her honour,
Splendour of the priesthood,
Founder of Friars Preachers,
Confounder of the Albigenses.

Pray for us.

Thaumaturgus of thy age.
Reviver of ecclesiastical discipline,
St. Dominic, most humble,
St. Dominic, most obedient,
St. Dominic, most charitable,
St. Dominic, most poor,
Glorious patriarch,
Father of saints,
Treasure of divine love,
Enjoying the beatific vision in the splendour
    of the saints,

Pray for us.

Lamb of God, who takest away the sins of the world.
    Spare us, O Lord.
Lamb of God, who takest away the sins of the world.
    Graciously hear us. O Lord.
Lamb of God, who takest away the sins of the world,
    Have mercy on us, O Lord.

Ant. Greater love than this no man hath, that he lay down his life for his friends.

V. Pray for us, O holy Father St. Dominic.

R. That we may be made worthy of the promises of Christ.

LET US PRAY.

O God, who hast vouchsafed to enlighten thy Church by the eminent merits and doctrine of blessed Dominic, thy confessor and our father, mercifully grant, that by his intercession we may find relief in our temporal necessities, and ever be assisted in arriving at perfection. Through Christ our Lord. Amen.

SECOND TUESDAY.

Consideration 1. Immediately after his incarnation, Jesus, in quality of Saviour, blesses the house of Zachary.

2. St. Dominic is the herald of divine blessings wherever he goes. In the distress of his brethren he provides food for them through the ministry of angels·

Prayer.

O BLESSED Father St. Dominic, happy those who beheld thy countenance, who listened to thy words, and enjoyed thy conversation! Thy presence was an earnest of blessings, spiritual and temporal. Come, then, most loving Father, to the assistance of my soul. Visit me in mercy, and obtain for me of Jesus and Mary the favour I petition.

R. Oh, admirable hope, and *Litany*, page 234.

THIRD TUESDAY.

Consideration 1. On the day of his birth, Jesus brings peace to men of good will.

2. St. Dominic brings peace by reconciling sinners to God. He interposes between heaven and earth the resplendent rainbow of the Rosary ; error disappears, and calm succeeds the tempest.

Prayer.

O GREAT Father St. Dominic, be my mediator with Jesus and Mary ; obtain for me the pardon of my sins, the gift of peace, and the favour I petition.

R. Oh, admirable hope, and *Litany*, page 234.

FOURTH TUESDAY.

Consideration 1. Jesus, offered up by his Mother, in the Temple of Jerusalem, presents himself as High Priest to his heavenly Father, for the redemption of mankind.

2. St. Dominic offers himself to become a slave for the deliverance of his brethren.

Prayer.

O BLESSED Father St. Dominic, how greatly do I need thy charitable assistance. Offer thyself, I beseech thee, once more to the adorable Trinity, in union with Jesus and Mary, to deliver my soul from the slavery of sin, and to restore it to the liberty of the children of God. Obtain for me also the grant of my present petition.

R. Oh, admirable hope, and *Litany,* page 234.

FIFTH TUESDAY.

Consideration 1. Jesus, lost in Jerusalem, is found in the Temple, conferring with the doctors of the law.

2. St. Dominic, by frequent conferences and continuous instructions, convinces the Albigensian heretics of their errors, commands their admiration, and brings them back to the path of truth.

Prayer.

O HOLY Father St. Dominic, whose entire life was consecrated to the glory of God; shining light, who didst confound so many errors, enlighten my ignorance, show me the true way of salvation, increase my love and devotion towards the Holy Catholic Church, and beg for me from Jesus and Mary the grant of my present petition.

R. *Oh, admirable hope*, and *Litany*, page 234.

SIXTH TUESDAY.

Consideration 1. Jesus in the Garden of Olives, is seized with a mortal sadness. His body is bathed in a bloody sweat: and he prays to obtain pardon of our sins.

2. St. Dominic, moved with compassion for sinners, spends whole nights in prayer for their conversion. He uses a holy violence with God ; his earnest supplications appease the heart of the Almighty. His prayer is more efficacious than his preaching.

Prayer.

O LOVING Father St. Dominic, to whom God never refused anything, how powerful must thou be in heaven ! Show thy greatness, O good Father, by obtaining for me true contrition for all my past sins, and also the grant of my present petition.

R. *Oh, admirable hope,* and *Litany,* page 234.

SEVENTH TUESDAY.

Consideration 1. Jesus is scourged for our sins.

2. St. Dominic takes every night three bloody disciplines with a chain of iron. The first for his own sins, the second for the conversion of sinners, and the third for the souls in purgatory.

Prayer.

O BLESSED Father St. Dominic, I am one of those sinners for whom thou didst offer thy blood. Obtain for me, then, pardon of my sins, my entire conversion, and the grant of my present petition.

R. Oh, admirable hope, and *Litany,* page 234.

EIGHTH TUESDAY.

Consideration 1. Jesus is crowned with thorns by the Roman soldiers, in mockery of his royalty.

2. St. Dominic accepts, with resignation and with joy, ignominy and contempt. He rejoices to be treated as a fool.

Prayer.

O BLESSED Father St. Dominic, faithful imitator of Jesus, obtain for me grace to repair the scandals of my past life. May I henceforth serve no other King but Jesus; may I adore and love him alone. Beg also for me, O my dear and blessed Father, the grant of my present petition.

R. Oh, admirable hope, and *Litany,* page 234.

NINTH TUESDAY.

Consideration 1. Jesus carries his cross loaded with the weight of our innumerable sins, to deliver us from our miseries.

2. St. Dominic embraces the cross of his Saviour, and carries it perseveringly to the end of his life, practising assiduously self-abnegation.

Prayer.

O MIRROR of penance. my holy Father and protector, St. Dominic. deign to intercede for me, that imitating thee in suffering and in mortification. I may hereafter enjoy with thee the reward of eternal glory. Amen.

R. *Oh, admirable hope*, and *Litany*, page 234.

TENTH TUESDAY.

Consideration 1. Jesus is nailed to the cross.

2. St. Dominic is crucified in a spiritual sense. His fast is continual; his body is girt with an iron chain; he sleeps sometimes on the bare ground; sometimes on the altar steps.

He is consumed with an ardent desire of martyrdom; he burns to shed his blood for love of Jesus Christ.

Prayer.

O BLESSED Father St. Dominic, crucified in spirit with thy Divine Master, obtain that the Blood of Jesus may wash away the defilements of my sinful soul, that after death I may enjoy with thee a glorious and immortal life in heaven. Amen.

R. *Oh, admirable hope*, and *Litany*, page 234.

ELEVENTH TUESDAY.

Consideration 1. Jesus, by his Resurrection, attains to immortal glory, and fills the whole world with joy.

2. St. Dominic resuscitates the dead, and shares in the empire of Jesus over death.

Prayer.

O BLESSED Father St. Dominic, I am in thy presence as one dead. O good Father, show now the greatness of thy power. Speak, break the bonds of sin which fetter me. Raise me from the tomb of my evil habits. Give me a new life, hidden in Jesus Christ, and beg for me the grant of my present petition.

R. *Oh, admirable hope*, and *Litany*, page 234.

TWELFTH TUESDAY.

Consideration 1. Jesus ascends to heaven, there to prepare for us a place at the eternal feast of love.

2. The place being ready and the feast prepared, he sends St. Dominic to invite us to come.

Prayer.

O BLESSED Father St. Dominic, I hear thy voice and I will follow thee. From thy intercession I hope for all good things, and for the grant of my present earnest request.

R. *Oh, admirable hope*, and *Litany*, page 234.

THIRTEENTH TUESDAY.

Consideration 1. Jesus sends down the Holy Ghost upon the Apostles, and they spread the fire of divine love throughout the earth.

2. St. Dominic is an Apostle; he spreads the divine fire throughout France, Spain, and Italy, and after his death his work is continued by his children, renowned alike for their zeal and charity.

Prayer.

O BLESSED Father St. Dominic, take pity on me, and obtain through thy merits, that Jesus may graciously extend his hand to assist me in my numerous wants. Beg for me also the favour I now so earnestly petition. Amen.

R. *Oh, admirable hope*, and *Litany*, page 234.

FOURTEENTH TUESDAY.

Consideration 1. The Blessed Mother of God is triumphantly assumed into heaven, and there seated at the right hand of her beloved Son.

2. Jesus and Mary receive the soul of St. Dominic on the day of his death. A year before the event, he is shown by an angel of the Lord the palms and crowns reserved as the reward of his labours.

Prayer.

O BLESSED Father St. Dominic, may my last end be like unto thine! I implore thy assistance for the moment which shall decide my eternity. Abandon me not; by thy protection I hope to escape eternal punishment, and by fidelity to thy holy Rosary I shall mount the mysterious ladder which will lead me to heaven. Beg for me also the favour I now petition.

R. *Oh, admirable hope*, and *Litany*, page 234.

FIFTEENTH TUESDAY.

Consideration 1. Jesus crowns his most holy Mother, Queen of heaven and earth.

2. Jesus and Mary share their power with St. Dominic, granting him extraordinary powers over the diseases, miseries, and afflictions of humanity.

Prayer.

O RENOWNED Father St. Dominic, I rejoice in the glory conferred upon thee. I have chosen thee for my Father; receive me as thy child; deliver me from my enemies; protect me from their assaults; beg for me all the graces necessary to work out my eternal salvation; and ask for me also the grant of my present earnest petition.

R. Oh, admirable hope, and *Litany*, page 234.

Devotions of the Fifteen Saturdays

This Devotion is a course of spiritual exercises performed, and of communions received, on fifteen consecutive Saturdays in honour of the Fifteen Mysteries of the Rosary. It had its origin in the city of Toulouse, towards the end of the seventeenth century, and it received at once the approbation of the Church. It is a most efficacious means of obtaining from God signal blessings, spiritual and temporal, and it is enriched with numerous indulgences.

It is usually practised before the Feast of the Holy Rosary, which is always celebrated on the first Sunday of October.

MEDITATIONS BEFORE AND AFTER COMMUNION.

PRACTICE AND EXAMPLE FOR EACH SATURDAY.

FIRST SATURDAY.

The Annunciation.

Before Communion.—It appears to me, my good Angel, that thou invitest me to holy communion and that thou addressest to me the words of Gabriel to the Holy Virgin, before the mystery of her miraculous Conception of the Son of God: Fear not; thou hast found grace before God: approach then, lovingly, and receive his sacred body.

With Mary, I answer: *Ecce ancilla Domini.* Behold the most unworthy of thy creatures. I refuse not, my adorable Saviour, the grace thou offerest to me. Oh, grant that I may never be separated from thee.

After Communion.—My God, I possess thee; I adore thee with humility, gratitude, and love.

Prayer.—O holy Virgin, Queen of the Rosary, by the joy which filled thy heart in the mystery of the Annunciation, obtain for me the favours I petition.

Practice.—Humility.

Example.—St. Thomas of Aquin belonged to the illustrious family of the Lords of Aquino, in Naples. He possessed the most astonishing amount of knowledge, and was always remarkable for simplicity, modesty, silence, and prayer.

When questioned on one occasion by his gifted master, Albertus Magnus, on some very obscure matters of science, Thomas replied with so much clearness, that Albert in a transport of joy exclaimed: We call Thomas a dumb ox; but he will one day make such a bellow in learning that he shall be heard throughout the universe. Such a flattering eulogium excited no motion of vanity in the saint. Sensible of the greatness of God and of his own nothingness, he was totally indifferent to praise or commendation

SECOND SATURDAY.

The Visitation.

Before Communion.—I adore thee, divine Jesus, in the chaste womb of thy holy Mother. Thy presence purifies from original sin the little John Baptist. Ah! wash away my sins in the adorable Sacrament I am about to receive. Whence is this to me? Oh, goodness of my God! My Jesus comes himself to visit me in person and to load me with his benefits.

After Communion.—O Jesus, thy presence, and that of Mary filled the house of Zachary with a thousand blessings. Bless my poor soul, and let nothing in life or death ever separate me from thee.

Prayer.—O glorious Virgin Queen of the holy Rosary, by the joy which filled thy soul in the mystery of the Visitation, obtain for me the favours I petition.

Practice.—Charity towards the neighbour.

Example.—St. Catherine de Ricci exercised a charity most agreeable to God in delivering from purgatory many souls by her prayers. She sometimes endured for them the sensible torments of that place of suffering. The fire which consumed her then was so great, that drops of water poured on her flesh, produced the same effect that they would have produced on red hot iron.

THIRD SATURDAY.

The Nativity of our Lord.

Before Communion.—The Blessed Virgin seeks in

vain in Bethlehem a lodging wherein she may give birth to the Redeemer of the world. She must be satisfied with a stable. O Mary! I present thee my heart, defiled as it is by sin ; purify it and make it a dwelling worthy of thy divine Son.

After Communion.—Adorable Jesus, my heart is now the dwelling-place of the divine Majesty. I adore thee, O Jesus, in union with thy holy Mother, St. Joseph, the angels, the shepherds, and the kings. Preserve me, dear Lord, from relapsing into sin. Let me never act towards thee the cruel part of Herod.

Prayer.—O holy Virgin, Queen of the Rosary, by the joy which filled thy blessed heart in the mystery of the Nativity, obtain, I beseech thee, the grant of my present petition.

Practice.—Disengagement from the riches of the world.

Example.—Blessed Margaret of Castello, of the Third Order of St. Dominic, was blind from birth. She exercised an extraordinary devotion towards the Babe of Bethlehem. After her death three stones were found in her heart ; on one of them was engraven an image of the infant Jesus, on another that of the holy Virgin, and on the third, the image of St. Joseph.

FOURTH SATURDAY.

The Presentation of our Lord in the Temple.

Before Communion. — Holy Simeon had received from God the promise that he should not die until he had seen the Redeemer. In Mary's arms, on the Feast of the Purification, he beholds with joy the Messias—the Christ of the Lord. "Now, O Lord," he exclaims, "thou dost dismiss thy servant in peace." My happiness, O divine Jesus, is still greater, for thou comest in this sweet sacrament to take entire possession of my heart.

After Communion.—O my God! when the holy old man Simeon bore thee in his arms, he pressed thee with raptures to his heart; but thou hast entered into my very soul to become one with me. Assist me, O my Jesus, to love thee, to do in all things thy holy will; and then, with confidence, I may say: *Nunc dimittis servum tuum, Domine.*

Prayer.—O glorious Virgin, Queen of the most holy Rosary, by the joy which filled thy soul in the mystery of the Presentation of our Lord in the Temple, I beseech thee, obtain for me the grant of my present petition.

Practice.—Purity of heart.

Example.—The blessed Dominica of Paradiso, a village in the vicinity of Florence, was remarkable for the purity and modesty of her life. One day, when very young, she met a poor woman, with a little child in her arms. Remarking that the hands, feet, and breast of the child were wounded, she inquired if he suffered much pain. A pensive smile was his only answer. Perceiving a sweet odour from the child's wounds, Dominica inquired of his mother with what ointment she dressed them, and whether she could purchase some. "You can buy it," was the reply, "by faith and good works."

The delightful odour continued to increase until, overcome by its sweetness, Dominica swooned away On recovering, she found the vision changed, and recognised her heavenly visitants to be Jesus and Mary. Dominica subsequently became a nun of the Order of St. Dominic, and died in the odour of sanctity, A.D. 1633.

FIFTH SATURDAY.
The Finding of our Lord in the Temple.

Before Communion.—The child Jesus disappears. How profound the grief of Mary and of her holy Spouse! with what earnestness they seek their lost treasure! Alas! my Jesus, how often have I lost thee by my sins. I shall seek thee then with all the fervour of my soul. I behold thee upon this altar—thou callest me—thou invitest me to receive thee. Come, then, thou light of mine eyes, thou happiness of my soul, thou only treasure of my life! Come, and may I never again separate myself from thee.

After Communion.—Oh, heaven! oh, earth! I have found my beloved. I hold him, I will never let him go. Bless him, praise him, glorify him with me. Oh, what shall henceforth separate me from his love? I am certain that neither hunger, nor thirst, nor cold, nor heat, nor torments, nor hell itself, nor paradise, nor life, nor death, shall ever separate me from thee. my God.

Prayer.—O blessed Virgin, Queen of the most holy Rosary, by the joy which filled thy heart in the mystery of the Finding of our Lord in the Temple, obtain for me the favours I petition.

Practice.—Fidelity to grace.

Example. St. Lewis Bertrand once ordered a novice, during religious service, to lift up some burning coals. "Where shall I put them, my Father?" asked the religious. "In your scapular," replied the saint. The obedience of the young novice was rewarded by a miracle. He carried the burning coals in the folds of his scapular, and the stuff received not the slightest injury therefrom.

SIXTH SATURDAY.

The Agony of our Saviour in the Garden.

Before Communion.—Jesus, prostrate before his Eternal Father, overwhelmed with sorrow, sweating blood, accepts the bitter chalice of his passion. What a difference between the chalice offered thee in the Garden of Olives and that which thou presentest to me at thy holy table, O merciful Jesus! The brothers of Joseph esteemed it a great happiness to eat at his table and drink out of his cup. My happiness is infinitely greater, for I partake of the food of angels, and drink the blood of Jesus Christ.

After Communion.—O sacred banquet, admirable feast, joy of the elect! thou art my nourishment, my strength, my consolation, in this valley of tears!

Most sweet Jesus, I pray thee to detach my heart from all created things; unite me so closely to thyself that I may love thee with a perfect love through all eternity. Amen.

Prayer.—O holy Virgin, Queen of the most holy Rosary, by the sword of sorrow which pierced thy tender heart during the agony of thy Son, I beseech thee obtain the grant of my present petitions.

Practice.—Perseverance in Prayer.

Example.—St. Rose of Lima devoted twelve hours every day to the exercise of mental prayer.

For a very long period she experienced in it aridities and fearful dryness: nevertheless, she persevered as a *rose of patience.* In her infancy she was never known to cry; insults and injuries were her delight.

SEVENTH SATURDAY.
The Scourging.

Before Communion.—O my sweet Saviour, what an example of patience thou art to me in this painful mystery! I unite my sufferings to thine: I detest my sins which bound thee to the pillar. May thy precious blood obtain for me pardon and mercy.

After Communion.—O sweet Lamb! delivered up to the inhuman fury of the wicked, I thank thee for having taken refuge in my poor heart. Oh! how sincerely I desire by love and affection to make thee forget the scourges and affronts thou didst receive in Pilate's house. I bitterly repent of my past sins. O most merciful Mother, pray to Jesus for me.

Prayer.—O sacred Virgin, Queen of the most holy Rosary, by that sword of sorrow which transpierced thy most holy heart during the scourging of thy beloved Son, obtain for me, I beseech thee, the favours I petition.

Practice.—Patience.

Example.—The saints of the Order of Friars Preachers have borne in their bodies the mortification of Jesus Christ in an eminent degree. Their blessed founder, St. Dominic, scourged himself to blood three times every night. St. Catherine, of Sienna, worthy daughter of the blessed patriarch, imitated him in this severe penance. St. Vincent Ferrer, to obtain fruit in his missionary labours, scourged himself unmercifully; and when in sickness he had not sufficient strength to mortify himself as he desired, he humbly begged the assistance of his brethren, and received from their hands the discipline. St. Catherine, of Sienna, subsisted on herbs; on one occasion she passed eighty days without any other nourishment than the blessed Eucharist. She contented herself with a half hour's sleep during the night. St. Catherine de Ricci went still farther in the practice of this mortification: during one entire month, she slept only for the space of four hours.

Let us admire these heroic examples, and if we cannot imitate them, let us at least cultivate the spirit of self-denial, without which we cannot attain to salvation.

EIGHTH SATURDAY.

The Crowning with Thorns.

Before Communion.—My divine Saviour, crowned with thorns, covered with a purple mantle of derision, and bearing a reed in his hand, is presented by Pilate to the people. *Ecce homo,* behold the man! Soon shall the priest present to me the King of Heaven concealed under the Eucharistic veils. *Ecce Agnus Dei;* behold the Lamb of God. O King of Glory, I adore thee in the humiliations of thy passion and in those of the Blessed Sacrament. I acknowledge thee with faith and love as my Lord and Master.

After Communion.—O divine Jesus, thy crown of thorns is the burning bush which Moses saw, and which was not consumed by the flames. Thy royalty is eternal. Reign then over my heart and affections. This crown teaches me likewise that the kingdom of heaven suffers violence, and that the violent alone bear it away.

Ah! Lord, may thy example teach me to accept the crown of thorns in this world, that I may wear the crown of glory in the next.

Prayer.—O Blessed Virgin, Queen of the most holy Rosary, by the sword of sorrow which pierced thy heart when thou didst see thy dear Son crowned with thorns, obtain for me the favours I petition.

Practice.—Love of contempt and humiliation.

Example.—St. Dominic having been asked why he more willingly abode in Carcasonne than in Toulouse replied : " Because in Toulouse they consider me a saint, whereas in Carcasonne I am scoffed, ridiculed, and despised by all."

When travelling, before entering town or country he was accustomed to offer a most fervent prayer to God, beseeching him not to destroy the place on account of his sins, and yet he never committed a grievous sin during his whole life. In death he wished to make a general confession in the presence of twelve religious of the convent at Bologna. And, asked by his children where he wished to be buried, he humbly answered : "at the feet of all my brethren."

NINTH SATURDAY.

The Carrying of the Cross.

Before Communion.—Jesus bends under the weight of his cross. Whence proceeds this weight? From my sins. . . O Lord! I desire with the daughters of Jerusalem to weep over thy sufferings. Thou comest to me. Thou presentest to me thy holy cross. Oh, I accept it with all my heart. I will die in its embraces.

After Communion.—O my God, thou hast entered into my heart. Permit not, that it should be to thee as a new Calvary, an ungrateful, barren, unfruitful soil. May thy precious blood blot out my sins. May the memory of thy dolorous passion be to me a most powerful protection of soul and body against all the deceits, temptations and molestations of my cruel enemies. Amen.

Prayer.—O sweet Virgin Mary, Queen of the holy Rosary, by the sword of sorrow which pierced thy heart on beholding Jesus carrying the cross, obtain for me the grant of my earnest petitions. Amen.

Practice.—Resignation under all trials to the will of God.

Example.—St. Dominic braved every danger when there was question of saving a soul. He was once warned of a party of heretics who lay concealed in a certain place, to assassinate him. He treated the information with indifference, and passed on. On their next meeting, the heretics accosted him, thus: "And so thou dost not fear death? Tell us what wouldst thou have done if thou hadst fallen into our hands?" "I would have prayed you," said the great Dominic, "not to have taken my life at a single blow, but little by little, cutting off each member of my body one by one; and having done that, that you should have plucked out my eyes, and then have left me so, to prolong my torments and to enrich my crown."

TENTH SATURDAY.
The Crucifixion.

Before Communion.—Jesus, God of love and of compassion, I thank thee for the infinite love thou didst manifest towards me in sacrificing thyself for me on the altar of the cross. Accept, I beseech thee, the sacrifice I now make to thee, of my soul and all its powers ; my body and all its senses.

After Communion.—Jesus, taken down from the cross, is laid in the arms of his Blessed Mother.

O divine Master, I offer thee my heart, that thou mayest repose therein in peace. What shall I render unto thee, O my well-beloved, for all thy benefits ? O Jesus, my one good, I have nothing else besides. O Jesus, my sweetest peace, when shall I lay me down and take my rest in thee ?

Prayer.—O Blessed Virgin, Queen of the holy Rosary, by the sword of grief which pierced thy soul during the crucifixion of thy divine Son, I beseech thee, obtain the grant of my earnest petitions ?

Practice.—Charity towards our enemies.

Example.—Blessed Clare Gambacorta, of the Order of St. Dominic, gave refuge in her convent to the murderer of her father who was pursued by assassins. After the death of the murderer she supported his widow and educated his children.

ELEVENTH SATURDAY.

The Resurrection of our Lord.

Before Communion.—I rejoice, O divine Jesus, with Mary thy Mother, in thy glorious Resurrection. I adore thee in all the majesty and loveliness of thy most dear soul and glorified body. An angel said to the holy women who sought thee in the sepulchre : *Surrexit. Non est hic.* He is risen ; he is not here.

And so, O dearest Lord, my soul, resuscitated from sin to grace, is no longer what it was. Yesterday, it fed on the onions of Egypt, that is. on sin ; to-day it eats the bread of Angels ; it hungers for the body of Jesus, it thirsts for his precious blood.

After Communion.—The joy of Mary was extreme in beholding her divine Son risen from the dead. Let us too rejoice and sing alleluias to the King of Glory ; because he has redeemed his people and is triumphant over the powers of hell. Happy the Apostles, saluted by our glorified Saviour in the words, *pax vobis.* O sweet Redeemer, I possess *thee* who art the peace of our souls. Give me then thy peace, that peace which will calm my passions and establish in my soul the reign of thy grace.

Practice.—Mortification of the passions to obtain interior peace.

Prayer.—O glorious Virgin, Queen of the most holy Rosary, by the joy which filled thy heart in the mystery of the Resurrection of thy dearly-beloved Son, obtain for me, I beseech thee, the grant of my earnest petitions.

Example.—St. Peter Martyr, the son of heretical parents, became one of the brightest ornaments of the Order of St. Dominic. He received the habit from the holy Patriarch himself.

To an angelic innocence of life he united an extraordinary courage in the profession of the Catholic faith. "Hammer of the heretics," as he was commonly called, he died by their hands, writing on the ground in his blood the word *Credo.* During this act his beautiful soul ascended to heaven, and received the palm of victory.

TWELFTH SATURDAY.
The Ascension of our Lord.

Before Communion.—Jesus quits the earth, and takes with him to heaven the holy patriarchs.

O my God, vouchsafe that we may seek the things that are above. Dwell in our hearts by faith, and pour down upon us thy plenteous benedictions. Come, O Bread of Angels, sweet viaticum ; fortify me on my journey to eternity, and take me to thyself, that where thou art I also may be.

After Communion.—In leaving us, O sweet Jesus, thou didst find by means of the Holy Eucharist, the secret of remaining with us to the end of the world. Eternal thanks be given to thee for this wonderful invention of thy charity. I know not how to thank thee, my God, for the favour thou hast just bestowed upon me in feeding me with the body and blood of thy Divine Son.

Henceforth I will visit thee as often as I am able; I will come to thy altar to adore thee, to praise thee, to lament my sins before thee, to seek light and comfort in all my difficulties, until the day arrives when I shall behold thee unveiled, and when thou wilt receive me to thy love for ever. Amen.

Prayer.—O glorious Virgin, Queen of the most holy Rosary, by the joy which filled thy soul in the mystery of the Ascension of thy dear Son, obtain for me, I beseech thee, the grant of my earnest petitions.

Practice.—Contempt of the riches and honours of the world.

Example.—Fra Girolamo Monsignori, of the Third Order of Preachers, was chiefly distinguished for his love of prayer and his indifference to the world. The money which he earned by his artistic works was hung up in an old box without a lid, so that anyone who wished might use it.

When Mantua was visited by the plague and every one fled in alarm, he, moved by charity, attended the sick with his own hands. Thus, sacrificing his life to God, he caught the contagion, and died at the age of sixty.

THIRTEENTH SATURDAY.

The Descent of the Holy Ghost.

Before Communion.—O King of Glory! thou art about to favour me, as thou didst favour the Apostles and disciples assembled in the upper room at Jerusalem. A thousand times blessed be thine infinite charity which moves thee to repair our miseries by bestowing upon us a gift wherein is contained all good! Purify then, my heart, O God, as thou didst sanctify the hearts of thy Apostles, and kindle in it the fire of thy love.

After Communion.—O sweet Saviour, I adore thee as true God, together with the Father and the Holy Ghost. Most Holy Spirit create a new heart within me. A thousand times I bless thee, and with the Seraphim

before thy throne, I cry : *Sanctus, Sanctus, Sanctus!*
Thou art the giver of all heavenly gifts ; animate me
with thy charity and save me by thy mercy, that I may
praise and love thee in time and in eternity. Amen.

Prayer.—O Blessed Virgin, Queen of the most holy
Rosary, by the joy which filled thy soul at Pentecost,
obtain for me, I beseech thee, the grant of my earnest
petitions.

Practice.—Zeal for the salvation of souls.

Example.—St. Hyacinth, of the Order of Friars
Preachers, laboured incessantly for the glory of God
and for the salvation of sinners. For the space of
forty years he preached successively in Poland,
Silesia, Prussia, Denmark, Sweden, Russia, the borders
of the Black and Caspian Seas, Tartary, &c. He
penetrated even into Thibet and China. On one
occasion, to save a statue of our Blessed Lady from
profanation, he took it in his arms, though it was of
enormous weight, and charged with his precious
burden, he walked upon the waters of a deep and
rapid river, as if it had been firm land.

He expired on the Feast of the Assumption, being
seventy-two years old.

FOURTEENTH SATURDAY.

The Assumption of the Blessed Virgin.

Before Communion.—" Let us all rejoice in the Lord,
on account of the honour done the Blessed Virgin
Mary, at whose Assumption the angels rejoice and
adore the Son of God."

What must have been the transports of the heart of Mary at the approach of death! How perfect her security: how ardent her love and her desire to be re-united to her beloved Son, for whom alone she lived.

O most amiable Saviour, draw my heart to thee; fill it with the insatiable desire of seeing thee, of contemplating thee, and of loving thee under the sacramental veils, and in the full light of thy glory.

After Communion.—O Saviour of souls, why can I not, with thy Holy Mother, die of love, now that I hold thee in my heart? Ah! mayest thou be hence-forth my sole delight, the God of my heart, and my portion for ever.

Prayer.—O Glorious Virgin, Queen of the holy Rosary, by the joy which filled thy soul on the day of thy Assumption into heaven, obtain for me the grant of my present petitions.

Practice.—Desire of enjoying God in heaven.

Example.——About the year 1393, it happened that some little children were about to receive their first Holy Communion in a Dominican Convent at Bologna. One knelt alone in sadness and tears, because she had been pronounced too young to receive Him whom she loved. As the celebrating priest held in his hand the Blessed Sacrament, saying: *Ecce Agnus Dei,* a ray of dazzling light went forth from it, and the Sacred Host, which, a few minutes before he held in his hand at the altar, stood in the air above the head of Imelda. With trembling hand, he com-municated the child. Shortly after, she was seen to lean on one side as if she were ill. The nuns thought she had fainted; her arms were crossed over her breast, an angelic smile lighted up her countenance ; her heart was too weak to bear the excessive joy she felt in receiving her Jesus ; the thread of life was broken. . . The soul of the little child was gone to heaven !

FIFTEENTH SATURDAY

The Coronation of the Blessed Virgin in Heaven.

Before Communion.—The glorious Mother of Jesus is assumed into heaven, enthroned there as Queen of the Universe, seated at the right hand of her Son. The sacrament of the Eucharist is the pledge of future glory. " He who eats my flesh and drinks my blood," says Jesus Christ, " shall live for ever." Come, then, O heavenly food, open to me the gates of a blessed eternity, support me in life, and at the awful moment of my death. Amen.

After Communion.—O divine Majesty, thou hast crowned thy holy Mother with a royal diadem, and now thou condescendest to feed a wretched sinner with thy body and blood. Oh! what unspeakable goodness, what infinite mercy !

Mary, Queen of Angels and of men, show thyself our Mother ; in pity look upon our miseries, and rule us by the gentle sway of thy protection. Amen.

Prayer.—O glorious Virgin, Queen of the holy Rosary, by the joy with which thou wert replenished in the mystery of thy Coronation, I beseech thee obtain for me the grant of my earnest petitions. Amen.

Practice.—Confidence in Mary. Renew your consecration to the Queen of the holy Rosary, and beg of her to obtain for you the precious gift of final perseverance.

Example.—In the year 1259, when the Tartars made frequent and sudden irruptions into the Polish territories, there existed at Sandomir a Convent of Dominicans wherein forty young religious led most perfect lives under the direction of one Sadoc, a man full of faith and zeal. On the 1st of June, all the brethren being seated at supper, the lector, who, according to custom, was reading the martyrology of the next day, saw written in the book the following words, which he read aloud:—" At Sandomir, the martyrdom of forty-one Christians." These words were applied to the 2nd of June. The lector paused; the astonished religious knew not what the words could signify; no one had ever seen them in the book before. It seemed like a warning that they should prepare for death. They spent the night in prayer. At daybreak, the pious Sadoc celebrated the sacred mysteries; all received the holy Communion as Viaticum; and as they chanted the *Salve* after Mass, they were startled by a loud noise and by terrific screams. The Tartars had broken into the town, massacred the inhabitants, and in a few moments, entered the Convent of the Dominicans, brandishing swords and axes, which they used for the murder of the brothers, who still continued their holy chant. Sadoc was the last to fall by a blow from an axe, just as he had finished alone the last words of the hymn : " *O clemens, O pia, O dulcis Virgo Maria.*"

These martyrs have been honoured at Sandomir since the thirteenth century. Every evening they recited in common the Rosary and Salve Regina. Sadoc had never once been absent from the devotion.

Our blessed Lady assists in a particular manner at the hour of death those who are faithful to honour her in the devotion of the holy Rosary.

The Rosary Confraternity.

" Preach the Rosary ; it will be a remedy against all evils.
—*Words of B. V.M. to St. Dominic, A.D. 1206.*

Of all the Confraternities, that of the Holy Rosary is the most important. Scarcely any has so long a history behind it—no other is so widely spread ; has produced such abundant fruits of holiness ; has brought so many blessings on the Church ; has received so many favours and privileges at the hands of the Popes ; or is so well suited to the spiritual needs of the times. It is the most richly indulgenced Confraternity in the Church, and membership in it is necessary for all who would gain in their fullness the advantages of the saving devotion of the Rosary.

In order to *join* the Confraternity all that is necessary is to get your name enrolled on the Register in a Dominican Church, or Parish Church, where the Confraternity has been established by authority of the Master-General of the Dominican Order.

To *gain the advantages*, you must have your beads blessed by a Dominican Priest (or a priest having special faculties from the Master-General of the Dominican Order), and say the fifteen decades of the Rosary once each week, meditating on the Mysteries while doing so. This obligation does not bind under sin. You need not say the whole Rosary together, but recite the decades, one or more at a time, as you please.

The Advantages of the Confraternity are, briefly, as follows :—

(*a*) The special protection of Our Lady, Queen of the Rosary.

(*b*) A share in all the good works and spiritual benefits of the members of the Dominican Order, and of the Rosary Confraternity the world over.

(*c*) A share, after death, in the prayers and suffrages offered by the same for the dead.

(*d*) Very great indulgences, daily, monthly, and annually, all of which are applicable to the dead.

(*e*) A special indulgence for every work of charity or piety you do.

(*f*) An indulgence of 2,025 days for each *Hail Mary* in the Rosary.

(*g*) An indulgence of 100 years and 4,000 days daily for merely carrying the blessed beads about with you.

(*h*) A plenary indulgence every day (applicable to the dead) for those members who go to Confession and Communion, visit a Church, and offer the Fifteen Mysteries of the Rosary *for the triumph of the Catholic Church.*

(*i*) A plenary indulgence at the hour of death.

Act of Consecration to Our Blessed Lady of the Rosary.

O VIRGIN Mary, Mother of God, Queen of the most holy Rosary, thou beholdest at thy feet the most miserable of sinners. I deserve not to be called thy child, for I have too grievously offended thy divine Son. But thou art my Mother, my merciful Mother, the Mother of contrite sinners. Oh, reject me not; I acknowledge my sins, I hate them, I detest them, I deplore them in the bitterness of my soul. I firmly purpose never to commit them again. I give thee my heart, I consecrate myself to thee; O Mary, I promise thee an eternal fidelity.

O Queen of the Rosary, take possession of my whole being; rule me as my sovereign; banish from my heart all that displeases thee; sanctify my soul, purify my intentions. I wish to love all that thou lovest; thy desires shall be my desires, thy joy shall be my joy, thy sorrows my sorrows. O most holy Mother of Jesus, hear me. Queen of the holy Rosary, hear me, through thy joys, thy sorrows, thy triumphs, have pity on a poor sinner who implores thy mercy. Protect me during life, assist me at the hour of my death; receive my soul, and present it to the Sovereign Judge. Grant me a safe retreat in the fountain of mercy, that with thee I may glorify the Sacred Heart of thy dear Son, for ever and ever. Amen.

On the Rosary of the Blessed Virgin.

About the year 1206, when war and bloodshed raged in France, the celebrated devotion of the Rosary began to be propagated by Saint Dominic.

The universal voice of tradition affirms that the Rosary devotion was revealed to him by the Blessed Virgin herself; and, indeed, if we consider its almost supernatural character, and the extraordinary power with which it has been blessed, we can have no difficulty in recognising in it the gift and most precious token of the love of our dear and blessed Mother.

"To pray in the presence of Christ," says a holy bishop, "and to trust in the help of Mary, these are the impulses of the Christian heart." The Rosary helps us to do both. It might have been hard to fix our minds on the invisible and unapproachable Deity. But the infinite God became a little child, a boy, a man with a human soul, and heart, and feelings. He spoke to us, he blessed us, he pitied us, he suffered and died for us. He went up to heaven and left us, but we have still in the holy name of Jesus the vivid picture of all that he was and all that he did.

Since he came amongst us, our worship and our love are very easy and natural; for we may speak to him as to a friend and brother, offer him our gifts, sympathise with him in his sufferings, and lament our sins at his feet. The Beads are placed in our fingers to rouse our attention; and then a picture is set before us of our Lord or of his blessed Mother, and we are told to utter some of the sweetest words that ever brought hope and healing to man. A little picture is put before us: "Let us contemplate the Annunciation of the most holy Virgin, by the angel;" or. "Let us meditate upon the birth of our Lord Jesus Christ at Bethlehem," or upon his "Crucifixion." or upon the "assumption of the B'essed Virgin Mary." Words like these fix our hearts in the presence of our Saviour.

Then we say Our Father; and all the worship, the praise, the asking and affection of that glorious prayer are poured out at the feet of him who is at once our God and our Brother. As it dies away, we take up the Hail Mary. When the world was first b'essed with the sight of Jesus, he was shown to it in the arms of Mary his Mother. The shepherds offered him their earliest gifts and homage as she held him there. It has been so ever since, and it will be so always.

To recite the Hail Mary, is to honour the prophetic announcement of the coming of Jesus; it is to bless him; to bless his Mother.

By the Son of Mary, all good has come to the earth. To lift up the banner of Mary, the Mother of Jesus, is to lift up the Ark of the

New Covenant, and God arises and his foes are scattered. So it was with the early heresies; so it was when the Turks menaced Christendom, and so it must be now.

The Rosary is a grand crusade of prayer. Next to the Divine Office it is the most Catholic prayer in the Church, and the most authoritatively approved, even so far as to have a special festival in its honour. To have it recited as family prayer in every household, would be an earnest of the abundant blessings of heaven.

PART FIRST.

THE JOYFUL MYSTERIES.

Assigned for the Mondays and Thursdays throughout the year, the Sundays of Advent, and the Sundays after Epiphany till Lent.

IN the name of the Father, and of the Son, and of the Holy Ghost. Amen.

V. Hail Mary, full of grace, the Lord is with thee.

R. Blessed art thou amongst women, and blessed is the fruit of thy womb, Jesus.

V. Thou, O Lord, wilt open my lips.

R. And my tongue shall announce thy praise.

V. Incline unto my aid, O God.

R. O Lord, make haste to help me.

V. Glory be to the Father, and to the Son, and to the Holy Ghost.

R. As it was in the beginning, is now, and ever shall be, world without end. Amen.

I.—*The Annunciation.*

Let us contemplate in this mystery, how the

angel Gabriel saluted our Blessed Lady with
the title "Full of Grace," and declared unto her
the Incarnation of our Lord and Saviour Jesus
Christ.

*† Be still, and let our hearts adore in language
higher than that of words, the amazing wonders of
the infinite goodness of God, in thus offering himself
a holocaust for us, poor miserable sinners, who had
deserved to be thrown from his mercy for ever.
Let us imagine to ourselves that we see the angel of
God descending from heaven with the joyful news
to our Blessed Lady : " *Hail, full of grace . . .
thou shalt conceive . . . . the power of the Most
High shall overshadow thee . . . . thou shalt bear
a Son, and thou shalt call his name Jesus.*"

Oh, miracle of love! the co-eternal Son of the
living God, seeing the miseries into which we were
plunged, descends from heaven, that we might
ascend thither, and becomes the Son of man, that we
might become the children of God.

Our Father, *once.*

Hail Mary, *ten times.*

Glory be to the Father, *once.*

O Holy Mary, Queen of Virgins, by the most
high mystery of the Incarnation of thy beloved Son,
our Lord Jesus Christ, by which our salvation was
so happily begun, obtain for us, by thy intercession.
light to know this so great benefit which he hath

---

* This mark (†) here, as in the other mysteries, indicates the
additional reflections, to be made use of, as devotion shall suggest.

bestowed upon us, vouchsafing in it to make himself our Brother, and thee, his own most beloved Mother, our Mother also. Amen.

II.—*The Visitation*

Let us contemplate in this mystery, how the Blessed Virgin Mary, understanding from the angel that her cousin St. Elizabeth had conceived went with haste into the mountains of Judea to visit her, and remained with her three months.

† Let us imagine here, that we see our Blessed Lady preparing herself for the journey, and let us devoutly accompany her. She enters the house of Zachary and salutes Elizabeth. Oh, blessed Salutation, at which the infant Precursor leaps for joy in his mother's womb, is sanctified and cleansed from original sin! Oh, let us here make one moment's stay where the Mother of God stayed three months exercising every virtue, every kind office, and work of charity.

My soul doth magnify the Lord, and my spirit rejoiceth in God my Saviour.

Our Father, &c.

O Holy Virgin, most spotless mirror of humility, by that exceeding charity which moved thee to visit thy holy cousin, St. Elizabeth, obtain for us by thy intercession that our hearts may be so visited by thy most holy Son, that, being free from all sin, we may praise him and give him thanks for ever. Amen.

III.—*The Nativity.*

Let us contemplate, in this mystery, how the Blessed Virgin Mary, when the time of her delivery had come, brought forth our Redeemer Christ Jesus at midnight, and laid him in a manger, because there was no room for him in the inns at Bethlehem.

† Let us imagine ourselves here surrounded by a divine brightness, and flying to Bethlehem with the watchful shepherds. Let us imagine we hear the melodious harmony of the heavenly musicians, singing—*Glory in the highest to God,* upon account of those tidings of great joy which were brought to us ; *because this day is born to us a Saviour, who is Christ the Lord, in the city of David.*

Let us now enter into the stable, and humbly fall prostrate before our divine Jesus. Oh, what amazing mysteries ! A pure creature gives life to her Creator ! a Virgin becomes a Mother without ceasing to be a virgin ! the Son of God the Father without a Mother from all eternity, becomes in time, the Son of a Virgin Mother without a Father, and He whom the heavens cannot comprehend is wrapped in swaddling clothes and laid in a manger ! O Blessed Jesus ! thou art my King and my Lord I bless and praise thee for having become a little Babe for love of me.

Our Father, &c.

O most pure Mother of God, by thy virginal and most joyful delivery, by which thou gavest unto the world thy only Son, our Saviour, we beseech thee obtain for us by thy intercession grace to lead such pure and holy lives in this world, that we may worthily sing without ceasing, both by day and night, the mercies of thy Son, and his benefits to us by thee. Amen.

IV.—*The Presentation of our Blessed Lord in the Temple.*

Let us contemplate in this mystery, how the Blessed Virgin Mary, on the day of her Purification, presented the child Jesus in the temple, where holy Simeon, giving thanks to God, with great devotion, received him into his arms.

† Let us place ourselves here in the temple of Jerusalem, and imagine we see the Mother of God coming with the child Jesus in her arms, to offer him to his Eternal Father, and to submit to the ceremony of Purification, in obedience to the laws of Moses. Hear the devout Anna praising the Lord; see holy Simeon taking the Divine Infant into his arms, blessing God, and saying : "*Now, thou dost dismiss thy servant, O Lord, according to thy word, in peace; because my eyes have seen thy salvation.*"

Oh, may we, most Sacred Virgin, receive thy Blessed Son into our hearts, and there enjoy in the closest embraces, Him who is the life of our souls, our light and *the glory of his people Israel.*

Our Father, &c.

O holy Virgin, most admirable Mistress and pattern of obedience, who didst present in the Temple

the Lord of the Temple, obtain for us of thy
beloved Son, grace, that with holy Simeon and devout
Anna, we may praise and glorify him for ever.
Amen.

V.—*The Finding of the Child Jesus in the Temple.*

Let us contemplate in this mystery, how the most
Blessed Virgin Mary, having lost, without any fault
of hers, her beloved Son in Jerusalem, sought him
for the space of three days, and at length found
him, on the fourth day, in the Temple, in the midst of
the doctors disputing with them, being but twelve
years of age.

† Let us imagine here that we see the holy Virgin,
now come homewards a day's journey, missing
Jesus, and, all drowned in tears, seeking him among
her acquaintances. She hastens back to Jerusalem, and
there finds him, questioning the doctors of the law.

Our Father. &c.

Most blessed Virgin, more than martyr in thy
sufferings, and yet the comfort of such as are
afflicted, by that unspeakable joy, wherewith thy
soul was ravished in finding thy beloved Son in the
Temple, in the midst of the doctors, disputing with
them, obtain of him for us, so to seek him and to
find him in the Holy Catholic Church, that we may
never be separated from him   Amen

PART SECOND.

THE DOLOROUS MYSTERIES.

For Tuesdays and Fridays throughout the year, and the Sundays in Lent.

I.—*The Prayer and Bloody Sweat of our Blessed Saviour in the Garden.*

Let us contemplate in this mystery, how our Lord Jesus Christ was so afflicted for us in the Garden of Gethsemani, that his body was bathed in a bloody sweat, which ran trickling down in great drops to the ground.

† Let us imagine ourselves here with Jesus and his three beloved disciples, in the mournful garden, and that we hear him say : *My soul is exceeding sorrowful, even unto death.*

Ah! woe is me, my dearest Jesus, that thou shouldst be so afflicted for me. Let us consider what our sins have done--let us see the Son of God lying prostrate on the ground, struggling under the most dismal agonies of mind, sweating blood from every pore, and praying that if it were possible the bitterness of that cup might pass away from him. *Nevertheless*, he adds: *not my will but thine be done.*

Our Father, &c.

O most holy Virgin, more than martyr, by that ardent prayer which thy beloved Son poured forth unto his Father in the garden. vouchsafe to intercede for us, that our passions being reduced to the obedience of reason, we may always, and in all things, conform and subject ourselves to the will of God. Amen.

II.—*The Scourging of our Blessed Lord at the Pillar.*

Let us contemplate in this mystery, how our Lord Jesus Christ was most cruelly scourged in Pilate's house, the number of stripes they gave him being above five thousand, as it was revealed to St. Bridget.

† Let us imagine here that we see our dearest Jesus, after he had been apprehended, blindfolded, buffeted, spit upon, and insulted in the most ignominious manner, stripped of all his clothes, and bound to a pillar. His skin is torn off with knotty scourges! His blood springs out in streams, pieces of flesh fly in the air, and his bones are laid uncovered!—one wound from head to foot. Oh! the heinousness, the monstrous heinousness of sin, and the fierceness of God's anger against it.

Our Father, &c.

O Mother of God, overflowing fountain of patience, by those stripes thy only and most beloved Son vouchsafed to suffer for us, obtain of him for us, grace, that we may know how to mortify our rebellious senses, and cut off all occasions of sinning with that sword of grief and compassion which pierced thy most tender soul. Amen.

III.—*The Crowning of our Blessed Saviour with Thorns.*

Let us contemplate in this mystery, how those cruel ministers of Satan plaited a crown of sharp

thorns, and most cruelly pressed it on the most
sacred head of our Lord and Saviour Jesus Christ.

† Let us imagine that we behold our suffering
Jesus, clothed with the purple of derision as if he
had pretended to some royalty that did not belong
to him. See the thorny crown struck deep into
his sacred temples, and the blood gushing out from
every wound. *Wounded for our iniquities, bruised for
our sins.* Behold his sacred head, bruised with the
reed, that mock sceptre which they put into his
hands, whilst they bend the knee before him and cry:
Hail, King of the Jews. Ecce Homo—Behold the man!
That divine Man-God, laid as low for our pride, as
grief and sorrow and pain and shame could lay him!
Behold the uncreated Wisdom of his Eternal Father
ridiculed—Omnipotence injured and affronted; and
Divine Majesty crowned with ignominy!

Our Father, &c.

O Mother of our eternal Prince and King of Glory,
by those sharp thorns wherewith his most holy head
was pierced, we beseech thee, that by thy intercession
we may be delivered here from all motions of pride,
and in the day of judgment, from that confusion
which our sins deserve. Amen.

IV.—*Jesus carrying His Cross.*

Let us contemplate in this mystery, how our Lord
Jesus Christ being sentenced to die, bore with great
patience the cross which was laid upon him for his
greater torment and ignominy.

† Let us imagine to ourselves here, that we see those inhuman, spiteful, pitiless wretches, tear off his cleaving purple, and ay upon Jesus, now agonising and exhausted, the heavy load of a rude, unwieldy cross, under whose weight he falls, unable to bear the ignominious instrument of his own pains.

See how they drag our dearest Lord amidst insults, scorn and reproach, to the top of that fatal mountain. Oh! let us, who have had so great a hand in his blood, with Simeon of Cyrene, bear part of his burden; let us accompany him with his dearest afflicted Mother, and bathe his bloody footsteps with our tears.

Our Father, &c.

O Holy Virgin, example of patience, by the most painful carrying of the cross, on which thy Son, our Lord Jesus Christ, bore the heavy weight of our sins, obtain for us of him, by thy intercession, courage and strength to follow his steps, and bear our cross after him to the end of our lives. Amen.

V.—*The Crucifixion of our Lord Jesus Christ.*

Let us contemplate in this mystery, how our Lord Jesus Christ, being come to Mount Calvary, was stripped of his clothes, and his hands and feet most cruelly nailed to the cross in the presence of his most afflicted Mother.

† Let us imagine ourselves here under the cross *looking upon him whom we have pierced.* Methinks I see him, the Priest sacrificing, and the Lamb

sacrificed for the sins of the whole world and for
mine in particular, fastened by three gross nails to
the tree of the cross. Methinks, I hear the strokes
of the hammer, enough to rend the rocks and make
heaven and earth tremble. O! how fast the blood
gushes forth whilst he prays for his enemies;
languishing, agonising, thirsting, fainting, bleeding,
dying. But, oh! my sweetest Jesus, am I the
cause of thy death? *Oh! that my head were waters,
and mine eyes a fountain of tears*, that I might weep
both day and night, lament and sympathise with thee.

Our Father, &c.

Holy Mary, Mother of God, as the body of thy
beloved Son was for us extended on the cross, so
may our desires be daily more and more stretched
out in his service. and our hearts wounded with
compassion for his most bitter passion; and thou,
O most Blessed Virgin, vouchsafe to negociate for
and with us the work of our salvation, by thy
powerful intercession. Amen.

PART THIRD.

THE GLORIOUS MYSTERIES.

For Wednesdays and Saturdays throughout the year, and Sundays
from Easter to Advent.

I.--*The Resurrection.*

Let us contemplate in this mystery, how our
Lord Jesus Christ, triumphing gloriously over death,
rose again the third day, immortal and impassible.

† Let us imagine to ourselves here, that we see our blessed Lord arising out of the sepulchre, disfigured the other day, and hacked and mangled, but now immortal, clothed with splendour, and endowed with all the gifts of a glorified body, never to die any more.

Let us fix our eyes upon him, and behold him going to visit his Blessed Mother, to cheer and clear up that eclipsed heaven, to dry up the tears of her chaste eyes, and to give her the kiss of peace. Oh! what a heaven of joy filled her soul when she saw her beloved Son, our triumphant conqueror of sin and Satan, not hanging any more between two thieves, but environed by multitudes of angels, not covered with blood and gore. but enrobed with immortality and glory.

Sweetest Jesus, give us grace to die to sin, that, rising again to life, we may conquer as thou hast done, and trample under foot every unruly passion.

Our Father, &c.

O glorious Virgin Mary, by that unspeakable joy thou receivedst in the resurrection of thy only-beloved Son, we beseech thee obtain of him for us, that our hearts may never go astray after the false joys of this world, but may be ever and wholly employed in pursuit of the only true and solid joys of heaven. Amen.

II.—*The Ascension.*

Let us contemplate in this mystery, how our Lord Jesus Christ, forty days after his resurrection.

ascended into heaven, attended by angels, in sight of his most holy Mother, and his Apostles and disciples, to the great admiration of them all.

† Let us imagine ourselves here upon the mountain of Olives, and that we see the glorious champion of our salvation taking leave of his blessed Mother and disciples, comforting them, *lifting up His hands and blessing them*, and that we hear the angels sing, *Arise, O Lord, and go to the place of thy repose.* See him mounting up upon a cloud, ascending victorious from the wars, all dyed in blood, and leading captivity captive, whilst the heavenly chorus sing : *Who is this that cometh from Edom, with dyed garments from Bosra; this beautiful one in his robe, walking in the greatness of his strength? (Isaias* lxiii. 1.) *Who is this King of Glory? Our Lord strong and mighty; our Lord mighty in battle. Be ye lifted up, O eternal gates, and the King of Glory shall enter in.*

Our Father, &c.

O Mother of God, comfort of the afflicted, as thy beloved Son, when he ascended into heaven, lifted up his hands and blessed his Apostles, so vouchsafe, most holy Mother, to lift up thy pure hands to him for us, that we may enjoy the benefit of his blessing and thine here on earth, and hereafter in heaven. Amen.

III.—*The Descent of the Holy Ghost.*

Let us contemplate in this mystery, how our Lord Jesus Christ, being seated at the right hand of

God, sent (as he had promised) the Holy Ghost, upon his Apostles, who, after he had ascended, returning to Jerusalem, continued in prayer and supplication with the Blessed Virgin Mary, expecting the performance of his promise.

† Let us imagine ourselves here in the holy company of the Apostles, assembled with them, and Mary, the Mother of Jesus, in an upper room in Jerusalem, persevering with one mind in prayer, preparing our souls for the coming of the Holy Ghost, the blessed Comforter and Spirit of Truth. Let us imagine that we hear the noise, which all of a sudden *came from heaven as of a violent, rushing wind, which filled the whole house where they were sitting. And there appeared to them cloven tongues, as it were of fire, and it sat upon each of them. And they were all filled with the Holy Ghost.* O holy Mary, blessed and happy Apostles, we congratulate you, and beseech you to obtain that the Divine Spirit may visit us also and take full possession of our hearts for time and eternity. Amen.

Our Father, &c.

O sacred Virgin, Tabernacle of the Holy Ghost, we beseech thee obtain by thy intercession, that this most sweet Comforter, whom thy beloved Son sent down upon his Apostles, filling them thereby with spiritual joy, may teach us in this world the true way of salvation, and make us walk in the paths of virtue and good works. Amen.

IV.—*The Assumption.*

Let us contemplate in this mystery, how the glorious Virgin, twelve years after the resurrection of her Son, passed out of this world unto him, and was by him assumed into heaven, accompanied by the holy angels.

† Let us imagine to ourselves here, that we see the most glorious procession upon which the sun ever shone, the glorious, the glorified Virgin Mary, three days after she had given up her soul into the hands of that King of Glory, to whom she had given flesh, mounting up, body and sou through the air with all incredible joy and triumph.

Hear the music, the applause, and acclamations of angels. *Who is this that ascends on high like the morning light, beautiful as the moon, chosen as the sun?* Oh, may we so imitate her virtues, that at the hour of death we may be met by the angels as she was, and welcomed to the joys of heaven.

Our Father, &c.

O most prudent Virgin, who, entering into the heavenly palace, didst fill the holy angels with joy, and man with hope, vouchsafe to intercede for us in the hour of our death, that, being free from the illusions and temptations of the devil, we may joyfully and securely pass out of this temporal state, to enjoy the happiness of eternal life. Amen.

V.—*The Coronation of the Most Blessed Virgin Mary.*

Let us contemplate in this mystery, how the

glorious Virgin Mary was, with great jubilee and exultation of the whole court of heaven, and with particular glory of all the saints. crowned by her Son with the brightest diadem of glory.

† Let us imagine to ourselves here, that we see the solemnity of this heavenly coronation, that we see her blessed Son, circling her brows with an imperial crown, investing her sacred body with a most peculiar glory, and proclaiming her Queen of all creatures.

See all the choirs of angels coming to pay their homage and obedience to her. casting down their crowns before her, and congratulating her as their Queen and their Lady.

Oh! let us leave off gazing upon trifles here below, and look up to our eternal inheritance in heaven ; let us run with joy the race that is set before us, that with our Queen we may live eternally in glory.

Our Father, &c.

O Glorious Queen of all the heavenly citizens, we beseech thee to accept this Rosary, which (as a crown of roses) we offer at thy feet; and grant, most gracious Lady, that by thy intercession, our souls may be inflamed with so ardent a desire of seeing thee so gloriously crowned, that it may never die in us, until it shall be changed into the happy fruition of thy blessed sight. Amen.

HAIL, holy Queen. Mother of mercy, hail our life, our sweetness, and our hope. To thee do we cry, poor banished children of Eve; to thee do we send up our sighs, mourning and weeping, in this vale of tears.   Turn, then, most gracious advocate, thine eyes of mercy towards us; and after this our exile, show unto us the blessed fruit of thy womb, Jesus. O clement, O loving, O sweet Virgin Mary!

V. Pray for us, O holy Mother of God.

R. That we may be made worthy of the promises of Christ.

LET US PRAY.

O GOD, whose only-begotten Son, by his life, death, and resurrection, has purchased for us the rewards of eternal life, grant, we beseech thee, that meditating upon these mysteries in the most holy Rosary of the Blessed Virgin Mary, we may imitate what they contain, and obtain what they promise; through the same Christ our Lord.   Amen.

Litany of the Blessed Virgin.

Ant. Sub tuum præsidium confugimus sancta Dei Genitrix, nostras deprecationes ne despicias in necessitatibus nostris, sed a periculis cunctis libera nos, semper Virgo gloriosa et benedicta.

Ant. We fly to thy patronage, O holy Mother of God, despise not our petitions in our necessities, but deliver us from all dangers, O ever glorious and blessed Virgin.

KYRIE, eleison.
Christe, eleison.
Kyrie, eleison.
Christe, audi nos.
Christe, exaudi nos.
Pater de cœlis Deus,
Miserere nobis.

Lord, have mercy on us.
Christ, have mercy on us.
Lord, have mercy on us.
Christ, hear us.
Christ, graciously hear us.
God, the father of heaven,
Have mercy on us.

Fili, Redemptor mundi Deus,	God, the Son, Redeemer of the world,
Miserere nobis.	*Have mercy on us.*
Spiritus Sancte Deus,	God, the Holy Ghost,
Miserere nobis.	*Have mercy on us.*
Sancta Trinitas, unus Deus,	Holy Trinity, one God,
Miserere nobis.	*Have mercy on us.*
Sancta Maria,	Holy Mary,
Sancta Dei Genitrix,	Holy Mother of God,
Sancta Virgo virginum,	Holy Virgin of virgins,
Mater Christi,	Mother of Christ,
Mater divinæ gratiæ,	Mother of divine grace,
Mater purissima,	Mother most pure,
Mater castissima,	Mother most chaste,
Mater inviolata,	Mother inviolate,
Mater intemerata,	Mother undefiled,
Mater amabilis,	Mother most amiable,
Mater admirabilis,	Mother most admirable,
Mater boni consilii,	Mother of good counsel,
Mater Creatoris,	Mother of our Creator,
Mater Salvatoris,	Mother of our Redeemer,
Virgo prudentissima,	Virgin most prudent,
Virgo veneranda,	Virgin most venerable,
Virgo prædicanda,	Virgin most renowned,
Virgo potens,	Virgin most powerful,
Virgo clemens,	Virgin most merciful,
Virgo fidelis,	Virgin most faithful,
Speculum justitiæ,	Mirror of justice,
Sedes sapientiæ,	Seat of wisdom,
Causa nostræ letitiæ,	Cause of our joy,
Vas spirituale,	Spiritual vessel,
Vas honorabile,	Vessel of honour,
Vas insigne devotionis,	Vessel of singular devotion,
Rosa mystica,	Mystical rose,
Turris Davidica,	Tower of David,
Turris eburnea,	Tower of ivory,
Domus aurea,	House of gold,
Fœderis arca,	Ark of the covenant,
Janua cœli,	Gate of heaven,
Stella matutina,	Morning star,
Salus infirmorum,	Health of the weak,
Refugium peccatorum,	Refuge of sinners,
Consolatrix afflictorum,	Comforter of the afflicted,

Ora pro nobis.

Pray for us.

Auxilium Christianorum,		Help of Christians,
Regina angelorum,		Queen of angels.
Regina patriarcharum,		Queen of patriarchs,
Regina prophetarum,		Queen of prophets,
Regina apostolorum,	*Ora pro nobis.*	Queen of apostles,
Regina martyrum,		Queen of martyrs,
Regina confessorum,		Queen of confessors,
Regina Virginum,		Queen of virgins,
Regina sanctorum omnium,		Queen of all saints,

Regina sine labe originali concepta,

Regina sacratissimi rosarii,

Agnus Dei, qui tollis peccata mundi:

Parce nobis, Domine.

Agnus Dei, qui tollis peccata mundi:

Exaudi nos, Domine.

Agnus Dei, qui tollis peccata mundi:

Miserere nobis.

V. Ora pro nobis, sancta Dei Genitrix.

R. Ut digni efficiamur promissionibus Christi.

Queen conceived without original sin,

Queen of the most Holy Rosary,

Lamb of God, who takest away the sins of the world:

Spare us, O Lord.

Lamb of God, who takest away the sins of the world:

Graciously hear us, O Lord.

Lamb of God, who taketh away the sins of the world:

Have mercy on us.

V. Pray for us, O holy Mother of God.

R. That we may be made worthy of the promises of Christ.

Pray for us.

OREMUS.

Concede nos famulos tuos, quæsumus Domine Deus, perpetua mentis et corporis sanitate gaudere : et gloriosa beatæ Mariæ semper Virginis intercessione, a præsenti liberari tristitia, et æterna perfrui lætitia. Per Christum Dominum nostrum. Amen.

LET US PRAY.

Grant we beseech thee, O Lord God, that we thy servants may enjoy perpetual health of mind and body; and by the glorious intercession of the blessed Mary ever Virgin, we may be freed from present sorrow, and come to possess eternal joy. Through Christ our Lord. Amen.

V. Divinum auxilium maneat semper nobiscum.

R. Amen.

V. Et fidelium animæ per misericordiam Dei requiescant in pace.

R. Amen.

V. May the divine assistance remain always with us.

R. Amen.

V. And may the souls of the faithful departed, through the mercy of God, rest in peace.

R. Amen.

De Profundis.

V. De profundis clamavi ad te Domine :* Domine exaudi vocem meam.

R. Fiant aures tuæ intendentes * in vocem deprecationis meæ.

V. Si inquitates observaveris, Domine : * Domine, quis sustinebit ?

R. Quia apud te propitiatio est : * et propter legem tuam sustinui te, Domine.

V. Sustinuit anima mea in verbo ejus : * speravit anima mea in Domino.

R. A custodia matutina usque ad noctem : * speret Israel in Domino.

V. Quia apud Dominum misericordia : * et copiosa apud eum redemptio.

R. Et ipse redimet Israel,* ex omnibus iniquitatibus ejus.

V. Out of the depths have I cried unto thee, O Lord : Lord, hear my voice.

R. Let thine ears be attentive to the voice of my supplication.

V. If thou, O Lord, wilt mark iniquities : Lord, who shall abide it ?

R. For with thee there is merciful forgiveness : and because of thy law I have waited for thee, O Lord.

V. My soul hath waited on his word : my soul hath hoped in the Lord.

R. From the morning watch even until night : let Israel hope in the Lord.

V. For with the Lord there is mercy: and with him is plenteous redemption.

R. And he shall redeem Israel from all his iniquities.

V. Requiem æternam dona eis Domine.

R. Et lux perpetua luceat eis.

V. A porta inferi.

R. Erue Domine animas eorum.

V. Requiescant in pace.

R. Amen.

V. Domine exaudi orationem meam.

R. Et clamor meus ad te veniat.

OREMUS.

Fidelium Deus, omnium Conditor et Redemptor, animabus famulorum famularumque tuarum, remissionem cunctorum tribue peccatorum, ut indulgentiam quam semper optaverunt piis supplicationibus consequantur. Qui vivis, &c.

V. Requiem æternam dona eis Domine.

R. Et lux perpetua luceat eis.

V. Requiescant in pace.

R. Amen.

V. Eternal rest give to them, O Lord.

R. And let perpetual light shine upon them.

R. From the gate of hell,

V. O Lord deliver their souls.

V. May they rest in peace.

R. Amen.

V. O Lord hear my prayer,

R. And let my cry come unto thee.

LET US PRAY.

O God, the Creator and Redeemer of all the faithful, give to the souls of thy servants departed the remission of all their sins; that through pious supplications they may obtain the pardon which they have always desired. Who livest, &c.

V. Eternal rest give to them, O Lord.

R. And let perpetual light shine upon them.

V. May they rest in peace.

R. Amen.

EJACULATION TO BE REPEATED EVERY DAY.

HOLY Mary, Mother of God, fix deeply in my heart the wounds of Jesus crucified.—*Indulgence of* 100 *days.*

Devotions for the Months of the Year.

It is a pious custom to set apart the months of the year for special devotion. Some of these arrangements are generally recognised; whilst in others the custom varies in different places. The order observed in this manual is that of a series of Italian devotions for the months of the year.

January: The Holy Name of Jesus.

February: Lent and Passion.

March: St. Joseph.

April: The Glorified Life of Jesus.

May: The Blessed Virgin Mary.

June: The Sacred Heart of Jesus.

July: The Precious Blood of Our Lord.

August: The Sacred Heart of Mary.

September: The Seven Dolours of the B.V.M.

October: The Holy Angels.

November: The Holy Souls in Purgatory.

December: Advent and the Nativity.

DEVOTIONS FOR JANUARY.

The Holy Name of Jesus.

The devout invocation of the holy name of Jesus, implies an act of faith, of hope, and of love. Jesus means Saviour. The name is wonderful in power; it is our strength in temptation, our help in weakness, our light in darkness, our buckler in the battle of life. When we pronounce with love the name of Jesus, we invoke our blessed Lord as Father, Brother, Friend, and we believe that he will realise in our regard all that is signified by each of those titles. Let us, then, frequently repeat the name of Jesus; that sacred name of salvation which, "is as a lamp to our feet, and a light to our paths," a refuge in temptation, and a remedy in our evils.

PRAYER FOR THE FEAST OF THE HOLY NAME OF JESUS.

O BLESSED name of Jesus, I adore thee as a name of grandeur and of majesty; I invoke thee as a name, the foundation of all my hopes ; I love thee as a name worthy of my tenderest affections.

O Jesus, be incessantly in my mind, that I may think of thee ; be upon my lips, that I may speak of thee ; be in my heart, that I may love but thee. And since, under heaven, no other name has been given to man whereby he must be saved. oh! be to me a Jesus during life, be to me a Jesus at the hour of my death, for my eternal salvation. Amen.

ANOTHER PRAYER.

O SWEET Jesus! grant me a lively devotion to thy sacred name ; teach me thyself to understand its meaning and to realise its efficacy ; to relish its sweetness and to trust in its power ; teach me to call on it worthily in all my difficulties and afflictions. May it be the last sound of my dying lips as I go forth to meet thee in judgment. Oh! be to me then, dear Lord, a merciful Saviour, not an angry Judge!

PETITION TO JESUS.

O MOST compassionate Jesus, full of pity and of mercy, who despisest not the sighing of the wretched ; alas, my whole life is perished and gone without fruit, nor have I ever done anything good in thy sight. To thee, therefore, I betake myself, imploring thy clemency. Do thou speak for me, do thou satisfy for me. Wash away all the defilement of my sinful eyes with the pure tears of thy most glorious eyes. By the sweet compassion of thy blessed ears, take away the iniquity of my sinful ears. By the pure intention of thy most holy thoughts, and by the ardent love of thy pierced heart, wash away all the guilt of my evil thoughts and of my wicked heart. By the thrilling power of the sweet words of thy blessed mouth, blot out all the offences of my polluted mouth. By the perfection of thy actions and the crucifixion of thy hands, wash away all the offences of my impious hands. By the painful weariness of thy blessed feet, and by their cruel piercing with the nails, wash away all the defilement of my sinful feet. By the majestic innocence of thy life, and by thy unblemished holiness, wash away the foulness of my corrupt life. Finally, do thou wash away, efface, extinguish all the sins of my heart and my soul in the abundant streams of thy most precious blood, that so, by thy most holy merits I may be thoroughly cleansed, and henceforward keep all thy commandments blameless. Amen.

The Psalter of Jesus.

" There is no other name under heaven given to men, whereby we must be saved."—*Acts* iv. 12.

Begin by a devout bending of the head, or genuflection, at the adorable name of JESUS.

PART I.

"At the name of Jesus let every knee bow, of things in heaven, of things on earth, and of things in hell; and let every tongue confess that our Lord Jesus Christ is in the glory of God the Father."—*Phil.* ii. 10, 11.

First Petition.

Jesus, Jesus, Jesus,
Jesus, Jesus, Jesus, } have mercy on me.
Jesus, Jesus, Jesus,

Jesus, have mercy on me, O God of compassion, and forgive the many and great offences I have committed in thy sight.

Many have been the follies of my life, and great are the miseries I have deserved for my ingratitude.

Have mercy on me, dear Jesus, for I am weak; O Lord heal me, who am unable to help myself.

Deliver me from setting my heart upon any of thy creatures, which may divert my eyes from continually looking up to thee.

Grant me grace henceforth, for the love of thee, to hate sin; and out of a just esteem of thee to despise all worldly vanities.

Have mercy on all sinners, O Jesus, I beseech thee; turn their vices into virtues, and, making them true observers of thy law, and sincere lovers of thee, bring them to bliss in everlasting glory. Have mercy also on the souls in purgatory, for thy bitter passion, I beseech thee, and for thy glorious name, Jesus.

O blessed Trinity, one eternal God, have mercy on me.

V. Glory be to the Father, and to the Son, and to the Holy Ghost.

R. As it was in the beginning, is now, and ever shall be, world without end. Amen.

Our Father, &c.　　Hail Mary, &c.

Second Petition.

Jesus, Jesus. Jesus,)
Jesus, Jesus. Jesus. > help me.
Jesus. Jesus. Jesus.)

Jesus, help me to overcome all temptations to sin, and the malice of my ghostly enemy.

Help me to spend my time in virtuous actions, and in such labours as are acceptable to thee.

To resist and repress the motions of my flesh to sloth, gluttony, and impurity.

To render my heart enamoured of virtue, and inflamed with desires of thy glorious presence.

Help me to deserve and keep a good name, by a peaceful and pious living, to thy honour, O Jesus, to my own comfort, and the benefit of others.

Have mercy on all sinners, &c.

Third Petition.

Jesus, Jesus, Jesus,)
Jesus. Jesus, Jesus. > strengthen me.
Jesus. Jesus, Jesus,)

Jesus, strengthen me in soul and body. to please thee in doing such works of virtue as may bring me to thy everlasting joy and felicity.

Grant me a firm purpose, most merciful Saviour, to amend my life. and atone for the years past :

Those years which I have misspent to thy displeasure. in vain or wicked thoughts, words, deeds, and evil habits.

Make my heart obedient to thy will ; and ready, for thy love, to perform all the works of mercy.

Grant me the gifts of the Holy Ghost, which, through a virtuous life, and a devout frequenting of thy most holy sacraments, may at length bring me to thy heavenly kingdom.

Have mercy on all sinners, &c.

Fourth Petition.

Jesus, Jesus, Jesus,
Jesus, Jesus, Jesus, } comfort me.
Jesus, Jesus, Jesus,

Jesus, comfort me, and give me grace to place my chief, my only joy and felicity in thee.

Send me heavenly meditations, spiritual sweetness, and fervent desires of thy glory : ravish my soul with the contemplation of heaven, where I shall everlastingly dwell with thee.

Bring often to my remembrance thy unspeakable goodness, thy gifts, and thy great kindness shown to me.

And when thou bringest to my mind the sad remembrance of my sins, whereby I have so unkindly offended thee, comfort me with the assurance of obtaining thy grace, by the spirit of perfect penance, purging away my guilt, and preparing me for thy kingdom.

Have mercy on all sinners, &c.

Fifth Petition.

Jesus, Jesus, Jesus,
Jesus, Jesus, Jesus, } make me constant.
Jesus, Jesus, Jesus,

Jesus, make me constant in faith, hope, and charity, with continuance in all virtues, and resolution not to offend thee.

Make the memory of thy passion, and of those bitter pains thou sufferedst for me, sustain my patience, and refresh me in all tribulations and adversity.

Make me ever hold fast the doctrines of thy holy Catholic Church, and be a diligent frequenter of all holy duties.

Let no false delight of this deceitful world blind me, no fleshly temptation or fraud of the devil shake my heart:

My heart, which has for ever set up its rest in thee, and is resolved to give up all things for thy eternal reward.

Have mercy on all sinners, &c.

" Our Lord Jesus Christ humbled himself, becoming obedient unto death, even the death of the cross."—*Phil.* ii. 8.

Hear these my petitions, O most merciful Saviour, and grant me thy grace so frequently to repeat and consider them, that they may prove easy steps, whereby my soul may climb up to the knowledge, love, and performance of my duty to thee and to my neighbour, through the whole course of my life. Amen.

Our Father, &c.

Hail Mary, &c.

I believe in God, &c

Part II.

Sixth Petition.

Jesus, Jesus, Jesus,
Jesus, Jesus, Jesus, } enlighten me with
Jesus, Jesus, Jesus, } spiritual wisdom.

Jesus, enlighten me with spiritual wisdom, to know thy goodness, and all those things which are most acceptable to thee.

Grant me a clear apprehension of my only good, and discretion to order my life according to it.

Grant that I may wisely proceed from virtue to virtue, till at length I arrive at the clear vision of thy glorious Majesty.

Permit me not, dear Lord, to return to those sins for which I have sorrowed, and of which I have purged myself by confession.

Grant me grace to benefit the souls of others by my good example, and to convert those by good counsel who have used me ill.

Have mercy on all sinners, &c.

Seventh Petition.

Jesus, Jesus, Jesus,
Jesus, Jesus, Jesus, } grant me grace to
Jesus, Jesus, Jesus, } fear thee.

Jesus, grant me grace inwardly to fear thee, and to avoid all occasions of offending thee.

Let the threats of the torments which shall befall sinners, the fear of losing thy love and thy heavenly inheritance, ever keep me in awe.

Let me not dare to remain in sin, but call me soon to repentance : lest through thine anger the dreadful sentence of endless death and damnation fall upon me.

May the powerful intercession of thy blessed Mother and all the saints, and, above all, thy own merits and mercy, O my Saviour, be ever between thy avenging justice and me.

Enable me, O my God, to work out my salvation with fear and trembling ; and may the apprehension of thy secret judgments render me a more humble and diligent suitor at the throne of grace.

Have mercy on all sinners, &c.

Eighth Petition.

Jesus, Jesus, Jesus,
Jesus, Jesus, Jesus, } grant me grace truly
Jesus, Jesus, Jesus, to love thee.

Jesus, grant me grace truly to love thee for thy infinite goodness, and those great bounties I have received, and hope for ever to receive from thee.

Let the remembrance of thy kindness and patience conquer the malice and evil inclinations of my perverse nature.

Let the consideration of my many deliverances, and thy gracious calls and continued protection through life, shame me out of my ingratitude.

And what dost thou require of me, for and by all thy mercies, but to love thee ; and why, but because thou art my only good?

O my dear Lord! my whole life shall be nothing

but a desire of thee ; and because I truly love thee, I will most diligently keep thy commandments.

Have mercy on all sinners, &c.

Ninth Petition.

Jesus, Jesus, Jesus,
Jesus, Jesus, Jesus, } grant me grace to remember my death.
Jesus, Jesus, Jesus,

Jesus grant me grace always to remember my death, and the great account I then must render ; that so being kept continually disposed, my soul may depart out of this world rightly in thy grace.

Then by the gracious intercession of thy blessed Mother, and the assistance of the glorious St. Michael, deliver me from the danger of my soul's enemies ; and do thou, my good angel, I beseech thee, help me at the hour of death.

Then, dear Jesus, remember thy mercy, and turn not for my offences, thy face away from me.

Secure me against the terrors of that day, by causing me now to die daily to all earthly things, and to have my continual conversation in heaven.

Let the remembrance of thy death teach me how to esteem my life ; and the memory of thy resurrection encourage me cheerfully to descend into the grave.

Have mercy on all sinners, &c.

Tenth Petition.

Jesus, Jesus, Jesus,
Jesus, Jesus, Jesus, } send me here my purgatory.
Jesus, Jesus, Jesus,

Jesus, send me here my purgatory, and so prevent the torments of that cleansing fire, which, after this life, awaits unpurged souls.

Vouchsafe to grant me those merciful crosses and afflictions, which thou seest are necessary to break off my affections from all things here below.

Since none can see thee that loves anything but for thy sake, permit not my heart to find here any rest but in seeking after thee.

Too bitter, alas! will be the anguish of a separated soul that desires, but cannot come to thee, clogged with the heavy chains of sin.

Here, then, O my Saviour, keep me continually mortified in this world; that purged thoroughly by the fire of thy love, I may immediately pass into the everlasting possessions.

Have mercy on all sinners, &c.

"Our Lord Jesus Christ humbled himself, becoming obedient unto death, even the death of the cross."—*Phil.* ii. 8.

Hear these my petitions. Page 294.
Our Father, &c.
Hail Mary, &c.
I believe in God, &c.

PART III.

Eleventh Petition.

Jesus, Jesus, Jesus, ⎫
Jesus, Jesus, Jesus, ⎬ grant me grace to fly evil company.
Jesus, Jesus, Jesus, ⎭

Jesus, grant me grace to fly evil company: or, if

I chance to come among such, I beseech thee, by the merits of thy uncorrupt conversation among sinners, preserve me from being overcome by any temptations to mortal sin.

Make me, O blessed Lord, to remember always with dread, that thou art present and hearest; who wilt judge us according to our words and actions.

How, then, dare I converse with slanderers, liars, drunkards, or swearers, or those whose discourse is quarrelsome, dissolute, or vain?

Repress in me, dear Jesus, all inordinate affection for the pleasures of taste and of the flesh; and grant me grace to avoid all such as would excite the fire of these unhappy appetites.

May thy power defend, thy wisdom direct, thy fatherly pity chastise me, and make me so to live here among men, as may fit me for the conversation of angels hereafter.

Have mercy on all sinners, dear Jesus, I beseech thee; turn their vices into virtues, and having made them true observers of thy law, and sincere lovers of thee, bring them to bliss in everlasting glory.

Have mercy also on the souls in purgatory, for thy bitter passion, I beseech thee, and for thy glorious name, Jesus.

O blessed Trinity, one Eternal God, have mercy on me.

Glory be to the Father.

Our Father.

Hail Mary.

Twelfth Petition.

Jesus, Jesus. Jesus. }
Jesus, Jesus, Jesus, } grant me grace to call
Jesus, Jesus. Jesus. } for help to thee.

Jesus, grant me grace in all my necessities to call for help to thee, and faithfully to remember thy death and resurrection for me.

Wilt thou be deaf to my cries, who wouldst lay down thy life for my ransom? or canst thou not save me, who couldst take it up again for my crown?

Whom have I to invoke but thee, O my Jesus, whose own blessed mouth has pronounced, *Call upon me in the day of trouble, and I will relieve thee.*

Thou art my sure rock of defence against all kinds of enemies: thou art my ever present grace, able to strengthen me to fight and conquer.

In all my sufferings, therefore, in all my weakness and temptations, will I confidently call upon thee: hear me, O my Jesus, and when thou hearest, have mercy.

Have mercy on all sinners, &c.

Thirteenth Petition.

Jesus, Jesus, Jesus. }
Jesus, Jesus, Jesus, } make me to persevere
Jesus, Jesus, Jesus, } in virtue.

Jesus, make me to persevere in virtue and in a good life; and never to draw back from serving thee, till thou bringest me to my reward in thy kingdom.

In all pious customs and holy duties, in my honest

and necessary employments, continue and strengthen, O Lord, both my soul and body.

Is my life anything but a pilgrimage upon earth towards the new Jerusalem, at which he that sits down, or turns out of the way, can never arrive?

O Jesus, make me always consider thy blessed example, through how many and great pains and how little pleasure thou pressedst on to a bitter death; because it is the way to a glorious resurrection.

Make me, O my Redeemer, seriously to ponder those severe words of thine, *He only that persereres to the end shall be saved.*

Have mercy on all sinners, &c.

Fourteenth Petition.

Jesus, Jesus, Jesus,
Jesus, Jesus, Jesus, } grant me grace to fix
Jesus, Jesus, Jesus) my mind on thee.

Jesus, grant me grace to fix my mind on thee; especially in the time of prayer, when I aspire to converse directly with thee.

Control the wanderings of my mind and the affections of my heart; repress the power of my spiritual enemies, who could then draw off my mind from heavenly things, to thoughts and imaginations of vanity.

So shall I, with joy and gratitude, behold thee, as my deliverer from all the evils I have escaped, and as my benefactor for all the good I have received or can hope for.

I shall see that thou thy very self art my only good and that all other things are but means ordained by thee to make me fix my mind on thee, to make me love thee more, and be eternally happy.

O beloved of my soul, absorb all my thoughts here, that I may become worthy to behold thee for evermore face to face in thy glory.

Have mercy on all sinners, &c.

Fifteenth Petition.

Jesus, Jesus, Jesus. \
Jesus, Jesus, Jesus, } give me grace to order \
Jesus, Jesus, Jesus. my life to thee.

Jesus, give me grace to order my life to thee, heartily intending and wisely designing all the operations of my body and soul, for obtaining the reward of thy infinite bliss and eternal felicity.

For what else is this world but a school to discipline souls, and fit them for the other? and how are they fitted for it but by an eager desire of enjoying God, their only end?

Break my froward spirit, O Jesus; make it humble and obedient; grant me grace to depart hence with a contempt for this world, and with a joyful hope of coming to thee in the next.

Let the memory of thy passion make me cheerfully embrace all occasions of suffering here for thy love; while my soul breathes after that blissful life and immortal glory, which thou hast ordained in heaven for thy servants.

O Jesus, let me frequently and attentively consider, that whatsoever I gain, if I lose thee, all is lost; and whatsoever I lose, if I gain thee, all is gained.

Have mercy on all sinners, &c.

"Our Lord Jesus Christ humbled himself, becoming obedient unto death, even the death of the cross."—*Phil.* ii. 8.

Hear these my petitions.   Page 294.

DEVOTIONS FOR FEBRUARY.

Lent.—Passion.

"Let us do penance, lest suddenly overtaken by the day of our death, we seek for time to do penance, and cannot find it."

"Be converted to me with all your heart, in fasting, in weeping and in mourning.   Blow the trumpet in Sion and sanctify a fast."

Let us unite with the whole Church during this penitential season in honouring the sufferings of our dear Redeemer, and let us unite, to his great sacrifice of atonement the oblation of voluntary penance for the sins which must be expiated either in this life or in the next.   Let us determine that with the divine assistance this Lent shall be the epoch of our entire conversion to God.

The Thirty Days' Prayer.

TO THE BLESSED VIRGIN MARY, IN HONOUR OF THE SACRED PASSION OF OUR LORD JESUS CHRIST, BY THE DEVOUT RECITAL OF WHICH, FOR THE ABOVE SPACE OF TIME, WE MAY CONFIDENTLY HOPE TO OBTAIN OUR LAWFUL REQUEST.

It is particularly recommended as a proper devotion for every day in Lent, and all the Fridays throughout the year.

EVER glorious and blessed Mary, Queen of Virgins, Mother of Mercy, hope and comfort of dejected and desolate souls; through that sword of sorrow which pierced thy tender heart, whilst thine only Son, Jesus Christ our Lord, suffered death and ignominy on the cross; through that filial tenderness and pure love he had for thee, grieving in thy grief, whilst from his cross he recommended thee to the care and protection of his beloved disciple St. John; take pity, I beseech thee, on my poverty and necessities; have compassion on my anxieties and cares; assist and comfort me in all my infirmities and miseries. Thou art the Mother of mercies, the sweet comforter and only refuge of the needy and the orphan, of the desolate and the afflicted. Cast, therefore, an eye of pity on a poor child of Eve, and hear my prayer; for since, in just punishment of my sins, I find myself encompassed by a multitude of evils, and oppressed with much anguish of spirit, whither can I fly for more secure shelter, O amiable Mother of my Lord and Saviour Jesus Christ! than to the wings of thy maternal protection? Attend, therefore, I beseech thee, with an ear of pity and compassion, to my humble and earnest request. I ask it through the mercy of thy dear Son; through that love and condescension wherewith he embraced our nature, when, in compliance with the divine will, thou gavest thy consent; and whom, after the expiration of nine months, thou didst bring forth from thy chaste womb to visit this world, and bless it with his presence. I ask it through that anguish of mind wherewith thy beloved Son, our dear Saviour, was overwhelmed on the Mount of Olives, when he besought his Eternal Father to remove from him, if possible, the bitter chalice of his Passion. I ask it through the threefold repetition of his prayer in the garden, from whence afterwards, with sorrowing steps, and mournful tears, thou didst accompany him to the doleful theatre of his death and sufferings. I ask it through the wounds and sores of his virginal flesh, occasioned by the cords and whips wherewith he was bound and scourged, when stripped of his seamless garment, for which his executioners afterwards cast lots. I ask it through the scoffs and ignominies wherewith he was insulted; the false accusations and unjust sentence by which he was condemned to death, and which he bore with heavenly patience. I ask it through his bitter tears and bloody sweat, his silence and resignation, his sadness and grief of heart. I ask it through the blood which trickled from his royal and sacred head, when struck with his sceptre of a reed, and pierced with his crown of thorns. I ask it through the excruciating torments he suffered, when his hands and feet were fastened with gross nails to the tree of the cross. I ask it through his vehement thirst, and bitter portion of vinegar and gall. I ask it through his dereliction on the cross, when he exclaimed, *My God! My God! why hast thou forsaken me?* I ask it through his mercy extended to the good thief, and through his recommending his precious soul and spirit into the hands of his Eternal Father before he expired, saying, *It is finished.* I ask it through the blood, mixed with water, which issued from his sacred side when pierced with a lance, from whence a plenteous stream of grace and mercy hath flowed to us. I ask it through his immaculate life, his bitter passion, and ignominious death on the cross, at which nature itself was thrown into convulsions, by the bursting of rocks, rending of the veil of the temple, the earthquake, and darkness of the sun and moon. I ask it through his descent into hell, where he comforted the saints of the old law with his presence, and led captivity captive. I ask it through his glorious victory over death, when he rose again to life on the third day, and through the joy which his appearance for forty days after gave thee, his Blessed Mother, his Apostles, and the rest of his disciples, when in thy presence and in theirs he miraculously ascended into heaven. I ask it through the grace of the Holy Ghost, infused into the hearts of the disciples, when he descended upon them in the form of fiery tongues, and by which they were inspired with zeal in the conversion of the world when they went to preach the Gospel. I ask it through the awful appearance of thy Son at the last dreadful day, when he shall come to judge the living and the dead, and the world by fire. I ask it through the compassion he bore thee in this life, and the ineffable joy thou didst feel at thine assumption into heaven, where thou art eternally absorbed in the sweet contemplation of his adorable perfections. O Glorious and ever blessed Virgin! comfort the heart of thy supplicant by obtaining for me. [*Here mention or reflect on your lawful request, under the reservation of its being agreeable to the will of God, who sees whether it will contribute towards your spiritual good*]. And as I am persuaded my Divine Saviour doth honour thee as his beloved Mother, to whom he can refuse nothing, let me speedily experience the efficacy of thy powerful intercession, according to the tenderness of thy maternal affection, and his filial loving heart, who mercifully grantest the requests and compliest with the desires of those that love and fear him. O most blessed Virgin! besides the object of my present petition, and whatever else I may stand in need of, obtain for me of thy dear Son, our Lord and our God, a lively faith, firm hope, perfect charity, true contrition, a horror of sin, love of God and my neighbour, contempt of the world, and patience and resignation under the trials and afflictions of this life. Obtain likewise for me, O Sacred Mother of God! the great gift of final perseverance, and grace to receive the last sacraments worthily at the hour of death. Lastly, obtain, I beseech thee, for the souls of my parents, brethren, relations and benefactors, both living and dead, life everlasting. Amen.

Devotions to the Holy Face of our Lord.

Protector noster aspice Deus; et respice in faciem Christi tui. Behold, O God our protector; and look on the face of thy Christ.— Ps. lxxxiii. 10.

This touching devotion, which our Lord Himself seems to have instituted on the day of his death, by imprinting miraculously the traces of his blood-stained features on the veil of Veronica, has always been practised in the Church. Lately, the devotion has spread considerably. It is a shield against the scourges of Divine justice, a powerful means of obtaining the conversion of sinners.

PRAYER OF POPE PIUS IX.

O MY Jesus ! cast upon us a look of mercy ; turn thy Face towards each of us as thou didst to Veronica ; not that we may see it with our bodily eyes, for this we do not deserve ; but turn it towards our hearts, so that, remembering thee, we may ever draw from this fountain of strength the vigour necessary to sustain the combats of life.   Amen.

BLESSING OF THE HIGH PRIEST AARON.

Benedicat tibi Dominus, et custodiat te ;
Ostendat Dominus Faciem suam tibi, et misereatur tui.
Convertat Dominus vultum suum ad te et det tibi pacem.

The Lord bless thee and keep thee.

The Lord show his Face to thee and have mercy on thee.   The Lord turn his countenance to thee, and give thee peace.   (*Numbers* vi. 24, 25, 26.)

ASPIRATIONS.

Eternal Father, we offer thee the Adorable Face of thy well-beloved Son, for the honour and glory of thy holy name and for the conversion of France and England.   (*Sister Marie de Saint-Pierre.*)

May I die consumed by an ardent thirst to see the desirable Face of our Lord and Saviour Jesus Christ. (*Thought of Saint Edmund which M. Dupont frequently repeated towards the close of his life.*)

OTHER PRAYERS.

O MNIPOTENT God, Eternal Father, look upon the Face of thy Son Jesus ! we confidently present it to thee, imploring thy pardon. He is himself our Advocate, he pleads our cause. Hear his cries; see his tears, O my God; and because of his infinite merits, hear him pleading for us poor and miserable sinners.

O adorable Face of my Jesus! bowed so mercifully from the tree of the cross, on the day of thy Passion for the salvation of the world, now in pity bend towards us, cast upon us a look of compassion, and receive us to the kiss of peace. Amen.

Supplication for the Time of Lent.

V. Have pity on us, O most merciful Lord, and spare thy people;

R. For, we have sinned against thee.

V. We prostrate before thee, and pour out our tears; we confess unto thee our hidden sins, and beseech thee, O God, to pardon us.

R. For, we have sinned against thee.

V. Thou art angry against us: our heinous crimes have bowed us down to the earth: and we have grown faint, because there is no hope within us.

R. For, we have sinned against thee.

V. We have been made a prey to evils that we know not, and every evil has come upon us.

R. For, we have sinned against thee.

V. We all cry unto thee: we all seek thee; we are repentant, and weeping follow thee, for, we have provoked thy anger.

R. For, we have sinned against thee.

V. We beseech thee: O Jesus, we prostrate before thee and petition thee: let thy power raise us from our misery.

R. For, we have sinned against thee.

V. Receive thy people's confession : full of sorrow, we pour it out before thee : and our hearts are sad for the sins we have committed.

R. For, we have sinned against thee.

V. We sue for peace; grant us peace ! avert the scourge of war, and deliver us, we humbly beseech thee, O Lord !

R. For, we have sinned against thee.

V. Bow down thine ear, O most merciful God ; cleanse us from the stains of our sins, and in thy pity, deliver us from all dangers.

R. Have mercy on us, and spare us.

ASSOCIATION OF PRAYER IN HONOUR OF THE SACRED THIRST AND AGONY OF JESUS, TO REPRESS INTEMPERANCE.

Let us pray for those who tamper with drink, for those who drink habitually, and for those in danger of death from drink. Let us say for them daily, in honour of the Sacred Thirst of Jesus, and the transfixed Heart of Mary—

One Pater and three Aves.

"That the Scripture might be fulfilled, Jesus said, I thirst."— *St. John* xix. 28.

O MOST sweet Jesus, what thirst is it that torments thee ? What else but a thirst for our salvation and our healing? " I thirst." O my Saviour, who will give thee refreshment? Who will bring back a wandering sheep to thee? I will, O Lord. I will seek for sinners ; I will endeavour to bring them back to thee. I will endeavour to assuage thy thirst by tears of repentance, sorrow and contrition.

O Sacred Heart of Jesus, through thy thirst and agony on the cross, have mercy on us.

Immaculate Virgin, through the sorrow which

pierced thy heart on beholding the refreshment offered to thy Divine Son on the cross, deign to assist us, children of thy grief : protect us from the enemy, and receive us at the hour of death.

V. From a sudden and unprovided death.

R. Deliver us, O Lord.

V. From the snares of the devil.

R. Deliver us, O Lord.

V. From everlasting death.

R. Deliver us, O Lord.

O God of my heart, by those five wounds, which thy love for us inflicted on thee, succour thy servants whom thou hast redeemed with thy precious blood.

DEVOTIONS FOR MARCH.
Month Dedicated to the Honour of St. Joseph.

The Incarnate Word dethroned the world: its atheisms, its idolatries, its superstitions were swept away in the light of the incarnation. Hence, the person of our Divine Lord has been from the beginning the centre of all the chief heresies that have tormented the Christian world. In this nineteenth century the Church has been, and is, most violently assailed by her enemies ; and to it, also, God has specially reserved two consoling devotions—devotion to the Sacred Heart and devotion to St. Joseph; the one to revive in hearts grown cold the love of God; the other to secure in heaven for the Church a new Protector in the days of bitter trial.

In answer to the prayers of almost all the Bishops of Christendom, assembled at the Vatican Council, the illustrious Pontiff. Pope Pius IX., by a decree of the Sacred Congregation of Rites, published on the 8th December, 1870, proclaimed, to the joy of all the faithful, St. Joseph Patron of the Universal Church.

He also ordained that the Feast of St. Joseph, March 19th, should be raised to the rite of a double of the first class.

MEMORARE TO ST JOSEPH.

REMEMBER, O most illustrious and glorious Patriarch, St. Joseph, that no one ever had recourse to thy protection without obtaining relief. Confiding, therefore, in thy goodness, my most loving Father, I fly unto thee, humbly begging of thee to procure for me all the graces I require for my eternal salvation. Do not, O Guardian of the Word made Flesh, reject my petition, but graciously hear and grant it. Amen.

O blessed St. Joseph, who hadst the happiest of all deaths, obtain for us grace to die as thou didst in the arms of Jesus and of Mary, and with thee to enjoy their blessed company for all eternity. Amen

PRAYER TO ST. JOSEPH.

To obtain his Guidance through life.

O BLESSED St. Joseph, faithful Guide of Jesus Christ in his childhood and youth: thou who didst lead him safely in his flight to Egypt, and didst dwell with him during thirty years of thy earthly pilgrimage; be also my guide and companion in my pilgrimage through life, and never permit me to turn aside from the way of God's commandments. Be my refuge in adversity, my support in temptation, my solace in affliction, and conduct me at last to the land of the living, where, with thee and with Mary, thy most holy spouse, I may eternally bless, praise, and thank my God. Amen.

ADDRESS TO THE HEART OF ST. JOSEPH.

O MOST holy heart of Joseph! heart of the most venerable of Patriarchs! heart of the most holy

Spouse of the Mother of Jesus! heart of the reputed Father of our Saviour and Redeemer! obtain that my heart may resemble thine in the virtues of silence, meekness, humility, charity, recollection, obedience, and purity.   O heart of Joseph, deign to watch over me and assist me during life, and obtain for me the grace of expiring, like thee, in the arms of Jesus and of Mary.   Amen.

PRAYER TO ST. JOSEPH.

Special favours have been obtained by reciting the following short invocation and versicle in honour of St. Joseph.

O GLORIOUS St. Joseph, faithful follower of Jesus Christ, to thee we raise our hearts and hands, to implore through thy powerful intercession, from the benign Heart of Jesus, all the helps and graces necessary for our spiritual and temporal welfare, the grace of a happy death, and the special favours we hope to obtain.   [*Name them.*]

O Guardian of the word Incarnate, we have the most unbounded confidence that thy prayers in our behalf will be graciously heard before the throne of God.

[Here say the following versicle seven times, in honour of the seven Dolours and Joys of St. Joseph] :—

V. O Glorious St. Joseph, through the love thou dost bear to Jesus Christ, and for the glory of his name,

R. Hear our prayers, and obtain the grant of our petitions.

PRAYER.

O GLORIOUS St. Joseph, spouse of the ever Immaculate Virgin Mary, the Mother of God, obtain for me a pure, humble, and charitable mind;

the spirit of prayer, interior recollection, and perfect resignation to the divine will. Be my guide, my father, and model during life, and obtain that, like thee, I may expire in the arms of Jesus and Mary. Amen.

PRAYER TO ST. JOSEPH.

GLORIOUS St. Joseph, model of all those who are devoted to labour, obtain for me the grace to work in a spirit of Penance for the expiation of my many sins; to work conscientiously, putting the call of duty above my inclinations; to work with gratitude and joy, considering it an honour to employ and develop by means of labour the gifts received from God; to work with order, peace, moderation, and patience, without ever recoiling before weariness or difficulties; to work, above all, with purity of intention and with detachment from self, having always death before my eyes and the account which I must render of time lost, of talents wasted, of good omitted, of vain complacency in success, so fatal to the work of God.

All for Jesus, all for Mary, all after thy example, O Patriarch Joseph, such shall be my watchword in life and in death. Amen.—(*Pius X.*)

PRAYER TO ST. JOSEPH.
To obtain a Temporal Favour.

GREAT St. Joseph, whose influence over the Sacred Hearts of Jesus and Mary is all powerful, thou whom no one has ever invoked in vain, prostate in spirit before thee, I ask with the most firm and lively confidence the grant of my personal request.

Do, dear saint, obtain for me the object of my prayer, if it be for the glory of God and my own salvation; if not, obtain for me the grace lovingly to resign myself to the will of my heavenly Father, who, in the affliction he sends, as well as in the temporal favours he grants, has ever in view my happiness here and my eternal salvation. Amen.

PRAYER TO ST. JOSEPH, ORDERED BY HIS HOLINESS LEO XIII. TO BE SAID AS PART OF THE DEVOTIONS FOR THE MONTH OF OCTOBER.

To thee, O Blessed Joseph, we have recourse in our tribulations, and while imploring the aid of thy most holy Spouse, we confidently invoke thy patronage also. By that love which united thee to the Immaculate Virgin Mother of God, and by the fatherly affection with which thou didst embrace the Infant Jesus, we humbly beseech thee graciously to regard the inheritance which Jesus Christ purchased by his blood, and to help us in our necessities by thy powerful intercession.

Protect, O most provident guardian of the Holy Family, the chosen children of Jesus Christ: ward off from us, O most loving Father, all taint of error and corruption; graciously assist us from heaven, O most powerful Protector, in our struggle with the powers of darkness; and as thou didst once rescue the Child Jesus from imminent peril to His life, so now defend the Holy Church of God from the snares of her enemies and from all adversity. Shield each one of us with thy unceasing patronage, that imitating thy example, and supported by thy aid, we may be enabled to live a good life, die a holy death, and secure everlasting happiness in heaven. Amen.

(*300 days' indulgence—applicable to the souls in Purgatory—once every day of the year for recital even in private.*)

(*Indulgence of seven years and seven quarantines for each public recital during month of October.*)

DEVOTIONS FOR APRIL.

The Glorified Life of Jesus.

On the great Feast of the Resurrection, we solemnize with holy joy the triumph of our Blessed Redeemer over sufferings and death. We exult in the consciousness of his bliss, "Christ rising from the dead, dieth now no more." He is risen with the same flesh that quivered on Calvary, the very same blood that purpled the hard rock. He is clothed with light so sparkling that the eyes of the Roman soldiers are struck blind; so beautiful, that the hearts of Mary and the devout women are emptied of sorrow, "Oh grave! where is thy victory? Oh, death! where is thy sting?"

AN EXERCISE

In Honour of the Mysteries of Jesus Risen.

O MY blessed Jesus, I adore thee, bright and beautiful in thy Resurrection; I adore thee in all the mysteries of thy Risen Life on earth, and in all the majesty and loveliness of thy most dear Soul and glorified Body, as seen and worshipped in heaven at this hour. I acknowledge thee to be my Lord and my God; I bless thee for thy sweet victory over death, and for thy faithful love in retaining thy five holy Wounds, wherewith we sinners wounded thee on earth. Grant, I beseech thee, O my dearest Jesus, that I may so often and so tenderly meditate upon thee Risen and Glorified, that my heart may become daily more and more inflamed with love of thee, so that thy beauty may make the world dull and intolerable, and that I may thirst exceedingly with pure and disinterested love for the hour when thou shalt admit me to behold thee as thou art, my dearest Lord, at this very moment on thy throne in heaven ; who livest and reignest, with the Father and the Holy Ghost, God, world without end. Amen.

I believe in God, &c.

O Queen of heaven and earth, Mother of God, Mother of mercy, conceived without stain of original sin, and gloriously crowned in heaven, I desire with all the love of my poor heart to congratulate thee on those wonderful delights which thou didst and which thou dost still enjoy in the glory and splendour of Jesus Risen from that first dawn when he appeared to thee in thy sorrows even to the present hour ; and I beseech thee to accept this my devotion to thy maternal joys, and to obtain for me an increase of love to Jesus in this world, and in the world to come the never-fading light of his most blessed countenance. Amen.

Hail Mary.

O glorious and affectionate St. Joseph, Foster-father of Jesus and Spouse of Mary, by the joy of thy meeting with Jesus in the place of departed spirits, and by the joy thou hast this hour in thy nearness to his risen beauty and most sweet splendour, present unto him, I beseech thee, O my dear father and protector, this my devotion to the mysteries of his Risen Life; and as he spared thee the bitterness of his Sacred Passion, obtain for me the peace of his Resurrection and the gift of spiritual joy, that I may find no delight but in God, in Jesus, in Mary, and in thyself. Amen.

Our Father.

V. Pray for us, O holy angels of God. Alleluia.

R. That we may be made worthy of the vision of Jesus Glorified. Alleluia.

O Eternal Father, who, of thine infinite goodness, didst give unto us thine eternal and only-begotten Son Jesus Christ, and hast now raised his sacred humanity to the high places of heaven: grant, we beseech thee, that by our devotion to the mysteries of his Risen and Glorified Life both on earth and in heaven, we may so please thee, that by thy clemency we may attain to the vision and enjoyment of thee in the world to come: through the same Jesus Christ, thy Son, our Lord, who with thee and the Holy Ghost liveth and reigneth, God, world without end. Amen.

LET US PRAY.

O MOST blessed Lord and Saviour Jesus Christ, who in various ways and places, during the forty days of thy Risen Life on earth, didst

appear to thy Mother and thine Apostles; vouchsafe, we beseech thee, to manifest thy will to us
on earth ; so that by the help of thy grace, following
thy divine vocation in this life, we may come to see
thee in the unfading vision of thy glory in the life
to come.

O Lord Jesus Christ, eternal Shepherd of thy
chosen flock, desert not thy Church, which thou hast
gathered out of the nations, and redeemed by thy
Precious Blood ; but for the sake of the joyful and
glorious mysteries of thy Risen Life, vouchsafe to
grant unto her in all lands an increase of the peace
of thy Resurrection, and the sevenfold gifts of thy
Blessed Spirit, that she may grow in holiness before
thee, till thou comest to judge the world ; and we
beseech thee, for her sake, to pour down most
abundantly the anointing of the Holy Spirit upon
thy Vicar, the Sovereign Pontiff; that the Spirit
of St. Peter may rest upon him, as the double
spirit of Elias rested upon Eliseus, and that by thy
clemency he may come, with the flock committed
to his care, to the blessed vision of thy glory in
heaven. Who livest and reignest, with the Father
and the same Holy Spirit, God, world without end.
Amen.

Let us say one *Our Father* and one *Hail Mary* for the soul in
purgatory most devoted to the mysteries of Jesus Risen.

DEVOTIONS FOR MAY.

The Blessed Virgin Mary.

Love and devotion to the Mother of God form a part of Christianity —they are an earnest of salvation. The Saints have numbered them amongst the marks of predestination. There is no shorter, no easier way to Christ than by his Mother. We pray to her, we praise her, and we know with certainty that she draws us to God. Always bearing in mind and promoting the honour of her Son, this loving Mother exercises her wondrous power over us in a thousand winning and tender ways. Let us then respond to her love—let us cling to her and join with the universal Church in consecrating to her this sweet Month of May. We are her children, she is the guardian of our peace, placed on the highest summit of power and glory which any pure creature can possess in heaven, that she may give the aid of her protection to all who call upon her.

ACT OF CONSECRATION
To be said every day during the Month of May.

O MOST august and blessed Virgin Mary, holy Mother of God, glorious Queen of heaven and earth, powerful protectress of those who love thee, and unfailing advocate of all who invoke thee, look down, I beseech thee, from thy throne of glory, on thy devoted child; accept the solemn offering I present thee of this month, specially dedicated to thee, and receive my ardent, humble desire, that by my love and fervour, I could worthily honour thee, who, next to God, art deserving of all honour. Receive me, O Mother of mercy! among thy best beloved children, extend to me thy maternal tenderness and solicitude, obtain for me a place in the Heart of Jesus, and a special share in the gifts of his grace. Oh, deign I beseech thee, to recognise my claims on thy protection, to watch over my spiritual and temporal interests, as well as those of all who are dear to me, to infuse into my soul the spirit of Christ, and to teach me thyself to become meek, humble, charitable, patient, and submissive to the will of God. May my heart burn with the love of thy divine Son, and of thee, his blessed Mother, not for a month alone, but for time and eternity; may I thirst for the promotion of his honour and thine, and contribute as far as I can to its extension. Receive me, O Mary, the Refuge of sinners! Grant me a Mother's blessing and a Mother's care, now and at the hour of my death.   Amen.

Litany of our Lady of the Rosary.

Lord have mercy on us,
Christ have mercy on us.
Lord have mercy on us,
Christ hear us.
Christ graciously hear us.
God, the Father of heaven, *have mercy on us.*
God the Son, Redeemer of the world, *have mercy on us.*
God the Holy Ghost, *have mercy on us.*
Holy Trinity, one God, *have mercy on us*
Queen of the Holy Rosary,
Queen, conceived without sin.
Queen of the Rosary, wonderful in thy joys, sorrows, and glory.
Who didst teach St. Dominic this efficacious devotion,

Pray for us.

22

Who didst select his children to preserve, protect and spread it throughout the universe, *Pray for us.*

By the joy which filled thy soul in the mystery of the Annunciation,

By the benedictions which thy presence brought to the house of Zachary,

By the bliss which thou didst impart to the world in the birth of our Saviour,

By the consolations infused into the heart of holy Simeon in the mystery of the presentation,

By thy joy in finding thy beloved child in the temple,

By the bitter agony of Jesus,

By his cruel scourging,

By his thorny crown,

By the weight of his holy cross,

By his crucifixion and his blood shed for the remission of our sins,

By the glorious Resurrection of thy Son,

By his triumphant Ascension,

By the coming of the Holy Ghost the Comforter,

By thy glorious Assumption into heaven,

By thy resplendent Coronation and thine immortal empire,

That the children of St. Dominic may be faithful to their vocation,

That sinners may be converted,

That the agonising may be assisted in their distress,

Queen of the holy Rosary, hear us.

That the souls in Purgatory may be delivered
from their sufferings.

That in our last moments we may be fortified with the holy Sacraments of the
Church,

That thou mayest receive our souls and present
them before the Judge,

That thou mayest grant us in heaven the seats
of predilection promised to the children of
thy Confraternity,

Queen of the Holy Rosary, hear us.

Lamb of God, who takest away the sins of the
world, *Spare us, O Lord.*

Lamb of God, who takest away the sins of the
world, *Hear us, O Lord.*

Lamb of God, who takest away the sins of the
world, *Have mercy on us, O Lord.*

V. Queen of the Holy Rosary, pray for us.

R. That we may be made worthy of the promises
of Christ.

LET US PRAY.

O MARY, sweet Queen of the Rosary, take pity
on our miseries, and give us thy holy benediction.
Thou art our refuge. Speak for us to the Heart of
thy Divine Son; appease his indignation; restrain
his arm so justly raised to strike.

O Mary, obtain pardon for sinners, pardon and
grace for all, peace and triumph for the Church,
through thy holy Rosary. Amen.

PRAYER TO THE VIRGIN MOTHER OF GOOD COUNSEL.

MOST holy Virgin, seat of wisdom, Immaculate Mother of Good Counsel, all hail to thee, through whom the Blessed Trinity is adored! to thee, through whom Angels and Archangels are filled with gladness, through whom heaven exults, through whom demons are put to flight; I beseech thee mercifully to take me under thy powerful protection. By that gift of Counsel with which thy beloved Son enriched thee, instruct my ignorance, guard and keep me, thy poor helpless child. Look upon me, O Virgin Mother of Good Counsel, with an eye of pity. Be thou my light, my guide, my consolation. Forsake me not; give peace to my soul. Obtain for me the pardon of my sins, grace to imitate thy virtues, and a holy, happy death. O my tender Mother, at that tremendous hour, come and receive my soul, present it to the Sovereign Judge, and obtain for me a favourable sentence. I deserve not this grace; but I am thy child. I love thee. I desire to make all hearts love thee, O my amiable Queen, my Virgin Mother of Good Counsel. Amen.

PRAYER TO OUR BLESSED LADY OF LOURDES.

"I am the Immaculate Conception."

O IMMACULATE Virgin, most pure Mother of God, model of all sweetness, hasten to the aid of thy wretched children; convert those who sin, give courage and patience to those who suffer. O

most sweet, tender and holy Virgin, Queen of
Lourdes, hear the cry of our misery and trouble—
listen to the whisperings of thy maternal compassion
and mercy whilst we cry : Merciful Lady of Lourdes,
pray for us.   Thou art our Mother—bequeathed to
us from the cross, come therefore to our aid ; come
and cure us, covered as we are with the leprosy of
sin.   Humbly prostrate at thy feet, we consecrate
ourselves to thee, O Lady of Lourdes—to thee we
confide the direction of our lives.   Be henceforward
our hope and our strength, our consolation and our
support—our joy and our love.   And when we are
about to appear before our Almighty Judge, may we
repeat with our dying lips : Immaculate Mother,
Queen of Lourdes, pray for us.

PRAYER TO THE MADONNA OF PERPETUAL SUCCOUR.

"Have confidence in me. I have suffered, I can therefore compassionate thy miseries. I am strong. I am able to assist thee. I am
the Mother of Perpetual Succour."

MOST Holy Virgin of Perpetual Succour, my
dearest Mother and my hope, I consecrate
myself entirely to thee.   I take refuge under thy
mantle.   Oh, take me by the hand, keep me at thy
side until all danger shall have passed away and
until my happy lot shall be secured for ever.   Again
and again I cry to thee for protection in my journey
through this valley of tears.   I salute thee, Mother
of my Lord and God, Mother of him who pardons
and of sinners who are pardoned.   Oh! hear us,
hear us, Holy Mary; pray for us, intercede for us,

disdain not to help us, for thou canst obtain whatsoever thou wilt of thy beloved Son. O Mother of Perpetual Succour, deign to cast an eye of compassion on my poverty, and to help me in every need. All my wants and petitions, all my concerns and interests for time and eternity, I place in thy sacred hands. O my Mother and my refuge, be thou my perpetual, unfailing succour. Stand by me in the hour of trial, intercede for me in my temptations, hasten to me in my afflictions, bring with thee Jesus my salvation, and may his mercy be shown unto me according to the hope I have placed in him. Mother of Jesus, show thyself my Mother, for I have tried to prove myself thy child. Be to me a powerful and merciful protectress—come unto me in my last moments; vouchsafe to me thy maternal blessing ; succour me with a Mother's tenderness, that I may be rescued from peril, and with thee attain to everlasting gladness. Amen.

COVENANT WITH THE HOLY MOTHER OF GOD.

O MOTHER of God, and my most dear Mother, by the Heart of Jesus, I beg of thee each time I shall say, "O Mother of God, remember me," to adore then for me the Heart of thy Divine Son, and to offer my unworthy heart to him, asking pardon for all that is amiss in it—telling that God of love, how much it desires perfectly to love him ; and obtain by thy powerful intercession, a love that may consume in it all earthly affections, and that he may replenish it to the full extent of its small capacity. This, dear Mother, I beg, through the Heart of Jesus, to which thou canst refuse nothing, and by which I know thou canst not be rejected. Oh, show thyself then my Mother, and comply with the desires of thy poor unworthy child.

DEVOTIONS FOR JUNE.

The Sacred Heart of Jesus.

The Devotion to the Sacred Heart of Jesus, now so approved and cherished by the Church, is in substance identified with the devotion to the Blessed Sacrament. The object of this devotion is the material Heart of flesh that beat within the breast of Jesus; the Heart that was formed at the moment of the Incarnation; the Heart that **was** pierced on Calvary, and that is now enthroned as part of the Sacred Humanity, at the right hand of his Father in heaven. Special devotion to the Sacred Heart has been, as it were, inaugurated by our Lord himself in that sublime sentence which contains in itself the whole philosophy of Christian life: "Learn of Me because I am meek and humble of heart." If you desire to make atonement for the sins of your past life, offer to the Eternal Father the merits of his Divine Son. "Honour the adorable Heart of Jesus by constant acts of fervent devotion," says Lanspergius; "offer all your petitions to God through that Divine Heart; in your troubles and perplexities seek refuge in the Sacred Heart, and be convinced that though all the world should forget and forsake you, Jesus will ever be your faithful friend, and his Heart your secure asylum."

ACT OF CONSECRATION.

To be made every day during the Month.

O LORD Jesus, I consecrate my heart to thee: place it in thine. It is therein I wish to breathe, to love, to live unknown to men and known only to thee. It is in this Sacred Heart I shall derive those loving ardours which should consume mine; it is there I shall find strength, light, courage and true consolation. When sad, it will rejoice me: when languishing, it will animate me; when troubled and disquieted, it will encourage and uphold me. O Heart of Jesus, may my heart be the altar of thy love. May my tongue publish thy bounty, my mind meditate on thy perfections, my memory preserve for ever the precious remembrance of thy mercies. May all in me express my love for *thy* Heart, O Jesus, and may *my* heart be disposed to offer thee every sacrifice.

O Heart of Mary, the most amiable, compassionate and merciful after that of Jesus, present to his Divine Heart, my love, my resolutions, my consecration. It will be moved by my miseries; it will deliver me from them; and, O Blessed Mother, having been my protectress on earth, thou wilt be my Queen in heaven. Amen.

Memorare to the Sacred Heart

REMEMBER, O Jesus, meek and humble of Heart, that thou hast never yet beheld misery without being moved to mercy and compassion. Animated, therefore, with boundless confidence in thy unwearied love, I come to thee, sweet Saviour; burdened with miseries, I fly to thee: laden with sorrows, I throw myself upon thy compassionate mercy. Do not, O my Lord, my Father, cast me off, but graciously receive me into thy munificent Heart, nor suffer me ever to be separated therefrom.

Aid me, I beseech thee, in all my difficulties; bless me, O benign Heart of Jesus, in the name of the Father, and of the Son, and of the Holy Ghost; and let thy blessing descend upon all those for whom I desire to pray. Amen.

THE AGONIZING HEART OF JESUS.

The end of this devotion is :

1st. To pay a tribute of homage to the sufferings which the Heart of Jesus endured for the salvation of souls throughout the whole course of his life, and especially during his Sacred Passion.

2ndly. To obtain, through the merits of this long agony, the grace of a happy death for those who, in number about 80,000, die each day throughout the world; a number in nothing exaggerated—it is an ascertained fact.

PRAYER.

To be said daily on behalf of those who are in their agony, and of all those who are that day to die.

O clementissime Jesu, amator animarum, obsecro te per agoniam Cordis tui sanctissimi, et per dolores Matris tuæ immaculatæ, lava in sanguine tuo peccatores totius mundi, nunc positos in agonia, et hodie morituros. Amen.

O most merciful Jesus, fond lover of souls, purify, I implore thee by the agony of thine own most Sacred Heart, and by the grief of thy Immaculate Mother— purify in the laver of thy blood all sinners who are in their agony, and who are this day to die. Amen.

Cor Jesu in agonia factum, miserere morientium.

Agonizing Heart of Jesus, have pity on the dying!

PIOUS PRACTICE.

Offer up together with this prayer some of your daily actions to the agonizing Heart of Jesus, on behalf of those who are this day in their agony.

PRAY!

To-day *eighty thousand* souls are falling in the harvest of death; they are standing before the awful judgment-seat of God; they are entering on an eternity either of weal or woe; and, oh, of that number thousands perhaps are in the state of mortal sin!

PRAY THEN!

Christian, blessed with a heart to feel, it is the Heart of Jesus that asks this of you, that Heart which has loved you so dearly, that Heart which has suffered such anguish for you and for these poor souls. Pray then, and above all, for sinners now in their agony and *about to die*. All that is wanting to save them from hell is a *well-made confession* or a *perfect act of contrition*. Ask of the agonizing Heart of Jesus to grant them the one or the other of these two graces. Ask it without delay; *time, urges—to-morrow will be too late*.

Pray for the agonizing, they are your brethren in Jesus Christ, your relations perhaps, your friends, your benefactors.

Pray for the agonizing; and you will do what Jesus Christ did—you will save souls. How sublime a mission!

Pray for the agonizing. St. James says:—" He who causeth a sinner to be converted from the error of his way, shall save his soul from death, and shall cover a multitude of sins."

Pray for the agonizing. Prayers will one day be offered for you when you are in your agony. How sweet a consolation in this last terrible struggle!

Make " the devotion to the agonizing Heart of Jesus " known to those who are ignorant of it ; introduce it into your families and into your communities, and the Sacred Heart will heap blessings upon you.

If by the favour of your prayers you succeed in saving one soul each day, at the end of the year the number will amount to 365 ; at the end of ten years to 3,650. How rich this harvest! What a diadem for eternity !

ACT OF REPARATION.

O adorable Heart of Jesus, my soul is filled with grief to see the tokens of thy love received with so great contempt or indifference by so many men, and I am ashamed, and mourn that I myself have been numbered amongst those ungrateful ones. In reparation for all these insults I offer thee, O Divine Heart, the love of all just souls, the glowing ardours of the love of Mary and of Joseph. Deign, O most loving

Jesus, to accept with these the offering of all the affections of my heart and all its good desires. Amen.

O Good Shepherd, have pity on thy sheep, seek the lost, bring back the wanderers, heal the sick, strengthen the weak, preserve those whom thou hast led into thy fold. I pray especially for all who are to die to-day. O Lord, forgive thy people and let not thine inheritance fall into contempt. Save us, and we will never cease to sing thy praise.

DEVOTIONS FOR JULY.

The Precious Blood.

The Precious Blood of Jesus should be the object of our reverential, grateful love, since it has rescued us from eternal misery. Our loving Saviour first shed his Blood, as an infant, on the eighth day after his birth. Mute as a lamb, he opposed no resistance to the knife of Circumcision. The Angels wondered and our Lady wept on beholding the Blood of her most precious, holy child. In the Garden of Olives, the Sacred Blood bedewed the earth. In the cruel Scourging and Crowning with Thorns, streams of the same divine balsam flowed from the Body of Jesus; but oh, on the sad way to Calvary his footprints were marked with his Blood! He died to complete his sacrifice, shedding for us the very last drop of his most precious Blood. Let us therefore, love God, says St. John, because God first loved us. This Divine Blood placed in the scales of God's justice far outweighs our crimes. Its power has broken the very gates of hell and severed our chains. Let us therefore wash our wounds in it, and sign our foreheads with it, as with an indelible mark, which may protect us on the day of wrath.

THREE OFFERINGS OF THE PRECIOUS BLOOD.

In thanksgiving for the gifts and privileges with which the most holy Virgin Mary, Mother of God, was enriched, more especially for those which she received in her Immaculate Conception.

1. Eternal Father, in union with the most Holy and Immaculate Virgin, and in her name, and in union with, and in the name of all the blessed in heaven, and of all the elect upon earth, I offer thee the most Precious Blood of Jesus Christ, in thanksgiving for the gifts and privileges with which thou hast enriched Mary, as thy most obedient Daughter, particularly in her Immaculate Conception. I offer thee also this Precious Blood for the conversion of poor sinners, for the propagation and exaltation of thy holy Church, for the safety and prosperity of our chief pastor the Bishop of Rome, and according to his intentions.

Glory be to the Father, &c.

2. Eternal and Incarnate Word, in union with the most Holy and Immaculate Virgin, and in her name, and in union with, and in the name of all the blessed in heaven, and of all the elect upon earth, I offer thee thine own most Precious Blood, in thanksgiving for the gifts and privileges with which thou hast enriched Mary, as thy most loving Mother, particularly in her Immaculate Conception. I offer thee also this Precious Blood for the conversion of poor sinners, for the propagation and exaltation of thy holy Church, for the safety and prosperity of our chief pastor the Bishop of Rome, and according to his intentions.

Glory, &c.

3. Holy and Eternal Spirit, in union with the most Holy and Immaculate Virgin, and in her name,

and in union with, and in the name of all the blessed in heaven, and of all the elect upon earth. I offer thee the most Precious Blood of Jesus, in thanksgiving for the gifts and privileges with which thou hast enriched Mary. as thy most faithful Spouse, particularly in her Immaculate Conception. I offer thee also this Precious Blood for the conversion of poor sinners, for the propagation and exaltation of thy holy Church, for the safety and prosperity of our chief pastor the Bishop of Rome, and according to his intentions.

Glory. &c.

PRAYER TO THE MOST HOLY VIRGIN.

Mary, Mother of God, most Holy and Immaculate Virgin, by the love thou dost ever bear to God, by the gratitude thou hast towards him, for the manifold graces and favours with which thou wast enriched by him, particularly for the privilege granted to thee alone, of thy Immaculate Conception, and by the infinite merits of Jesus Christ, thy divine Son our Lord, we pray thee most earnestly to obtain for us a most perfect and constant devotion towards thyself. and a full trust that through thy most mighty intercession we shall receive all the graces which we ask ; certain henceforth of obtaining them from thy great goodness, with hearts overflowing with joy and thankfulness we venerate thee, repeating the salutation which the holy archangel Gabriel made to thee.

Hail Mary.

Prayer to Jesus Agonizing.

In honour of his Bloody Sweat.

REMEMBER, O my Divine Saviour, thine anguish and fear, when, being in an agony, thou didst pray the longer, and water the ground with thy Blood.

O tender Lamb, permit me with the deepest reverence and love, to gather up every drop of thy Precious Blood, and present it to thee for my own salvation and that of the dying. Deign to apply its merits to us, and, having purified us by its virtue from all our stains, bring us to the dwelling of eternal joy. O Mary, glorious Mother of Perpetual Succour, thou didst stand at the foot of the Cross of thy dying Son, receive the last sighs of those, who, after God, place all their hopes in thy maternal protection. Amen.

DEVOTIONS FOR AUGUST.

The Sacred Heart of Mary.

The Heart of Mary is the most perfect copy of the ever adorable Heart of Jesus. We have no easier means of gaining admission to our Saviour's Heart than through devotion to the Immaculate Heart of His most dear Mother. "She is an infinite treasure to man, which they that use, become the friends of God." (*Wisdom* vii. 14.)

The Heart of Mary is all love, all tenderness. How great soever our crimes may be, Mary stretches out her hand, opens her heart to receive us. And when *she* pleads, she must be heard.

O my Sovereign Lady, receive me into thy sacred Heart, pray for me, bless me, and obtain that I may have perpetual recourse to thy powerful protection.

Prayer of St. Gertrude

To the Sacred Heart of Mary.

O IMMACULATE Heart of Mary! I have nothing in myself to offer that is worthy of thee; but what thanks do I not owe thee for all the favours which thou hast obtained for me from the Sacred Heart of Jesus! what reparation ought I not to make to thee for all my tepidity in thy service! I desire to return thee love for love. I offer thee the Heart of thy beloved Son; it is a treasure of infinite price—receive with it my poor heart and I shall be for ever blessed. Amen.

PRAYER TO THE SACRED HEART OF THE BLESSED VIRGIN MARY.

O HEART of Mary, Mother of God, and our Mother also; O Heart most worthy of love, in which the most Holy Trinity is well pleased; O Heart worthy to be loved and honoured by angels and men, most similar to the Sacred Heart of Jesus, whose clear and perfect image thou reflectest: O Heart of Mary, seat of mercy, full of the bowels of compassion towards us wretched creatures; warm, I beseech thee, the cold hearts of thy children, and make them henceforth think of nothing, love nothing, desire nothing, but the Heart of Jesus Christ. Infuse into our breasts the love of thy virtues, and kindle in them the flame of thy unfailing charity. Watch over the Church, and continually defend it; be thou the sweet refuge of all faithful Christians; be thou their impregnable tower, wherein they may abide secure against the assaults of the enemy. Through thee, O Heart of Mary, may we have access to thy Son, through thee may we obtain all graces necessary to our eternal salvation

Assist us in all straits and necessities, comfort us when sorrowful, strengthen us when tempted, be thou our refuge in persecution, our succour in danger; but especially at the hour of death, in our last awful agony, when the powers of hell assail us that they may take away our souls—in that terrible day, and at that tremendous hour, on which our eternity depends, then, O most compassionate Virgin, make thy servants feel the goodness of thy maternal Heart; then be mindful, we beseech thee, of that power which the Saviour of the world, who was born of thee, hath given to thee. Grant us a most safe retreat in the very fountain of mercy, that one day we may be made worthy to glorify with thee in the heavens, the most Sacred Heart of thy dear Son, for ever and ever. Amen.

May the Divine Heart of Jesus and the Immaculate Heart of Mary be always, and in all places, acknowledged, praised, blessed, loved, and faithfully honoured and glorified. Amen.

Act of Reparation

To the Sacred Heart of Mary.

O HEART of Mary, I honour thee as the Heart most pleasing to our Lord, and most intimately united to his. I love thee as the Heart of the best of Mothers, and I rejoice in thy glorious prerogatives. Prostrate before thee, O Heart of Mary, I make thee this humble act of reparation for all the outrages which thou hast received from me and from all mankind. I humbly confess that I have been guilty of the greatest ingratitude towards thee : but seeing that, through thee, the Divine mercy has so often had regard unto me, I venture, even yet, to hope that thou wilt not abandon me. In this sweet confidence I am animated by a most earnest desire to be more faithful and more devoted to thee. I pray thee to accept all the good that henceforth I am resolved to do, to present it to thy dear Son Jesus, so that, through thee, my most loving Saviour may pour down his benedictions more and more on me, and on all who are dear unto me. Amen.

O Holy Virgin ! thou art my good Mother, and by excellence the Mother of pure love. Thou hast obtained for me many favours during life ; beg for me one more which will crown all the rest : that is, to love my God—to love him purely—to love him ardently—to love him constantly as long as I shall live on earth—that I may have the happiness to love him eternally with thee in heaven. Amen.

DEVOTIONS FOR SEPTEMBER.

The Dolours of the Blessed Virgin Mary.

Mary became our Mother amidst unutterable anguish and pain. She was solemnly declared our Mother when standing at the foot of the Cross, whilst the Blood flowed in streams from the wounds of her dying Jesus. We are told that the beloved disciple, St. John, yearning for a vision of his dear Mother after her Assumption into heaven, the favour was granted him. Whilst he looked upon her in an ecstacy of love, he heard her ask her Divine Son what particular graces he would grant to those who honour her dolours. "I will give them," replied our Lord, "the grace of sincere contrition before death; I will be with them in their tribulations, and especially at the hour of death: I will engrave on their hearts the memory of my passion, and I will reward them in heaven for having sympathised in my sufferings: I will commit the care of their souls in a special manner to thee, my Mother, that thou mayest dispose of them according to the tenderness of thy maternal heart."

Rosary or Chaplet
Of the Seven Dolours.

1. The Prophecy of Simeon. *One Our Father and seven Hail Marys.*

2. The Flight into Egypt. *One Our Father and seven Hail Marys.*

3. The Loss of Jesus for three days. *One Our Father and seven Hail Marys.*

4. Mary meeting Jesus carrying his Cross. *One Our Father and seven Hail Marys.*

5. Mary standing beneath the Cross on Calvary. *One Our Father and seven Hail Marys.*

6. Mary receiving on her lap the Sacred Body of Jesus taken down from the cross. *One Our Father and seven Hail Marys.*

7. Mary witnessing the burial of the Sacred Body of her Son. *One Our Father and seven Hail Marys.*

In honour of the tears shed by our Lady during these dolours. *Three Hail Marys.*

V. Pray for us, O most sorrowful Virgin.

R. That we may be made worthy of the promises of Christ.

LET US PRAY.

Grant, we beseech thee, O Lord Jesus Christ, that the Blessed Virgin Mary, thy Mother, may intercede for us with thy clemency now and at the hour of our death, who in the hour of thy Passion was pierced in her most holy soul by the sword of sorrow; grant this, O Jesus Christ, Saviour of the world, who, with the Father and the Holy Ghost, liveth and reigneth, world without end. Amen.

Act of Consecration

To the Compassionate Heart of Mary.

O MARY, Immaculate Virgin, Mother of God and our Mother. I consecrate myself to thee and lovingly offer thee, my body and my soul, my life and my death. O Queen of Martyrs, I offer thee my sufferings and my sorrows. O most compassionate Virgin, by the Agonizing Heart of Jesus thy Son, deign to take pity on the afflictions of the Holy Church, our Mother; remember our Sovereign Pontiff; beg mercy for our dear country; mercy for the faithful of this diocese; mercy for all the members of our families, for our benefactors, our friends, and our enemies; mercy for all sinners, especially for all the dying. O most afflicted of Mothers, do not reject the sincere homage of our compassion and sorrow, pray for us now, and at the hour of our death. Amen.

PRAYER TO THE MOTHER OF DOLOURS FOR LAST HOUR.

O MOTHER of Dolours! by the anguish and love with which you stood beneath the Cross of Jesus, stand by me in my last agony. To your maternal heart I commend the last hours of my life, offer these hours to the Eternal Father in union with the agony of our dearest Lord. Offer frequently, in atonement for my sins, the Precious Blood of Jesus which mingled with your tears on Calvary to obtain for me the grace to receive Holy Communion immediately before my death, and to breathe forth my soul in the actual presence of Jesus in the Blessed Sacrament; and O dearest Mother, when the moment of my death has at length arrived, present me as your child to Jesus—say to him in my behalf—" Son, forgive her, for she knew not what she did. Receive her this day into thy Kingdom!" Amen.

DEVOTIONS FOR OCTOBER.

The Holy Angels.

The life of man on earth is a warfare. He has to fight against temptations from within and temptations from without. We must combat against the devils, powerful in might, cruel in rage, countless in number. On our victory depends our eternal fate. Whence look for help in such dangers? God has provided it for us. "He hath given his Angels charge of thee, to keep thee in all thy ways." (*Ps.* xc. 11.) The Angels obtain for us victory over our passions, they invite us to penance, they support us in the way of virtue, they console us in sufferings, quiet our fears, and impart to us holy joy and divine peace. Souls devoted to the Angels during life, shall receive extraordinary helps from them at the hour of death. After death, the Angels present our souls before the bar of divine justice and most zealously plead our cause. If heaven be awarded us, transported with joy, they accompany us thither; if condemned to Purgatory, they visit us there and render to us in its flames very great consolation. Let us then in all spiritual and corporal dangers, recur to the powerful patronage of the Holy Angels whom the Lord has appointed for our defence, through a marvellous excess of love.

Memorare.

REMEMBER, O Holy Angels, that Jesus, the Eternal Truth, assures us, you " rejoice more at the conversion of one sinner, than at the perseverance of many just." Encouraged thereby, I, the least of creatures, humbly entreat you to receive me as your servant, and make me unto you a cause of true joy. Do not, O blessed spirits, reject my petition, but graciously hear and grant it. Amen.

PRAYER TO THE GUARDIAN ANGEL.

O MOST faithful companion, whom God has appointed to watch over me, my guide and protector, ever at my side, what thanks can I offer thee for thy love, thy constancy, and thy innumerable benefits? Thou watchest over me in sleep: thou consolest me in sorrow; thou raisest me when I fall; thou wardest off danger; thou preparest me for the future: thou withdrawest me from sin; thou urgest me to good, and movest me to do penance, and reconcilest me with my God. Already, perhaps, I should have been thrust into hell, unless thou by thy prayers hadst averted from me the dreadful wrath of God. Desert me not, then, I beseech thee: encourage me in adversity; restrain me in prosperity; protect me in dangers: and assist me in temptations, lest at any time I yield to them. Offer to the Divine Majesty all my prayers and sighs and works, and obtain for me the grace to die in the friendship of God, and so to enter into life eternal. Amen.

O most holy Angel of God, appointed by him to be my guardian, I give thee thanks for all the benefits which thou hast ever bestowed on me in body and in soul. I praise and glorify thee that thou dost condescend to assist me, miserable and worthless as I am, with such patient fidelity, and to defend me against all the assaults of my enemies. Blessed be the hour in which thou wast assigned me for my guardian, my defender, and my patron. Blessed be all thy love to me, and all thy care for me, wherewith thou dost unwearyingly further my salvation. In acknowledgment of and return for all thy loving ministries to me from my youth, I offer thee the infinitely precious and noble Heart of Jesus, full and overflowing with all blessedness: beseeching thee to forgive me for having so often striven against thy holy inspirations, and saddened thee my nearest, dearest friend, firmly purposing to obey thee henceforward, and most faithfully to serve my God. Amen. (*St. Gertrude.*)

TO ST. MICHAEL ARCHANGEL.

MICHAEL, glorious prince, chief and champion of the heavenly host, guardian of the souls of men, conqueror of the rebel angels, steward of the palace of God, our worthy captain under Jesus Christ, endowed with superhuman excellence and virtue; vouchsafe to free us from every evil, who with full confidence have recourse to thee; and by thy powerful protection enable us to make progress every day in the faithful service of our God.

V. Pray for us, most blessed Michael, Prince of the Church of Jesus Christ.

R. That we may be made worthy of his promises.

LET US PRAY.

Almighty and eternal God, who in thine own marvellous goodness and pity didst, for the common salvation of man, choose the glorious Archangel Michael to be the Prince of thy Church; make us worthy, we pray thee, to be delivered by his beneficent protection from all our enemies, that at the hour of our death no one of them may approach to harm us, and that by the same Archangel Michael we may be introduced into the presence of thy high and heavenly Majesty. Amen.

PRAYER TO ST. GABRIEL.

O GABRIEL, might of God, who didst announce to the Virgin Mary the incarnation of the only Son of God, and in the garden didst console and strengthen Christ oppressed with fear and sorrow; I praise thee, I worship thee, O chosen spirit, and humbly pray thee to be my advocate with Jesus Christ my Saviour, and with Mary, his blessed Virgin Mother; in all my trials do thou assist me, lest overcome by temptation I offend my God and Sovereign Good. Amen.

PRAYER TO ST. RAPHAEL.

O HEAVENLY physician and faithful companion St. Raphael, who didst restore sight to the elder Tobias, and guide the younger in his long journey and preserve him in safety; be thou the physician of my soul and body, disperse the dark clouds of ignorance, defend me from the dangers of

my earthly pilgrimage, and lead me to that heavenly
country where, with thee, I may gaze for ever on
the face of God. Amen.

DEVOTIONS FOR NOVEMBER.

The Holy Souls in Purgatory.

The **existence** of Purgatory is defined by the Church as an
Article of Faith. The souls in Purgatory always sigh after the
possession of God; their sufferings are excessive. St. Thomas
asserts, that, one quarter of an hour's suffering in Purgatory is
more insupportable than the united pangs of all the martyrs.

Who are those who suffer in Purgatory? . . . They are the
members of Jesus Christ; they are perhaps our parents or our
best friends. What do they suffer? . . . Of this, we can form
no conception—but, we know for certain that we can procure for
them the greatest, the most precious of comforts, the clear vision
and entire possession of God. The ordinary means of relieving the
dead are these: Prayer, Fasting, and Alms-deeds. There is no
prayer comparable to the oblation of the Holy Sacrifice of the
Mass—it affords the greatest help to those for whom it is offered.

St. Austin praised his deceased mother in these words: "She
thought not of having her body sumptuously buried or embalmed,
but she desired that her memory might be made at God's altar."

Another most powerful means of assisting the souls in Purgatory,
is to gain Indulgences for them. We may also offer for their relief
all our good acts, thoughts, words, and sufferings, inasmuch as they
are *satisfactory*, whilst we remain free to apply the same works, as
they are *impetratory*, to obtain anything we desire or pray for.

Offering of the Passion of Christ

For the Faithful Departed.

LOOK down, O Father of compassion, from thy
high and holy seat upon the hapless souls
detained in Purgatory. Look upon all the pains
and torments wherewith they are so grievously
chastised: regard now the plaintive groans and
tears which they pour forth unto thee; and be

merciful unto their sins. Remember, O most compassionate Father, all the sufferings which thy Son hath endured for them; remember his Precious Blood shed in such abundance for them; call to mind the most bitter death which he suffered for them, and have mercy on them. For all the sins they have ever committed against thee, I offer thee the most holy life and conversation of thy most beloved Son; for all their negligences, I offer thee his most fervent desires towards thee: for all their omissions, I offer thee the great abundance of his merits; for their every insult and wrong to thee, I offer thee the sweet submission with which he honoured thee. Finally, for all the chastisements which they have ever incurred, I offer thee all the mortifications, fastings, watchings, the labours and afflictions, wounds and stripes, passion and death, which he endured in such spotless innocence and with such loving eagerness; beseeching thee now to suffer thy anger to be appeased towards them, and to lead them forth into everlasting joy. Amen.

BEADS OF THE DEAD.

The Forty small Beads of which this Chaplet is composed, are in honour of the Forty Hours our Blessed Lord spent in the Sepulchre.

On the Cross, say

The De Profundis, or a Pater and Ave.

On the Large Beads.

Eternal rest grant to them, O Lord,
And let perpetual light shine upon them.

Act of Faith. My God, I believe in thee, because thou art Truth itself.

Act of Hope. My God, I hope in thee, because thou art infinitely good.

Act of Charity. My God, I love thee with my whole heart and above all things, because thou art infinitely perfect, and for thy sake, I love my neighbour as myself.

On the Small Beads.

Sweet Heart of Mary, be my Salvation.

Conclude with a Pater and Ave.

Large Indulgences may be gained each time above Rosary is recited.

SUPPLICATION TO THE MOST HOLY MARY.

TO thee, O most holy Virgin Mary, my Mother I turn in supplication, and through that sword which pierced thy heart, when thou didst behold thy beloved Son Jesus Christ bow down his head and give up the ghost. I pray and implore thee, with the greatest confidence, to succour the poor holy souls in Purgatory, and particularly those of which an especial commemoration has been made. O Mother of Sorrows, O Queen of Martyrs, for the love of Jesus, who died for us upon the Cross, do thou with thy powerful prayers give succour also unto us, who are in danger not only of falling into Purgatory, but even of losing ourselves for ever. O Mary, our dear Mother, Mother of grace, Mother of mercy, have pity upon us.

Prayer for a Happy Death.

By St. Vincent Ferrer, O.P.

O MOST dear and adorable Jesus! who desirest that no one should perish, but was crucified for the redemption of mankind, I beseech thee by thy dolorous passion, by thy dreadful agony, by thy countless wounds, by the effusion of thy precious blood, by the recommendation of thy sacred soul, into the hands of thy Eternal Father, and by thy ignominious death on the Altar of the Cross, that thou wilt graciously vouchsafe to me at my last hour a sincere contrition, a true faith, an ardent hope, a perfect charity, and then to receive me into the bosom of thy mercy. Amen.

INDULGENCED ASPIRATIONS.

My Jesus Mercy.—100 *days.*

Divine Heart of Jesus, convert sinners, save the dying, deliver the Holy Souls in Purgatory.—300 *days.* (*Pius X., 13th July,* 1906.)

DEVOTIONS FOR DECEMBER.

Advent. Christmas.

Et Verbum caro factum est: " *The Word was made Flesh.*"

The Incarnation is the fundamental article of the Christian religion. Above all other mysteries, it challenges our most profound homage and constant devotion. It is the joy of joys to the whole earth. Let us draw near to Bethlehem to study the mystery of the sacred Infancy. We shall see more at Bethlehem than we can understand, and even what we cannot understand will fill us full of love, and it is love which makes us wise unto salvation. See the divine Infant laid in the manger. He assumes all the weakness of a tender infant—he offers himself to his Eternal Father to bear unceasingly during his whole life sorrow and affliction, hunger and fatigue, contempt and excess of pain—to be in every respect a victim—a lamb prepared for sacrifice.

Let us next fix our eyes upon the wonderful tenderness of the Heart of our Infant Saviour, remembering all the while, that if he be the most affectionate being that ever trod his own earth, it is because he is God. Oh, how beautiful and how adorable was the holy Child as he "grew in wisdom and in age and in grace before God and man." It is little enough that the Gospel tells us of his exterior, but enough is known to show that the majesty of a sweet and winning love shone forth in all his actions. The prophets foretold that he should be "beautiful exceedingly above the sons of men:" and when in very deed he came on earth, he drew all hearts to him by the blandness and suavity of his every look and gesture. He passed through the years of infancy for the very purpose of winning us the more surely to himself. "O sweet Babe of Bethlehem, we consecrate ourselves to thee. When shall we kneel before thy face? When shall we see thee smile—smile on us our welcome into heaven, smile on us with that smile which will sit upon thy lips as our own glory and possession for evermore." Amen.

Rorate Cœli.

(ADVENT.)

RORATE cœli desuper, et nubes pluant Justum.

Ne irascaris, Domine, et ne ultra memineris iniquitatis : ecce, civitas Sancti facta est deserta : Sion deserta facta est : Jerusalem desolata est : domus sanctificationis

DROP down dew, ye heavens, from above. and let the clouds rain down the Just One.

Be not very angry, O Lord, and remember no longer our iniquity; behold, the city of the Holy One is become deserted : Sion is become a desert : Jerusalem is desolate; the

tuæ et gloriæ tuæ, ubi, laudaverunt te patres nostri.

Rorate, &c.

Peccavimus, et facti sumus tamquam immundi nos: et cecidimus quasi folium universi, et iniquitates nostræ quasi ventus abstulerunt nos: abscondisti faciem tuam a nobis, et allisisti nos in manu iniquitatis nostræ.

Rorate, &c.

Vide Domine, afflictionem populi tui, et mitte quem missurus es: emitte Agnum dominatorem terræ, de Petra deserti, ad montem filiæ Sion; ut auferat ipse jugum captivitatis nostræ.

Rorate, &c.

Consolamini, consolamini, popule meus: cito veniet salus tua: quare mœrore consumeris? quia innovavit te dolor: salva-

house of thy sanctification and of thy glory, where our fathers praised thee.

We have sinned, and are become as unclean: and we have all fallen as a leaf, and our iniquities like the wind have carried us away: thou hast hidden thy face from us, and hast crushed us in the hand of our iniquity.

Behold, O Lord, the affliction of thy people, and send him whom thou wilt send: send forth the Lamb, the ruler of the earth, from Petra of the desert, to the mount of the daughter of Sion: that he may take away the yoke of our captivity.

Be comforted, be comforted, my people: thy salvation cometh quickly: why with grief art thou consumed? for

bo te : noli timere : ego enim sum Dominus Deus tuus, Sanctus Israel, Redemptor tuus.

Rorate, &c.

sorrow hath stricken thee I will save thee, fear not ; for I am the Lord thy God, the Holy One of Israel, thy Redeemer.

Act of Offering to the Most Holy Mary.

O VIRGIN and Mother, O sacred temple of the Divinity, O marvel of heaven and earth, my great Mother Mary, it is but just that, whilst thou hast brought forth for us an Infant God, we should venerate in thee the most exalted dignity of the Mother of God, and should consecrate to so worthy a Mother all the homage of our whole being. I therefore offer myself and give myself up wholly unto thee this day, and desire with a resolute will to serve and love thy holy Child Jesus, my Saviour and my God. I know that in doing so I shall give thee pleasure, and the homage which I pay to the Son will be also a homage paid unto the Mother.

Accept, then, O most loving Mother, this my offering of love, which, that it may be still more acceptable to thee, I present to thee by the hands of the Infant Jesus. Ah ! by those swathing bands in which thou didst wrap him in the manger, bind my will so that I may never retract the offering which I have made of myself this day to thee, and to thy Holy Infant ; place me under thy most holy mantle, guard me, help me, and defend me to the last moment of my life. Amen.

Prayer to the Infant Jesus.

ALL hail! most lovely, most holy, most amiable and most loving Infant Jesus, King of my soul. O most beautiful above the children of men, come into my heart; give me the true spirit of thy holy nativity—the spirit of humility, silence, docility, meekness, true and ardent charity. Give me grace daily to advance in devotion to thy blessed infancy, and faithfully to persevere in my good purposes. Bless me, divine Infant, as thou didst bless the humble Shepherds, watching over their flocks. May my only treasure be henceforth thy graces; my only pleasure, thy service and love, and my only desire, the accomplishment of thy most holy will. Amen.

Offerings to the Most Holy Infant.

O MY most adorable Infant Jesus, my King, my Father, and my Lord, I dedicate myself to thee this day, giving up to thee my whole being, my soul, my body, my will, the goods which thou hast given me, and in short, all that belongs to me; I beseech thee to take possession and absolute dominion of all, as I desire no longer to live but in thee, nor to possess anything in the world, except it be according to thy will, permission, and divine appointment, so that henceforth I must look upon myself simply as an instrument in thy hands, O most holy Infant Jesus, to do whatsoever thou desirest of me, with a simple heart.

I beg these graces of thee, through the intercession of the most holy Virgin Mother and my advocate, and of my protector, St. Joseph. Amen.

Consecration to the Infant Jesus.

SWEET Infant Jesus, I give thee my soul, fill it with thy divine love.

Holy Infant Jesus, I give thee my heart, renovate it in thy crib.

Divine Infant Jesus, I give thee my crosses and pains, through thee alone they will merit.

Amiable Infant Jesus, I give thee my mouth; may it bless thee in time and in eternity.

Adorable Infant Jesus, I give thee my thoughts, that thou mayest be the sole object of them.

Jesus, Infant King, I give thee my eyes which desire to behold thee alone.

Jesus, Infant Creator, I give thee my hands; may they henceforth be employed in thy service alone.

Jesus, Infant Saviour, I give thee my feet, that they may conduct me to thee alone.

Jesus, Infant Redeemer, I give thee my will; may thine in exchange be the sole rule of my conduct.

Jesus, Infant God, my Lord and my all, my joy and my happiness, my life and my strength, I give myself entirely to thee. Thou shalt be mine for ever.

Novenas.

NOVENA FOR THE FEAST OF THE IMMACULATE CONCEPTION.

O PURE and Immaculate Virgin, who wert dignified by thy Divine Son with that happy
privilege of exemption from sin, which the God of
all sanctity alone could claim, I commemorate, with
the liveliest gratitude towards thy Divine Benefactor,
that happy moment in which thou didst begin to
live to grace. I return thanks to Him, who in
the instant of thy Immaculate Conception, began
to do *great things* to thee. (*Luke* i. 49.) O incorruptible Ark, which was prepared to enclose the true
Manna descended from heaven! O sanctuary of the
Incarnate Word! thou art among the children of
Adam like the lily among thorns—thou art the
most privileged of all creatures, the parent of all
virgins, the most perfect image of thy Divine
Creator. Thou didst not partake of that general
misery, in those fatal evils which overwhelmed mankind. Ah! since thou wert chosen among all
creatures to bring forth the Saviour of men, deign
to distil on me some drops of that heavenly dew of
grace with which thou wert replenished. Preserve
me by thy powerful intercession, from yielding to
those perverse inclinations which never disturbed the
tranquillity of thy pure soul. Repress my fatal pro-
pensity to evil, and obtain for me such courage and

perseverance in surmounting my passions, such fervour and resolution in the practice of self-denial and penance, that I may recover the treasure of innocence I have so often forfeited, and thus attain to that mansion of rest, where nothing defiled can gain admittance. Amen.

NOVENA FOR THE FEAST OF THE NATIVITY OF OUR LORD.

O SON of the living God, *O Desired of all nations* (*Agg.* ii. 8), the Expectation, the Saviour of the world, do not permit that this glorious solemnity, which transported the angels with joy, and satisfied the longing desires of all the just, should pass without recalling to my mind the greatness of thy mercy, and the excess of that love which brought thee on earth. *O Word made flesh and dwelling among us* (*St. John* i. 14), O infinite Goodness, who wouldst rather save than condemn us; Eternal Greatness, who wouldst teach us to practise virtue by thy own example, prostrate at thy crib, there *will I dwell, for I have chosen it* (*Ps.* cxxxi. 14), or rather, O most *beautiful above the sons of men* (*Ps.* xliv. 3), I present thee my heart, that thou mayest prepare it to become the crib of thy nativity. I offer thee my memory, that it may dwell on the wonders of love, which the manger of Bethlehem exhibits to the world. I offer thee my will, that the view of my Lord and Master become subject to his creatures, may totally destroy its perverse inclinations

O' drop down dew, ye heavens, from above, and let the clouds rain the Just One; let the earth be opened and bud forth a Saviour. (*Isa.* xlv. 8.) *O brightness of eternal light* (*Wisd.* vii. 26), come and show us the vanity of all that the world calls great. Adorable Infant, Sacred Babe of Bethlehem, in whose very name thy saints have found inexpressible sweetness. I wish I could unite in my heart the faith of the ancient patriarchs; the desires of the just who preceded thy coming; the purity of the angels who longed to announce thy birth; the tender love, the ineffable transports, which thy infant humanity has since excited in thy saints: that thus I may invite thee with more fervour, and receive thee with less indignity into the cold, wretched mansion of my heart. But, my sovereign Lord, though the dispositions of thy angels and saints are far beyond my reach, yet I have a resource of which thou wilt not forbid me to profit. I unite my heart to thine. O adorable Treasure of all thy creatures; I desire to become thy sanctuary, in union with the eternal charity with which thou didst long to be born, for man's redemption. I unite my heart to that of thy Sacred Mother, and desire to receive thee with the transports of love with which she sighed to behold thee. O most pure Mother of God, deign to prepare the dwelling of thy Divine Infant in my heart —lay thy Sacred Babe therein; but I entreat of thee, by the anguish thou didst endure from the cold and misery to which thou wert obliged to expose him at his birth, that his tears may soften my heart. his love inflame it, and his mercy adorn it with a share in the perfect dispositions of thy pure soul. Amen.

NOVENA IN HONOUR OF THE NAME OF JESUS.

O MERCIFUL Jesus, who didst in thy early infancy commence thy office of Saviour, by shedding thy precious blood, and assuming for us that name which is above all names; we thank thee for such proofs of thy infinite love; we venerate thy sacred name, in union with the profound respect of the angel who first announced it to the earth, and unite our affections to the sentiments of tender devotion which the adorable name of Jesus has in all ages enkindled in the hearts of thy servants. Animated with a firm faith in thy unerring word, and penetrated with confidence in thy mercy, we now most humbly remind thee of the promise thou hast made, that when two or three should assemble in thy name, thou thyself wouldst be in the midst of them. Come, then, into the midst of us, most amiable Jesus! for it is in thy Sacred Name we are here assembled. Come into our hearts, that thy Holy Spirit may pray in and by us; and mercifully grant us, through that adorable Name which is the joy of heaven, the terror of hell, the consolation of the afflicted, and the solid ground of our unlimited confidence, all the petitions we make in this Novena.

Oh! Blessed Mother of our Redeemer! who didst

participate so sensibly in the sufferings of thy dear Son, when he shed his Sacred Blood, and assumed for us the Name of Jesus; obtain for us, through that adorable Name, the favours we petition in this Novena. Beg also, that the most ardent love may imprint on our hearts that Sacred Name, that it may be always in our minds, and frequently on our lips; that it may be our defence in temptations, and our refuge in danger, during our lives, and our consolation and support in the hour of death. Amen.

NOVENA IN HONOUR OF THE EPIPHANY.

O ADORABLE Infant, infuse into our hearts the holy dispositions of the three kings, that, animated with a lively faith, we may seek thee as faithfully and perseveringly as they did. Infant God! Infant King! Adorable Emmanuel! God with us! permit us to adore thee. May our tribute of praise ascend as the sweet odour of *incense* to thy throne above. We offer thee the affection of our hearts as *gold*, that will be purified by the application of thy merits. We offer thee our senses, that they may be instrumental to thy glory, and that by the *myrrh* of mortification whatever tends not to that end, may be retrenched. Adorable Infant, deign to cast on us one look of mercy; graciously receive our offering; forgive us our sins; clothe us with thy merits; inflame our hearts with thy holy love; grant that we may serve thee faithfully during life, and that we may reign with thee in eternal glory. Amen.

TO ST. RAYMUND OF PENNAFORT, C., O.P.

O GOD, who didst choose the Blessed Raymund for a glorious minister of the sacrament of penance, and didst guide him wonderfully across the waves of the sea, grant that we, through his intercession, may bring forth worthy fruits of penance, and at length reach the haven of salvation. Through Christ our Lord. Amen.

NOVENA TO ST. BRIGID.

O GLORIOUS St. Brigid, Mother of the Churches of Erin, patroness of our missionary race, wherever their lot may be cast! be thou our guide in the paths of virtue, protect us amid temptation, shield us from danger. Preserve to us the heritage of chastity and temperance; keep ever brightly burning on the altar of our hearts the sacred fire of Faith, Charity, and Hope, that thus we may emulate the ancient piety of Ireland's children, and the Church of Erin may shine with peerless glory as of old. Thou wert styled by our fathers " *The Mary of Erin*," secure for us by thy prayers the all-powerful protection of the Blessed Virgin, that we may be numbered here among her most fervent clients, and may hereafter merit a place together with Thee and the countless Saints of Ireland in the ranks of her triumphant children in paradise. Amen.

NOVENA TO THE HOLY FAMILY.

O MOST loving Jesus, who through thy ineffable virtues and the example of thy domestic life didst sanctify on earth the family chosen by thee, graciously look down on this our family which throws itself at thy feet and implores thy grace. Remember that this family is thy property, because it has given and consecrated itself to thy love and service. Graciously protect it, save it from dangers, lend it thy assistance in tribulation and bestow on it strength to persevere in the imitation of thy Holy Family, so that after having faithfully continued in obedience and love during the time of its earthly pilgrimage, it may one day sing thy praise for ever in heaven.

O Mary, most sweet Mother, we implore thy protection, trusting with confidence that thy divine Son will hear thy requests.

And thou also, most glorious Patriarch, Saint Joseph, come to our assistance with thy mighty protection, place our resolutions in the hands of Mary, that she may present them to Jesus Christ.

NOVENA FOR THE PURIFICATION OF THE B.V.M.

O ETERNAL God, whose adorable Majesty was so imperfectly honoured by the sacrifices of the Old Law, we rejoice from the bottom of our hearts, in the homage thou didst receive from thy beloved Son, on his presentation in the Temple. Sacrifices and sin-offerings had ceased to please thee; when behold! he came, in whom, from eternity, thou wert

well pleased, to offer thee that victim of adoration,
which thy infinite Majesty expected—that sacrifice
of expiation, which thy justice required—that victim
of thanksgiving, which thy benefits deserved—and
that host of impetration to which thy mercy had
reserved the most precious favours. O most happy
Virgin! from whom the Almighty first received a
victim worthy of himself, let us not be excluded
from a share in the graces, which through thee have
been granted to the world. Give us thyself, thy
Divine Infant, in each of our communions, as thou
didst to holy Simeon. Obtain that, like him, a
lively faith may discover to us, our Lord and salvation, in the mystery of his humiliation; that our
hearts may love him therein ardently, and that
frequent union with Jesus, in the sacrament of his
infinite goodness, may so detach us from the world,
that we may never cease to sigh after that kingdom
of peace, where we shall never sin, and never cease to
love. Amen.

NOVENA IN HONOUR OF ST. CATHERINE DE RICCI.

O PRIVILEGED Virgin, most blessed St.
Catherine de Ricci, I rejoice from my heart in
thy bliss, the exceeding great reward of thy crucified
life on earth. Thou didst early burst every human
tie and generously offer the morning of thy life to
God. Oh, let not thy bright example be lost on
me; pray that now, at least, I may begin to love my

God—that his cross may become my delight; his sufferings, the study of my life ; and intimate union with him, the only joy of my soul. O victim of charity, take pity on my miseries, beg for me sincere sorrow for my past sins, and full remission of them. Obtain that by constant meditation on the bitter Passion of my Redeemer, I may find as thou didst, in the wounded Heart of Jesus, an asylum of security and a haven of peace and rest. Amen.

The Litany of St. Thomas of Aquin.

O THOU, the Most High, *have mercy on us.*
    Mighty One of Jacob, *have mercy on us.*
Divine Spirit, *have mercy on us.*
Great Triune God, *have mercy on us.*
Glorious Mother of the King of kings,
Saint Thomas of Aquin,
Worthy child of the Queen of Virgins,
Aquinas most chaste,
Aquinas most patient,
Prodigy of science,
Silently eloquent,
Reproach of the ambitious,
Lover of that life which is hidden with Christ in
    God,
Fragrant flower in the parterre of St. Dominic.
Glory of Friars Preachers,
Illumined from on high,
Angel of the Schools,
Oracle of the Church,

Pray for us.

Incomparable scribe of the Man-God,
Satiated with the odour of his perfumes,
Perfect in the school of his cross,
Intoxicated with the strong wine of his charity,
Glittering gem in the cabinet of the Lord,
Model of perfect obedience,
Endowed with the true spirit of holy poverty,
    Lamb of God, &c., *three times.*

ANT.—Oh, how beautiful is the chaste generation with glory, for the memory thereof is immortal, because it is known with God and man, and it triumpheth crowned for ever.

V. Oh! what have I in heaven, or what do I desire on earth?

R. Thou art the God of my heart, and my portion for ever.

PRAYER.

O God, who hast ordained that blessed Thomas should enlighten thy Church, grant that through his prayers we may practise what he taught, through Christ our Lord. Amen.

A NOVENA TO ST. PATRICK.

O BLESSED Apostle of Ireland! glorious St. Patrick! who didst become my Father and Benefactor long before my birth, receive my prayers and accept the sentiments of gratitude and veneration with which my heart is filled towards thee.

Pray for us.

Thou wert the channel of the greatest graces to me; deign then to become also the channel of my grateful thanksgivings to God for having granted me, through thee, that precious gift of faith, which is dearer than life. O most blessed Father, and patron of my country! do not, I beseech thee, despise my weakness. Remember, that the cries of little children were the mysterious invitation thou didst receive to come among us. Listen, then, to my most humble supplications; I unite them to the praises and blessings which will ever follow thy name and thy memory throughout the Irish Church; I unite them to the prayers of the multitude of my ancestors, who now enjoy eternal bliss, and owe their salvation, under God, to thy zeal and charity. They will eternally share thy glory, because they listened to thy word and followed thy example. Ah! since I am descended from saints, may I blush to differ from them; may I begin from this moment to love God with all my heart, and serve him with all my strength. For this end I most humbly beg thy blessing, O great St. Patrick! and thy particular intercession, for obtaining whatever grace thou seest to be most necessary for me, and also the particular intentions of this Novena. (*Name them.*)

O charitable Shepherd of the Irish Flock! who wouldst have laid down a thousand lives to save one soul, take my soul, and the souls of all Christians under thy special care, and preserve us from the dreadful misfortune of sin. Thy zealous preaching provided us the blessing of religious instructions which we now enjoy; obtain that none of us may receive them in vain. Thou didst teach our ancestors how to connect the pursuit of virtue with that of science; deign also to take my studies under thy protection, and to obtain for me the grace to sanctify them by a pure motive of pleasing God and my superiors. I most humbly recommend to thee this country, which was so dear to thee while on earth. Protect it still; and above all, obtain for its pastors, principally for those who instruct us, the grace to walk in thy footsteps, that they may share in thy eternal bliss.

NOVENA TO ST. JOSEPH.

O GLORIOUS Patriarch, Virgin Spouse of the Virgin Mother of God, faithful guardian of the Word Incarnate, I consecrate myself to thee, I place all my concerns under thy care and protection. Accept me as thy child; take charge of my salvation; watch over me day and night; preserve me from the occasions of sin; obtain for me purity of body and soul, the spirit of prayer, the spirit of humility and of self-denial.

Obtain for me a burning love for Jesus in the Blessed Sacrament, a sweet and tender love for Mary my Mother, and also the particular favours I ask in this Novena. O great St. Joseph, be with me living, be with me dying, and obtain for me a

favourable judgment from Jesus, thy loving care
and my most merciful Saviour.   Amen.

NOVENA IN HONOUR OF THE ANNUNCIATION.

O ADMIRABLE Virgin, the most exalted, yet the
most humble among all creatures, I salute thee
in union with the respect and veneration of the angel
who was deputed from heaven to *hail* thee *full
of grace,* and to choose thee for the Mother and
Sanctuary of the Author of grace.   O most happy
Mother, most pure Virgin, most favoured among all
women, shall not I join with all generations in
calling thee blessed?   Why cannot I share in
the profound feelings of humiliation which filled
thy soul, even in the moment of thy glorious
exaltation?   O most humble, but most privileged
"handmaid of the Lord," since thou hast found
grace before God, obtain for me that invaluable
treasure, and fidelity to practise all that it requires.
Since thou hast never felt the anguish which springs
from sin, and wert never degraded by a single imperfection, thou hast no cause to fear those tremendous
judgments which should make me tremble.   O
powerful Protectress of those who trust in thee,
O refuge of sinners, whose misfortunes thou well
knowest how to compassionate, shield me from the
anger of thy divine Son, and since it is by thee he
comes to us, may we by thee attain to the enjoyment
of his adorable presence in heaven.   Amen.

NOVENA IN HONOUR OF THE DOLOURS OF THE B.V.M.

O MOST holy and afflicted Virgin, Queen of Martyrs, thou who didst stand motionless beneath the cross, witnessing the agony of thy expiring Son, through the unceasing sufferings of thy life of sorrow, and the bliss which now more than amply repays thee for thy past trials, look down with a Mother's tenderness and pity on me, who kneel before thee to venerate thy dolours and place my requests with filial confidence in the sanctuary of thy wounded Heart; present them, I beseech thee, on my behalf to Jesus Christ, through the merits of his own most sacred death and passion, together with thy sufferings at the foot of the cross, and through the united efficacy of both, obtain the grant of my present petition. To whom shall I recur in my wants and miseries, if not to thee, O Mother of mercy, who having so deeply drunk of the chalice of thy Son, canst compassionate the woes of those who still sigh in the land of exile. Offer for me to my Saviour one drop of the blood which flowed from his sacred veins, one of the tears which trickled from his divine eyes, one of the sighs which rent his adorable Heart. O Refuge of the universe and Hope of the whole world, do not reject my earnest prayer, but graciously obtain the grant of my petition. Amen.

NOVENA TO JESUS CHRIST CRUCIFIED.

JESUS Christ crucified! Son of the most holy
Virgin Mary, incline thy sacred head, and listen
to my prayers and sighs, as thou didst listen to
thy Eternal Father on Mount Thabor. Hail
Mary, &c.

Jesus Christ crucified! Son of the most holy
Virgin Mary, open thy sacred eyes, and look on me
as thou didst look on thy afflicted Mother from the
cross. Hail Mary, &c.

Jesus Christ crucified! Son of the most holy
Virgin Mary, open thy sacred lips, and speak to my
sad heart as thou didst to St. John, when recommending to him thy blessed Mother. Hail Mary,
&c.

Jesus Christ crucified! Son of the most holy
Virgin Mary, open thy sacred arms, and receive me
thy poor child, as thou didst embrace the hard wood
of the cross, for love of me and all sinners. Hail
Mary, &c.

Jesus Christ crucified! Son of the most holy
Virgin Mary, open thy Sacred Heart, that seat of
love and mercy : receive mine into it : make it
wholly thine; hear my prayers, and mercifully grant
my petitions. Hail Mary, &c.

O Eternal Father! look down on me, for whom
thy beloved Son Jesus Christ, was delivered up to
the death of the cross; and as he did not refuse
to die for my salvation, do not thou refuse, O

heavenly Father! to grant me pardon and eternal life, through the merits of thy Son Jesus on the Cross. Amen.

TO ST. VINCENT FERRER, CONF., O.P.

O GOD, who didst bring multitudes of nations to the knowledge of thy holy Name, by the wonderful preaching of the blessed Vincent, thy confessor; grant, we beseech thee, that we may deserve to find in heaven a bountiful rewarder in him whom he preached upon earth as the Judge to come, Christ our Lord. Amen.

TO ST. PETER GONZALES, CONF., O.P.

O GOD, who dost afford singular help through blessed Peter to such as are in the dangers of the sea, grant, through his intercession, that in all the storms of this life the light of thy grace may ever shine upon us, whereby we may be able to gain the port of eternal salvation. Through Christ our Lord. Amen.

TO ST. AGNES OF MONTE PULCIANO. V., O.P.

O GOD, who wast often pleased to shed a heavenly dew over thy holy virgin, the blessed Agnes, and to deck the places of her prayer with divers fresh-blown flowers; mercifully grant that we, through her prayers, may be sprinkled with the unfailing dew of thy blessing, and made fit to receive the fruits of immortality. Through Christ our Lord. Amen.

TO ST. PETER, MARTYR, O.P.

GRANT, we beseech thee, Almighty God, that we may imitate with due devotion the faith of blessed Peter, thy martyr, who for the spreading of that same faith was made worthy to obtain the palm of martyrdom. Through Christ our Lord. Amen.

Litany of St. Catherine of Sienna. V., O.P.

LORD have mercy on us,
    Christ have mercy on us.
Lord have mercy on us.
Eternal Fountain of all being, *have mercy on us.*
Unspotted Mirror of God's Majesty, *have mercy.*
Love of the Father and of the Son, *have mercy.*
Sacred Trinity of persons, in unity of essence, *have mercy.*
August Mary, tabernacle of God with men,
Holy father Saint Dominic,
Saint Catherine of Sienna,
Saint Catherine, our holy Mother and Patroness,
Chaste Spouse of Jesus Christ,
Fervent lover of our Lord,
Faithful follower of the Cross,

Contemplative soul, instructed by the Holy
    Ghost,

Enemy of vanity,

Vanquisher of the evil one,

Pattern of obedience and docility,

Humble Catherine,

Rigidly austere,

Immaculate Catherine,

Most devout to the Blessed Sacrament,

Entirely devoted to the Sacred Heart of Jesus,

Lustre of Dominicanesses,

Heroically meek and patient,

Transcendently charitable,

Powerful in converting souls,

Mediatrix for sinners,

Angel of peace,

Guide in the interior life,

Replenished with eternal knowledge,

Filled with divine gifts,

Caught up to the throne of the divinity,

Following the Lamb whithersoever he goeth,

Encompassed with glory, and inebriated with
    the plenitude of the house of God,

Pray for us.

Brightness of Eternal Light, *Have mercy on us.*

Teacher of St. Catherine, *Have mercy on us.*

Increated Beauty, rewarder of St. Catherine,
    Have mercy on us.

    V. Pray for us, O blessed St. Catherine.

    R. That we may be made worthy of the promises
of Christ.

LET US PRAY.

O GOD, who didst adorn blessed Catherine with a special privilege of purity and patience, and didst enable her to triumph over malignant spirits, and to persevere unshaken in the love of thy holy name; grant, we beseech thee, that by her example, contemning the world, and overcoming all its deceits, we may securely pass to the enjoyment of thy glory. Through Jesus Christ our Lord. Amen.

TO ST. PIUS V., POPE AND CONF., O.P.

O GOD, who wast pleased to elect the blessed Pius to the office of chief Pontiff for the defeat of the enemies of the Church, and the consecration of divine worship; grant that we may be defended by his watchful guardianship, and be so intent upon thy holy service, that overcoming all the wiles of our enemies, we may enjoy eternal peace. Through Christ our Lord. Amen.

TO ST. ANTONINUS, B. CONF., O.P.

MAY we be assisted, O Lord, by the merits of thy blessed confessor and bishop Saint Antoninus; that as we confess thee wonderful in him, so we may glory in that thou art merciful unto us. Through Christ our Lord. Amen.

TO B. COLUMBA OF RIETI, V., O.P.

COME, O my chosen one, and I will establish my throne within thee, for the King hath greatly desired thy beauty.

V. **Pray** for us, O blessed Columba.

R. That we may be made worthy of the promises of Christ.

LET US PRAY.

O GOD, who wast pleased that thy holy Virgin, the blessed Columba, graced with the spotless white of purity and innocence, should shine forth with heavenly splendours, grant, we beseech thee, by her intercession, that serving thee here with pure minds, we may deserve to enjoy the brightness of thy glory in heaven. Through Christ our Lord. Amen.

PRAYER

To implore the Descent of the Divine Spirit, particularly suitable for the ten days preceding Pentecost.

O JESUS, triumphant Conqueror of sin and death, who hast taken possession of that seat of bliss purchased by thy blood, remember thy tender promise, that thou wouldst "not leave us orphans." (*St. John* xiv. 18.) Send down upon us, and upon thy whole Church, that Spirit of light, of truth, and of love, who alone can bring to our minds, and imprint on our hearts the divine lessons thou hast taught us. But, alas, how can I hope for his descent into a heart defiled like mine by a thousand imperfect and sinful inclinations? O my God, if thou desirest to give me thy Divine Spirit, prepare thyself his dwelling in my soul; unite my heart and affections to the ardent sighs and perfect dispositions with which thy blessed Mother and thy Apostles awaited his coming. And thou, O adorable *Spirit*, who *breathest where* thou willest, deign to descend on me, and on all the members of that Church, to which thou dost "teach all truth" to the end of time. O Spirit of purity, Spirit of peace, whom the foulest stains of sin cannot resist, purify our souls, and infuse therein that peace which the world cannot give. "Oh, rend the heavens and come down," consoling Spirit, that, strengthened and encouraged by thee, we may never be attached to this wretched world, so as to prefer its consolations to the perfect accomplishment of God's holy will. Amen.

NOVENA FOR THE FEAST OF CORPUS CHRISTI.

O AMIABLE Jesus, who hast given us in the adorable Eucharist, so convincing a proof of thy infinite love, permit us to thank thee in the name of all thy creatures for the blessings included in this one precious gift. We adore thee, O hidden Deity! and most ardently wish we could offer thee such love as would atone for our own offences, and those committed by all mankind against this most amiable mystery. We firmly purpose to become from this moment the devoted adorers of this sacrament of love, and to take thy Eucharistic life for the rule and model of ours. O living Bread of eternal life, we humbly beseech thee to remove all obstacles to our frequently and worthily receiving thee ; and to grant us so tender a devotion to this mystery of love, that our hearts and thoughts may ever be turned to thee, present on our altars, and every action of our lives be directed to the perfect accomplishment of thy holy will. Amen.

FOR THE FEAST OF THE SACRED HEART.

O ADORABLE· Jesus, who hast discovered to us thy most Sacred Heart, that we may form some idea of the extent of thy love, grant that we may value as we ought so precious a favour. We adore thee, O infinitely amiable Heart, and beseech thee to receive our adorations, in unison with those thou thyself renderest to the Divinity on our altars— in unison with the perfect homage of all thy saints, —and in particular in unison with the unceasing adorations of the heavenly spirits, who crowd thy sanctuary during this glorious solemnity. We humbly represent all our necessities to thee, O adorable Heart, the fountain of all graces, the ocean of mercy, and exhaustless source of consolation and strength! We most fervently entreat of thee to infuse into our hearts the dispositions thou requirest; and then, for thy own sake, to grant the earnest petitions of this Novena.

Thou art, O Furnace of Love, a public victim, thy mercies and graces are now offered to all, who will only ask, that they may receive; but thy tenderest compassion seems peculiarly directed to all unhappy sinners. For them, thou wert overwhelmed with sorrow in the Garden of Olives, and wounded on the cross—for them we most particularly pray, and most earnestly entreat the grace of conversion. Assist us all to learn of thee who art *meek and humble of heart*, that thereby we may find rest to our souls in this life, and everlasting repose in a happy eternity. Amen.

NOVENA IN HONOUR OF OUR BLESSED LADY OF PERPETUAL SUCCOUR.

FEAST.—*First Sunday before 24th of June.*

MOST tender Mother of Perpetual Succour, grant us, under our present necessity, those maternal consolations and that peculiar protection thou hast promised to all who invoke thee. Relying on thy sacred word, we humbly entreat thee to obtain from thy Divine Son our earnest request. May the light we burn before thy loved image stand as a memorial of the lively confidence we repose in thee. May it consume in honour of that inflamed love and joy with which thy Sacred Heart was replenished in holding in thy arms thy Blessed Son. We offer to thee the sentiments of our poor hearts, and beseech thee to comfort us, by obtaining from thy dear Son a favourable answer to the petition we make to thy compassionate mercy and benevolence. Amen.

NOVENA IN HONOUR OF ST. ALOYSIUS.

O GLORIOUS St. Aloysius! prostrate in spirit before thy resplendent throne, I rejoice in thy happiness, and bless the most adorable Trinity for the magnificent rewards which have crowned thy virtues. Thy purity, thy penance, and thy perfect charity rendered thee dear to the Heart of Jesus Obtain for me, I beseech thee, a share in all thy virtues. Assist me to pursue the road of sanctity undeterred by the difficulties I shall meet on the way. May the remembrance of thy earthly combats support me in my struggles, and the thought of thy glory encourage me in my trials. Conduct me safely through this region of sin and temptation; pray for me until I shall have reached my true and happy home in heaven. Assist me especially in my last hour; comfort me then by thy sweet presence, and strengthen me with thy holy blessing. Oh! obtain that by imitating thy life, I may deserve to share in the peace and joy of thy saintly death. Amen.

NOVENA IN HONOUR OF SS. PETER AND PAUL.

O HOLY Apostles Peter and Paul! I (N.) do choose you this day and for ever, as my special protectors and advocates. I humbly rejoice with thee, Saint Peter, Prince of the Apostles, because thou art that Rock on which God built his Church, and with thee, Saint Paul, chosen by God for a vessel of election, and a preacher of the truth,

through the entire world. Obtain for me, I pray
you, a lively faith, a firm hope, and a perfect charity,
and a total disengagement from myself, a contempt for the world, patience in adversity, and
humility in prosperity, attention in prayer, purity of
heart, an upright intention in my actions, diligence
in fulfilling the obligations of my state, constancy in
my resolutions, resignation to the will of God, and
perseverance in the divine grace, until death. Grant
that, through your intercession and glorious
merits, I may overcome the temptations of the
world, of the devil, and of the flesh, and may become worthy to appear before the supreme and
eternal Pastor of souls, Jesus Christ, in order to
enjoy and love him eternally, who, with the Father
and the Holy Ghost, liveth and reigneth for ever
and ever. Amen.

NOVENA FOR THE FEAST OF THE VISITATION.

O PURE and holy Mother! deign to visit the poor
lodging of my soul as thou didst visit and
sanctify the dwelling of St. Elizabeth. Visit me in
life ; visit me especially at the hour of death when I
shall so peculiarly require thy consoling help, and
lead me by thy prayers to the glorious kingdom
where thou wilt reign in peace for ever. Ask for me
also, I beseech thee, the particular intention of this
Novena.

Aspiration.—Comfortress of the afflicted, pray for
us.

Litany of St. Vincent of Paul.

L ORD have mercy on us.
Christ have mercy on us.

Father, Son, and Holy Ghost, *Have mercy on us.*

God creating, God begotten, God proceeding from both, *Have mercy on us.*

Holy Mary, Mother of Jesus Christ,

St. Vincent of Paul,

St. Vincent, confessor of Christ,

St. Vincent, most humble and patient,

St. Vincent, perfectly mortified,

St. Vincent, deeply imbued with the spirit of the Apostles,

St. Vincent, indefatigable in extending the kingdom of God,

St. Vincent, abounding in the charity of Jesus Christ,

St. Vincent, father of the poor,

St. Vincent, succour of the indigent,

St. Vincent, refuge of the miserable,

St. Vincent, honour of the priesthood,

St. Vincent, reviver of the ecclesiastical spirit,

St. Vincent, founder of the Fathers of the Mission,

St. Vincent, institutor and patron of the Sisters of Charity,

St. Vincent, promoter of conventual discipline,

St. Vincent, prudent in counsel,

St. Vincent, truly devoted to divine Providence,

Pray for us.

St. Vincent, good and faithful servant,
St. Vincent, man according to God's own heart,
St. Vincent, highly exalted in the heavenly city,
By the merits of blessed Vincent,
By his ardent zeal,
By his burning charity,
By all the good he has operated,
By the bliss he now enjoys in thy kingdom,

O Lord, deliver us.

Lamb of God, &c., *three times.*

Ant. When thou didst pray with tears, and bury the dead. I offered thy prayer to the Lord.

V. He distributed ; he gave to the poor.

R. His justice remains for ever.

PRAYER.

O GOD, who didst enable blessed Vincent of Paul to evangelize the poor, and promote the honour of the ecclesiastical order, grant that we who honour his memory, may be helped by his prayers, and profit by the example of his eminent virtues. Through Jesus Christ, thy Son, &c. Amen.

Litany of St. Mary Magdalen.

LORD have mercy on us.
Christ have mercy on us.
God the Father, Son, and Holy Ghost, *Have mercy on us.*
Holy Trinity one God, *Have mercy on us.*
Holy Mary,
Holy Mother of God,
St. Mary Magdalen,

Pray for us.

Anchor of the afflicted,
Sister of Lazarus raised from the dead,
Apostle of the apostles,
Disciple of our Lord,
Bright shining gem, restored from darkness to
    light,
Wounded with the love of God,
Sweet advocate of sinners,
Inflamed with the love of Christ,
Thou who wert unclean and wert made whole,
Constant woman,
Thou who wert called by Christ to penance.
St. Mary Magdalen,
Thou who didst wash the feet of Jesus with thy
    tears,
Who didst wipe them with thy hair,
Who from Jesus didst obtain pardon of thy sins,
Who wert enamoured with the Saviour of the
    world,

Pray for us.

    Lamb of God, &c., *three times.*

    V. Pray for us, holy St. Magdalen,

    R. That we may be made worthy of the promises
of Christ.

LET US PRAY.

O ALMIGHTY and merciful God, who by the
    intercession of St. Mary Magdalen, didst raise
Lazarus from the dead after he had been four days
in the tomb, we beseech thee, by the intercession of
the same, to raise us from all our sins, and without

impediment, to grant us a speedy passage to life everlasting. Who livest and reignest world without end. Amen.

NOVENA TO ST. ANNE.

O MOST amiable mother of the ever Immaculate Virgin Mary, with unbounded confidence I have recourse to thy powerful intercession. Deign to accept me as thy devoted client, and to assist me in every necessity of soul and body. I rejoice with thee for all the good gifts of nature and of grace which thou didst receive from God. I rejoice in the bliss which for all eternity thou wilt possess in beholding the glory of thy blessed child, the holy Mother of God. And I pray thee to obtain for me true and persevering devotion to her, that I may be partaker of thy happiness in paradise. Amen.

NOVENA TO ST. DOMINIC.

O RENOWNED champion of the faith of Christ, most holy father, St. Dominic, look down from that throne of glory where thou enjoyest the reward of all thy labours, upon me, thy poor unworthy child.

I praise and thank God for the exalted degree of sanctity to which he has raised thee, and the special privileges by which he has distinguished thee; and I conjure thee by that gratitude with which thou shalt for all eternity be penetrated to thy divine Benefactor, to root out of my heart whatever is not agreeable in his sight, especially that evil habit by which I most frequently offend him. Obtain, likewise, the favours I request in this Novena.

O glorious Mother of God, Queen of the Sacred Rosary, who didst love Dominic with the affection of a mother, and wert most tenderly loved and honoured by him, vouchsafe to look upon me for his sake with an eye of pity: deign to join with him in presenting my petitions to thy most blessed Jesus, whom I sincerely desire from this moment to love with all my heart, and to serve with all my strength.

Mother of my Redeemer, I place myself now under thy powerful protection, as a certain means of obtaining all necessary grace here, and eternal happiness hereafter. Amen.

MEMORARE TO ST. DOMINIC.

REMEMBER, O most dear and holy Father St. Dominic, that, at the close of thy mortal career, thou didst raise thy pure hands to heaven and pray: " Holy Father, since by thy mercy I have ever accomplished thy will, and have kept and preserved those whom thou hast given to me, now I recommend them to thee; do thou keep them, do thou preserve them." Animated with unbounded confidence in thee, O tender Father, I cast myself at thy feet, beseeching thee to plead still for thy poor helpless children, to protect us amidst the dangers of our earthly pilgrimage, to guard and keep us. Be mindful, O great Father, of the comforting assurance thou didst make in thy last moments to thy weeping brethren, promising that after death thou wouldst assist thy children.

O Father, fulfil thy word, and help us by thy prayers.

THE ASSUMPTION OF OUR BLESSED LADY.

O GLORIOUS Queen of all the heavenly host, whose sacred body, the immaculate temple of the Divinity, is now assumed into heaven, I unite my voice to the choirs of angels who celebrate thy triumph. " Winter is now past " for thee, O fervent follower of thy crucified Son. In this world, like him, thou hadst not any part in its perishable possessions, but now all the treasures of heaven are thine —they are thine to enjoy, and thine to distribute, for thy intercession " is now an infinite treasure to man, which they that use, become the friends of God." Thou wert buried in obscurity in this valley of tears, but now thou " art compared with the light," and " art found before it." O Mother of God, elevated to the highest pinnacle of glory, should not thy triumphant exaltation encourage us to despise this world, and aspire after the next; for, O amiable Virgin, how short were thy sufferings on earth, yet, for all eternity, thou " shalt be admired in the holy assembly: among the elect thou shalt have praise, and among the blessed thou shalt be blessed." Look down then with compassion on us poor banished children of Eve—draw our hearts after thee by filial confidence and vigorous exertions to imitate thy virtues; above all, obtain for us that true humility, which neither seeks nor values any earthly distinction; detachment from the things of the world; purity of heart, and such ardent love for Jesus Christ as may cause us to despise this earth, and incessantly sigh after those eternal joys, which *the eye hath not seen, nor the ear heard, neither hath it entered into the heart of man to conceive.*

TO ST. HYACINTH, CONFESSOR, O.P.

O God, who didst make blessed Hyacinth, thy confessor, glorious amongst the people of divers nations, for the holiness of his life, and the glory of his miracles; grant that by his example we may amend our lives, and be defended by his help in all adversities. Through Christ our Lord. Amen.

TO ST. AUGUSTINE, B. CONF.

ANT.—Hail, O gem of confessors, tongue of Christ, voice of heaven, scribe of life, light of the learned, most blessed prelate: may those who venerate thee as a father, under thy guidance, obtain that life in which the souls of the blessed exult.

V. The just man shall bloom as a lily.

R. And flourish for ever in the sight of the Lord.

PRAYER.

Give ear, O Lord, to our prayers, and by the intercession of blessed Augustine, thy confessor and bishop, favourably bestow the effects of thy accustomed mercy on us, to whom thou hast given reason to trust in thy goodness, through Christ our Lord. Amen.

TO ST. ROSE OF LIMA, V., O.P.

Almighty God, the giver of all good gifts, who wast pleased that blessed Rose, early watered by the dew of thy grace. should flourish in the Indies in all the beauty of virginity and patience, grant unto us, thy servants, that running in the odour of her sweetness, we may be found worthy to become the good odour of Christ; who liveth and reigneth with thee, in the unity of the Holy Ghost, God, world without end. Amen.

NOVENA FOR THE NATIVITY OF THE BLESSED VIRGIN.

O Mary, the channel of God's tenderest mercies to man. thou wert promised from the beginning of the world to crush the serpent's head, to bring forth the Redeemer of mankind. In thy sacred birth appears the dawn of that glorious day of grace, for which all nations ardently sighed. O blessed Infant, already thou beginnest to accomplish the predictions of the prophets, and to satisfy the longing desires of the just; already thou hast conceived in thy heart, by the most perfect love. that adorable Being who was afterwards to be born of thee. O happy Virgin, who on entering this world didst become a victim of charity, perfectly and unreservedly submissive to the will of God, may I, even at the last hour of my life, be enriched with a share in the dispositions which animated thy sacred infancy. Thou art the dignified descendant of kings, patriarchs, and prophets, yet thy birth so little corresponds with thy rank, that even the earliest part of thy life may liken thee to Him whom thou wert destined to resemble in all things. Inspire me then by thy example and intercession with that spirit of renunciation, detachment from the world, and self-contempt which I promised at baptism. Thou knowest the weakness and perverse inclinations which I brought into the world, and which unhappily have gained strength with increasing years. Pray for me then, O most holy Mary, whose nativity I commemorate, obtain for me strength to fulfil my duties as a Christian, and fidelity to co-operate with the graces of heaven. Beg for me also the favours I petition in this Novena.

NOVENA IN HONOUR OF THE NAME OF MARY.

O MARY! what would be our poverty and misery if the Father of mercies had not drawn thee from his treasury to give thee to earth. O my life and consolation! I trust and confide in thy holy name. My heart wishes to love thee; my mouth to praise thee; my mind to contemplate thee; my soul sighs to be thine. Receive me, defend me, preserve me. I cannot perish in thy hands. Let the demons tremble when I pronounce thy holy name, since thou hast ruined their empire. We shall esteem it our greatest honour to rank among the number of thy servants. Let thy glory, blessed Mother, be equal to the extent of thy name; reign after God, over all that is beneath God; but, above all, reign in my heart. Thou shalt be my consolation in suffering, my strength in weakness, my counsel in doubt. At the name of Mary my hope shall be enlivened, my love inflamed. Oh, that I could deeply engrave thy dear name on every heart, suggest it to every tongue, and make all celebrate it with me. Mary! sacred name, under which no one should despair. Mary! sacred name often assaulted, but always victorious. Mary! it shall be my life, my strength, my comfort. Every day shall I invoke it and the divine name of Jesus. Jesus and Mary! this is what my heart shall say at the last hour, if my tongue cannot. I shall hear these names on my death-bed; they shall be wafted on my expiring breath, and I with them, to see, know, bless and love Jesus and Mary for eternity. Amen.

PRAYER OF ST. THOMAS.

O MERCIFUL God, grant that I may eagerly desire, carefully search out, truthfully acknowledge, and ever perfectly fulfil all things that are pleasing to thee, to the praise and glory of thy name. Amen.

(300 *days' Indulgence, Leo XIII.*)

TO BLESSED IMELDA, V., O.P.

SHE is a wise and glorious virgin, for the Lord of all hath loved her.

LET US PRAY.

O LORD Jesus Christ, who wounding the blessed virgin Imelda with the fire of thy love, and miraculously feeding her with the Immaculate Host, didst receive her into heaven, grant us, through her intercession, to approach the holy Table with the same fervour of charity, that we may long to be dissolved, and deserve to be with thee, who livest and reignest for ever and ever. Amen.

NOVENA FOR THE FEAST OF THE ANGEL GUARDIANS.

O PURE and happy spirits, whom the Almighty selected to become the angels and guardians of men, I most humbly prostrate before you to thank you for the charity and zeal with which you execute this commission. Alas! how many pass a long life without ever thanking that invisible friend to whom they a thousand times owed its preservation. O charitable guardians of those souls for whom Christ died! O burning Spirits, who cannot avoid loving those whom Jesus eternally loved, permit me to address you on behalf of all those committed to your care, and to implore for them all in general a grateful sense of your many favours, and also the grace to profit of your charitable assistance. O angels of those happy infants, who as yet " are without spot before God," preserve their innocence, I earnestly conjure you. Angels of youth, who are exposed to so many dangers, conduct them safely to the bosom of God, as Tobias was conducted back to his father. Angels of those who employ themselves in the instruction of youth, animate them with your zeal and love ; teach them to emulate your purity and incessant view of God, that they may worthily and successfully co-operate with the invisible guardians of their young charge. O angels of the clergy, "who have the eternal Gospel to preach to them that sit upon earth," present their words, their actions, and their intentions to God, and purify them in that fire of love which consumes you. Angels of infidels whom the true faith has never enlightened, intercede for them, that, practising what they know, they may at length discover the hidden secrets of the kingdom of God. O angels of all those who throughout the world are deprived of religious instruction, open for them some source of salvation; raise up someone to break for them the bread of the word. And you, O guardian angels of sinners charitable guides of those unhappy mortals, whose perseverance in sin would embitter even your unutterable joys, were you not established in the peace of God, oh! join me, I ardently beseech you, in imploring their conversion. Angels of all those who at this moment struggle in the agonies of death, strengthen, encourage, and defend them against the attacks of their infernal enemy. O faithful guides, holy spirits, ardent adorers of the Divinity, guardian angels of all creatures, protect us all—teach us to love, to pray, to combat on earth, and rather obtain for us instant death, than permit us to commit one mortal sin. Amen.

NOVENA IN HONOUR ST. LEWIS BERTRAND, CONF., O.P.

O GLORIOUS St. Lewis Bertrand, perfect disciple of our crucified Redeemer, vouchsafe to cast upon me a look of pity and of love. I have recourse to thee with confidence. Throughout thy whole life, thou didst ever labour most zealously to secure the salvation of thy neighbour, seeking by all means in thy power to win hearts to God. Oh, pray for me thy devoted client, that together with the pardon of my sins, I may become like thee, an apostle of charity, that I may compassionate the miseries of my fellow-creatures, wipe away the tears from their eyes, and assist them as far as I can in all their spiritual and corporal necessities. Beg for me, O great saint, from the adorable Heart of Jesus, a constant increase of divine love. Be thou my protector during life; obtain for me a death calm and peaceful, under the protection of Mary, the Virgin Mother of Good Counsel, the Immaculate Mother of God. Amen.

NOVENA IN HONOUR OF ALL SAINTS.

I PRAISE thee, O God, in thy saints, for having created them and given them thy abundant grace. Thou knowest the merits of all thy friends. Thou didst foresee them for thy beloved from the beginning of the world. Thou didst choose them out of the world, and draw them to thyself by many attractions; thou didst pour celestial consolations into their souls. Strengthened by thee, they persevered in good. And how affectionately didst thou crown their virtue! With what unspeakable love dost thou love them all! Yes, O thou who art holy and incomprehensible, I praise thee in thy saints. Thou hast delivered them, O Jesus. from darkness, sin and death ; thou hast brought them to thy kingdom, the kingdom of light, of life, and of love. O beloved saints, you are as the fairest flowers in the garden of my God. O happy company of God, you are seen, you love, you flourish in God's eternity ; you shine in the truth of God, you exult in the good things of God. I will fix my abode with you on high, I will leave this world in affection, and mix in your holy society, and with you, become one heart, one soul, one continued homage of praise to God. Thither I direct my eyes. To that abode on high and to you, I lift up my heart. To you, O ye saints of God, I direct my prayers. Oh ! that they may be directed in one everlasting alleluia with you ! And to your Creator and mine, to your Redeemer and mine, to your Sanctifier and mine, to the most Blessed Trinity, to God and to the Lamb, be glory, praise, and benediction for all eternity. - Amen.

NOVENA FOR THE SOULS IN PURGATORY.

O MOST sweet Jesus! through the bloody sweat which thou didst suffer in the Garden of Gethsemani, have mercy on these blessed souls.

Have mercy on them, O Lord! have mercy on them.

O most sweet Jesus! through the pains which thou didst suffer during thy most cruel scourging, have mercy on them.

R. Have mercy on them, &c.

O most sweet Jesus! through the pains which thou didst suffer in thy most painful crowning with thorns, have mercy on them.

R. Have mercy on them, &c.

O most sweet Jesus! through the pains which thou didst suffer in carrying thy cross to Calvary, have mercy on them.

R. Have mercy on them, &c.

O most sweet Jesus! through the pains which thou didst suffer in thy most cruel crucifixion, have mercy on them.

R. Have mercy on them, &c.

O most sweet Jesus! through the pains which thou didst suffer in thy most bitter agony on the cross, have mercy on them.

R. Have mercy on them, &c.

O most sweet Jesus! through that immense pain which thou didst suffer in breathing forth thy blessed soul, have mercy on them.

R. Have mercy on them, &c.

Blessed souls! we have prayed for you; we entreat you who are so dear to God, and who are secure of never losing him, to pray for us, miserable sinners, who are in danger of being damned and of losing God for ever.

LET US PRAY.

O GOD! the author of mercy, the lover of the salvation of mankind, we address thy clemency on behalf of our brethren, relations and benefactors, who are departed this life, that by the intercession of blessed Mary ever Virgin, and of all the saints, thou wouldst receive them into the enjoyment of eternal happiness, through Christ our Lord. Amen.

NOVENA IN HONOUR OF ALL SAINTS OF THE ORDER OF ST. DOMINIC.

Anthem.

THE Lord hath raised up the needy from the earth, and hath placed them among princes; making Dominic, in his heavenly home, a joyful father of children.

LET US PRAY.

O GOD, who hast vouchsafed to make the Order of Preachers fruitful in an abundant progeny of saints, and hast gloriously crowned in them the merits of all heroic virtues; grant unto us to follow their footsteps, that we may at last be united in perpetual festivity with those in heaven, whom we venerate to-day under one celebration upon earth. Through Christ our Lord. Amen.

NOVENA FOR THE FEAST OF THE PRESENTATION B.V.M.

O INCOMPARABLE Virgin! destined from all eternity to become the living temple of the Most High, permit thy devoted clients to remind thee of that entire, fervent, and most perfect oblation which thou didst make of thyself on the day of thy Presentation in the Temple. We beseech thee, by the singular graces bestowed on thee then, to employ thy powerful interest in our behalf, and to obtain for us the intentions of this Novena.

Teach us to commemorate thy consecration of thyself to God, on the day of thy Presentation, by a fervent renewal of our Baptismal Vows; pray that we may love God ardently and all creatures for his sake; that his adorable will may be ours; and that every exertion of our mind and body, may be happily consecrated to the promoting of his greater glory. Amen.

Prayers and Devotions.

PRAYER FOR ONE'S CONFESSORS.

O JESUS, great king, good shepherd, my wisdom, my hope, my reward; with Mary my Mother, I adore thy wounded heart. I pray to thee for all priests, especially for those whose charity has aided me; for those who have guided, instructed, absolved me; for those who have commended themselves to my prayers.

Preserve them for the glory of thy name, for they have proclaimed thy praise; regard them with mercy, for they have shown mercy; gladden them in their troubles, for they have brought joy to the sorrowful; keep unstained their anointed hands, for they have blessed; keep unearthly their hearts sealed with the sublime marks of thy priesthood. Bless their labours, the souls they love, the souls they seek, the souls they pray for. May those to whom they have ministered be here their joy and consolation, and in heaven their beautiful crown. Amen.

PRAYER TO "JESUS CRUCIFIED," FOR THE CONVERSION OF SINNERS.

O JESUS. my Crucified Lord! look down with pity and compassion upon sinful man; suffer not those souls for whom thou didst die upon the Cross to be lost to thy Heavenly Kingdom, and to be punished eternally.

By that compassion which moved thee to raise Thine Adorable Head, crowned with Thorns, and agonizing with pain, to listen to the prayer of the good thief, have pity on us; and out of that immense charity which consumed thee on the Cross, pardon us!

Let not thy Precious Blood be shed in vain, O Lord, but may each drop fall with mercy upon all poor sinners, for whom thou didst suffer and die!

PRAYER OF MADAME ELIZABETH.

I KNOW not, O my God. what may befall me to-day, but this I know, that nothing will happen which thou hast not foreseen and ordained from eternity. I adore thy eternal and impenetrable designs; I submit to them for thy love; I sacrifice myself in union with the sacrifice of Jesus Christ. my divine Saviour. I ask in his holy name, for patience and resignation in my sufferings, and perfect conformity of my will to thine in all things, past, present, and to come. My God, I have nothing worthy of thy acceptance to offer thee. I know nothing, I can do nothing; I have but my heart to give thee. I may be deprived of health, reputation, and even life, but my heart is my own; I consecrate it to thee, hoping never to resume it, and desiring not to live if not for thee. Amen.

ACT OF ABANDONMENT TO DIVINE PROVIDENCE.

O SWEET and tender Providence of my God into thy hands I commend my spirit: to thee I abandon my hopes and fears, my desires and repugnances, my temporal and eternal prospects. To thee I commit the wants of my perishable body; to thee I commit the far more precious interests of my immortal spirit for whose lot I have nothing to apprehend whilst I withdraw it not from thy bosom. Though my faults are many, my miseries great, my spiritual poverty extreme, my hope in thee surpasses all; it is superior to my weakness, greater than my difficulties, stronger than death. Though temptation should assail me, I will trust in thee; though I should sink, beneath my weakness I will hope in thee still; though I should break my resolutions, I will look to thee with confidence for grace to keep them at last; though thou shouldst kill me, even then will I trust in thee, for thou art my Father, my God, and the protector of my life; thou art my kind, my tender, my indulgent Parent, and I am thy devoted child who cast myself into thy arms and beg thy blessing, who put my trust in thee and so trusting shall not be confounded.

PRAYERS IN TIMES OF SICKNESS OR TROUBLE.

MERCY of God, encompass us, and deliver us from every plague.

Glory be to the Father, &c.

Eternal Father, sign us with the blood of the Immaculate Lamb, as thou didst sign the dwellings of thy people.

Glory, &c.

Most precious blood of Jesus, our love, cry for mercy for us from thy Divine Father, and deliver us.

Glory, &c.

Wounds of my Jesus, mouths of love and mercy, speak for us in pity to the Eternal Father; hide us within yourselves, and deliver us.

Glory, &c.

Eternal Father, Jesus is ours; ours his blood; ours his infinite merits; to thee we offer ourselves wholly; then, if thou lovest him, and holdest precious this gift we make thee, thou oughtest to deliver us; and for this we hope with fullest confidence.

Glory, &c.

Eternal Father, thou desirest not the death of a sinner, but rather that he should be converted and live: in thy mercy grant that we may live before thee, and be ever thine.

Glory, &c.

Save us, Christ our Saviour, by the virtue of thy holy cross; thou who didst save Peter in the sea, have mercy on us.

Mary, Mother of mercy, pray for us, and we shall be delivered; Mary our advocate, speak for us, and we shall be saved.

The Lord justly scourgeth us for our sins; but do thou, Mary, plead for us, for thou art our most tender mother.

Mary, in thy Jesus and in thee have we put our hope; oh! let us never be confounded.

Salve Regina.

PRAYER FOR PEACE.

Ant.—Give peace, O Lord, in our days; for there is none other who fighteth for us, but only thou, our God.

V. Let peace be in thy strength, O Lord.

R. And plenty in thy strong places.

LET US PRAY.

O GOD, from whom proceed all holy desires, all right counsels and just works; grant unto us, thy servants, that peace which the world cannot give, that our hearts may be devoted to thy commands; and that, being delivered from the fear of our enemies, we may pass our time in peace under thy protection. Through Christ our Lord. Amen.

On the Rosary of Jesus.

IN the thirteenth century, when the abominable vices of cursing, swearing, and blasphemy raged throughout the world, and called loudly to heaven for the severest punishments that an all-powerful God could inflict, the blessed Pope Gregory X. addressed a *Bull* to the Master-General of the Order of Preachers, entreating and requiring him and his brethren to propagate devotion to the all-saving name of Jesus. As soon as the Master-General, *John of Vercelli*, had received the *Bull*, he wrote a circular letter, full of piety, exhorting his subjects in all parts of the world to exert themselves in the execution of the Supreme Pontiff's pious intention. This they did with so much unction and constancy that a singular devotion and respect for the Most Sacred Name was introduced amongst the faithful, and the execrable vices of cursing, swearing, and blaspheming most remarkably decreased.

To perpetuate this happy change, the sons of St. Dominic resolved, that in all their churches, an altar should be erected and dedicated solely to the most holy and august name of Jesus.

In this state the devotion continued till the year 1432, at which time the kingdom of Portugal was visited by a most dreadful plague, which swept away such multitudes that the kingdom appeared almost depopulated, and Lisbon, its capital, seemed little more than a receptacle for the dead. The few that survived imputed these chastisements to the just judgment of heaven for their crimes, and particularly for those of cursing and swearing. They earnestly sought forgiveness, and firmly purposed amendment. The children of St. Dominic were singularly active in promoting so desirable a reformation. Foremost amongst them in the important cause was *Andrew Diaz*, for some time Bishop of

Megara, an ancient city in Greece, but who, having renounced his pastoral charge, had retired to his Convent at Lisbon. This venerable Prelate, afflicted at the distresses of the people, and perceiving that heaven seemed deaf to their lamentations, ascended the pulpit, and most pressingly exhorted all to have recourse to the merciful name of Jesus. The people responded to his entreaties—the plague suddenly ceased—the corruption of morals banished, the contagion also disappeared. Universal joy and thanks were diffused throughout all Europe, whose every nation had dreaded the spreading infection.

To engage future generations to praise the all-gracious name of Jesus, the zealous Prelate founded a *Sodality* or *Confraternity* sacred to the most holy name of Jesus.

This Sodality was not to be confined to Spain and Portugal. It spread, by the labours of the Dominican Fathers, into the most distant climes, and by it numberless sinners were everywhere reclaimed.

As Almighty God had inspired and appointed St. Dominic to be the founder and preacher of the Rosary of the Blessed Virgin Mary, so the same all-gracious God singled out St. Dominic's children to be the happy instruments of instituting and preaching the Sodality and Rosary sacred to the most holy name of Jesus.

This Rosary is an efficacious form of prayer: it was framed by Blessed *John Micon*, of the Order of Preachers, and modelled after the Rosary of the B. V. M. It is a summary of the life, sufferings, and triumphs of Jesus Christ. By the devout and constant recital of it we give great glory to God. To praise God's adorable name is a most acceptable homage; 'tis the language, 'tis the employment of the angels and saints in paradise. In the agonies of death, when the world, with all its momentary pleasures, is bidding us an eternal farewell, the devout invocation of the most holy name of Jesus will administer to us unutterable comfort. By accustoming ourselves to glorify the name of Jesus with heart and mouth on earth, it will be quite familiar to us when we happily arrive at the regions of bliss and glory. *Save us, O Lord our God, that we may give thanks to thy holy name, and may glory in thy praise. Blessed be the Lord, the God of Israel, from everlasting to everlasting ; and let all the people say : So be it, so be it.* (Ps. cv. 47, 48.)

Rosary of the Blessed Name of Jesus.

In the Name of the Father, and of the Son, and of the Holy Ghost. Amen.

O THOU the Son and Image of the Almighty Father, anointed Saviour of mankind! O thou who art! O Jehovah! O Emmanuel! O Adonai! O thou the holy One! O thou the dreadful One! O thou the Wonderful! O thou our God! O thou the strong One! O thou the Prince of Peace! O thou the Father of the future age! we adore thee in all thy names. But thou hast humbled thyself, being made obedient unto death, even the death of the cross, for which God hath exalted thee. and given thee a name above all names, that in the name of Jesus every knee may bend, of those that are in heaven, on earth, and in hell. I offer thee my thanks for uniting me in this holy Society. O grant me to partake of those benefits which were obtained by the merits of the glorious Order of St. Dominic. I purpose for ever to honour thee in all thy sacred names, and never to profane them. I purpose to hinder and prevent so great a crime in others, to the best of my ability. Inspire me with reverence and zeal to fulfil this purpose. I implore thee in virtue of the mysteries of thy most holy Rosary— O thou the Son of David, miraculously made man, and born from the womb of a Virgin—O thou the King of the Jews, who bore for me a most bitter passion—O thou the Son of the living God, risen from death, and the Judge of the living and the dead, grant to me and to all our Society, to perform this great devotion in the spirit of thy Church, that we may duly celebrate thy mysterious greatness : and obtain grace and merit in this life, and happiness in the next : through thee, who with the Father and the Holy Ghost, livest and reignest God for all eternity. Amen.

V. Thou O Lord, wilt open my lips.

R. And my tongue shall announce thy praise.

V. Incline unto my aid, O God.

R. O Lord, make haste to help me.

V. Glory be to the Father, &c.

R. As it was in the beginning, &c.

PART I.

I.—*The Incarnation of our Lord Jesus Christ.*

THE Son of God assumes human flesh, of the pure blood of the Blessed Mary ever Virgin, and is made man in her womb.

O Jesus, Son of David, have mercy on us [*ten times*]. Glory be to the Father, &c.

II.—*Birth of our Lord Jesus Christ.*

THE Saviour of the world is born for our redemption, his Mother remaining a Virgin.

O Jesus, Son of David, have mercy on us [*ten times*]. Glory be to the Father, &c.

III.—*The Circumcision of our Lord Jesus Christ.*

OUR Saviour being eight days old begins to suffer for our sins, and his blood already flows for us. He is circumcised according to the law, as if he had been himself a sinner.

O Jesus, Son of David, have mercy on us [*ten times*]. Glory be to the Father, &c.

IV.—*Our Lord Jesus Christ found in the Temple.*

OUR Saviour being twelve years old shows himself more than mortal by his knowledge and wisdom, teaching the teachers of the Jews.

O Jesus, Son of David, have mercy on us [*ten times*]. Glory be to the Father, &c.

V.—*The Baptism of our Lord Jesus Christ.*

THE Saviour of the world is baptized by St. John. The Eternal Father declares him to be his Son.

O Jesus, Son of David, have mercy on us [*ten times*]. Glory be to the Father, &c.

THE PRAYER.

O JESUS, whose name is above all names, that at the name of Jesus, every knee may bend, of those that are in heaven, on earth, or in hell. Who, at the time appointed by the Eternal Wisdom, assumedst flesh in the womb of the blessed Mary ever Virgin, and thus becamest the Son of David; whose birth gladdened men and angels; who began so early to suffer for us, and to shed, on our account, that blood which washeth away the sins of the world; whose immortal wisdom appeared at the age of twelve years; to whose baptism all heaven was attentive; grant to us to celebrate those mysteries to thy honour and our own salvation; who with the Father and the Holy Ghost, livest and reignest, God for all eternity. Amen.

PART II.

I.—*Our Saviour washes his Disciples' feet.*

OUR Saviour, to show us an example of humility, and how much we ought to serve each other, descendeth so low as to wash the feet of his disciples, though he is the God whom heaven and earth adore.

O Jesus of Nazareth, King of the Jews, have mercy on us [*ten times*]. Glory be to the Father, &c.

II.—*The Prayer of our Lord Jesus Christ in the Garden.*

OUR Saviour, knowing his passion to be now at hand, is so affected with the thoughts of it, and so oppressed with the load of our sins, that he prays to his Almighty Father that the bitter chalice might pass away from him.

O Jesus of Nazareth, King of the Jews, have mercy on us [*ten times*]. Glory be to the Father, &c.

III.—*Our Saviour is apprehended.*

OUR Saviour, as if he had been no more than man, yields to the power of men, and permits himself, for our redemption, to be apprehended, as if he were a malefactor.

O Jesus of Nazareth, King of the Jews, have mercy on us [*ten times*]. Glory be to the Father, &c.

IV.—*Our Saviour carries his Cross.*

OUR Saviour being torn with scourges and pierced with thorns, to expiate our sins, is obliged to carry the cross on which he is to die, and moves on, labouring with sorrow, towards the place of execution.

O Jesus of Nazareth, King of the Jews, have mercy on us [*ten times*] Glory be to the Father, &c.

V.—*The Descent of our Saviour into Hell.*

THE soul of our Saviour being separated by death from the body, descends to that place where the Saints were expecting their redemption.

O Jesus of Nazareth, King of the Jews, have mercy on us [*ten times*]. Glory be to the Father, &c.

THE PRAYER.

O JESUS. whose name is above all names, that at the name of Jesus every knee may bend, of those that are in heaven, on earth, or in hell; whose mysterious humiliations and sorrows, appointed for thee on account of our sins, appeared in the washing of the feet of thy servants and creatures; in thy distress, and prayer, and bloody sweat; in thy being secured and brought before courts as a criminal : in thy bearing the load of the cross ; and in the separation of thy soul from thy body, and its descent to the regions below ; grant to us to celebrate those mysteries to thy honour and our own salvation ; who with the Father and the Holy Ghost, livest and reignest God for all eternity. Amen.

PART III.

I.—*The Resurrection of our Lord Jesus Christ.*

THE soul of our Lord Jesus Christ, which had been separated from the body, is re-united to it by a miracle of the Almighty Power; and that body, which had been dead, rises to die no more.

O Jesus, Son of the living God, have mercy on us [*ten times*]. Glory be to the Father, &c.

II.—*The Ascension of our Lord Jesus Christ.*

THE body of our Lord Jesus Christ ascends into the highest heaven, where the Saviour of mankind sits at the right hand of God the Almighty Father.

O Jesus, Son of the living God, have mercy on us [*ten times*]. Glory be to the Father, &c.

III.—*Our Lord Jesus Christ sends down the Holy Ghost.*

OUR Saviour, now seated at the right hand of God, his Almighty Father, sends down the Holy Ghost, to inspire and animate his disciples, that they may be qualified to publish to mankind his cross and his glory.

O Jesus, Son of the living God, have mercy on us
[*ten times*].   Glory be to the Father, &c.

IV.—*Our Lord Jesus Christ crowning the Blessed Virgin and Saints.*

OUR Saviour, having by his passion, resurrection,
and ascension, opened the way for the Sons of
Adam to the heaven which they had lost by sin,
bestows on his Mother and his saints crowns of
immortal glory.

O Jesus, Son of the living God, have mercy on us
[*ten times*].   Glory be to the Father, &c.

V.—*Our Lord Jesus Christ coming to Judgment.*

OUR Saviour will come, in power and majesty, to
judge the living and the dead, and to render
to everyone according to his works.

O Jesus, Son of the living God, have mercy on us
[*ten times*].   Glory be to the Father, &c.

THE PRAYER.

O JESUS, whose name is above all names, that at
the name of Jesus every knee may bend, of
those that are in heaven, on earth, or in hell: whose
body, that was murdered by mankind, the Almighty
raised from death glorious and immortal; who by
thy ascension triumphed over death and led captivity
captive ; who, according to thy promise, didst send
down the Spirit, that proceedeth from the Father
and thee, the Comforter and Enlivener: who, stretching forth the bounty of thy Almighty hand, didst

shed upon the chosen children of Adam, that glory which neither eye hath seen, nor ear hath heard, nor hath it entered into the heart of man to conceive; and who will come forth in power and majesty to judge the living and the dead; before whose throne all mortals shall appear: grant to us to celebrate these mysteries to thy honour and our own salvation: who, with the Father and the Holy Ghost, livest and reignest God for all eternity. Amen.

O God, who hast made the most glorious name of Jesus Christ, thy Son, our Lord, most lovely to thy faithful, by the great and affecting sweetness of it, and at the same time dreadful to malignant spirits, grant propitiously that all who venerate it on earth may obtain the sweetness of consolation for the present, and afterwards the joy of happiness without end; through the same Jesus Christ, thy Son, our Lord, who with thee and the Holy Ghost liveth and reigneth, God, world without end. Amen.

Prayer to the Sacred Heart.

O JESUS! I cast myself and all my concerns into your Sacred Heart, overflowing with all sweetness. I commit to you with perfect confidence all my spiritual and temporal interests. I beg of you in the hours of my weakness and excitement, when I forget and neglect to call upon you for help, to be still my Protector and Guide. Give me light to see your will, strength to do it, and the grace not to offend you by the least deliberate fault. Amen.

PRAYER TO OBTAIN THE GRACE OF A HAPPY DEATH.

MY Lord Jesus Christ, through that bitterness which thou didst suffer of on the Cross, when thy blessed Soul was separated from thy Sacred Body, have pity on my sinful soul, when it shall depart from my miserable body, and shall enter into eternity. Amen. (*One Hail Mary.*)

O Mary, watch the hour when my departing soul shall lose its hold on earthly things, and shall stand unveiled in the presence of its Creator. Oh! be then to me a powerful advocate and a tender Mother, and place the merits of thy Son Jesus in the scales of justice in my behalf. Amen. (*One Hail Mary.*)

O blessed St. Joseph, who hadst the happiest of all deaths, obtain for us grace to die as thou didst in the arms of Jesus and of Mary, and with thee to enjoy their blessed company for all eternity. Amen. (*One Hail Mary.*)

LET US PRAY.

O GOD, who hast doomed all men to die, but hast concealed from all the hour of their death, grant that I may pass my days in the practice of holiness and justice, and that I may deserve to quit this world in the peace of a good conscience, and in the embrace of thy love. Through Christ our Lord. Amen.

PREPARATION FOR DEATH.

LORD have mercy on her. *Christ have mercy on her.* Lord have mercy on her.

Holy Mother of God, *pray for her.*

All ye Angels and Archangels, *pray for her.*

All ye blessed Company of the Just,
All ye holy Patriarchs and Prophets,
All ye holy Apostles and Evangelists,
All ye holy Disciples of our Lord,
All ye holy Martyrs,
All ye holy Bishops and Confessors,
All ye holy Virgins and Widows,
All ye holy Saints of God, *make intercession for her.*

Pray for her.

Have mercy, O Lord! and spare her.
Have mercy, O Lord! and hear her.
From all her offences, and the punishment
    due to them,
From all the snares and temptations of the devil,
From all impatience and repining at thy just
    chastisements,
From dejection of spirit, and diffidence in thy
    mercies,
From all undue fear of death, and immoderate
    desires of life,
From distraction of mind, and neglect of pre-
    paration for eternity,
By thy Cross and Passion,
By thy Death and Burial,
By thy glorious Resurrection and Ascension,
By the grace of the Holy Ghost, the Comforter,
In the hour of death, and in the day of judgment,
    We sinners, *beseech thee to hear us.*

Deliver her, O Lord.

That it would please thee to comfort her in her
    anguish, and enable her to look to a happy futurity,
    We beseech thee to hear us.

That it would please thee to remind her of all
thy mercies, and encourage her to confide in
thy goodness,

That thou wouldst vouchsafe to grant her the
grace to forgive those by whom she may have
been offended, and to satisfy those whom she
may have injured in word or deed,

That being thus reconciled to thee, and all
creatures, she may, with assured hope, and
steadfast faith, receive the sacrament of thy
Blessed Body, and by this heavenly food be
strengthened against the pangs of death,

That patient submission under the pains of sickness, may expiate the punishment due to her
sins, diminish her love of this world, and increase
her desire of the happiness which awaits the just,

That she may readily acquiesce in the orders of
thy providence, both in life and death,

Son of God, *we beseech thee to hear us.*

Lamb of God, &c., &c.

Lord have mercy on us, &c.

Our Father, &c.

O Lord, hear my prayer.

And let my cry come unto thee.

We beseech thee to hear us.

LET US PRAY.

ALMIGHTY and Eternal God, in whose hands are
life and death, whose infinite wisdom disposes
all things advantageously for those who love thee,
behold thy servant whom thou hast laid on the bed

of sickness; comfort, we beseech thee, her afflicted spirit; increase her faith, strengthen her hope, and perfect her charity. Enable her to sanctify all her sufferings, by patient resignation, and if thy mercy shall restore her to health, may she carefully correct all that is displeasing in thy sight. If it please thee to call her out of this world, grant that she may pass safely through the shades of death, transported by thy holy angels into the mansions of bliss, where no fear shall trouble her, no pain afflict her, no grief disquiet her mind; but pure delight, unspeakable joys, and perfect security shall be for ever confirmed to her, through Christ our Lord. Amen.

PRAYERS FOR THE AGONIZING.

DEPART. Christian soul, out of this world, in the name of God the Father Almighty, who created thee; in the name of Jesus Christ, Son of the living God, who suffered for thee; in the name of the Holy Ghost, who was poured out upon thee; in the name of the Angels, Archangels; in the name of the Thrones and Dominations; in the name of the Principalities and Powers : in the name of the Cherubim and Seraphim; in the name of the Patriarchs and Prophets ; in the name of the holy Apostles and Evangelists; in the name of the holy Martyrs and Confessors; in the name of the holy Monks and Hermits: in the name of the holy Virgins, and of all the Saints of God: let thy place be this day in peace, and thy abode in holy Sion, through Christ our Lord. Amen.

God of mercy, God of goodness! who, according to the multitude of thy mercies, forgivest the sins of such as repent, and graciously remittest the guilt of their past offences, mercifully regard this thy servant N. and hear her asking most earnestly a full remission of her sins. Renew, O merciful Father, whatever is corrupt in her through human frailty, or by the snares of the enemy; make her a true member of the Church, and let her partake of the fruit of thy redemption. Have compassion, Lord, on her sighs, take pity on her tears, and admit her to the Sacrament of thy reconciliation, for she has no hope but in thee. Through Christ our Lord. Amen.

I recommend thee, dear Sister, to Almighty God, and leave thee to his mercy, whose creature thou art, that, having paid the common debt by surrendering thy soul, thou mayest return to thy Maker, who formed thee out of the earth. Let, therefore, the holy angels meet thy soul at its departure: let the court of the apostles receive thee, let the triumphant army of glorious martyrs conduct thee; let the crowds of joyful confessors encompass thee; let the choir of blessed virgins go before thee; and let a happy rest be thy portion in the company of the patriarchs: let Jesus Christ appear to thee with a mild and cheerful countenance, and give thee a place among those who are to be in his presence for ever. Mayest thou be a stranger to all that is punished with darkness, that is chastised with flames, and that suffers in torments. May all the ministers of hell be filled with confusion and shame, and let no evil spirit dare to stop thee in thy way. Christ Jesus be thy deliverer, who was crucified for thee ; Christ Jesus deliver thee from death, who vouchsafed to die for thee ; Christ Jesus, Son of the living God, place thee in the possession of the ever new delights of paradise : and may he, the true Shepherd, own thee for one of his flock ; may he absolve thee from all thy sins, and place thee on his right hand, in the inheritance of his elect. We pray it may be thy happy lot to behold thy Redeemer face to face ; to be for ever in his presence. and in the vision of that truth which is the joy of the blessed. Amen.

LET US PRAY.

WE recommend to thee. O Lord. the soul of this thy servant, and beseech thee, Jesus Christ, Redeemer of the world, that as in mercy to her thou becamest man. so now thou wouldst vouchsafe to admit her into the number of the blessed. Remember, Lord, she is thy creature, not made by strange gods, but by thee. the only true and living God; for there is no other God but thee. none that can work thy wonders. Let her soul find comfort in thy sight, and remember not her former sins, nor any of those excesses which she has fallen into, through the violence of passion and corruption. For although she has sinned, yet she has still retained true faith in thee, Father, Son, and Holy Ghost: she has had zeal for thy honour, and faithfully adored thee, her God, and the Creator of all things.

Remember not, O Lord, we beseech thee, the sins and ignorance of her youth; but according to thy great mercy, be mindful of her in thy eternal glory. Let the heavens be opened to her, and the angels rejoice with her. Receive, O Lord, thy servant into thy kingdom. Let the Archangel St. Michael, the chief of the heavenly host, conduct her. Let the holy Angels of God meet her, and bring her into the city of the heavenly Jerusalem. May blessed Peter the Apostle, to whom were given the keys of the kingdom of heaven, receive her. May holy Paul the Apostle, who was a vessel of election, help her. May St. John, the beloved Disciple, to whom God revealed the secrets of heaven, intercede for her. May all the holy Apostles, to whom was given the power of binding and loosing, pray for her. May all the blessed and chosen servants of God, who, in this world, have suffered torments for the name of Christ, pray for her, that, being delivered from this body of corruption, she may be admitted into the kingdom of heaven; through the assistance and merits of our Lord Jesus Christ, who liveth and reigneth with the Father and the Holy Ghost, **world** without **end.** Amen.

If further prayers are required, any of the Penitential Psalms may be said.

Immediately after the sick person has expired, the following Responsory is said.

Come to her assistance, all ye saints of God; meet her, all ye angels of God; receive her soul, and present it now before the Most High. May Jesus Christ receive her, who called her, and the angels conduct her to Abraham's bosom ; may they receive her soul, and present it now before the Most High.

Grant her, O Lord, eternal rest,
And let perpetual light shine on her.
Lord, have mercy on us.
Christ, have mercy on us.
Lord, have mercy on us.
Our Father, &c.
And lead us not into temptation, &c.
Grant her, O Lord, eternal rest, &c.
From the gates of hell,
Deliver her soul, O Lord.
May she rest in peace.
Amen.
O Lord, hear my prayer.
And let my cry come unto thee.

LET US PRAY.

TO thee, Lord, we recommend the soul of thy servant *N.*, that being dead to this world, she may live to thee ; and whatever sins she has committed through human frailty, we beseech thee, in thy goodness, mercifully to pardon through Christ our Lord. Amen.

The Seven Penitential Psalms,

Prayer to be recited on **Fasting Days**, and at other penitential times.

Ant. Remember not.

PSALM VI. *Domine, ne in furore.*

1. David, in deep affliction, prays for a mitigation of the divine anger; 4. in consideration of God's mercy; 5. his glory; 6. his own repentance. 8. By faith triumphs over his enemies.

O Lord, rebuke me not in thine indignation, nor chastise me in thy wrath.

Have mercy on me, O Lord, for I am weak: heal me, O Lord, for my bones are troubled.

And my soul is troubled exceedingly: but thou, O Lord, how long?

Turn thee, O Lord, and deliver my soul: O save me for thy mercy's sake.

For there is no one in death that is mindful of thee: and who shall confess to thee in hell?

I have laboured in my groanings; every night I will wash my bed, and will water my couch with my tears.

Mine eye is troubled through indignation: I have grown old among all my enemies.

Depart from me, all ye workers of iniquity: for the Lord hath heard the voice of my weeping.

The Lord hath heard my supplication: the Lord hath received my prayer.

Let all my enemies be ashamed, and be very much troubled : let them be turned back, and be ashamed very speedily. Glory be, &c.

Psalm XXXI. *Beati quorum.*

1. Blessings of remission of sins. 3. Misery of impenitence. 6. Confession of sin bringeth ease. 8. Safety. 14. Joy.

Blessed are they whose iniquities are forgiven, and whose sins are covered.

Blessed is the man to whom the Lord hath not imputed sin, and in whose spirit there is no guile.

Because I was silent, my bones grew old whilst I cried out all the day long.

For day and night thy hand was heavy upon me : I am turned in mine anguish, whilst the thorn is fastened.

I have acknowledged my sin unto thee : and my injustice I have not concealed.

I said, I will confess against myself my injustice to the Lord : and thou hast forgiven the wickedness of my sin.

For this shall every one that is holy pray to thee : in a seasonable time.

And yet in a flood of many waters; they shall not come nigh unto him.

Thou art my refuge from the trouble which hath encompassed me : my joy, deliver me from them that surround me.

I will give thee understanding, and I will instruct thee in this way, in which thou shalt go : I will fix my eyes upon thee.

Do not become like the horse and the mule, who have no understanding.

With bit and bridle bind fast their jaws ; who come not near unto thee.

Many are the scourges of the sinner : but mercy shall encompass him that hopeth in the Lord.

Be glad in the Lord, and rejoice ye just ; and glory all ye right of heart. Glory be, &c.

PSALM XXXVII. *Domine, ne in furore.*

1. David's extreme anguish. 15. He hopeth in God. 18. His resignation, grief. 22. Fervent prayer.

Rebuke me not, O Lord. in thine indignation : nor chastise me in thy wrath.

For thine arrows are fastened in me: and thy hand hath been strong upon me.

There is no health in my flesh, because of thy wrath ; there is no peace to my bones, because of my sins.

For mine iniquities are gone over my head: and, as a heavy burden, are become heavy upon me.

My sores are putrefied and corrupted : because of my foolishness.

I am become miserable, and am bowed down even to the end : I walked sorrowful all the day long.

For my loins are filled with illusions : and there is no health in my flesh.

I am afflicted and humbled exceedingly : I roared with the groaning of my heart.

Lord, all my desire is before thee : and my groaning is not hidden from thee.

My heart is troubled, my strength has left me: and the light of mine eyes itself is not with me.

My friends and my neighbours have drawn near, and stood against me.

And they that were near me stood afar off : and they that sought my soul used violence.

And they that sought evils to me spoke vain things : and studied deceits all the day.

But I, as a deaf man, heard not : and was as a dumb man, not opening his mouth.

And I became as a man that heareth not; and that hath no reproofs in his mouth.

For in thee, O Lord, have I hoped : thou wilt hear me, O Lord my God.

For I said, lest at any time mine enemies rejoice over me : and whilst my feet are moved, they speak great things against me.

For I am ready for scourges : and my sorrow is continually before me.

For I will declare my iniquity : and I will think for my sin.

But my enemies live, and are stronger than I : and they that hate me wrongfully are multiplied.

They that render evil for good have detracted me, because I followed goodness.

Forsake me not, O Lord my God : do not thou depart from me.

Attend unto my help, O Lord, the God of my salvation. Glory, &c.

PSALM L. *Miserere.*

1. David prayeth for remission of his sins; 3. for perfect sanctity; 17. God delighteth not in sacrifice. but in a contrite heart; 19. he prayeth for the building of a temple in Jerusalem, figuratively the exaltation of the Church.

Have mercy upon me, O God : according to thy great mercy.

And according to the multitude of thy tender mercies : blot out my iniquity.

Wash me yet more from my iniquity : and cleanse me from my sin.

For I know my iniquity: and my sin is always before me.

To thee only have I sinned, and have done evil before thee . that thou mayst be justified in thy words, and mayst overcome when thou art judged.

For behold, I was conceived in iniquities : and in sins did my mother conceive me.

For behold, thou hast loved truth : the uncertain and hidden things of thy wisdom thou hast made manifest to me.

Thou shalt sprinkle me with hyssop, and I shall be cleansed: thou shalt wash me, and I shall be made whiter than snow.

To my hearing thou shalt give joy and gladness : and the bones that have been humbled shall rejoice.

Turn away thy face from my sins : and blot out all my iniquities.

Create a clean heart in me, O God: and renew a right spirit within my bowels.

Cast me not away from thy face : and take not thy holy spirit from me.

Restore unto me the joy of thy salvation : and strengthen me with a perfect spirit.

I will teach the unjust thy ways: and the wicked shall be converted to thee.

Deliver me from blood, O God, thou God of my salvation : and my tongue shall extol thy justice.

O Lord, thou will open my lips : and my mouth shall declare thy praise.

For if thou hadst desired sacrifice, I would indeed have given it : with burnt-offerings thou wilt not be delighted.

A sacrifice of God is an afflicted spirit : a contrite and humble heart, O God, thou wilt not despise.

Deal favourably, O Lord, in thy good will with Sion : that the walls of Jerusalem may be built up.

Then shalt thou accept the sacrifice of justice, oblations, and whole burnt-offerings : then shall they lay calves upon thine altar.   Glory be, etc.

PSALM CI.   *Domine, exaudi.*

1. The extreme affliction of the Psalmist. 12. The eternity and mercy of God. 19. To be recorded and praised by future generations. 26. The unchangeableness of God.

Hear O Lord, my prayer : and let my cry come to thee.

Turn not away thy face from me : in the day when I am in trouble, incline thine ear unto me.

In what day soever I shall call upon thee, hear me speedily.

For my days are vanished like smoke: and my bones are grown dry like fuel for the fire.

I am smitten as grass, and my heart is withered: because I forgot to eat my bread.

Through the voice of my groaning, my bone hath cleaved to my flesh.

I am become like to a pelican of the wilderness: I am like a night-raven in the house.

I have watched, and am become as a sparrow all alone on the house-top.

All the day long my enemies reproached me: and they that praised me did swear against me.

For I did eat ashes like bread, and mingled my drink with weeping.

Because of thy anger and indignation: for having lifted me up thou hast thrown me down.

My days have declined like a shadow, and I am withered like grass.

But thou, O Lord, endurest for ever: and thy memorial to all generations.

Thou shalt arise and have mercy on Sion: for it is time to have mercy on it, for the time is come.

For the stones thereof have pleased thy servants: and they shall have pity on the earth thereof.

And the Gentiles shall fear thy name, O Lord, and all the kings of the earth thy glory.

For the Lord hath built up Sion: and he shall be seen in his glory.

He hath had regard unto the prayer of the humble: and he hath not despised their petition.

Let these things be written unto another generation: and the people that shall be created shall praise the Lord.

Because he hath looked forth from his high sanctuary: from heaven the Lord hath looked upon the earth.

That he might hear the groans of them that are in fetters: that he might release the children of the slain.

That they may declare the name of the Lord in Sion: and his praise in Jerusalem.

When the people assemble together, and kings to serve the Lord.

He answered him in the way of his strength: declare unto me the fewness of my days.

Call me not away in the midst of my days: thy years are unto generation and generation.

In the beginning, O Lord, thou foundedst the earth: and the heavens are the works of thy hands.

They shall perish, but thou remainest: and all of them shall grow old like a garment.

And as a vesture thou shalt change them, and they shall be changed: but thou art always the self-same, and thy years shall not fail.

The children of thy servants shall continue: and their seed shall be directed for ever.

Glory be to the Father, &c.

PSALM CXXIX. *De profundis.*

An excellent model for sinners imploring the divine mercy.

Out of the depths I have cried to thee, O Lord: Lord, hear my voice

Let thine ears be attentive to the voice of my supplication.

If thou, O Lord, wilt mark iniquities: Lord, who shall stand it?

For with thee there is merciful forgiveness: and by reason of thy law, I have waited for thee, O Lord.

My soul hath relied on his word: my soul hath hoped in the Lord.

From the morning watch even until night, let Israel hope in the Lord.

Because with the Lord there is mercy: and with him plentiful redemption.

And he shall redeem Israel from all his iniquities.

Glory be, &c.

PSALM CXLII. *Domine, exaudi.*

1. David prayeth for favour in judgment; 3. represents his distress. 7. He prayeth for grace; 9. for deliverance; 10. for sanctification; 12. victory over his enemies.

Hear, O Lord, my prayer: give ear to my supplication in thy truth; hear me in thy justice.

And enter not into judgment with thy servant: for in thy sight no man living shall be justified.

For the enemy hath persecuted my soul: he hath brought down my life to the earth.

He hath made me to dwell in darkness, as those that have been dead of old: and my spirit is in anguish within me; my heart within me is troubled.

I remembered the days of old, I meditated on all thy works: I mused upon the works of thy hands.

I stretched forth my hands to thee: my soul is as earth without water unto thee.

Hear me speedily, O Lord: my spirit hath fainted away.

Turn not away thy face from me: lest I be like unto them that go down into the pit.

Cause me to hear thy mercy in the morning: for in thee have I hoped.

Make the way known to me wherein I should walk: for I have lifted up my soul to thee.

Deliver me from mine enemies, O Lord; to thee have I fled: teach me to do thy will, for thou art my God.

Thy good spirit shall lead me into the right land: for thy name's sake, O Lord, thou wilt quicken me in thy justice.

Thou wilt bring my soul out of trouble: and in thy mercy thou wilt destroy mine enemies.

And thou wilt cut off all them that afflict my soul: for I am thy servant. Glory be, &c.

Ant. Remember not, O Lord, our offences, nor those of our parents; and take not revenge of our sins.

The Litany of the Saints.

KYRIE eleison.
Christe eleison.
Kyrie eleison.
Christe audi nos.
Christe exaudi nos.
Pater de cœlis Deus, miserere nobis.
Fili Redemptor mundi, Deus, miserere nobis.

Spiritus Sancte Deus, miserere nobis.
Sancta Trinitas, unus Deus, miserere nobis.
Sancta Maria, ora pro nobis
Sancta Dei Genitrix,
Sancta Virgo Virginum,
Sancte Michael,
Sancte Gabriel,
Sancte Raphael,
Omnes sancti Angeli et Archangeli, Orate, etc.
Omnes sancti beatorum spirituum ordines, Orate, etc.

Ora pro nobis.

Lord, have mercy on us.
Christ, have mercy on us.
Lord, have mercy on us.
Christ, hear us.
Christ, graciously hear us.
God the Father of heaven have mercy on us.
God the Son, Redeemer of the world, have mercy on us.
God the Holy Ghost have mercy on us.
Holy Trinity, one God, have mercy on us.
Holy Mary, pray for us.
Holy Mother of God,
Holy Virgin of Virgins,
St. Michael,
St. Gabriel,
St. Raphael,
All ye holy Angels and Archangels,
All ye holy orders of blessed spirits,

Pray for us.

Sancte Joannes Baptista, *Ora pro nobis.*	St. John Baptist,
Sancte Joseph, *Ora, etc.*	St. Joseph,
Omnes sancti Patriarchæ et Prophetæ, *Orate, etc.*	All ye holy Patriarchs and Prophets,
Sancte Petre,	St. Peter,
Sancte Paule,	St. Paul,
Sancte Andrea,	St. Andrew,
Sancte Jacobe,	St. James,
Sancte Joannes,	St. John,
Sancte Thoma,	St. Thomas,
Sancte Jacobe,	St. James,
Sancte Philippe,	St. Philip,
Sancte Bartholomæe,	St. Bartholomew,
Sancte Matthæe,	St. Matthew,
Sancte Simon,	St. Simon,
Sancte Thaddæe,	St. Thaddeus,
Sancte Matthia,	St. Matthias,
Sancte Barnaba,	St. Barnaby,
Sancte Luca,	St. Luke,
Sancte Marce,	St. Mark,
Omnes sancti Apostoli et Evangelistæ, *Orate, etc.*	All ye holy Apostles and Evangelists,
Omnes sancti Discipuli Domini, *Orate, etc.*	All ye holy Disciples of our Lord,
Omnes sancti Innocentes, *Orate, etc.*	All ye holy Innocents,
Sancte Stephane,	St. Stephen,
Sancte Laurenti,	St. Laurence,
Sancte Vincenti,	St. Vincent,

Ora pro nobis.

Pray for us.

Sancti Fabiane et Sebastiane, *Orate pro nobis.* — SS. Fabian and Sebastian,

Sancti Joannes et Paule, *Orate, etc.* — SS. John and Paul,

Sancti Cosmaet Damiane, *Orate, etc.* — SS. Cosmas and Damian,

Sancti Gervasi et Protasi, *Orate, etc.* — SS. Gervase and Protase

Omnes sancti Martyres, *Orate, etc.* — All ye holy Martyrs,

Sancte Sylvester, — St. Sylvester,

Sancte Gregori, — St. Gregory,

Sancte Ambrosi, — St. Ambrose,

Sancte Augustine, — St. Augustine,

Sancte Hieronyme, — St. Jerome,

Sancte Martine, — St. Martin,

Sancte Nicolæ, — St. Nicholas,

Ora pro nobis.

Omnes sancti Pontifice et Confessores, *Orate, etc.* — All ye holy Bishops and Confessors,

Omnes sancti Doctores, *Orate, etc.* — All ye holy Doctors,

Sancte Antoni, — St. Anthony,

Sancte Benedicte, — St. Benedict,

Sancte Bernarde, — St. Bernard,

Sancte Dominice, — St. Dominic,

Sancte Francisce, — St. Francis,

Omnes sancti Sacerdotes et Levitæ, *Orate, etc.* — All ye holy Priests and Levites,

Omnes sancti Monachi et Eremitæ, *Orate, etc.* — All ye holy Monks and Hermits,

Pray for us.

Sancta Maria Magdalena,	St. Mary Magdalene,
Sancta Agatha,	St. Agatha,
Sancta Lucia,	St. Lucy,
Sancta Agnes,	St. Agnes,
Sancta Cæcilia,	St. Cecily,
Sancta Catharina,	St. Catharine,
Sancta Anastasia,	St. Anastasia,

Ora, etc.   *Pray for us.*

Omnes Sanctæ Virgines et Viduæ, *Orate, etc.* — All ye holy Virgins and Widows.

Omnes sancti et sanctæ Dei, *Intercedite pro nobis.* — All ye men and women, saints of God, *Make intercession for us.*

Propitius esto, *Parce nobis, Domine.* — Be merciful unto us. *Spare us, O Lord.*

Propitius esto, *Exaudi nos, Domine.* — Be merciful unto us, *Graciously hear us, O Lord.*

Ab omni malo, *Libera nos, Domine.* — From all evil, *O Lord deliver us.*

Libera nos, Domine.   *O Lord, deliver us.*

Ab omni peccato, — From all sin,

Ab ira tua, — From thy wrath,

A subitanea et improvisa morte, — From a sudden and unprovided death,

Ab insidiis diaboli, — From the deceits of the devil,

Ab ira, et odio, et omni mala voluntate, — From anger, hatred, and all ill-will,

A spiritu fornicationis, — From the spirit of fornication,

A fulgure et tempestate,

From lightning and tempest,

A flagello terræmotus,

From the scourge of earthquake,

A peste, fame et bello,

From plague, famine, and war,

A morte perpetua,

From everlasting death,

Per mysterium Sanctæ Incarnationis tuæ,

Through the mystery of thy holy incarnation,

Per Adventum tuum,

Through thy coming,

Per Nativitatem tuam,

Through thy nativity,

Perbaptismum et sanctum jejunium tuum,

Through thy baptism and holy fasting,

Per crucem et passionem tuam,

Through thy cross and passion,

Per mortem et sepulturam tuam,

Through thy death and burial,

Per sanctam resurrectionem tuam,

Through thy holy resurrection,

Per admirabilem ascensionem tuam.

Through thy admirable ascension,

Per adventum Spiritus Sancti Paracliti,

Through the coming of the Holy Ghost, the Comforter,

In die Judicii,

In the day of Judgment,

Peccatores, *Te rogamus audi nos.*

We sinners, *beseech thee to hear us.*

Ut nobis parcas, *Te rogamus audi nos.*

That thou spare us, *We beseech thee to hear us.*

Libera nos, Domine.

O Lord, deliver us.

Ut nobis indulgeas,

Ut ad veram pœnitentiam nos perducere digneris,

Ut Ecclesiam tuam sanctam, regere et conservare digneres,

Ut Dominum Apostolicum, et omnes Ecclesiasticos Ordines in sancta religione conservare digneris,

Ut inimicos sanctæ Ecclesiæ humiliare digneris,

Ut Regibus et Principibus Christianis pacem et veram concordiam donare digneris,

Ut cuncto populo Christiano pacem et unitatem largiri digneris,

Ut nos metipsos in tuo sancto servitio confortare et conservare digneris,

Ut mentes nostras ad cœlestia desideria erigas,

Te rogamus audi nos.

That thou pardon us.

That thou vouchsafe to bring us to true penance.

That thou vouchsafe to govern and preserve thy holy Church,

That thou vouchsafe to preserve our Apostolic Lord, and all Ecclesiastical Orders in holy religion.

That thou vouchsafe to humble the enemies of the holy Church,

That thou vouchsafe to give peace and true concord to Christian kings and princes,

That thou vouchsafe to grant peace and unity to all Christian people,

That thou vouchsafe to confirm and preserve us in thy holy service,

That thou lift up our minds to heavenly desires,

We beseech thee to hear us.

Ut omnibus benefactoribus nostris sempiterna bona retribuas,

Ut animas nostras, fratrum, propinquorum, et benefactorum nostrorum ab æterna damnatione eripias,

Ut fructus terræ dare et conservare digneris,

Ut omnibus fidelibus defunctis requiem æternam donare digneris.

Ut nos exaudire digneris,

Fili Dei,

Agnus Dei, qui tollis peccata mundi, *Parce nobis Domine.*

Agnus Dei, qui tollis peccata mundi, *Exaudi nos Domine.*

Agnus Dei, qui tollis peccata mundi, *Miserere nobis.*

Te rogamus audi nos.

That thou render eternal good things to all our benefactors,

That thou deliver our souls and those of our brethren, kinsfolk, and benefactors, from eternal damnation,

That thou vouchsafe to give and preserve the fruits of the earth,

That thou vouchsafe to give eternal rest to all the faithful departed,

That thou vouchsafe graciously to hear us.

Son of God,

Lamb of God, who takest away the sins of the world, *Spare us, O Lord.*

Lamb of God, who takest away the sins of the world, *Graciously hear us, O Lord*

Lamb of God, who takest away the sins of the world, *Have mercy on us.*

We beseech thee to hear us.

Christe audi nos. Christe exaudi nos. Kyrie eleison. Christe eleison. Kyrie eleison. Pater noster, *secreto.*

Christ, hear us. Christ, graciously hear us. Lord, have mercy on us. Christ, have mercy on us. Lord, have mercy on us. Our Father, *in secret.*

V. Et ne nos inducas in tentationem.

V. And lead us not into temptation.

R. Sed libera nos a malo. *Amen.*

R. But deliver us from evil. *Amen.*

PSALM LXIX.

DEUS in adjutorium meum intende ;* Domine ,ad adjuvandum me festina.

INCLINE unto my aid O God ; * O Lord, make haste to help me.

Confundantur et revereantur, * qui quærunt animam meam.

Let them be confounded and ashamed * that seek my soul.

Avertantur retrorsum, et erubescant,* qui volunt mihi mala.

Let them be turned backward, and blush for shame, * that desire evils to me.

Avertantur statim erubescentes, * qui dicunt mihi, Euge, euge.

Let them be presently turned away blushing for shame, * that say to me, 'Tis well, 'tis well.

Exultent et lætentur in te omnes qui quærunt te, * et dicant semper ; Mag-

Let all that seek thee rejoice, and be glad in thee, * and let such as love

nificetur Dominus qui diligunt salutare tuum.

Ego vero egenus et pauper sum ; * Deus adjuva me.

Adjutor meus, et liberator meus es tu ; *Domine ne moreris.

Gloria Patri, etc.

V. Salvos fac servos tuos. *R.* Deus meus sperantes in te. *V.* Esto nobis Domine turris fortitudinis. *R.* A facie inimici. *V.* Nihil proficiat inimicus in nobis. *R.* Et filius iniquitatis non apponat nocere nobis.. *V.* Domine, non secundum peccata nostra facias nobis. *R.* Neque secundum iniquitates nostras retribuas nobis. *V.* Oremus pro Pontifice nostro *N.* *R.* Dominus conservet eum, et vivificet eum, et beatum faciat eum in terra, et non tradat eum in animam inimicorum

thy salvation say always The Lord be magnified.

But I am needy and poor. * O God, help me.

Thou art my helper and my deliverer ; * O Lord, make no delay.

Glory be to the Father etc.

V. Save thy servants. *R.* Trusting in thee, O my God. *V.* Be unto us, O Lord, a tower of strength. *R.* From the face of the enemy. *V.* Let not the enemy prevail against us at all. *R.* Nor the son of iniquity have any power to hurt us. *V.* O Lord, deal not with us according to our sins. *R.* Neither reward us according to our iniquities. *V.* Let us pray for our chief Bishop. *R.* Our Lord preserve him, and give him life, and make him blessed upon earth, and deliver him not to the will of

ejus. *V.* Oremus pro benefactoribus nostris. *R.* Retribuere dignare Domine, omnibus nobis bona facientibus, propter nomen tuum, vitam æternam. Amen. *V.* Oremus pro fidelibus defunctis. *R.* Requiem æternam dona eis Domine, et lux perpetua luceat eis. *V.* Requiescant in pace. *R.* Amen. *V.* Pro fratribus nostris absentibus. *R.* Salvos fac servos tuos, Deus meus, sperantes in te. *V.* Mitte eis Domine auxilium de sancto. *R.* Et de Sion tuere eos. *V.* Domine exaudi orationem meam. *R.* Et clamor meus ad te veniat.

his enemies. Let us pray for our benefactors. *R.* Vouchsafe, O Lord, for thy mame's sake, to reward with eternal life all them that have done us good. Amen. *V.* Let us pray for the faithful departed. *R.* Eternal rest give to them, O Lord; and let perpetual light shine upon them. *V.* May they rest in peace. *R.* Amen. *V.* For our absent brethren. *R.* O my God, save thy servants trusting in thee. *V.* Send them help, O Lord, from thy holy place. *R.* And from Sion protect them. *V.* O Lord, hear my prayer. *R.* And let my cry come unto thee.

LET US PRAY.

O GOD, whose attribute it is, always to have mercy and to spare, receive our petition, that we, and all thy servants who are bound by the chains of sin, may, by the compassion of thy goodness, mercifully be absolved.

Hear, we beseech thee, O Lord, the prayers of thy suppliants, and pardon the sins of them that confess to thee; that, in thy bounty, thou mayest give us both pardon and peace.

Out of thy clemency, O Lord, show thy unspeakable mercy to us, that so, thou mayest both acquit us of our sins, and deliver us from the punishment we deserve for them.

O God, who by sin art offended. and by penance pacified, mercifully regard the prayers of thy people making supplication to thee, and turn away the scourges of thy anger, which we deserve for our sins.

O Almighty and Eternal God, have mercy on thy servant *N.*, our chief Bishop, and direct him according to thy clemency. in the way of everlasting salvation ; that by thy grace he may desire those things that are agreeable to thee, and perform them with all his strength.

O God, from whom are all holy desires, right counsels, and just works, give to thy servants that peace which the world cannot give ; that our hearts may be disposed to keep thy commandments, and the fear of enemies being removed, the times, by thy protection, may be peaceable.

Inflame, O Lord, our reins and hearts with the fire of thy Holy Spirit, that we may serve thee with a chaste body, and please thee with a clean heart.

O God, the Creator and Redeemer of all the faithful, give to the souls of thy servants departed the remission of all their sins ; that through pious supplications they may obtain the pardon which they have always desired.

Prevent, we beseech thee, O Lord, our actions by thy holy inspirations, and carry them on by thy gracious assistance; that every prayer and work of ours may always begin from thee, and by thee be happily ended.

O Almighty and Eternal God. who hast dominion over the living and the dead, and art merciful to all whom thou foreknowest shall be thine by faith and good works; we humbly beseech thee that they for whom we have determined to offer up our prayers, whether this world still detains them in the flesh, or the world to come has already received them out of their bodies, may, by the clemency of thy goodness, all thy saints interceding for them, obtain pardon and full remission of all their sins, through our Lord Jesus Christ, thy Son, who liveth and reigneth, etc. Amen.

V. O Lord, hear my prayer.

R. And let my cry come unto thee.

V. May the Almighty and most merciful Lord graciously hear us. *R.* Amen.

V. And may the souls of the faithful departed, through the mercy of God, rest in peace. *R.* Amen.

A Universal Prayer

FOR ALL THINGS NECESSARY TO SALVATION.

O MY God, I believe in thee, do thou strengthen my faith. All my hopes are in thee; do thou secure them. I love thee with my whole heart; oh! teach me to love thee daily more and more. I am sorry that I have offended thee: do thou increase my sorrow.

I adore thee as my first beginning; I aspire after thee as my last end; I give thee thanks as my constant benefactor: I call upon thee as my sovereign protector.

Vouchsafe, O my God, to conduct me by thy wisdom, to restrain me by thy justice, to comfort me by thy mercy, to defend me by thy power.

To thee I desire to consecrate all my thoughts, words, actions and sufferings; that henceforward I may think of thee, speak of thee, willingly refer all my actions to thy greater glory, and suffer willingly whatever thou shalt appoint.

Lord, I desire that in all things thy will may be done, because it is thy will, and in the manner thou willest.

I beg of thee to enlighten my understanding, to inflame my will: to purify my body, and to sanctify my soul.

Give me strength, O my God, to expiate my offences, to overcome my temptations, to subdue my passions, and to acquire the virtues proper for my state.

Fill my heart with a tender affection for thy goodness, a hatred for my faults, a love for my neighbour, and a contempt of the world.

Let me always remember to be submissive to my superiors, condescending to my inferiors, faithful to my friends, and charitable to my enemies.

Assist me to overcome sensuality by mortification, avarice by alms-deeds, anger by meekness, and tepidity by devotion.

O my God, make me prudent in my undertakings, courageous in dangers, patient in afflictions, and humble in prosperity.

Grant that I may be ever attentive at my prayers, temperate at my meals, diligent in my employments, and constant in my resolutions.

Let my conscience be ever upright and pure, my exterior modest, my conversation edifying, and my comportment regular.

Assist me, that I may continually labour to overcome nature, to correspond with thy grace, to keep thy commandments, and to work out my salvation.

Discover to me, O my God, the nothingness of this world, the greatness of heaven, the shortness of time, and the length of eternity.

Grant that I may prepare for death, that I may fear thy judgments, that I may escape hell, and in the end obtain heaven: through Jesus Christ. Amen

The Office for the Dead.

When the whole Office is said, the *Vespers* should be recited in the evening, and the *Matins* and *Lauds* on the following morning, concluding with one or more appropriate prayers. The *Antiphons* are doubled, that is, said completely before and after each Psalm on All Souls' Day, the Day of Burial, and on the third, seventh, and thirtieth days after Decease, as also on the Anniversary. On other occasions, only one or two words of the Antiphon are recited before each Psalm, and the whole of the Antiphon at the end thereof.

VESPERS.

Ant. I will please the Lord in the land of the living.

PSALM CXIV. *Dilexi, quoniam.*

I have loved, because the Lord will hear the voice of my prayer.

Because he hath inclined his ear unto me : and in my days I will call upon him.

The sorrows of death have compassed me : and the perils of hell have found me.

I met with trouble and sorrow : and I called upon the name of the Lord.

O Lord, deliver my soul. The Lord is merciful and just, and our God showeth mercy.

The Lord is the keeper of little ones : I was humbled, and he delivered me.

Turn, O my soul, into thy rest : for the Lord hath been bountiful to thee.

For he hath delivered my soul from death ; my eyes from tears, my feet from falling.

I will please the Lord in the land of the living.

Grant them eternal rest, O Lord :
And let perpetual light shine on them.

Ant. I will please the Lord in the land of the living.

Ant. Wo is me, O Lord, that my sojourning is prolonged.

PSALM CXIX *Ad Dominum, cum tribularer.*

In my trouble I cried to the Lord; and he heard me.

O Lord, deliver my soul from wicked lips, and a deceitful tongue.

What shall be given to thee, or what shall be added to thee, to a deceitful tongue ?

The sharp arrows of the mighty, with coals that lay waste.

Wo is me that my sojourning is prolonged ! I have dwelt with the inhabitants of Cedar ; my soul hath been long a sojourner.

With them that hated peace I was peaceable ; when I spoke to them they fought against me without cause.

Grant them eternal rest, &c.

Ant. Wo is me, O Lord, that my sojourning is prolonged.

Ant. The Lord keepeth thee from all evil; may the Lord keep thy soul.

PSALM CXX. *Levavi oculos.*

I have lifted up my eyes to the mountains, from whence help shall come to me.

My help is from the Lord, who hath made heaven and earth.

May he not suffer thy foot to be moved; neither let him slumber that keepeth thee.

Behold he shall neither slumber nor sleep, that keepeth Israel.

The Lord is thy keeper, the Lord is thy protection upon thy right hand.

The sun shall not burn thee by day : nor the moon by night.

The Lord keepeth thee from all evil; may the Lord keep thy soul.

May the Lord keep thy coming in and thy going out, from henceforth, now, and for ever.

Grant them eternal rest, &c.

Anth. The Lord keepeth thee from all evil; may the Lord keep thy soul.

Anth. If thou, O Lord, wilt mark iniquities; Lord, who shall stand it?

PSALM CXXIX. *De profundis* (page 118).

Ant. If thou, O Lord, wilt mark iniquities; Lord, who shall stand it?

Ant. Despise not, O Lord, the works of thy hands.

PSALM CXXXVII. *Confitebor tibi.*

I will praise thee, O Lord, with my whole heart : for thou hast heard the words of my mouth.

I will sing praise to thee in the sight of the angels : I will worship towards thy holy temple, and I will give glory to thy name.

For thy mercy, and for thy truth ; for thou hast magnified thy holy name above all.

In what day soever I shall call upon thee, hear me : thou shalt multiply strength in my soul.

May all the kings of the earth give glory to thee : for they have heard all the words of thy mouth.

And let them sing in the ways of the Lord : for great is the glory of the Lord.

For the Lord is high, and looketh on the low ; and the high he knoweth afar off.

If I shall walk in the midst of tribulation, thou wilt quicken me ; and thou hast stretched forth thy hand against the wrath of my enemies ; and thy right hand hath saved me.

The Lord will repay for me : thy mercy, O Lord, endureth for ever.   Oh, despise not the works of thy hands.

Grant them eternal rest, &c.

Anth. Despise not, O Lord, the works of thy hands.

V. I heard a voice from heaven saying to me,

R. Blessed are the dead that die in the Lord.

Ant. All that the Father giveth to me, shall come to me ; and him that cometh to me, I will not cast out.

Canticle of the Blessed Virgin Mary (p. 502).

Grant them eternal rest, &c.

Ant. All that the Father giveth to me, shall come to me ; and him that cometh to me I will not cast out.

The following Prayers are said kneeling.

Our Father, &c., *in secret.*

V. And lead us not into temptation.

R. But deliver us from evil.

PSALM CXLV. *Lauda anima.*

Praise the Lord, O my soul, in my life I will praise the Lord : I will sing to my God as long as I shall be.

Put not your trust in princes : in the children of men, in whom there is no salvation.

His spirit shall go forth, and he shall return into his earth : in that day all their thoughts shall perish.

Blessed is he who hath the God of Jacob for his helper, whose hope is in the Lord his God : who made heaven and earth, the sea, and all things that are in them.

Who keepeth truth for ever ; who executeth judgment for them that suffer wrong ; who giveth food to the hungry.

The Lord looseth them that are fettered : the Lord enlighteneth the blind.

The Lord lifteth up them that are cast down : the Lord loveth the just.

The Lord keepeth the strangers : he will support the fatherless and the widow ; and the ways of sinners he will destroy.

The Lord shall reign for ever; thy God, O Sion, unto generation and generation.

* This Psalm is omitted on All Saints' Day, and on the day of Burial.

Grant them eternal rest, &c.

V. From the gates of hell.

R. Deliver their souls, O Lord.

V. May they rest in peace.

R. Amen.

V. O Lord, hear my prayer.

R. And let my cry come to thee.

V. The Lord be with you.

R. And with thy spirit.

LET US PRAY.

O GOD, who among thy apostolic priests, hast bestowed on thy servants the dignity of bishops or priests: grant, we beseech thee, that these may also be joined with them in perpetual society.

O God, the giver of pardon, and lover of human salvation, we beseech thy clemency, that the brethren, relations, and benefactors of our congregation, who are departed this life, may, through the intercession of the blessed Mary, ever a virgin, and of all thy saints, attain to the fellowship of eternal bliss.

O God, the Creator and Redeemer of all the faithful, give to the souls of thy servants, men and women, the remission of all their sins; that by pious supplications they may obtain the pardon they have always desired. Who livest and reignest, world without end.

R. Amen.

V. Eternal rest give them, O Lord.

R. And let perpetual light shine on them.

V. May they rest in peace.

R. Amen.

[*On the Commemoration of All Souls, the last of the foregoing Prayers is said exclusively, with the following conclusion :* Who livest and reignest with God the Father, in the unity of the Holy Ghost, God, world without end.   Amen.]

A Prayer on the Day of the decease of a Man or Woman.

ABSOLVE, we beseech thee, O Lord, the soul of thy servant N., that being dead to the world, he (*or* she) may live to thee : and whatever sins he (*or* she) has committed through human frailty, do thou wipe away by the pardon of thy most merciful goodness : through our Lord Jesus Christ thy Son, who liveth and reigneth with thee in the unity of the Holy Ghost, God, world without end.

R. Amen.

V. Grant them eternal rest, O Lord.

R. And let perpetual light shine on them.

V. May they rest in peace.

R. Amen.

A Prayer for a Bishop or Priest deceased.   When it is for a Priest, the word Pontifical *is omitted, and* Priestly *introduced.*

O GOD, who among thy apostolic priests hast bestowed on thy servant N., the pontifical (*or* priestly) dignity; **grant,** we beseech thee, that he may also be joined with them in perpetual society. Through, &c.

For a Father and Mother deceased.

O GOD, who hast commanded us to honour our father and mother, have compassion, in thy mercy, on the souls of my father and mother, and forgive them their sins, and grant that we may meet in the joy of eternal bliss. Through, &c.

For a Father or Mother.

O GOD, who hast commanded us to honour our father and mother, have mercy through thy goodness on the soul of my father (*or* my mother), and forgive him (*her*) his (*her*) sins, and grant I may see him (*her*) in the joy of eternal bliss. Through, &c.

For a Man deceased.

INCLINE, O Lord, thy ear to our prayers, in which we humbly beseech thy mercy, that thou wouldst place the soul of thy servant, which thou hast caused to depart from this world, in the region of peace and light; and give him a share in the fellowship of thy saints. Through, &c.

For a Woman deceased.

WE beseech thee, O Lord, for thy goodness, have mercy on the soul of thy servant; and being freed from the corruption of mortality, restore to her the portion of eternal salvation. Through, &c.

On an Anniversary Day. If it be for one person only,
it is to be said in the singular number.

O LORD, the God of pardon, give to the souls of thy servants, men and women, whose anniversary day of departure we commemorate, the seat of refreshment, the happiness of rest, and the brightness of eternal light. Through, &c.

For Brethren, Relations, and Benefactors.

O GOD, the giver of pardon, and lover of human salvation, we beseech thy clemency to grant that the brethren, relations, and benefactors of our congregation, who are departed this world, may, by the intercession of the blessed Mary, ever virgin, and of all thy saints, attain to the fellowship of eternal beatitude. Through, &c.

For the Dead in general.

O GOD, the Creator and Redeemer of all the faithful, give to the souls of thy servants, men and women, the remission of all their sins, that, by pious supplications, they may obtain the pardon which they have always desired. Who livest and reignest world without end. R. Amen.

AT MATINS.

The following *Invitatory* is recited on All-Souls' Day, on day of Burial, and as often as the three *Nocturns* are said. At other times it is omitted, and the Office begins with the Antiphon of the Psalms of the Nocturn assigned to the day. The *first Nocturn* is assigned to Monday and Thursday; the *second*, to Tuesday and Friday; the *third*, to Wednesday and Saturday.

The Invitatory.

Come, let us adore the King, to whom all things live.

Come, let us adore the King, to whom all things live.

PSALM XCIV. *Venite exultemus.*

Come, let us praise the Lord with joy : let us joyfully sing to God our Saviour. Let us come before his presence with thanksgiving, and make a joyful noise to him with psalms.

Come, let us adore the King, to whom all things live.

For the Lord is a great God, and a great King above all gods : because the Lord repels not his people, for in his hand are all the ends of the earth : and the heights of the mountains are his.

Come, let us adore.

For the sea is his, and he made it : and his hands formed the dry land. Come, let us adore and fall down, and weep before the Lord that made us. For he is the Lord our God, and we are the people of his pasture, and the sheep of his hand.

Come, let us adore the King, to whom all things live.

To-day if you shall hear his voice, harden not your hearts : as in the provocation, according to the day of temptation in the wilderness : where your fathers tempted me, they proved me, and saw my works.

Come, let us adore.

Forty years long was I offended with that generation; and I said: These always err in heart. And these men have not known my ways: so I swore in my wrath that they shall not enter into my rest.

Come, let us adore the King, to whom all things live.

Grant them eternal rest, O Lord, and let perpetual light shine on them.

Come, let us adore.

Come, let us adore the King, to whom all things live.

FIRST NOCTURN.

On Monday and Thursday.

Ant. Direct.

PSALM V. *Verba mea.*

Give ear, O Lord, to my words, understand my cry.

Hearken to the voice of my prayer, O my King and my God.

For to thee will I pray: O Lord, in the morning thou shalt hear my voice.

In the morning I will stand before thee, and will see: because thou art not a God that willest iniquity.

Neither shall the wicked dwell near thee: nor shall the unjust abide before thy eyes.

Thou hatest all the workers of iniquity: thou wilt destroy all that speak a lie.

The bloody and the deceitful man the Lord will abhor: but as for me, in the multitude of thy mercy,

I will come into thy house : I will worship towards thy holy temple, in thy fear.

Conduct me, O Lord, in thy justice : because of my enemies, direct my way in thy sight.

For there is no truth in their mouth : their heart is vain.

Their throat is an open sepulchre : they dealt deceitfully with their tongues : judge them, O God.

Let them fall from their devices : according to the multitude of their wickednesses cast them out : for they have provoked thee, O Lord.

But let all them be glad that hope in thee : they shall rejoice for ever, and thou shalt dwell in them.

And all they that love thy name shall glory in thee : for thou wilt bless the just.

O Lord, thou hast crowned us, as with a shield of thy good-will.

Grant them eternal rest, &c.

Ant. Direct, O Lord my God, my steps in thy sight.

Ant. Turn to me, O Lord.

PSALM VI. *Domine, ne in furore.* (See p. 118).

Grant them eternal rest, &c.

Ant. Turn to me, O Lord, and deliver my soul : for there is none in death who will be mindful of thee

Ant. Lest at any time.

PSALM VII. *Domine, Deus meus.*

O Lord, my God, in thee have I put my trust : save me from all them that persecute me, and deliver me.

Lest at any time he seize upon my soul, like a lion, while there is no one to redeem me, nor to save.

O Lord, my God, if I have done this thing, if there be iniquity in my hands :

If I have rendered to them that repaid me evils let me deservedly fall empty before my enemies.

Let the enemy pursue my soul, and seize it, and tread down my life on the earth, and bring down my glory to the dust.

Rise up, O Lord, in thy anger; and be thou exalted in the borders of my enemies.

And arise, O Lord my God, in the precept which thou hast commanded. And a congregation of people shall surround thee.

And for their sakes return thou on high. The Lord judgeth the people.

Judge me, O Lord, according to my justice, and according to my innocence in me.

The wickedness of sinners shall be brought to nought, and thou shalt direct the just : the searcher of hearts and reins, is God.

Just is my help from the Lord: who saveth the upright of heart.

God is a just judge, strong and patient : is he angry every day ?

Except you will be converted, he will brandish his sword : he hath bent his bow, and made it ready.

And in it he hath prepared the instruments of death : he hath made ready his arrows for them that burn.

Behold he hath been in labour with injustice; he hath conceived sorrow, and brought forth iniquity.

He hath opened a pit and dug it; and he is fallen into the hole he made.

His sorrow shall be turned on his own head; and his iniquity shall come down upon his crown.

I will give glory to the Lord according to his justice; and will sing to the name of the Lord the most high.

Grant them eternal rest, &c.

Ant. Lest at any time he seize upon my soul, like a lion, while there is no one to redeem me nor to save.

V. From the gates of hell,

R. Deliver their souls, O Lord.

Our Father, &c., *in secret.*

The First Lesson. JOB VII.

Spare me, O Lord, for my days are nothing. What is man that thou shouldst magnify him? or why dost thou set thy heart upon him? Thou visitest him early in the morning, and thou provest him suddenly. How long wilt thou not spare me, nor let me alone to swallow down my spittle? I have sinned, what shall I do to thee, O keeper of men? why hast thou set me opposite to thee, and I am become burdensome to myself? Why dost thou not remove my sin, and why dost thou not take away my iniquity? Behold now I shall sleep in the dust; and if thou seek me in the morning I shall not be.

R. I believe my Redeemer liveth, and that in the last day I shall rise from the earth. And in my flesh I shall see God my Saviour.

V. Whom I myself shall see, and not another, and my eyes shall behold. And in my flesh.

The Second Lesson. JOB X.

My soul is weary of my life; I will let go my speech against myself, I will speak in the bitterness of my soul. I will say to God: Do not condemn me; tell me why thou judgest me so. Doth it seem good to thee that thou shouldst calumniate me, and oppress me, the work of thy own hands, and help the counsel of the wicked? Hast thou eyes of flesh; or shalt thou see as man seeth? Are thy days as the days of man, and are thy years as the times of men, that thou shouldst inquire after my iniquity, and search after my sin? And shouldst know that I have done no wicked thing, whereas there is no man that can deliver out of thy hand.

R. Thou who didst raise Lazarus stinking from the grave. Thou, O Lord, give them rest, and a place of pardon.

V. Who art to come to judge the living and the dead, and the world by fire. Thou, O Lord.

The Third Lesson. JOB X.

Thy hands have made me, and fashioned me wholly round about, and dost thou thus cast me down headlong on a sudden? Remember, I beseech thee, that thou hast made me as the clay, and thou wilt bring me into dust again. Hast thou not milked me as milk and curdled me like cheese? Thou hast clothed me with skin and flesh : thou hast put me together with bones and sinews : thou hast granted me life and mercy, and thy visitation hath preserved my spirit.

R. O Lord, when thou wilt come to judge the earth, where shall I hide myself from the face of thy wrath? For I have sinned exceedingly during my life.

V. I dread my misdeeds, and blush before thee : do not condemn me, when thou wilt come to judge. For I have sinned exceedingly during my life.

V. Grant them eternal rest, O Lord, and let perpetual light shine on them. For I have.

Here Lauds are recited when the first Nocturn only is said.

AT THE SECOND NOCTURN.
On Tuesday and Friday.

Ant. In a place of pasture.

PSALM XXII. *Dominus regit me.*

The Lord ruleth me ; and I shall want nothing. He hath set me in a place of pasture.

He hath brought me up on the water of refreshment ; he hath converted my soul.

He hath led me on the paths of justice, for his own name's sake.

For though I should walk in the midst of the shadow of death, I will fear no evils, for thou art with me.

Thy rod and thy staff, they have comforted me.

Thou hast prepared a table before me, against them that afflict me.

Thou hast anointed my head with oil; and my chalice which inebriateth me, how goodly is it!

And thy mercy will follow me all the days of my life.

And that I may dwell in the house of the Lord, unto length of days.

Grant them eternal rest, &c.

Ant. In a place of pasture he hath set me.

Ant. The offences.

PSALM XXIV. *Ad te, Domine, levavi.*

To thee, O Lord, have I lifted up my soul. In thee, O my God, I put my trust; let me not be ashamed.

Neither let my enemies laugh at me: for none of them that wait on thee shall be confounded.

Let all them be confounded that act unjust things without cause.

Show, O Lord, thy ways to me, and teach me thy paths.

Direct me in thy truth, and teach me: for thou art God my Saviour; and on thee have I waited all the day long.

Remember, O Lord, thy bowels of compassion; and thy mercies that are from the beginning of the world.

The sins of my youth and my ignorances do not remember.

According to thy mercy remember thou me: for thy goodness' sake, O Lord.

The Lord is sweet and righteous: therefore he will give a law to sinners in the way.

He will guide the mild in judgment: he will teach the meek his ways.

All the ways of the Lord are mercy and truth, to them that seek after his covenant and his testimonies.

For thy name's sake, O Lord, thou wilt pardon my sin : for it is great.

Who is the man that feareth the Lord? he hath appointed him a law in the way he hath chosen.

His soul shall dwell in good things : and his seed shall inherit the land.

The Lord is a firmament to them that fear him ; and his covenant shall be made manifest unto them.

My eyes are ever towards the Lord; for he shall pluck my feet out of the snare.

Look thou upon me, and have mercy on me; for I am alone and poor.

The troubles of my heart are multiplied ; deliver me from my necessities.

See my abjection and my labour ; and forgive me all my sins.

Consider my enemies, for they are multiplied, and have hated me with an unjust hatred.

Keep thou my soul, and deliver me : I shall not be ashamed, for I have hoped in thee.

The innocent and the upright have adhered to me ; because I have waited on thee.

Deliver Israel, O God, from all his tribulations.

Grant them eternal rest, &c.

Ant. The sins of my youth, and my ignorances do not remember, O Lord.

Ant. I believe to see.

PSALM XXVI. *Dominus illuminatio mea.*

The Lord is my light and my salvation, whom shall I fear?

The Lord is the protector of my life: of whom shall I be afraid?

Whilst the wicked draw near against me to eat my flesh,

My enemies that trouble me have themselves been weakened, and have fallen.

If armies in camp should stand together against me, my heart shall not fear.

If a battle should rise up against me, in this will I be confident.

One thing have I asked of the Lord, this will I seek after; that I may dwell in the house of the Lord all the days of my life.

That I may see the delight of the Lord, and may visit his temple.

For he hath hidden me in his tabernacle: in the day of evils, he hath protected me in the secret place of his tabernacle.

He hath exalted me upon a rock: and now he hath lifted up my head above my enemies.

I have gone round, and have offered up in his tabernacle a sacrifice of jubilation. I will sing, and recite a psalm to the Lord.

Hear, O Lord, my voice, with which I have cried to thee: have mercy on me, and hear me.

My heart hath said to thee: my face hath sought thee: thy face, O Lord, will I still seek.

Turn not away thy face from me : decline not in thy wrath from thy servant.

Be thou my helper, forsake me not; do not thou despise me, O God my Saviour.

For my father and my mother have left me : but the Lord hath taken me up.

Set me, O Lord, a law in thy way, and guide me in the right path, because of my enemies.

Deliver me not over to the will of them that trouble me : for unjust witnesses have risen up against me : and iniquity hath lied to itself.

I believe to see the good things of the Lord in the land of the living.

Expect the Lord, do manfully, and let thy heart take courage, and wait thou for the Lord.

Grant them eternal rest, &c.

Ant. I believe to see the good things of the Lord in the land of the living.

V. May the Lord place him with the princes.

R. With the princes of his people.

Our Father, &c., *in secret.*

The fourth Lesson. Job XIII.

Answer me : how many are my iniquities and sins? make me know my crimes and offences. Why hidest thou thy face, and thinkest me thy enemy? Against a leaf that is carried away with the wind, thou showest thy power, and thou pursuest a dry straw. For thou writest bitter things against me, and wilt consume me for the sins of my youth.

Thou hast put my feet in the stocks, and hast observed all my paths, and hast considered the steps of my feet, who am to be consumed as rottenness, and as a garment that is moth-eaten.

R. Remember me, O God, because my life is but wind. Nor may the sight of man behold me.

V. From the depths I have cried to thee, O Lord. Lord, hear my voice. Nor may.

The fifth Lesson. JOB XIV.

Man born of a woman, living for a short time, is filled with many miseries. Who cometh forth like a flower, and is destroyed, and fleeth as a shadow, and never continueth in the same state. And dost thou think it meet to open thy eyes upon such an one, and to bring him into judgment with thee? Who can make him clean that is conceived of unclean seed? Is it not thou who only art? The days of man are short, and the number of his months is with thee: thou hast appointed his bounds which cannot be passed. Depart a little from him, that he may rest, until his wished-for day come, as that of the hireling.

R. Woe is me, O Lord, because I have sinned exceedingly during my life: Oh! wretch, what shall I do, whither shall I fly but to thee, my God: Have mercy on me when thou comest at the last day.

V. My soul is greatly troubled; but thou, O Lord, succour it. Have mercy on me.

The sixth Lesson. JOB XIV.

Who will grant me this, that thou mayest protect me in hell, and hide me till thy wrath pass, and appoint me a time, when thou wilt remember me? Shall man that is dead, thinkest thou, live again? All the days in which I am now in warfare, I expect until my change come. Thou shalt call me, and I will answer thee : to the work of thy hands thou shalt reach out thy right hand. Thou indeed hast numbered my steps, but spare my sins.

R. Remember not my sins, O Lord, when thou wilt come to judge the world by fire.

V. Direct, O Lord, my God, my way in thy sight. When thou wilt come to judge the world by fire.

V. Grant them eternal rest, O Lord, and let perpetual light shine on them : When.

Here the Lauds are recited when the second Nocturn only is said.

THIRD NOCTURN.

On Wednesdays and Saturdays.

Ant. Be pleased.

PSALM XXXIX. *Expectans expectavi.*

With expectation I have waited for the Lord, and he was attentive to me.

And he heard my prayers, and he brought me out of the pit of misery and the mire of dregs.

And he set my feet upon a rock, and directed my steps.

And he put a new canticle into my mouth, a song to our God.

Many shall see, and shall fear: and they shall hope in the Lord.

Blessed is the man whose trust is in the name of the Lord: and who hath not had regard to vanities and lying follies.

Thou hast multiplied thy wonderful works, O Lord my God: and in thy thoughts there is no one like to thee.

I have declared and I have spoken: they are multiplied above number.

Sacrifice and oblation thou didst not desire: but thou hast pierced ears for me.

Burnt-offering and sin-offering thou didst not require: then said I, Behold I come.

In the head of the book it is written of me, that I should do thy will: O my God, I have desired it, and thy law in the midst of my heart.

I have declared thy justice in a great church: lo, I will not restrain my lips, O Lord, thou knowest it.

I have not hid thy justice within my heart: I have declared thy truth and thy salvation.

I have not concealed thy mercy and thy truth from a great council.

Withhold not thou, O Lord, thy tender mercies from me: thy mercy and thy truth have always upheld me.

For evils without number have surrounded me; my iniquities have overtaken me, and I was not able to see

They are multiplied above the hairs of my head : and my heart hath forsaken me.

Be pleased, O Lord, to deliver me ; look down, O Lord, to help me.

Let them be confounded and ashamed together, that seek after my soul to take it away.

Let them be turned backward and be ashamed that desire evils to me.

Let them immediately bear their confusion, that say to me, 'Tis well, 'tis well.

Let all that seek thee rejoice and be glad in thee : and let such as love thy salvation, say always, the Lord be magnified.

But I am a beggar and poor: the Lord is careful for me.

Thou art my helper and my protector : O my God be not slack.

Grant them eternal rest, &c.

Ant. Be pleased, O Lord, to deliver me · look down, O Lord, to help me.

Ant. Heal, O Lord.

PSALM XL. *Beatus qui intelligit.*

Blessed is he that understandeth concerning the needy and the poor : the Lord will deliver him in the evil day.

The Lord preserve him and give him life, and make him blessed upon the earth ; and deliver him not up to the will of his enemies.

The Lord help him on his bed of sorrow : thou hast turned all his couch in his sickness.

I said : O Lord, be thou merciful to me : heal my soul, for I have sinned against thee.

My enemies have spoken evils against me : when shall he die, and his name perish ?

And if he came in to see me, he spoke vain things ; his heart gathered together iniquity to itself.

He went out and spoke to the same purpose.

All my enemies whispered together against me : they devised evils to me.

They determined against me an unjust word : shall he that sleepeth rise again no more ?

For even the man of my peace, in whom I trusted, who ate my bread, hath greatly supplanted me.

But thou, O Lord, have mercy on me, and raise me up again : and I will requite them.

By this I know that thou hast had a good-will for me, because my enemy shall not rejoice over me.

But thou hast upheld me by reason of my innocence : and hast established me in thy sight for ever.

Blessed be the Lord the God of Israel from eternity to eternity. So be it. So be it.

Ant. Grant them eternal rest, &c.

Ant. Heal, O Lord, my soul, because I have sinned against thee.

Ant. My soul hath thirsted.

PSALM XLI. *Quemadmodum desiderat.*

As the hart panteth after the fountains of **waters** : so my soul panteth after thee, O God.

My soul hath thirsted after the strong living God ! when shall I come and appear before the face of God?

My tears have been my bread day and night, whilst it is said to me daily, Where is thy God?

These things I remembered, and poured out my soul in me: for I shall go over into the place of the wonderful tabernacle, even to the house of God:

With the voice of joy and praise ; the noise of one feasting.

Why art thou sad, O my soul, and why dost thou trouble me ?

Hope in God; for I will still give praise to him, the salvation of my countenance, and my God.

My soul is troubled within myself; therefore will I remember thee from the land of Jordan and Hermoniim, from the little hill.

Deep calleth on deep at the noise of thy floodgates.

All thy heights and thy billows have passed over me.

In the day-time the Lord hath commanded his mercy ; and a canticle to him in the night.

With me is prayer to the God of my life. I will say to God, thou art my support.

Why hast thou forgotten me ? and why go I mourning, whilst my enemy afflicteth me ?

Whilst my bones are broken, my enemies who trouble me have reproached me.

Whilst they say to me, day by day, Where is thy God?

Why art thou cast down, O my soul, and why dost thou disquiet me ?

Hope thou in God, for I will still give praise to him : the salvation of my countenance and my God.

Grant them eternal rest, &c.

Anth. My soul hath thirsted after the living God; when shall I come and appear before the face of the Lord?

V. Deliver not to beasts the souls that confess to thee.

R. And the souls of thy poor forget not to the end.

Our Father, &c., *in secret.*

The seventh Lesson. JOB XVII.

My spirit shall be wasted, my days shall be shortened, and only the grave remaineth for me. I have not sinned, and my eye abideth in bitterness. Deliver me, O Lord, and set me beside thee, and let any man's hand fight against me. My days have passed away, my thoughts are dissipated, tormenting my heart. They have turned night into day, and after darkness I hope for light again. If I wait, hell is my house, and I have made my bed in darkness. I have said to rottenness: thou art my father: to worms, my mother and my sister. Where is now then my expectation, and who considereth my patience?

R. The fear of death troubles me: sinning daily and not repenting: Because in hell there is no redemption, have mercy on me, O God, and save me.

V. O God, in thy name save me, and in thy strength deliver me: Because in hell.

The eighth Lesson. JOB XIX.

The flesh being consumed, my bone hath cleaved to my skin, and nothing but lips are left about my teeth. Have pity on me, have pity on me, at least you my friends, because the hand of the Lord hath touched me. Why do you persecute me as God, and glut yourselves with my flesh? Who will grant me that my words may be written? Who will grant me that they may be marked down in a book? With an iron pen, and in a plate of lead, or else be graven with an instrument in flint-stone? For I know that my Redeemer liveth, and in the last day I shall rise out of the earth. And I shall be clothed again with my skin, and in my flesh I shall see my God. Whom I myself shall see, and my eyes shall behold, and not another: this my hope is laid up in my bosom.

R. Judge me not, O Lord, according to my deeds, for I have done nothing worthy in thy sight; therefore I beseech thy majesty. That thou, O God, mayest blot out my iniquity.

V. Wash me, O Lord, yet more from my injustice, and cleanse me from my sin. That.

The Ninth Lesson. JOB X.

Why didst thou bring me forth out of the womb? Oh, that I had been consumed, that eye might not see me! I should have been as if I had not been carried from the womb to the grave. Shall not the fewness of my days be ended shortly? Suffer me, therefore, that I may lament my sorrow a little before I go and return no more, to a land that is dark and covered with the mist of death : a land of misery and darkness, where the shadow of death, and no order. but everlasting horror dwelleth.

R. Deliver me, O Lord, from the ways of hell, who hast broken the brazen gates, and hast visited hell, and hast given light to them, that they might behold thee who were in the pains of darkness.

V. Crying, and saying : thou art come, O our Redeemer. Who were.

V. Grant them eternal rest, O Lord, and let perpetual light shine on them. Who were.

This is always said in the Week-day office. But the following Responsory *is said on* All Souls' Day, *and when three* Nocturns *are said together.*

R. Deliver me, O Lord, from eternal death, in that dreadful day, when the heavens and earth are to be moved : when thou wilt come to judge the world by fire.

V. I tremble and do fear, when the examination is to be, and thy wrath to come, when the heavens and earth are to be moved.

V. That day is the day of anger, of calamity, and of misery, a great day and very bitter. When thou.

V. Grant them eternal rest, O Lord, and let perpetual light shine on them.

R. Deliver me, O Lord, from eternal death, in that dreadful day, when the heavens and earth are to be moved, when thou.

AT LAUDS.

Ant. The bones that have been humbled shall rejoice in our Lord.

Psalm L. *Miserere.* (See page 422).

Grant them eternal rest, &c.

Ant. The bones that have been humbled shall rejoice in our Lord.

Ant. Hear, O Lord.

Psalm LXIV. *Te decet hymnus.*

A hymn, O God, becometh thee in Sion ; and a vow shall be paid to thee in Jerusalem.

Oh, hear my prayer : all flesh shall come to thee.

The words of the wicked have prevailed over us : and thou wilt pardon our transgressions.

Blessed is he whom thou hast chosen and taken to thee : he shall dwell in thy courts.

We shall be filled with the good things of thy house ; holy is thy temple, wonderful in justice.

Hear us, O God our Saviour, who art the hope of all the ends of the earth, and in the sea afar off.

Thou who preparest the mountains by thy strength, being girded with power : who troublest the depth of the sea, the noise of its waves.

The gentiles shall be troubled, and they that dwell in the uttermost borders shall be afraid at thy signs : thou shalt make the outgoings of the morning and of the evening to be joyful.

Thou hast visited the earth, and hast plentifully watered it ; thou hast many ways enriched it.

The river of God is filled with water; thou hast prepared their food, for so is its preparation.

Fill up plentifully the streams thereof: multiply its fruits; it shall spring up and rejoice in its showers.

Thou shalt bless the crown of the year of thy goodness: and thy fields shall be filled with plenty.

The beautiful places of the wilderness shall grow fat: and the hills shall be girded about with joy.

The rams of the flock are clothed, and the vales shall abound with corn: they shall shout, yea, they shall sing a hymn.

Grant them eternal rest, O Lord.

Ant. Hear, O Lord, my prayer; all flesh shall come to thee.

Ant. Thy right hand.

PSALM LXII. *Deus, Deus meus.*

O God, my God, to thee do I watch at break of day.

For thee my soul hath thirsted; for thee my flesh, oh, how many ways!

In a desert land, and where there is no way, and no water; so in the sanctuary have I come before thee, to see thy power and thy glory.

For thy mercy is better than lives: thee my lips shall praise.

Thus will I bless thee all my life long: and in thy name I will lift up my hands.

Let my soul be filled as with marrow and fatness; and my mouth shall praise thee with joyful lips.

If I have remembered thee upon my bed, I will meditate on thee in the morning; because thou hast been my helper.

And I will rejoice under the covert of thy wings; my soul hath stuck close to thee: thy right hand hath received me.

But they have sought my soul in vain, they shall go into the lower parts of the earth: they shall be delivered into the hands of the sword, they shall be the portions of foxes.

But the king shall rejoice in God; all they shall be praised that swear by him: because the mouth is stopped of them that speak wicked things.

PSALM LXVI. *Deus misereatur nostri.*

May God have mercy on us, and bless us: may he cause the light of his countenance to shine upon us, and may he have mercy on us.

That we may know thy way upon earth, thy salvation in all nations.

Let people confess to thee, O God: let all people give praise to thee.

Let the nations be glad and rejoice: for thou judgest the people with justice, and directest the nations upon earth.

Let the people, O God, confess to thee; let all the people give praise to thee. The earth hath yielded her fruit.

May God, our own God, bless us: may God bless us, and all the ends of the earth fear him.

Grant them eternal rest, &c.

Ant. Thy right hand. O Lord, has received me.

Ant. From the gate of hell.

The Song of Ezechias. ISAIAS XXXVIII.

I said: in the midst of my days I shall go to the gates of hell.

I sought for the residue of my years. I said: I shall not see the Lord God in the land of the living.

I shall behold man no more, nor the inhabitant of rest.

My generation is at an end, and it is rolled away from me, as a shepherd's tent.

My life is cut off as by a weaver: whilst I was yet but beginning he cut me off: from morning even to night thou wilt make an end of me.

I hoped till morning; as a lion so hath he broken all my bones.

From morning even to night thou wilt make an end of me. I will cry like a young swallow, I will meditate like a dove.

My eyes are weakened with looking upward:

Lord, I suffer violence, answer thou for me. What shall I say, or what shall he answer for me, whereas he himself hath done it?

I will recount to thee all my years in the bitterness of my soul.

O Lord, if a man's life be such, and the life of my spirit be in such things as these, thou shalt correct me and make me to live. Behold in peace is my bitterness most bitter.

But thou hast delivered my soul, that it should not perish; thou hast cast all my sins behind thy back.

For hell shall not confess to thee, neither shall death praise thee; nor shall they that go down into the pit, look for thy truth.

The living, the living, he shall give praise to thee, as I do this day: the father shall make thy truth known to the children.

O Lord, save me, and we will sing our psalms all the days of our life in the house of the Lord.

Grant them eternal rest, &c.

Ant. From the gate of hell, deliver my soul, O Lord.

Ant. Let every spirit.

PSALM CXLVIII. *Laudate Dominum.*

Praise ye the Lord from the heavens: praise ye him in the high places.

Praise ye him all his angels: praise ye him all his hosts.

Praise ye him, O sun and moon: praise him all ye stars and light.

Praise him ye heavens of heavens: and let all the waters that are above the heavens praise the name of the Lord.

For he spoke, and they were made; he commanded, and they were created.

He hath established them for ever, and for ages of ages: he hath made a decree, and it shall not pass away.

Praise the Lord from the earth, ye dragons, and all ye deeps.

Fire, hail, snow, ice, stormy winds, which fulfil his word.

Mountains and all hills, fruitful trees and all cedars.

Beasts and all cattle: serpents and feathered fowls.

Kings of the earth, and all people; princes, and all judges of the earth.

Young men and maidens: let the old with the younger praise the name of the Lord: for his name alone is exalted.

The praise of him is above heaven and earth: and he hath exalted the horn of his people.

A hymn to all his saints: to the children of Israel, a people approaching to him.

PSALM CXLIX. *Cantate Domino.*

Sing ye to the Lord a new canticle: let his praise be in the church of the saints.

Let Israel rejoice in him that made him; and let the children of Sion be joyful in their king.

Let them praise his name in choir: let them sing to him with the timbrel and the psaltery.

For the Lord is well pleased with his people: and he will exalt the meek unto salvation.

The saints shall rejoice in glory: they shall be joyful in their beds.

The high praises of God shall be in their mouth: and two-edged swords in their hands.

To execute vengeance upon the nations, chastisements among the people:

To bind their kings with fetters, and their nobles with manacles of iron.

To execute upon them the judgment that is written; this glory is to all his saints.

Psalm CL. *Laudate Dominum in sanctis.*

Praise ye the Lord in his holy places: praise ye him in the firmament of his power.

Praise ye him for his mighty acts: praise ye him according to the multitude of his greatness.

Praise him with sound of trumpet: praise him with psaltery and harp.

Praise him with timbrel and choir: praise him with strings and organs.

Praise him on high sounding cymbals: praise him on cymbals of joy: Let every spirit praise the Lord.

Grant them eternal rest, &c.

Ant. Let every spirit praise the Lord.

V. I heard a voice from heaven saying to me.

R. Blessed are the dead that die in the Lord.

The Song of Zachary. Luke i.

Grant them eternal rest, &c.

Ant. I am the resurrection, and the life: he that

believeth in me, though he be dead, shall live : and every one that liveth and believeth in me, shall not die for ever.

The following Prayers are said kneeling.

Our Father, &c. (*in secret*).
V. And lead us not into temptation.
R. But deliver us from evil.

* Psalm. *De Profundis* (page 286.)

Grant them eternal rest, &c.
V. From the gates of hell.
R. Deliver their souls, O Lord.
V. May they rest in peace.
R. Amen.
V. O Lord, hear my prayer.
R. And let my cry come unto thee.
V. The Lord be with you.
R. And with thy spirit.

[*The* Prayer *is recited as at the end of the* Vespers *according to the rank, degree, or sex, of the person for the repose of whose Soul the Office has been said.*]

* This Psalm is omitted on the commemoration of All Souls, and on the day of Burial.

Devotions for the time of Jubilees,

OR OTHER INDULGENCES.

A PRAYER FOR THE WHOLE STATE OF CHRIST'S CHURCH
UPON EARTH, AND ALL THE INTENTIONS OF THE
INDULGENCE.

O ETERNAL Father of our Lord Jesus Christ,
Creator of all things, visible and invisible;
Source of all our good; infinitely good in thyself,
and infinitely gracious, bountiful and good to us;
behold, we, thy poor servants, the work of thy hands,
redeemed by the blood of thine only Son, come in
answer to his summons by his vicegerent, to present
ourselves, as humble petitioners, before the throne
of thy mercy. We come in communion with all thy
church in heaven, hoping to be assisted by their
prayers and merits; and with Jesus Christ as our
Head, our High Priest, and Mediator, in whose
precious blood we put all our trust.

We prostrate before thee, and humbly beseech
thee to sanctify thy own sacred name, by exalting
thy holy Catholic Church throughout the world.
O eternal King, who hast sent thine only Son from
thy throne above to this earth, to establish a kingdom
here amongst us, whence we might hereafter be
translated to thy eternal kingdom, look down, we
beseech thee, upon this kingdom of thy Son, and propagate it through all nations, and through all hearts.
Sanctify it in all truth; maintain it in peace, unity,

and holiness. Give it saints for its rulers, its chief pastors, and all its other prelates; enlighten them with heavenly wisdom, make them men according to thine own heart. Give thy grace and blessing to the clergy; send among them that heavenly fire, which thy Son came to cast on earth, and which he so earnestly desired should be enkindled. Assist and protect apostolic missionaries, that they may zealously and effectually promote thy glory, and the salvation of souls. Sanctify religious men and women of all orders; give them grace to serve thee, with perfection, according to the spirit of their institute, and to shine like lights to the rest of the faithful.

Have mercy on all Christian princes; grant them those graces that are necessary for the perfect discharge of their duty to thee and to their subjects; that they may be true servants to thee, the King of kings, fathers to their people, and nursing fathers to thy Church. Have mercy on magistrates and men in power; that they may fear thee, love thee, and serve thee, and ever remember that they are thy deputies, and ministers of thy justice. Have mercy on all thy people, and give thy blessing to thine inheritance; remember thy congregation, which thou hast possessed from the beginning; and give grace to thy children here upon earth, that they may do thy holy will in all things, even as the blessed do it in heaven.

Extend thy mercy also to infidels, who sit in darkness and the shadow of death; to those nations that have not yet received the faith and law of thy Son their Saviour; to Pagans, Mahometans, and Jews. Remember, O Lord, that these poor souls are made after thine own image and likeness, and redeemed by the blood of thy Son. Oh! let not Satan any longer exercise his tyranny over these thy creatures, to the great dishonour of thy name. Let not the precious blood of thy Son be shed for them in vain. Send among them zealous preachers and apostolic labourers, endued with the graces and gifts of thine Apostles, and bless them with the like success, for the glory of thy name: that these poor souls may be brought to know thee, love thee, and serve thee, here in thy Church, and bless thee hereafter for all eternity.

Look down also with an eye of pity and compassion on those deluded souls, who, under the name of Christians, have strayed from the one fold of the one Shepherd, thine only Son Jesus Christ, into the by-paths of error and schism. Oh! bring them back to thee and to thy Church. Dispel their darkness by thy heavenly light, take from them the spirit of obstinacy, pride, and self-conceit. Give them a humble and a docile heart, a strong desire of finding out thy truth, and grace to embrace it, notwithstanding the opposition of the world, the flesh, and the devil.

O Father of light, and God of all truth, purge the whole world from errors, abuses, corruptions, and vices. Beat down the standard of Satan, and set up the standard of Christ. Abolish the reign of sin, and establish the kingdom of grace in all hearts. Let humility triumph over pride and ambition; charity, over hatred, envy, and malice; purity and temperance, over lust and excess; meekness, over passion; disinterestedness and poverty of spirit, over covetousness and love of this perishable world. Let the Gospel of Jesus Christ, both in its belief and practice, prevail throughout the universe.

Grant to us thy peace, O Lord, in the days of our mortality, even that peace which thy Son bequeathed as a legacy to his disciples: a perpetual peace with thee, with one another, and within ourselves. Grant that all Christian princes and states may love, cherish, and maintain an inviolable peace among themselves. Give them an everlasting horror of the bloodshed, the devastation, and ruin of territories, the innumerable sacrileges, and the eternal loss of thousands of souls, which are the dismal consequences of war. Turn their hearts to another kind of warfare, teaching them to fight for a heavenly kingdom.

Remove, O Lord, thy wrath, which we have reason to apprehend for our sins. Deliver all Christians from the dreadful evil of mortal sin; make all sinners sensible of their misery; give them the grace of a sincere conversion and a truly penitential spirit, and discharge them from all their bonds. Preserve all Christendom, and in particular this nation, from the evils that threaten impenitent sinners, such as plagues, famines, earthquakes, fires, inundations, mortality of cattle, sudden and unprovided death, with thy many other judgments here, and eternal damnation hereafter. Comfort all that are under any affliction, sickness, or violence of pain ; support all that are under temptation ; reconcile those that are at variance ; deliver all that are in slavery or captivity ; defend all that are in danger ; grant relief to all in their respective necessities ; give a happy passage to those that are in their agony ; grant thy blessing, O Lord, to our friends and benefactors, and to all for whom we are particularly bound to pray, and have mercy on all our enemies. Give eternal rest to all the faithful departed, and bring us to everlasting life, through Jesus Christ our Lord. Amen.

RENEWAL OF THE BAPTISMAL VOWS.

O MY Lord and my God, humbly prostrate in spirit before thy Divine Majesty, I adore thy sovereign justice and thy infinite mercy. I am penetrated with fear at the consideration of thy awful judgments, and my great ingratitude for thy benefits since I was ranked by Baptism among thy children, raised to the glorious dignity of a Christian, and thus entitled to enjoy thee eternally in heaven. I was not then sensible of the precious grace bestowed upon me, nor of the awful obligations I contracted when I promised to renounce the devil, the world, and the flesh. But I am now fully sensible of both ; I most humbly thank thee for having brought me safely to the waters of Baptism, and I detest, from the bottom of my heart, every thought, word, and

action of my life which has been unworthy of a
Christian. Thou knowest, O my God, how often I
have stained the robe of innocence with which I was
then clothed, and how frequently I have violated my
sacred promises: but thou seest the contrition of
my heart, and the sincerity with which I now renew,
in the presence of heaven and earth, my profession
of faith in the doctrines proposed to my belief by
the holy Catholic Church, as well as the promises
made for me when I was regenerated in the waters of
Baptism. I firmly believe in God the Father
Almighty, Creator of heaven and earth—in Jesus
Christ his only Son our Lord, who was born and
suffered for us—in the Holy Ghost—the holy
Catholic Church—the Communion of Saints—the
Forgiveness of Sins—the Resurrection of the Body,
and Life Everlasting. I renounce the world, with its
pomps, vanities and false maxims, which I despise
because they are accursed by thee. I renounce the
flesh with all its temptations, and sincerely resolve
to endeavour to amend my faults, to conquer my
passions, and to sacrifice all that is most dear to me
rather than again deliberately sully that robe which
I promised to carry unstained before the judgment-
seat of Christ. O my good God, who didst love me
before I could love thee, and didst apply to my soul
the merits of Jesus Christ when I was unable to
implore that favour; look on me with compassion,
and grant me all those graces which will enable me
to keep my baptismal engagements without reproof.

Increase in my soul the heavenly virtues of faith, hope and charity, which I received at my Baptism, and teach me how to make faith the rule of my conduct, that it may avail me to life everlasting, through the infinite mercies and merits of my Lord and Saviour Jesus Christ, who with thee and the Holy Ghost liveth and reigneth, God, world without end. Amen.

Prayer to the Sacred Heart.

O SACRED Heart of Jesus, I fly, I come to thee! throwing myself into the arms of thy tender mercy. Thou art my sure refuge, my unfailing and only hope. Thou hast a remedy for all my evils, relief for all my miseries, reparation for all my faults. Thou canst supply for what is wanting in me, in order to obtain fully the graces that I ask for myself and others. Thou art for me, and for us all, the infallible, inexhaustible source of light, of strength, of perseverance, peace and consolation. I am certain that my importunity will never weary thee; certain, too, that thou wilt never cease to aid, to protect, to love me, because thy love for me, O Divine Heart, is infinite. Have mercy on me, then, O Heart of Jesus, and on all that I recommend to thee, according to thine own mercy, and do with us, for us, and in us, whatsoever thou wilt, for we abandon ourselves to thee with the full, entire confidence and conviction that thou wilt never abandon us either in time or eternity. Amen.

ACT OF CONSECRATION TO THE HOLY GHOST.

O HOLY Ghost, Divine Spirit of light and love, I consecrate to thee my mind, heart and will—my whole being for time and eternity. May my mind be ever docile to thy Divine Inspirations and to the teaching of the Holy Catholic Church, whose Infallible Guide thou art, my heart, ever inflamed with the love of God and my neighbour, my will ever conformable to the Divine Will, and my whole life a faithful imitation of the life and virtues of Our Lord and Saviour Jesus Christ, to whom, with the Father and thee, be honour and glory for ever. Amen.—300 *days' Indulgence once a day.*

—*Pius X.*, 1st *June*, 1908.

Anthems
For Particular Periods of the Year.

FROM THE FIRST SUNDAY OF ADVENT TILL THE PURIFICATION.

Mother of Jesus, heaven's open gate,
Star of the sea, support the falling state
Of mortals: thou whose womb thy maker bore,
And yet, O strange! a virgin, as before!
Who didst from Gabriel's "Hail!" the news
　　receive,
Repenting sinners by thy prayers relieve.

V. The angel of the Lord declared unto Mary.
R. And she conceived of the Holy Ghost.

LET US PRAY.

POUR forth, we beseech thee, O Lord, thy grace into our hearts, that we, to whom the incarnation of Christ, thy Son, was made known by the message of an angel, may by his passion and cross be brought to the glory of his resurrection : through the same Christ our Lord. Amen.

FROM THE FIRST VESPERS OF CHRISTMAS DAY, IS SAID :

V. After child-birth thou didst remain a pure virgin.

R. O Mother of God, intercede for us.

LET US PRAY.

O GOD, who by the fruitful virginity of blessed Mary, hast given to mankind the rewards of eternal salvation : grant, we beseech thee, that we may experience her intercession, by whom we received the Author of life, our Lord Jesus Christ, thy Son. Amen.

FROM THE PURIFICATION TILL HOLY THURSDAY.

Hail Mary, Queen of heavenly spheres !
Hail, whom the angelic host reveres !
Hail, fruitful root ! Hail sacred gate !
From whom our light derives its date
O Glorious Maid, with beauty blest !
Let joys eternal fill thy breast !
Thus crowned with beauty and with joy,
Thy prayers for us with Christ employ.

V. Vouchsafe, O sacred Virgin, to accept my praises.

R. Give me strength against thy enemies.

LET US PRAY.

GRANT us, O merciful God, strength against all our weakness ; that we, who celebrate the memory of the holy Mother of God, may by the help of her intercession, rise again from our iniquities ; through the same Christ, our Lord.   Amen.

FROM HOLY SATURDAY TILL TRINITY EVE.

Rejoice, O Queen of heaven, to see, Alleluia
The sacred infant born of thee, Alleluia,
Return in glory from the tomb, Alleluia,
And by thy prayers prevent our doom, Alleluia.
V. Rejoice and exult, O Virgin Mary, Alleluia.
R. For the Lord is truly risen, Alleluia.

LET US PRAY.

O GOD, who by the resurrection of thy Son, our Lord Jesus Christ, hast been pleased to fill the world with joy ; grant, we beseech thee, that by the intercession of the Virgin Mary, his Mother, we may receive the joys of eternal life ; through the same Christ, our Lord.   Amen.

FROM TRINITY EVE TILL ADVENT.

Hail to thee, the Queen of heaven,
    As a Mother to us giv'n ;
Rich in mercy, great in power,
    Be thou hailed at ev'ry hour !
Thee our life, our sweetness naming,
    Thee our cheering hope proclaiming ;
Eva's wretched children—we
    Spotless Virgin cry to thee.

At thy feet as suppliants lying,
　Weeping—wailing—mourning—crying ;
From this vale of tears we cry
　To thee, Mary, throned on high.
Then in pity for our fate,
　O thou chosen advocate ;
Turn to us, oh ! turn thine eyes
　In which mercy's dwelling lies.
And when exile here hath ended,
　Be to us thine arms extended ;
Show us thy most blessed child
　　　Jesus—with his face most mild.
　　　O most clement hear our pray'r ;
　　　　'Tis thy children claim thy care ;
　　　O most loving Mary, hear !
　　　　Sweetest, bend a list'ning ear.

V. Pray for us, O holy Mother of God.

R. That we may be made worthy of the promises
of Christ.

LET US PRAY.

O ALMIGHTY and Eternal God, who by the
co-operation of the Holy Ghost, didst prepare
the body and soul of the glorious Virgin Mary, that
she might become a habitation worthy of thy Son ;
grant that, as with joy we celebrate her memory, so
by her loving intercession we may be delivered from
present evils and eternal death : through the same
Christ, our Lord. Amen.

V. May the divine assistance always remain with us.

R. Amen.

VARIOUS

Hymns throughout the Year.

ADESTE FIDELES.

Adeste fideles,
Læti triumphantes:
Venite, venite in Bethlehem:
Natum videte
Regem angelorum:
Venite adoremus,
Venite adoremus,
Venite adoremus Dominum.

Come, all ye faithful,
Joyful and triumphant,
Oh, hasten, oh, hasten to
    Bethlehem;
See in a manger
The monarch of angels.

    Oh, come and let us worship
        Christ the Lord.

Deum de Deo,
Lumen de lumine,
Gestant puellæ viscera:
Deum verum,
Genitum, non factum:

   Venite adoremus, &c.

God of God eternal,
Light from light proceeding,
He deigns in the Virgin's
    womb to lie;
Very God of very God,
Begotten, not created.

   Oh, come, &c.

Cantet nunc Io,
Chorus angelorum:
Cantet nunc aula cœlestium,
Gloria
In Excelsis Deo!

   Venite, &c.

Sing alleluia,
All ye choirs of angels;
Sing, all ye citizens of heaven
    above,
Glory to God
In the highest,

   Oh, come, &c.

Ergo qui natus
Die hodierna,
Jesu tibi sit gloria:
Patris æterni
Verbum caro factum

   Venite, &c.

Yea, Lord, we greet Thee,
Born this happy morning;
To Thee, O Jesus, be glory
    given:
True word of the Father,
In our flesh appearing,

   Oh, come, &c.

STABAT MATER.

Stabat Mater dolorosa,

At the Cross her station keeping,

Juxta crucem lacrymosa,

Stood the mournful Mother weeping,

Dum pendebat Filius.

Close to Jesus to the last:

Cujus animam gementem,

Through her heart, His sorrow sharing,

Contristatam, et dolentem,

All His bitter anguish bearing,

Pertransivit gladius.

Now at length the sword has passed.

O quam tristis et afflicta

Oh, how sad and sore distressed

Fuit illa benedicta
Mater Unigeniti !

Was that Mother highly blest
Of the soul-begotten One !

Quæ mœrebat, et dolebat,

Christ above in torment hangs ;

Pia Mater dum videbat

She beneath beholds the pangs

Nati pœnas inclyti.

Of her dying glorious Son.

Quis est homo qui non fleret,

Is there one who would not weep,

Matrem Christi si videret
In tanto supplicio ?

Plunged in miseries so deep,
Christ's dear Mother to behold ?

Quis non posset contristari,
Christi Matrem contemplari
Dolentem cum Filio ?

Can the human heart refrain
From partaking in her pain,
In that Mother's pain untold ?

Pro peccatis suæ gentis,

Bruised, derided, cursed, defiled,

Vidit Jesum in tormentis,
Et flagellis subditum.

She beheld her tender Child
All with bloody scourges rent ;

Vidit suum dulcem natum

For the sins of His own nation

Moriendo, desolatum,
Dum emisit spiritum.

Saw Him hang in desolation,
Till His spirit forth He sent.

Eia Mater, fons amoris,

Me sentire vim doloris
  Fac, ut tecum lugeam.

Fac ut ardeat cor meum

In amando Christum Deum,

  Ut sibi complaceam.

Sancta Mater, istud agas,

Crucifixi fige plagas

  Cordi meo valide.
Tui Nati vulnerati,

Tam dignati pro me pati,
  Poenas mecum divide.

Fac me tecum pie flere,

Crucifixo condolere,

  Donec ego vixero.

Juxta crucem tecum stare,

Et me tibi, sociare,

  In planctu desidero.

Virgo virginum præclara,
Mihi jam non sis amara,
  Fac me tecum plangere.

Fac ut portem Christi mortem.
Passionis fac consortem,
  Et plagas recolere.

O thou Mother ! fount of love !

Touch my spirit from above,
  Make my heart with thine accord :

Make me feel as thou hast felt ;

Make my soul to glow and melt

  With the Love of Christ my Lord.

Holy Mother ! pierce me through :

In my heart each wound renew
  Of my Saviour crucified :
Let me share with thee His pain,

Who for all my sins was slain,
  Who for me in torments died.

Let me mingle tears with thee,

Mourning Him who mourned for me,
  All the days that I may live :

By the cross with thee to stay ;

There with thee to weep and pray
  Is all I ask of thee to give.

Virgin of all virgins blest !
Listen to my fond request
  Let me share thy grief divine,

Let me, to my latest breath,

In my body bear the death
  Of that dying Son of thine.

Fac me plagis vulnerari,
Wounded with His every wound,

Fac me cruce inebriari,
Steep my soul till it hath swooned

Et cruore Filii.
In His very blood away;

Flammis ne urar succensus
Be to me, O Virgin, nigh,

Per te, Virgo, sim defensus,
Lest in flames I burn and die

In die judicii.
In His awful judgment day.

Christe, cum sit hinc exire,
Christ, when Thou shalt call me hence,

Da per Matrem me venire
Be Thy Mother, my defence,

Ad palmam victoriæ.
Be Thy Cross, my victory.

Quando corpus morietur,
While my body here decays,

Fac ut animæ donetur
May my soul Thy goodness praise,

Paradisi gloria.
Safe in paradise with thee.

Amen.
Amen.

VEXILLA REGIS.

Vexilla regis prodeunt!
Behold the royal ensigns fly,

Fulget crucis mysterium,
Bearing the cross's mystery;

Qua vita mortem pertulit,
Where life itself did death endure,

Et morte vitam protulit.
And by that death did life procure.

Quæ vulnerata lanceæ
A cruel spear let out a flood

Mucrone diro, criminum,
Of water mix'd with saving blood;

Ut nos lavaret sordibus,
Which, gushing from our Saviour's side,

Manavit unda et sanguine,
Drown'd our offences in the tide.

Impleta sunt, quæ concinit
The mystery we now unfold,

David fideli carmine,
Which David's faithful verse foretold

Dicendo nationibus	Of our Lord's kingdom, whilst we see
Regnavit a ligno Deus.	God ruling nations from a tree.
Arbor decora, et fulgida,	O lovely tree, whose branches wore
Ornata regis purpura,	The royal purple of his gore ;
Electa digno stipite	How glorious does thy body shine,
Tam sancta membra tangere.	Supporting members so divine.
Beata, cujus brachiis,	The world's blest balance thou wast made,
Pretium pependit sæculi,	Thy happy beams its purchase weigh'd,
Statera facta corporis,	And bore his limbs, who snatched away
Tulitque prædam tartari.	Devouring hell's expecting prey.
O Crux ave spes unica !	Hail, Cross, our hope ! to thee we call,
Hoc passionis tempore.	Who keep this mournful festival.

On the finding of the Cross, is said :

* Paschale quæ fers gaudium,	* Now in this joyful Paschal time,

And on the exaltation of the Cross :

* In hac triumphi gloria,	* In this triumphant festival,
Piis adauge gratiam,	Grant to the just increase of grace,
Reisque dele crimina.	And every sinner's crimes efface.
Te, fons salutis Trinitas,	Blest Trinity we praises sing
Collaudet omnis spiritus :	To thee, from whom all graces spring :
Quibus crucis victoriam	Thou, through the Cross, the victory
Largiris, addo præmium.	Dost give ; oh, also give the prize. Amen.
Amen.	

O FILII ET FILIÆ.

O filii et filiæ,

Praise by mortals now be given

Rex cœlestis, Rex gloriæ,

On this day from death hath risen

Morte surrexit hodie, Alleluia,
    Et mane prima Sabbati.

The King of Glory, King of Heaven, Alleluia,
    The morn of Sunday scarce did beam,

Ad ostium monumenti,

When to his monument there came

Accesserunt discipuli, Alleluia.
    Et Maria Magdalene,

Disciples who adored his name, Alleluia.
    There Mary Magdalen anxious stood,

Et Jacobi, et Salome.

And James, and Salome the good ;

Venerunt corpus ungere, Alleluia.
    In albis sedens angelus.

His body fain embalm they would, Alleluia.
    The angel sat in white all robed,

Prædixit mulieribus,
In Galilea est Dominus, Alleluia.
Et Joannes apostolus,

And to the women he foretold
In Galilee you'll see the Lord, Alleluia.
    The message scarce did reach his ear,

Cucurrit Petro citius,

Swifter than Peter, John drew near

Monumento venit prius, Alleluia.

To the Lord's tomb, with hope, with fear, Alleluia.

Discipulis astantipus,

The disciples all assembled were ;

In medio stetit Christus,

Among them Jesus did appear ;

Dicens, pax vobis omnibus, Alleluia.
    Ut intellexit Didymus

His peace he gave, removed their fear, Alleluia.
    Thomas believed not, when 'twas said

Quia surrexerat Jesus,

That Christ had risen from the dead,

Remansit fere dubius. Alleluia.

Until he saw the wounds that bled, Alleluia.

Vide, Thoma, vide latus,

My hands, my side, my feet, O see!

Vide pedes, vide manus ;

Thomas, wounds that bled for thee :

Noli esse incredulus, Alleluia.

Renounce thine incredulity, Alleluia.

Quando Thomas vidit Christum

When Thomas Jesus had survey'd,

Pedes, manus, latus suum,

And on his wounds his fingers laid,

Dixit : Tu es Deus meus, Alleluia.

Thou art my Lord and God, he said. Alleluia.

Beati qui non viderunt,

Blessed are they who have not seen,

Et firmiter crediderunt.

And yet, whose faith entire hath been,

Vitam æternam habebunt, Alleluia.

Them endless joy from pain shall screen, Alleluia.

In hoc festo sanctissimo

On this most solemn feast let's raise

Sit laus et jubilatio :

Our hearts to God in hymns of praise,

Benedicamus Domino, Alleluia.

And bless the Lord in all his ways, Alleluia.

Ex quibus nos humillimas

Our grateful thanks to God let's give,

Devotas atque debitas

In humblest manner, whilst we live,

Deo dicamus gratias, Alleluia.

For all the favours we receive, Alleluia.

FOR WHITSUNTIDE

I.—Veni Creator.

Veni Creator Spiritus,

Come Holy Ghost, Creator come,

Mentes tuorum visita ;

From thy bright heavenly throne ;

Imple superna gratia

Quæ tu creasti pectora.

Come, take possession of our souls,
And make them all thy own.

Qui diceris Paraclitus,

Altissimi donum Dei.
Fons vivus, ignis, charitas :

Et Spiritalis unctio.

Thou who art called the Paraclete,
Best gift of God above ;
The living Spring, the living Fire,
Sweet Unction and true Love.

Tu septiformis munere

Digitus paternæ dexteræ

Tu rite promissum Patris,

Sermone ditans guttura.

Thou who art sevenfold in thy grace,
Finger of God's right hand ;
His promise teaching little ones
To speak and understand.

Accende lumen sensibus :

Infunde amorem cordibus

Infirma nostri corporis

Virtute firmans perpeti.

Oh ! guide our minds with thy blest light,
With love our hearts inflame ;
And with thy strength, which ne'er decays,
Confirm our mortal frame.

Hostem repellas longius

Pacemque dones protinus
Ductore sic te prævio

Vitemus omne noxium.

Far from us drive our hellish foe,
True peace unto us bring ;
And through all perils bring us safe
Beneath thy sacred wing.

Per te sciamus da Patrem,

Noscamus atque Filium

Teque utriusque Spiritum

Credamus omni tempore.

Through thee may we the Father know,
Through thee, the Eternal Son,
And thee the Spirit of them both,
Thrice blessed Three in One.

Deo Patri sit gloria,
  Et Filio qui a mortuis ;
Surrexit, ac Paraclito,

  Iu sæculorum sæcula.
  Amen.

All glory to the Father be,
  With his co-equal Son,
The like to thee, great Para-
  clete,
While endless ages run.
  Amen.

II.— VENI, SANCTE SPIRITUS.

Veni Sancte Spiritus,

Et emitte cœlitus

  Lucis tuæ radium.

Veni pater pauperum,

Veni dator munerum,

  Veni lumen cordium

Consolator optime,

Dulcis hospes auimæ,

  Dulce refrigerium.
Iu labore requies,

In æstu temperies,

  In fletu solatium.
O lux beatissima,

Reple cordis intima,

  Tuorum fidelium.

Sine tuo numine,

Nihil est in homine,

  Nihil est innoxium.

Come, Holy Ghost, send
  down those beams,
Which sweetly flow in
  silent streams,
From thy bright throne
  above.
Oh, come thou Father of the
  poor,
Oh, come thou source of all
  our store ;
Come, fill our hearts with
  love.
O thou, of Comforters the
  best,
O thou, the soul's delightful
  guest,
The pilgrim's sweet relief,
Thou art true rest in toil
  and sweat,
Refreshment in excess of
  heat,
And solace in our grief.
Thrice blessed light, shoot
  home thy darts
And pierce the centre of
  those hearts,
Whose faith aspires to
  thee ;
Without thy Godhead
  nothing can
Have any price or worth in
  man,
Nothing can harmless be.

Lava quod est sordidum,	Lord, wash our sinful stains away,
Riga quod est aridum,	Water from heaven our barren clay,
Sana quod est saucium	Our wounds and bruises heal;
Flecte quod est rigidum	To thy sweet yoke our stiff necks bow,
Fove quod est frigidum	Warm with thy fire our hearts of snow.
Rege quod est devium.	Our wandering feet recall.
Da tuis fidelibus,	Oh, grant thy faithful, dearest Lord,
In te confitentibus,	Whose only hope is thy sure word,
Sacrum septenarium.	The seven gifts of thy spirit.
Da virtutis meritum,	Grant us in life to obey thy grace,
Da salutis exitum,	Grant us in death to see thy face,
Da perenne gaudium. Amen.	And endless joys inherit. Amen.

ECCE PANIS.

Ecce panis Angelorum,	Lo! upon the altar lies,
Factus cibus viatorum:	Hidden deep from human eyes,
Vere panis filiorum,	Bread of Angels from the skies,
Non mittendus canibus.	Made the food of mortal man
In figuris præsignatur.	Children's meat to dogs denied;
Cum Isaac immolatur;	In old types foresignified;
Agnus paschæ deputatur:	In the manna heav'n-supplied,
Datur manna patribus.	Isaac, and the paschal lamb.

Bone pastor, panis vere,
Jesu nostri miserere :

Tu nos pasce, nos tuere :

Tu nos bona fac videre

  In terra viventium.
Tu, qui cuncta scis et vales,
Qui nos pascis hic mortales :

Tuos ibi commensales,

Coheredes, et sodales,
  Fac sanctorum civium.

            Amen.

Jesu ! Shepherd of the sheep !
Thou thy flock in safety
  keep.
Living bread ! thy life sup-
  ply ;
Strengthen us, or else we
  die ;
Fill us with celestial grace:
Thou, who feedest us below !
Source of all we have or
  know !
Grant that with thy saints
  above,
Sitting at the feast of love,
We may see Thee face to
  face.

            Amen.

PANGE LINGUA.

Pange lingua gloriosi

Corporis mysterium,

Sanguinisque pretiosi

Quem in mundi pretium,

Fructus ventris generosi,

Rex effudit gentium.

  Nobis datus, nobis natus,

Ex intacta virgine ;

Et in mundo conversatus

Sparso verbi semine,

Sing, O my tongue, adore
  and praise
The depth of God's mys-
  terious ways :
How Christ, the world's great
  King, bestow'd
His flesh concealed as human
  food,
And left mankind the blood
  that paid
The ransom for the souls he
  made.
Given from above, and
  born for man,
From virgin chaste his life
  began :
He lived on earth, and
  preach'd to sow
The seeds of heav'nly love
  below,

Sui moras incolatus	Then seal'd his mission from above
Miro clausit ordine !	With strange effects of power and love !
In supremæ nocte cœnæ.	'Twas on that ev'ning, when the last
Recumbens cum fratribus,	And most mysterious supper past ;
Observata lege plene	When Christ with his disciples sat,
Cibis in legalibus,	To close the law with legal meat ;
Cibum turbæ duodenæ	Then to the twelve himself bestow'd
Se dat suis manibus.	With his own hands to be their food.
Verbum caro, panem verum. Verbo carnem efficit :	The Word made flesh for love of man, His word turns bread to flesh again,
Fitque sanguis Christi merum, Et si sensus deficit, Ad firmandum cor sincerum	And wine to blood, unseen by sense, By virtue of omnipotence : And here the faithful rest secure,
Sola fides sufficit.	Whilst God can vouch and faith insure.
Tantum ergo sacramentum Veneremur cernui :	To this mysterious table now, Our knees, our hearts, and sense we bow :
Et antiquum documentum,	Let ancient rites resign their place
Novo cedat ritui : Præstet fides supplementum,	To nobler elements of grace : And faith for all defects supply,
Sensum defectui.	Whilst sense is lost in mystery.
Genitori Genitoque	To God the Father born of none,
Laus et jubilatio :	To Christ his co-eternal Son,

Salus, honor, virtus quoque : | And Holy Ghost, whose equal rays

Sit et benedictio : | From both proceed, be equal praise :

Procedenti ab utroque, | One honour, jubilee, and fame,

Compar sit laudatio. Amen. | For ever bless his glorious name. Amen.

V. Panem de cœlo præstitisti eis. Alleluia.
R. Omne delectamentum in se habentem. Alleluia.

V. Thou hast given them bread from heaven. Alleluia.
R. Replenished with all delights. Alleluia.

THE MAGNIFICAT

Or Canticle of the Blessed Virgin.

Magnificat anima mea Dominum.

1. My soul doth magnify the Lord.

Et exultavit spiritus meus, in Deo Salutari meo.

2. And my spirit hath rejoiced : in God my Saviour.

Quia respexit humilitatem ancillæ suae : ecce enim ex hoc beatam me dicent omnes generationes.

3. For he hath regarded the humility of his handmaid : for behold from henceforth all generations shall call me blessed.

Quia fecit mihi magna qui potens est : et sanctum nomen ejus.

4. For he that is mighty hath done to me great things : and holy is his name.

Et misericordia ejus a progenie in progenies : timentibus eum.

5. And his mercy is from generation to generation : unto them that fear him.

Fecit potentiam in brachio suo ; dispersit superbos mente cordis sui.

6. He hath shown strength in his arm : he hath scattered the proud in the conceit of their heart.

Deposuit potentes de sede : et exaltavit humiles.

7. He hath put down the mighty from their seat : and hath exalted the humble.

Esurientes implevit bonis : et divites dimisit inanes.

8. He hath filled the hungry with good things : and the rich he hath sent away empty.

Suscepit Israel puerum suum : recordatus misericordiæ suæ.

Sicut locutus est ad patres nostros : Abraham, et semini ejus in sæcula.

Gloria Patri, &c.

9. He hath received his servant Israel : being mindful of his mercy.

10. As he spoke unto our fathers : to Abraham and his seed for ever.

Glory be to the Father, &c.

FOR TIME OF THANKSGIVING

Te Deum

Te Deum laudamus : te Dominum confitemur.

We praise thee, O God : we acknowledge thee to be the Lord.

Te æternum Patrem : omnis terra veneratur.

Tibi omnes angeli : tibi cœli et universæ potestates;

Tibi cherubim et seraphim incessabili voce proclamant ;

Sanctus, sanctus, sanctus : Dominus Deus Sabaoth.

Pleni sunt cœli et terra : majestatis gloriæ tuæ.

Te gloriosus Apostolorum chorus.

Te Prophetarum laudabilis numerus.

Te Martyrum candidatus laudat exercitus.

Te per orbem terrarum, sancta confitetur Ecclesia.

Patrem immensæ majestatis.

All the earth doth worship thee: the Father everlasting.

To thee all angels : to thee the heavens and all the powers therein,

To thee cherubim and seraphim : continually cry :

Holy, holy, holy : Lord God of Sabaoth.

Heaven and earth are full of the majesty of thy glory.

The glorious choir of the Apostles,

The admirable company of the Prophets,

The white-robed army of Martyrs praise thee,

The Holy Church throughout all the world doth confess thee,

The Father of infinite majesty.

Venerandum tuum verum, et unicum Filium.

Sanctum quoque : Paraclitum Spiritum.

Tu rex gloriæ : Christe.

Tu Patris sempiternus es Filius.

Tu ad liberandum suscepturus hominem : non horruisti Virginis uterum.

Tu devicto mortis aculeo : aperuisti credentibus regna cœlorum.

Tu ad dexteram Dei sedes: in gloria Patris.

Judex crederis : esse venturus.

Te ergo quæsumus, tuis famulis subveni : quos pretioso sanguine redemisti.

Æterna fac cum Sanctis tuis : in gloria numerari.

Salvum fac populum tuum, Domine : et benedic hæreditati tuæ.

Et rege eos : et extolle illos usque in æternum.

Per singulos dies : benedicimus te.

Et laudamus nomen tuum in sæculum : et in sæculum sæculi.

Dignare, Domine, die isto : sine peccato nos custodire.

Miserere nostri, Domine : miserere nostri.

Thy adorable, true, and only Son.

Also the Holy Ghost : the Comforter.

Thou art the King of Glory, O Christ.

Thou art the everlasting Son of the Father.

When thou didst take upon thee to deliver man : thou didst not abhor the Virgin's womb.

When thou hadst overcome the sting of death : thou didst open the kingdom of heaven to all believers.

Thou sittest at the right hand of God : in the glory of the Father.

We believe that thou shalt come : to be our Judge.

We pray thee, therefore, help thy servants : whom thou hast redeemed with thy precious blood.

Make them be numbered with thy Saints : in glory everlasting.

O Lord, save thy people : and bless thine inheritance.

And govern them: and lift them up for ever.

Day by day : we bless thee.

And we praise thy name for ever : yea, for ever and ever.

Vouchsafe, O Lord, this day : to keep us without sin.

O Lord, have mercy upon us : have mercy upon us.

Fiat misericordia tua, Domine, super nos: quemadmodum speravimus in te.

In te, Domine, speravi: non confundar in æternum.

O Lord, let thy mercy be shown to us: as we have hoped in thee.

O Lord, in thee have I hoped: let me not be confounded for ever.

On occasions of Thanksgiving, the following Versicles are added:

V. Benedictus es, Domine, Deus, Patrum nostrorum.

R. Et laudabilis, et gloriosus in sæcula.

V. Benedicamus Patrem et Filium, cum Sancto Spiritu.

R. Laudemus et superexaltemus eum in sæcula.

V. Benedictus es, Domine Deus, in firmamento cœli.

R. Et laudabilis, et gloriosus, et superexaltatus in sæcula.

V. Benedic, anima mea, Dominum.

R. Et noli oblivisci retributiones ejus.

ADORE TE DEVOTE.

Hidden God, devoutly I adore thee,
  Truly present underneath these veils;
All my heart subdues itself before thee,
  Since it all before thee faints and fails.

Not to sight or taste or touch be credit,
  Hearing only do we trust secure:
I believe, for God the Son hath said it,
  Word of truth that ever shall endure.

On the Cross was veiled thy Godhead's splendour,
  Here thy manhood lieth hidden too
Unto both alike my faith I render,
  And, as sued the contrite thief, I sue.

Though I look not on thy wounds with Thomas
  Thee, my Lord, and thee, my God, I call,
Make me more and more believe thy promise,
  Hope in thee, and love thee over all.

O memorial of my Saviour dying!
  Living Bread that givest life to man!
May my soul, its life from thee supplying,
  Taste thy sweetness, as on earth it can.

Deign, O Jesus, Pelican of Heaven,
  Me a sinner in thy blood to lave,
To a single drop of which is given
  All the world from all its sin to save.

AVE MARIS STELLA.

Bright Mother of our Maker! hail,
  Thou virgin ever blest,
The ocean's star by which we sail,
  And gain the port of rest.

While we this *Ave* thus to thee
  From Gabriel's mouth rehearse,
Oh, grant that peace our lot may be,
  And Eva's name reverse.

Release our long entangled mind
  From all the snares of ill,
With heavenly light instruct the blind,
  And all our vows fulfil.

Exert for us a mother's care,
  And us thy children own
Prevail with Him to hear our prayer,
  Who chose to be thy Son.

O spotless maid, whose virtues shine
  With brightest purity,
Each action of our lives refine,
  And make us pure like thee.

Preserve our lives unstain'd with ill
  In this infectious way,
That heav'n alone our souls may fill,
  With joys that ne'er decay.

To God the Father endless praise;
  To God the Son the same,
And Holy Ghost, whose equal rays
  One equal glory claim.   Amen.

The Epistles and Gospels

FOR THE

Sundays and Principal Festivals

THROUGHOUT THE YEAR.

FIRST SUNDAY OF ADVENT.

EPISTLE. *Rom.* xiii. 11-14. *Brethren :* Know
that it is now the hour for us to rise from sleep.
For now our salvation is nearer than when we
believed. The night is past and the day is at hand.
Let us therefore cast off the works of darkness,
and put on the armour of light. Let us walk hon-
estly, as in the day : not in rioting and drunkenness,
not in chambering and impurities, not in con-
tention and envy : but put ye on the Lord Jesus
Christ.

GOSPEL. *Luke* xxi. 25-33. *At that time :*
Jesus said to his disciples : There shall be signs
in the sun, and in the moon, and in the stars ; and
upon the earth distress of nations, by reason of
the confusion of the roaring of the sea and of the
waves ; men withering away for fear and expectation
of what shall come upon the whole world. For
the powers of heaven shall be moved : and then
they shall see the Son of Man coming in a cloud,
with great power and majesty. But when these
things begin to come to pass, look up, and lift up
your heads, because your redemption is at hand.
And he spoke to them a similitude : See the fig-tree,
and all the trees : when they now shoot forth their
fruit, you know that summer is nigh ; so you also,
when you shall see these things come to pass,
know that the kingdom of God is at hand. Amen,

I say to you, this generation shall not pass away till all things be fulfilled. Heaven and earth shall pass away, but my words shall not pass away. CREDO.

SECOND SUNDAY OF ADVENT.

EPISTLE. *Rom.* xv. 4-13. *Brethren :* What things soever were written, were written for our learning, that through patience and the comfort of the Scriptures we might have hope. Now the God of patience and of comfort grant you to be of one mind one towards another, according to Jesus Christ : that with one mind and with one mouth you may glorify God and the Father of our Lord Jesus Christ. Wherefore receive one another, as Christ also hath received you unto the honour of God. For I say that Christ Jesus was minister of the circumcision for the truth of God, to confirm the promises made unto the fathers. But that the Gentiles are to glorify God for his mercy, as it is written : '' Therefore will I confess to thee, O Lord, among the Gentiles, and will sing to thy name.'' And again he saith : '' Rejoice, ye Gentiles, with his people.'' And again : '' Praise the Lord, all ye Gentiles, and magnify him, all ye people.'' And again Isaiah saith : '' There shall be a root of Jesse, and he that shall rise up to rule the Gentiles, in him the Gentiles shall hope.'' Now the God of hope fill you with all joy and peace in believing, that you may abound in hope and in the power of the Holy Ghost.

GOSPEL. *Matt.* xi. 2-10. *At that time :* When John had heard in prison the works of Christ, sending two of his disciples, he said to him : Art thou he that art to come, or look we for another ? And Jesus making answer, said to them : Go and relate to John what ye have heard and seen. The blind see, the lame walk, the lepers are cleansed.

tho deaf hear, the dead rise again, the poor have the gospel preached to them; and blessed is he that shall not be scandalised in me. And when they went their way, Jesus began to say to the multitudes, concerning John : What went ye out into the desert to see ? A reed shaken with the wind ? But what went ye out to see ? A man clothed in soft garments ? Behold, they that are clothed in soft garments are in the houses of kings. But what went ye out to see ? A prophet ? Yea, I tell you, and more than a prophet. For this is he of whom it is written : "Behold, I send my angel before thy face, who shall prepare thy way before thee." CREDO.

THIRD SUNDAY OF ADVENT.

EPISTLE. *Phil.* iv. 4-7. *Brethren :* Rejoice in the Lord always ; again, I say, rejoice. Let your modesty be known to all men. The Lord is nigh. Be nothing solicitous, but in every thing, by prayer and supplication, with thanksgiving, let your petitions be made known to God. And the peace of God, which surpasseth all understanding, keep your hearts and minds in Christ Jesus.

GOSPEL. *John* i. 19-28. *At that time :* The Jews sent from Jerusalem priests and Levites to John, to ask him : Who art thou ? And he confessed, and did not deny ; and he confessed : I am not the Christ. And they asked him : What then ? art thou Elias ? And he said : I am not. Art thou the prophet ? And he answered : No. They said therefore unto him : Who art thou, that we may give an answer to them that sent us ? What sayest thou of thyself ? He said : I am the voice of one crying in the wilderness : *Make straight the way of the Lord*, as said the prophet Isaias. And they that were sent were of the Pharisees. And they asked him and said to him : Why then dost thou baptize,

if thou be not Christ, nor Elias, nor the prophet ?
John answered them, saying : I baptize with
water, but there hath stood one in the midst of
you, whom you know not. The same is he that shall
come after me, who is preferred before me : the
latchet of whose shoe I am not worthy to loose.
These things were done in Bethania, beyond the
Jordan, where John was baptizing. CREDO.

FOURTH SUNDAY OF ADVENT.

EPISTLE. 1 *Cor.* iv. 1-5. *Brethren :* Let a man
so account of us as of the ministers of Christ and the
dispensers of the mysteries of God. Here now it
is required amongst the dispensers that a man be
found faithful. But to me it is a very small thing
to be judged by you or by man's day ; but neither
do I judge my own self. For I am not conscious to
myself of anything : yet am I not hereby justified ;
but he that judgeth me is the Lord. Therefore
judge not before the time until the Lord come,
who both will bring to light the hidden things of
darkness, and will make manifest the counsels
of the hearts : and then shall every man have praise
from God.

GOSPEL. *Luke* iii. 1-6. Now, in the fifteenth
year of the reign of Tiberius Cæsar (Pontius Pilate
being governor of Judea, and Herod tetrarch of
Galilee, and Philip, his brother, tetrarch of Iturea,
and the country of Trachonitis, and Lysanias
tetrarch of Abilina, under the high priests Annas
and Caiphas), the word of the Lord came to John,
the son of Zachary, in the desert. And he came
into all the country about the Jordan preaching
the baptism of penance for the remission of sins,
as it was written in the words of the book of Isaias
the prophet : "A voice of one crying in the wilderness : Prepare ye the way of the Lord ; make
straight his paths. Every valley shall be filled,

and every mountain and hill shall be brought low ; and the crooked shall be made straight and the rough ways plain, and all flesh shall see the salvation of God." CREDO.

CHRISTMAS DAY.

FIRST MASS. AT MIDNIGHT.

EPISTLE. *Tit.* ii. 11-15. *Dearly beloved :* The grace of God our Saviour hath appeared to all men ; instructing us, that, denying ungodliness, and worldly desires, we should live soberly, and justly and godly in this world looking for the blessed hope and coming of the glory of the great God and our Saviour Jesus Christ ; who gave himself for us, that he might redeem us from all iniquity, and might cleanse to himself a people acceptable, a pursuer of good works. These things speak, and exhort and rebuke with all authority. Let no man despise thee.

GOSPEL. *Luke* ii. 1-14. And it came to pass, that in those days there went out a decree from Cæsar Augustus, that the whole world should be enrolled. This enrolling was first made by Cyrinus, governor of Syria. And all went to be enrolled, every one into his own city. And Joseph also went up from Galilee out of the city of Nazareth into Judea to the city of David, which is called Bethlehem : because he was of the house and family of David, to be enrolled with Mary, his espoused wife, who was with child. And it came to pass, that when they were there, her days were accomplished, that she should be delivered. And she brought forth her first-born son, and wrapped him up in swaddling clothes, and laid him in a manger ; because there was no room for them in the inn. And there were in the same country shepherds watching and keeping the night-watches over their flocks. And behold

an angel of the Lord stood by them, and the brightness of God shone round about them ; and they
feared with a great fear.   And the angel said to
them : Fear not, for, behold, I bring you good
tidings of great joy, that shall be to all the people ;
for this day is born to you a SAVIOUR, who is Christ
the Lord, in the city of David.   And this shall be a
sign unto you : you shall find the infant wrapped in
swaddling clothes, and laid in a manger.   And
suddenly there was with the angel a multitude of
the heavenly army, praising God, and saying:
Glory to God in the highest ; and on earth peace
to men of good will.   CREDO.

SECOND MASS.   AT BREAK OF DAY.

EPISTLE. *Tit.* iii. 4-7.   *Most dearly beloved :*
The goodness and kindness of God our Saviour,
appeared : not by the works of justice which we
have done, but according to his mercy he saved us,
by the laver of regeneration, and renovation of the
Holy Ghost ; whom he hath poured forth upon us
abundantly, through Jesus Christ our Saviour,
that being justified by his grace, we may be heirs
according to hope of life everlasting, through Jesus
Christ our Lord.

GOSPEL.   *Luke* ii. 15-20.   *At that time :* The
shepherds said one to another : Let us go over to
Bethlehem, and let us see this word that has come
to pass, which the Lord has showed to us.   And
they came with haste : and they found Mary and
Joseph, and the infant lying in a manger.   And
seeing, they understood of the word that had been
spoken to them concerning this child.   And all that
heard wondered ; and at those things that were
told them by the shepherds.   But Mary kept all
these words, pondering *them* in her heart.   And
the shepherds returned, glorifying and praising

God for all the things they had heard and seen, as it was told unto them. CREDO.

THIRD MASS. IN THE DAY TIME.

EPISTLE. *Heb.* i. 1-12. God, who at sundry times, and in divers manners, spoke in times past to the fathers by the prophets, last of all, in these days hath spoken to us by his Son, whom he hath appointed heir of all things, by whom also he made the world ; who being the brightness of his glory, and the figure of his substance, and upholding all things by the word of his power, making purgation of sins, sitteth on the right hand of the majesty on high : being made so much better than the angels, as he hath inherited a more excellent name than they. For to which of the angels hath he said at any time : " Thou art my Son ; to-day have I begotten thee " ? And again : " I will be to him a Father, and he shall be to me a Son." And again, when he bringeth in the first-begotten into the world, he saith : "And let all the angels of God adore him." And to the angels indeed he saith : " He that maketh his angels spirits, and his ministers a flame of fire." But to the Son : " Thy throne, 'O God, is for ever and ever ; a sceptre of justice is the sceptre of thy kingdom. Thou hast loved justice and hated iniquity : therefore God, thy God, hath anointed thee with the oil of gladness, above thy fellows." And : " Thou, in the beginning, O Lord, didst found the earth, and the works of thy hands are the heavens. They shall perish, but thou shalt continue : and they shall grow old as a garment. And as a vesture shalt thou change them, and they shall be changed, but thou art the selfsame, and thy years shall not fail."

GOSPEL. *John* i. 1-14. In the beginning was the Word, and the Word was with God, and the

Word was God. The same was in the beginning with God. All things were made by him, and without him was made nothing that was made. In him was life, and the life was the light of men; and the light shineth in darkness, and the darkness did not comprehend it. There was a man sent from God, whose name was John. This man came for a witness to give testimony of the light, that all men might believe through him. He was not the light, but was to give testimony of the light. That was the true light which enlighteneth every man that cometh into this world. He was in the world, and the world was made by him, and the world knew him not. He came unto his own, and his own received him not. But as many as received him, to them he gave power to be made the sons of God, to them that believe in his name, who are born not of blood, nor of the will of the flesh, nor of the will of man, but of God. And *the Word was made flesh*, and dwelt among us : and we saw his glory, as it were the glory of the only begotten of the Father full of grace and truth.

Sunday within the Octave of Christmas.

EPISTLE. *Gal.* iv. 1-7. *Brethren :* As long as the heir is a child, he differeth nothing from a servant, though he be a lord of all, but is under tutors and governors until the time appointed by the father. So we also, when we were children, were serving under the elements of the world. But when the fulness of the time was come, God sent his Son, made of a woman, made under the law, that he might redeem them who were under the law, that we might receive the adoption of sons. And because you are sons, God hath sent the spirit of his Son into your hearts, crying : *Abba*, Father. Therefore now he is not a servant, but a son. And if a son, an heir also through God.

GOSPEL. *Luke* ii. 33-40. *At that time :* Joseph, and Mary the mother of Jesus, were wondering at those things which were spoken concerning him. And Simeon blessed them, and said to Mary his mother : Behold, this child is set for the fall, and for the resurrection of many in Israel, and for a sign which shall be contradicted. And thy own soul a sword shall pierce, that, out of many hearts thoughts may be revealed. And there was one Anna, a prophetess, the daughter of Phanuel, of the tribe of Aser ; she was far advanced in years, and had lived with her husband seven years from her virginity. And she was a widow until four score and four years ; who departed not from the temple, by fastings and prayer serving night and day. Now she, at the same hour coming in, confessed to the Lord, and spoke of him to all that looked for the redemption of Israel. And after they had performed all things according to the law of the Lord, they returned into Galilee, to their city Nazareth. And the child grew and waxed strong, full of wisdom ; and the grace of God was in him.

THE CIRCUMCISION.

EPISTLE. *Tit.* ii. 11-15. *Dearly beloved :* The grace of God our Saviour hath appeared to all men. Instructing us, that, denying ungodliness and worldly desires, we should live soberly and justly and godly in this world, looking for the blessed hope and coming of the glory of the great God and our Saviour Jesus Christ, who gave himself for us, that he might redeem us from all iniquity and might cleanse to himself a people acceptable, a pursuer of good works. These things speak, and exhort and rebuke with all authority. Let no man despise thee.

GOSPEL. *Luke* ii. 21. *At that time :* After eight days were accomplished that the child should be circumcised, his name was called JESUS, which was called by the angel, before he was conceived in the womb. CREDO.

THE EPIPHANY.

LESSON. *Isaias* lx. 1-6. Arise, be enlightened, O Jerusalem : for thy light is come, and the glory of the lord is risen upon thee. For behold darkness shall cover the earth, and a mist the people ; but the Lord shall arise upon thee, and his glory shall be seen upon thee. And the Gentiles shall walk in thy light, and kings in the brightness of thy rising. Lift up thy eyes round about and see : all these are gathered together, they are come to thee : thy sons shall come from afar, and thy daughters shall rise up at thy side. Then shalt thou see and abound, and thy heart shall wonder and be enlarged ; when the multitude of the sea shall be converted to thee, the strength of the Gentiles shall come to thee. The multitude of camels shall cover thee, the dromedaries of Madian and Epha : all they from Saba shall come, bringing gold and frankincense, and showing forth praise to the Lord.

GOSPEL. *Matt.* ii. 1-12. When Jesus therefore was born in Bethlehem of Juda, in the days of King Herod, behold, there came wise men from the East to Jerusalem, saying: Where is he that is born King of the Jews ? For we have seen his star in the East, and are come to adore him. And Herod hearing this was troubled, and all Jerusalem with him. And assembling together all the chief priests and scribes of the people, he inquired of them where Christ should be born. But they said to him : In Bethlehem of Juda. For so it is written by the prophet : "And thou Bethlehem in the land of Juda art not the least among the princes of Juda ; for out of thee shall come forth the captain that shall rule my people Israel." Then Herod, privately

calling the wise men, learned diligently of them
the time of the star which appeared to them ; and
sending them into Bethlehem, said : Go, and
diligently inquire after the child, and when you
have found him, bring me word again, that I also
may come and adore him. Who having heard the
king, went their way ; and behold, the star which
they had seen in the East went before them, until
it came and stood over where the child was. And
seeing the star, they rejoiced with exceeding great
joy. And entering into the house, they found the
child with Mary his mother, and falling down they
adored him ; and opening their treasures, they
offered him gifts, gold and frankincense, and
myrrh. And having received an answer in sleep
that they should not return to Herod, they went
back another way into their own country. CREDO.

FIRST SUNDAY AFTER EPIPHANY.

EPISTLE. *Rom.* xii. 1-5. *Brethren :* I beseech
you, by the mercy of God, that you present your
bodies a living sacrifice, holy, pleasing unto God,
your reasonable service. And be not conformed to
this world ; but be reformed in the newness of your
mind, that you may prove what is the good, and
the acceptable, and the perfect will of God. For
I say, by the grace that is given me, to all that are
among you, not to be more wise than it behoveth
to be wise, but to be wise unto sobriety, and according as God hath divided to every one the measure
of faith. For as in one body we have many members,
but all the members have not the same office ;
so we, being many, are one body in Christ, and
every one members of one another, in Jesus Christ
our Lord.

GOSPEL. *Luke* ii. 42-52. And when Jesus was
twelve years old, they going up to Jerusalem,

according to the custom of the feast, and having fulfilled the days, when they returned, the child Jesus remained in Jerusalem, and his parents knew it not. And thinking that he was in the company, they came a day's journey, and sought him among their kinsfolk and acquaintance. And not finding him they returned into Jerusalem, seeking him. And it came to pass, that, after three days, they found him in the temple, sitting in the midst of the doctors, hearing them and asking them questions. And all that heard him were astonished at his wisdom and his answers. And seeing him they wondered. And his mother said to him : Son, why hast thou done so to us ? Behold, thy father and I have sought thee sorrowing. And he said to them : How is it that you sought me ? Did you not know that I must be about my Father's business ? And they understood not the word that he spoke unto them. And he went down with them, and came to Nazareth, and was subject to them. And his mother kept all those words in her heart. And Jesus advanced in wisdom and age, and grace with God and men. Credo.

Second Sunday after Epiphany.

LESSON. *Acts* iv. 8-12. *In those days :* Peter being filled with the Holy Ghost, said to them : Ye princes of the people, and ancients, hear : If we this day are examined concerning the good deed done to the infirm man, by what means he hath been made whole, be it known to you all, and to all the people of Israel, that by the name of our Lord Jesus Christ of Nazareth, whom you crucified, whom God hath raised from the dead, even by him this man standeth here before you whole. " This is the stone which was rejected by you, the builders, which is become the head of the corner." Neither is there salvation in any other. For there is no

other name under heaven given to men whereby
we must be saved.

GOSPEL. *John* ii. 1-11. *At that time :* There
was a marriage in Cana of Galilee ; and the mother
of Jesus was there. And Jesus also was invited,
and his disciples, to the marriage. And the wine
failing, the mother of Jesus saith to him : They
have no wine. And Jesus saith to her : Woman,
what is it to me and to thee ? my hour is not yet
come. His mother said to the waiters : Whatsoever
he shall say to you, do ye. Now there were set
there six water-pots of stone, according to the
manner of the purifying of the Jews, containing
two or three measures apiece. Jesus saith to them :
Fill the water-pots with water. And they filled
them up to the brim. And Jesus saith to them :
Draw out now, and carry to the chief steward of
the feast. And they carried it. And when the
chief steward had tasted the water made wine, and
knew not whence it was ; but the waiters knew who
had drawn the water ; the chief steward calleth
the bridegroom, and saith to him : Every man at
first setteth forth good wine, and when men have
well drank, then that which is worse. But thou
hast kept the good wine until now. This beginning
of miracles did Jesus in Cana of Galilee : and manifested his glory, and his disciples believed in him.

THIRD SUNDAY AFTER EPIPHANY.

EPISTLE. *Rom.* xii. 16-21. *Brethren :* Be not
wise in your own conceits. To no man rendering
evil for evil. Providing good things, not only in
the sight of God, but also in the sight of all men.
If it be possible, as much as is in you having peace
with all men. Not revenging yourselves, my dearly
beloved ; but give place unto wrath. For it is
written : " Revenge to me ; I will repay," saith

the Lord. But " if thy enemy be hungry, give him to eat : if he thirst, give him to drink : for doing this, thou shalt heap coals of fire on his head." Be not overcome by evil, but overcome evil by good.

GOSPEL. *Matt.* viii. 1-13. *At that time :* When Jesus was come down from the mountain, great multitudes followed him ; and behold a leper came and adored him, saying : Lord, if thou wilt, thou canst make me clean. And Jesus stretching forth his hand, touched him, saying : I will ; be thou made clean. And forthwith his leprosy was cleansed. And Jesus saith to him : See thou tell no man, but go show thyself to the priests, and offer the gifts which Moses commanded for a testimony unto them. And when he had entered into Capharnaum, there came to him a centurion, beseeching him, and saying : Lord, my servant lieth at home sick of the palsy, and is grievously tormented. And Jesus saith to him : 1 will come and heal him. And the centurion making answer said : Lord, I am not worthy that thou shouldst enter under my roof ; but only say the word, and my servant shall be healed. For I also am a man subject to authority, having under me soldiers : and I say to this, Go, and he goeth ; and to another, Come, and he cometh ; and to my servant, Do this, and he doeth it. And when Jesus heard this, he marvelled, and said to them that followed him : Amen I say to you, I have not found so great faith in Israel. And I say unto you that many shall come from the east and the west, and shall sit down with Abraham and Isaac and Jacob in the kingdom of heaven ; but the children of the kingdom shall be cast out unto the exterior darkness ; there shall be weeping and gnashing of teeth. And Jesus said to the centurion : Go, and as thou hast believed so be it done to thee. And the servant was healed at the same hour. CREDO.

FOURTH SUNDAY AFTER EPIPHANY.

EPISTLE. *Rom.* xiii. 8-10. *Brethren :* Owe no man anything, but to love one another : for he that loveth his neighbour, hath fulfilled the law. For "thou shalt not commit adultery : Thou shalt not kill : Thou shalt not steal : Thou shalt not bear false witness : Thou shalt not covet " : And if there be any other commandment, it is comprised in this word : "Thou shalt love thy neighbour as thyself." The love of our neighbour worketh no evil. Love, therefore, is the fulfilling of the law.

GOSPEL. *Matt.* viii. 23-27. *At that time :* When Jesus entered into a boat, his disciples followed him ; and behold a great tempest arose in the sea, so that the boat was covered with waves ; but he was asleep. And his disciples came to him, and awakened him, saying: Lord, save us, we perish. And Jesus saith to them : Why are ye fearful, O ye of little faith ? Then rising up, he commanded the winds and the sea, and there came a great calm. But the men wondered, saying : What manner of man is this, for the winds and the sea obey him ? CREDO.

FIFTH SUNDAY AFTER EPIPHANY.

EPISTLE. *Colos.* iii. 12-17. *Brethren :* Put ye on therefore as the elect of God, holy and beloved, the bowels of mercy, benignity, humility, modesty, patience ; bearing with one another and forgiving one another, if any have a complaint against another. Even as the Lord hath forgiven you, so you also. But above all these things have charity, which is the bond of perfection, and let the peace of Christ rejoice in your hearts, wherein also you are called in one body ; and be ye thankful. Let the word of Christ dwell in you abundantly, in

all wisdom ; teaching and admonishing one another
in psalms, hymns, and spiritual canticles, singing
in grace in your hearts to God. All whatsoever you
do in word or in work, all things do ye in the name
of the Lord Jesus Christ, giving thanks to God and
the father by him.

GOSPEL. *Matt.* xiii. 24-30. *At that time :*
Jesus spoke this parable to the multitude, saying :
The kingdom of heaven is likened to a man that
sowed good seed in his field. But while men were
asleep, his enemy came and oversowed cockle among
the wheat, and went his way. And when the blade
was sprung up, and had brought forth fruit, then
appeared also the cockle. And the servants of the
good man of the house coming, said to him : Sir,
didst thou not sow good seed in thy field ? whence
then hath it cockle ? And he said to them : An
enemy hath done this. And the servants said to
him : Wilt thou that we go and gather it up ? And
he said : No, lest perhaps gathering up the cockle
you root up the wheat also together with it. Let
both grow until the harvest, and in the time
of the harvest I will say to the reapers : Gather
up first the cockle, and bind it in bundles to burn,
but gather the wheat into my barn.

Sixth Sunday after Epiphany.

EPISTLE. 1 *Thess* i. 2-10 *Brethren :* We give
thanks to God always for you all ; making a remembrance of you in our prayers without ceasing ;
being mindful of the work of your faith, and labour,
and charity, and of the enduring of the hope of our
Lord Jesus Christ, before God and our Father ;
knowing, brethren beloved of God, your election.
For our Gospel hath not been to you in word only,
but in power also, and in the Holy Ghost, and in
much fulness, as you know what manner of men

we have been among you for your sakes. And
you became followers of us and of the Lord, receiving
the word in much tribulation, with joy of the Holy
Ghost; so that you were made a pattern to all
that believe in Macedonia and in Achaia. For
from you was spread abroad the word of the Lord,
not only in Macedonia and in Achaia, but also in
every place your faith, which is towards God, is
gone forth, so that we need not to speak anything.
For they themselves relate of us, what manner of
entering in we had unto you; and how you turned
to God from idols, to serve the living and true God,
and to wait for his son from heaven (whom he raised
up from the dead), Jesus, who hath delivered us
from the wrath to come.

GOSPEL. *Matt.* xiii. 31-35. *At that time :* Jesus
spoke to the multitude this parable : The kingdom
of heaven is like to a grain of mustard seed, which
a man took and sowed in his field. Which indeed
is the least of all seeds ; but when it is grown up,
it is greater than all herbs, and becometh a tree,
so that the birds of the air come and dwell in the
branches thereof. Another parable he spoke to
them : The kingdom of heaven is like to leaven
which a woman took and hid in three measures of
meal, until the whole was leavened. All these
things Jesus spoke in parables to the multitudes, and
without parables he did not speak to them ; that
it might be fulfilled which was spoken by the prophet,
saying : " I will open my mouth in parables, I will
utter things hidden from the foundation of the
world." CREDO.

If there be not six Sundays between the Epiphany
and Septuagesima, what remain are omitted, and taken
in between the twenty-third and the last Sunday after
Pentecost.

SEPTUAGESIMA SUNDAY.

EPISTLE 1 *Cor.* ix. 24-27, *and* x. 1-5. *Brethren :*
Know you not that they that run in the race, all

run indeed, but one receiveth the prize ? So run that you may obtain. And every one that striveth for the mastery refraineth himself from all things ; and they indeed that they may receive a corruptible crown, but we an incorruptible one. I therefore so run, not as at an uncertainty ; I so fight, not as one beating the air ; but I chastise my body, and bring it into subjection, lest perhaps when I have preached to others, I myself should become a casta-way. [*Chap.* x. 1-5.] For I would not have you ignorant, brethren, that our fathers were all under the cloud, and all passed through the sea. And all in Moses were baptized in the cloud, and in the sea ; and did all eat the same spiritual food ; and all drank of the same spiritual drink (and they drank of the spiritual rock that followed them, and the rock was Christ). But with the most of them God was not well pleased.

GOSPEL. *Matt.* **xx. 1-16.** *At that time :* Jesus spoke to his disciples this parable : The kingdom of heaven is like to a householder who went out early in the morning to hire labourers into his vineyard. And having agreed with the labourers for a penny a day, he sent them into his vineyard. And going out about the third hour, he saw others standing in the market-place idle. And he said to them : Go you also into my vineyard, and I will give you what shall be just. And they went their way. And again he went out about the sixth and the ninth hour, and did in like manner. But about the eleventh hour he went out and found others standing, and he saith to them : Why stand you here all the day idle ? They said to him : Because no man hath hired us. He saith to them : Go you also into my vineyard. And when evening was come, the lord of the vineyard said to his steward : Call the labourers and pay them their hire, beginning from the last even to the first.

When, therefore, they were come that came about the eleventh hour, they received every man a penny. But when the first also came, they thought that they should receive more : and they also received every man a penny. And receiving it, they murmured against the master of the house, saying : These last have worked but one hour, and thou hast made them equal to us that have borne the burden of the day and the heats. But he answering said to one of them : Friend, I do thee no wrong : didst thou not agree with me for a penny ? Take what is thine and go thy way : I will also give to this last even as to thee. Or, is it not lawful for me to do what I will ? Is thy eye evil because I am good ? So shall the last be first, and the first last. For many are called but few chosen. CREDO.

SEXAGESIMA SUNDAY.

EPISTLE. 2 Cor. xi. 19-33, and xii. 1-9. Brethren : You gladly suffer the foolish : whereas yourselves are wise. For you suffer if a man bring you into bondage, if a man devour you. if a man take from you, if a man be lifted up. if a man strike you on the face. I speak according to dishonour, as if we had been weak in this part. Wherein if any man dare (I speak foolishly) I dare also. They are Hebrews ; so am I. They are Israelites ; so am I. They are the seed of Abraham ; so am I. They are the ministers of Christ (I speak as one less wise) ; I am more : in many more labours, in prisons more frequently, in stripes above measure, in deaths often. Of the Jews five times did I receive forty stripes, save one. Thrice was I beaten with rods, once I was stoned, thrice I suffered shipwreck ; a night and a day I was in the depth of the sea. In journeying often, in perils of waters, in perils of robbers, in perils from my own nation, in perils from the Gentiles, in perils in the city, in perils in the wilderness, in perils in the sea, in perils from false brethren. In labour and painfulness, in much watchings, in hunger and thirst, in fastings often, in cold and nakedness. Besides things which are without ; my daily instance, the solicitude for all the churches. Who is weak, and I am not weak ? Who is scandalized, and I am not on fire ? If I must needs glory, I will glory of the things that concern my infirmity. The God and Father of our Lord Jesus Christ, who is blessed for ever, knoweth that I lie not. At Damascus the governor of the nation under Aretas the king, guarded the city of the Damascenes, to apprehend me ; and through a window in a basket was I let down by the wall, and so escaped his hands. [*Chap.* xii. 1-9.] If I must glory (it is not expedient indeed) but I will come to the visions and revelations of the Lord. I know a man in Christ above fourteen years ago (whether in the body, I know not, or out of the body, I know not, God knoweth), such a one rapt even to the third heaven. And I know such a man (whether in the body or out of the body, I cannot tell, God knoweth), that he was caught up into paradise, and heard secret words, which it is not granted to man to utter. For such a one I will glory ; but for myself I will glory nothing but in my infirmities. For though I should have a mind to glory, I shall not be foolish ; for I will say the truth. But I forbear, lest any man should think of me above that which he seeth in me, or anything he heareth from me. And lest the greatness of the revelations should exalt me, there was given me a sting of my flesh, an angel of Satan to buffet me. For which thing I thrice besought the Lord, that it might depart from me : and he said to me : My grace is sufficient for thee : for power is made perfect in infirmity. Gladly, therefore, will I glory in my infirmities, that the power of Christ may dwell in me.

GOSPEL. *Luke* viii. 4-15. *At that time :* When a very great multitude was gathered together, and hastened out of the cities to meet Jesus, he spoke by a similitude. A sower went out to sow his seed ; and as he sowed some fell by the wayside, and it was trodden down and the fowls of the air devoured it. And other some fell upon a rock, and as soon as it was sprung up, it withered away, because it had no moisture. And other some fell among thorns, and the thorns growing up with it, choked it. And other some fell upon good ground ; and being sprung up, yielded fruit a hundred-fold. Saying these things he cried out : He that hath ears to hear, let him hear. And his disciples asked him what this parable might be. To whom he said : To you it is given to know the mystery of the kingdom of God : but to the rest in parables, that seeing they may not see, and hearing may not understand. Now the parable is this : The seed is the word of God. And they by the wayside are they that hear ; then the devil cometh, and taketh the word out of their heart, lest believing they should be saved. Now, they upon the rock *are they* who, when they hear, receive the word with joy ; and these have no roots : for they believe for a while, and in time of temptation fall away. And that which fell among thorns are they who have heard, and going their way are choked with the cares and the riches and pleasures of this life, and yield no fruit. But that on the good ground are they who, in a good and perfect heart, hearing the word, keep it, and bring forth fruit in patience.

Quinquagesima Sunday.

EPISTLE. 1 *Cor.* xiii. 1-13. *Brethren :* If I speak with the tongues of men and of angels, and have not charity, I am become as sounding brass or a tinkling cymbal. And if I should have prophecy and should know all mysteries and all knowledge, and if I should have all faith, so that I could remove mountains, and have not charity, I am nothing. And if I should distribute all may goods to feed the poor, and if I should deliver my body to be burned, and have not charity, it profiteth me nothing. Charity is patient, is kind. Charity envieth not, dealeth not perversely; is not puffed up, it is not ambitious, seeketh not her own, is not provoked to anger, thinketh no evil; rejoiceth not in iniquity, but rejoiceth with the truth; beareth all things, believeth all things, hopeth all things, endureth all things. Charity never falleth away; whether prophecies shall be made void, or tongues shall cease, or knowledge shall be destroyed. For we know in part, and we prophesy in part; but when that which is perfect is come, that which is in part shall be done away. When I was a child, I spoke as a child, I understood as a child, I thought as a child; but when I became a man, I put away the things of a child. We now see through a glass in a dark manner; but then face to face. Now I know in part; but then I shall know even as I am known. And now there remain faith, hope, charity, these three: but the greatest of these is charity.

GOSPEL. *Luke* xviii. 31-43. *At that time:* Jesus took unto him the twelve, and said to them: Behold, we go up to Jerusalem, and all things shall be accomplished which were written by the prophets concerning the Son of Man. For he shall be delivered to the Gentiles, and shall be mocked and scourged and spit upon: and after they have scourged him, they will put him to death, and the third day he shall rise again. And they understood none of these things. And this word was hid from them, and they understood not the things that were said. Now it came to pass, that when he drew nigh to Jericho, a certain blind man sat by the wayside begging. And when he heard the multitude passing by, he asked what this meant. And they told him that Jesus of Nazareth was passing by. And he cried out, saying : Jesus, son of David, have mercy on me. And they that went before, rebuked him, that he should hold his peace. But he cried out much more : Son of David, have mercy on me. And Jesus standing, commanded him to be brought unto him. And when he was come near, he asked him, saying : What wilt thou that I do to thee ? But he said : Lord, that I may see. And Jesus said to him : Receive thy sight ; thy faith hath made thee whole. And immediately he saw, and followed him, glorifying God. And all the people, when they saw it, gave praise to God. CREDO.

ASH WEDNESDAY.

LESSON. *Joel* ii. 12-19. Thus saith the Lord : Be converted to me with all your heart, in fasting, in weeping, and in mourning. And rend your hearts, and not your garments, and turn to the Lord your God, for he is gracious and merciful, patient and rich in mercy, and ready to repent of the evil. Who knoweth but he will return and forgive, and leave a blessing behind him ; sacrifice and libation to the Lord your God ? Blow the trumpet in Sion, sanctify a fast, call a solemn assembly, gather together the people, sanctify the church, assemble the ancients, gather together the little ones, and them that suck at the breasts : let the bridegroom go forth from his bed, and the bride out of the bride-chamber. Between the porch and the altar, the priests, the Lord's ministers, shall weep, and say : Spare, O Lord, spare thy people, and give not thine inheritance to reproach, that the heathens should rule over them. Why should they say among the nations : Where is their God ? The Lord hath been zealous for his land,

and hath spared his people. And the Lord answered, and said to his people : Behold, I will send you corn, and wine, and oil : you shall be filled with them, and I will no more make you a reproach among the nations, saith the Lord Almighty.

GOSPEL. *Matt.* vi. 16-21. *At that time :* Jesus said to his disciples : When you fast, be not as the hypocrites, sad. For they disfigure their faces, that they may appear to men to fast. Amen I say to you, they have received their reward. But thou, when thou fastest, anoint thy head and wash thy face, that thou appear not to men to fast, but to thy Father who is in secret ; and thy Father who seeth in secret, will repay thee. Lay not up to yourselves treasures on earth, where the rust and moth consume, and where thieves break through and steal ; but lay up to yourselves treasures in heaven, where neither the rust nor moth doth consume, and where thieves do not break through nor steal. For where thy treasure is, there is thy heart also.

First Sunday in Lent.

EPISTLE. 2 *Cor.* vi. 1-10. *Brethren :* We exhort you, that you receive not the grace of God in vain. For he saith : " In an accepted time have I heard thee ; and in the day of salvation have I helped thee." Behold, now is the acceptable time ; behold, now is the day of salvation. Giving no offence to any man, that our ministry be not blamed ; but in all things let us exhibit ourselves as the ministers of God, in much patience, in tribulation, in necessities, in distresses, in stripes, in prisons, in seditions, in labours, in watchings, in fastings, in chastity, in knowledge, in long suffering, in sweetness, in the Holy Ghost, in charity unfeigned, in the word of truth, in the power of God ; by the armour of justice on the right hand and on the left ;

by honour and dishonour ; by evil report and good
report : as deceivers and yet true ; as unknown and
yet known ; as dying and behold we live ; as
chastised and not killed ; as sorrowful yet always
rejoicing ; as needy yet enriching many : as having
nothing and possessing all things.

GOSPEL. *Matt.* iv. 1-11. *At that time :* Jesus
was led by the spirit into the desert, to be tempted
by the devil. And when he had fasted forty days
and forty nights, afterwards he was hungry. And
the tempter coming, said to him : If thou be the
Son of God, command that these stones be made
bread. Who answered and said : It is written :
"Not in bread alone doth man live, but by every
word that proceedeth out of the mouth of God."
Then the devil took him into the holy city, and set
him upon the pinnacle of the temple, and said to
him : If thou be the Son of God, cast thyself down ;
for it is written : "That he hath given his angels
charge over thee, and in their hands shall they bear
thee up, lest perhaps thou dash thy foot against a
stone." Jesus said to him : It is written again :
"Thou shalt not tempt the Lord thy God." Again
the devil took him up into a very high mountain,
and showed him all the kingdoms of the world,
and the glory of them, and said to him : All these
will I give thee, if falling down, thou wilt adore me.
Then Jesus said to him : Begone, Satan ; for it is
written : "The Lord thy God shalt thou adore,
and him only shalt thou serve." Then the devil
left him ; and behold angels came and ministered
to him. CREDO.

SECOND SUNDAY IN LENT.

EPISTLE. 1 *Thess.* iv. 1-7. *Brethren :* We
pray and beseech you in the Lord Jesus that as you
have received of us, how you ought to walk and to

please God, so also you would walk, that you may abound the more. For you know what precepts I have given to you by the Lord Jesus. For this is the will of God, your sanctification ; that you should abstain from fornication, that every one of you should know how to possess his vessel in sanctification and honour, not in the passion of lust, like the Gentiles that know not God ; and that no man over-reach nor circumvent his brother in business ; because the Lord is the avenger of all these things, as we have told you before, and have testified. For God hath not called us unto uncleanness, but unto sanctification.

GOSPEL. *Matt.* xvii. 1-9. *At that time :* Jesus taketh unto him Peter and James, and John his brother, and bringeth them up into a high mountain apart ; and he was transfigured before them. And his face did shine as the sun, and his garments became white as snow. And, behold, there appeared to them Moses and Elias talking with him. And Peter answering, said to Jesus : Lord, it is good for us to be here : if thou wilt, let us make here three tabernacles, one for thee, and one for Moses, and one for Elias. And as he was yet speaking, behold, a bright cloud overshaded them. And lo, a voice out of the cloud, saying : "This is my beloved Son, in whom I am well pleased ; hear ye him." And the disciples hearing, fell upon their face, and were very much afraid. And Jesus came and touched them, and said unto them : Arise, and fear not. And they lifting up their eyes saw no one, but only Jesus. And as they came down from the mountain, Jesus charged them, saying : Tell the vision to no man, till the Son of Man be risen from the dead. CREDO.

THIRD SUNDAY IN LENT.

EPISTLE. *Ephes.* v. 1-9. *Brethren :* Be ye therefore followers of God, as most dear children :

and walk in love, as Christ also hath loved us, and hath delivered himself for us, an oblation and a sacrifice to God, for an odour of sweetness. But fornication, and all uncleanness, or covetousness, let it not so much as be named among you, as becometh saints ; or obscenity, or foolish talking, or scurrility, which is to no purpose ; but rather giving of thanks. For know ye this, and understand that no fornicator, or unclean, or covetous person (which is a serving of idols) hath inheritance in the kingdom of Christ and of God. Let no man deceive you with vain words. For because of these things cometh the anger of God upon the children of unbelief. Be ye not, therefore, partakers with them. For you were heretofore darkness, but now light in the Lord. Walk then as children of the light. For the fruit of the light is in all goodness, and justice, and truth.

GOSPEL. *Luke* xi. 14-28. *At that time :* Jesus was casting out a devil, and the same was dumb ; and when he had cast out the devil, the dumb spoke, and the multitudes were in admiration at it. But some of them said : He casteth out devils by Beelzebub, the prince of devils. And others, tempting, asked of him a sign from heaven. But he, seeing their thoughts, said to them : Every kingdom divided against itself shall be brought to desolation, and house upon house shall fall. And if Satan also be divided against himself, how shall his kingdom stand ? because you say that through Beelzebub I cast out devils. Now, if I cast out devils by Beelzebub, by whom do your children cast them out ? Therefore they shall be your judges. But if I, by the finger of God, cast out devils, doubtless the kingdom of God is come upon you. When a strong man armed keepeth his court, those things are in peace which he possesseth. But if a stronger than he come upon him, and over-

come him, he will take away all his armour wherein
he trusted, and will distribute his spoils. He that
is not with me is against me ; and he that gathereth
not with me scattereth. When the unclean spirit
is gone out of a man, he walketh through places
without water, seeking rest ; and not finding, he
saith : I will return unto my house, whence I came
out. And when he is come, he findeth it swept and
garnished. Then he goeth and taketh with him
seven other spirits more wicked than himself, and
entering in they dwell there ; and the last state of
that man becomes worse than the first. And it came
to pass, as he spoke these things, a certain woman
from the crowd, lifting up her voice, said to him :
Blessed is the womb that bore thee, and the paps
that gave thee suck. But he said : Yea rather,
blessed are they who hear the word of God, and
keep it. CREDO.

FOURTH SUNDAY IN LENT.

EPISTLE. *Gal.* iv. 22-31. *Brethren :* It is
written that Abraham had two sons : the one by a
bond woman, and the other by a free woman.
But he who was of the bond woman was born
according to the flesh ; but he of the free woman
was by promise. Which things are said by an
allegory. For these are the two testaments. The
one from Mount Sina, engendering unto bondage,
which is Agar ; for Sina is a mountain in Arabia,
which hath affinity to that Jerusalem which now is,
and is in bondage with her children. But that
Jerusalem, which is above, is free, which is our
mother. For it is written : Rejoice, thou barren,
that bearest not : break forth and cry, thou that
travailest not : for many are the children of the
desolate, more than of her that hath a husband.
Now we, brethren, as Isaac was, are the children of
promise. But as then, he that was born according

to the flesh, persecuted him that was after the spirit, so also it is now. But what saith the scripture ? Cast out the bond woman and her son ; for the son of the bond woman shall not be heir with the son of the free woman. So then, brethren, we are not the children of the bond woman, but of the free ; by the freedom wherewith Christ has made us free.

GOSPEL. *John* vi. 1-15. *At that time :* Jesus went over the sea of Galilee, which is that of Tiberias ; and a great multitude followed him, because they saw the miracles which he did on them that were diseased. Jesus therefore went up into a mountain, and there he sat with his disciples. Now the pasch, the festival day of the Jews, was near at hand. When Jesus therefore had lifted up his eyes, and seen that a very great multitude cometh to him, he said to Philip : Whence shall we buy bread that these may eat ? And this he said to try him, for he himself knew what he would do. Philip answered him : Two hundred pennyworth of bread is not sufficient for them, that every one may take a little. One of his disciples, Andrew, the brother of Simon Peter, saith to him : There is a boy here that hath five barley loaves and two fishes ; but what are these among so many ? Then Jesus said : Make the men sit down. Now there was much grass in the place. The men therefore sat down, in number about five thousand. And Jesus took the loaves ; and when he had given thanks, he distributed to them that were set down. In like manner also of the fishes, as much as they would ; and when they were filled, he said to his disciples : Gather up the fragments that remain, lest they be lost. They gathered up therefore, and filled twelve baskets with the fragments of the five barley loaves, which remained over and above to them that had eaten. Now those men

when they had seen what a miracle Jesus had done,
said : This is of a truth the prophet that is to come
into the world.   Jesus therefore, when he knew
that they would come to take him by force and
make him king, fled again into the mountain
himself alone.   CREDO.

PASSION SUNDAY.

EPISTLE.   *Heb.* ix. 11-15.   *Brethren :* Christ,
being come a high priest of the good things to come,
by a greater and more perfect tabernacle not made
with hands, that is, not of this creation, neither by
the blood of goats or of calves, but by his own
blood, entered once into the Holies, having obtained
eternal redemption.   For if the blood of goats, and
of oxen, and the ashes of an heifer being sprinkled,
sanctify such as are defiled, to the cleansing of the
flesh ; how much more shall the blood of Christ
(who by the Holy Ghost offered himself unspotted
unto God) cleanse our conscience from dead works
to serve the living God ?   And therefore he is the
mediator of the New Testament ; that by means of
his death, for the redemption of those transgressions
which were under the former testament, they that
are called may receive the promise of eternal inheritance.

GOSPEL.   *John* viii. 46-59.   *At that time :*
Jesus said to the multitude of the Jews : Which of
you shall convince me of sin ?   If I say the truth to
you, why do you not believe me ?   He that is of
God, heareth the words of God.   Therefore you hear
them not, because you are not of God.   The Jews
therefore answered and said to him : Do not we say
well that thou art a Samaritan, and hast a devil ?
Jesus answered : I have not a devil : but I honour
my Father, and you have dishonoured me.   But I
seek not my own glory ; there is one that seeketh

and judgeth. Amen, amen, I say to you : If any man keep my word, he shall not see death for ever. The Jews therefore said : Now we know that thou hast a devil. Abraham is dead, and the prophets ; and thou sayest : If any man keep my word he shall not taste death for ever. Art thou greater than our father Abraham, who is dead ? And the prophets are dead. Whom dost thou make thyself ? Jesus answered : If I glorify myself my glory is nothing. It is my Father that glorifieth me, of whom you say that he is your God : and you have not known him, but I know him. And if I shall say that I know him not, I should be like to you, a liar. But I do know him, and do keep his word. Abraham your father rejoiced that he might see my day : he saw it, and was glad. The Jews therefore said to him : Thou art not yet fifty years old, and hast thou seen Abraham ? Jesus said to them : Amen, amen, I say to you, before Abraham was made, I am. They took up stones therefore to cast at him. But Jesus hid himself, and went out of the temple.

PALM SUNDAY.

EPISTLE. *Philip.* ii. 5-11. *Brethren :* Let this mind be in you, which was also in Christ Jesus ; who being in the form of God, thought it not robbery to be equal with God, but emptied himself, taking the form of a servant, being made in the likeness of men, and in habit found as a man. He humbled himself, becoming obedient unto death, even to the death of the cross. For which cause God also hath exalted him, and hath given him a name which is above all names ; that in the name of Jesus every knee should bow, of those that are in heaven, on earth, and under the earth. And that every tongue should confess that the Lord Jesus Christ is in the glory of God the Father.

GOSPEL. *The Passion of Our Lord Jesus Christ, according to* Matt. xxvi. *and* xxvii. *At that time :* Jesus said to his disciples : You know that after two days shall be the pasch, and the Son of Man shall be delivered up to be crucified. Then were gathered together the chief priests and ancients of the people, into the court of the high priest, who was called Caiphas ; and they consulted together, that by subtilty they might apprehend Jesus, and put him to death. But they said : Not on the festival day, lest perhaps there should be a tumult among the people. And when Jesus was in Bethania, in the house of Simon the leper, there came to him a woman having an alabaster box of precious ointment, and poured it on his head as he was at table. And the disciples seeing it, had indignation, saying : To what purpose is this waste ? For this might have been sold for much, and given to the poor. And Jesus knowing it, said to them : Why do you trouble this woman ? For she hath wrought a good work upon me. For the poor you have always with you, but me you have not always. For she, in pouring this ointment upon my body, hath done if for my burial. Amen I say to you, wheresoever this gospel shall be preached in the whole world, that also which she hath done shall be told for a memory of her. Then went one of the twelve who was called Judas Iscariot, to the chief priests, and said to them : What will you give me, and I will deliver him unto you ? But they appointed him thirty pieces of silver. And from thenceforth he sought opportunity to betray him. And on the first day of the Azymes the disciples came to Jesus, saying : Where wilt thou that we prepare for thee to eat the pasch? But Jesus said : Go ye into the city to a certain man, and say to him : "The Master saith, My time is near at hand, with thee I make the pasch with my disciples." And the disciples did as Jesus appointed to them, and they

prepared the pasch. But when it was evening he sat
down with his twelve disciples ; and whilst they were
eating, he said : Amen I say to you, that one of
you is about to betray me. And they being very
much troubled, began every one to say : Is it I,
Lord ? But he answering, said : He that dippeth
his hand with me in the dish, he shall betray me.
The Son of Man indeed goeth, as it is written of
him ; but woe to that man by whom the Son of
Man shall be betrayed. It were better for him if
that man had not been born. And Judas, that
betrayed him, answering, said : Is it I, Rabbi ?
He said to him : Thou hast said it. And whilst
they were at supper, Jesus took bread, and blessed,
and broke, and gave to his disciples, and said :
Take ye and eat : this is my body. And taking the
chalice he gave thanks, and gave to them, saying :
Drink ye all of this : for this is my blood of the New
Testament, which shall be shed for many unto
the remission of sins. And I say to you, I will not
drink from henceforth of this fruit of the vine,
until that day when I shall drink it with you new
in the kingdom of my Father. And a hymn being
said, they went out unto Mount Olivet. Then
Jesus saith to them : All you shall be scandalized
in me this night. For it is written : " I will strike
the shepherd, and the sheep of the flock shall be
dispersed." But after I shall be risen again, I
will go before you into Galilee. And Peter, answering
said to him : Although all shall be scandalized in
thee, I will never be scandalized. Jesus said to him :
Amen I say to thee, that in this night, before the
cock crow, thou wilt deny me thrice ; Peter saith
to him : Yea, though I should die with thee, I will
not deny thee. And in like manner said all the disciples. Then Jesus came with them into a country
place which is called Gethsemani ; and he said to
his disciples : Sit you here, till I go yonder and pray.
And taking with him Peter and the two sons of

Zebedee, he began to grow sorrowful, and to be sad. Then he saith to them : My soul is sorrowful even unto death : stay you here and watch with me. And going a little further he fell upon his face, praying, and saying : My Father, if it be possible, let this chalice pass from me. Nevertheless, not as I will, but as thou wilt. And he cometh to his disciples and findeth them asleep, and he saith to Peter : What, could you not watch one hour with me ? Watch ye, and pray that ye enter not into temptation. The spirit indeed is willing, but the flesh is weak. Again the second time he went and prayed, saying : My Father, if this chalice may not pass away, but I must drink it, thy will be done. And he cometh again, and findeth them sleeping ; for their eyes were heavy. And leaving them, he went again ; and he prayed the third time, saying the self-same word. Then he cometh to his disciples, and saith to them : Sleep ye now, and take your rest : behold the hour is at hand. and the Son of Man shall be betrayed into the hands of sinners. Rise, let us go : behold he is at hand that will betray me. As he yet spoke, behold, Judas, one of the twelve, came, and with him a great multitude, with swords and clubs, sent from the chief priests and the ancients of the people. And he that betrayed him, gave them a sign, saying : Whomsoever I shall kiss. that is he, hold him fast. And forthwith coming to Jesus, he said : Hail, Rabbi : and he kissed him. And Jesus said to him : Friend, whereto art thou come ? Then they came up, and laid hands on Jesus and held him. And behold one of them that were with Jesus, stretching forth his hand, drew out his sword ; and striking the servant of the high priest, cut off his ear. Then Jesus saith to him : Put up again thy sword into its place ; for all that take the sword shall perish with the sword. Thinkest thou that I cannot ask my Father, and he will give me presently more than twelve legions of angels ? How then shall the scriptures be fulfilled, that so it must be done ? In that same hour, Jesus said to the multitudes : You are come out as it were to a robber, with swords and clubs, to apprehend me. I sat daily with you teaching in the temple and you laid not hands on me. Now all this was done that the scriptures of the prophets might be fulfilled. Then the disciples all leaving him, fled. But they, holding Jesus, led him to Caiphas, the high priest, where the scribes and the ancients were assembled. And Peter followed him afar off, even to the court of the high priest ; and going in, he sat with the servants, that he might see the end. And the chief priests and the whole council sought false witness against Jesus, that they might put him to death ; and they found not, whereas many false witnesses had come in. And last of all there came two false witnesses : and they said : This man said, I am able to destroy the temple of God, and after three days to rebuild it. And the high priest rising up said to him : Answerest thou nothing to the things which these witness against thee ? But Jesus held his peace. And the high priest said to him : I adjure thee, by the living God, that thou tell us if thou be the Christ the Son of God. Jesus saith to him : Thou hast said it. Nevertheless I say to you, hereafter you shall see the Son of Man sitting on the right hand of the power of God, and coming in the clouds of heaven. Then the high priest rent his garments, saying : He hath blasphemed ; what further need have we of witnesses ? Behold, now you have heard the blasphemy, what think you ? But they answering, said : He is guilty of death. Then did they spit in his face. and buffeted him, and others struck his face with the palms of their hands, saying : Prophesy unto us, O Christ, who is he that struck thee ? But Peter sat without in the court ; and there came to him a servant maid saying : Thou also wast with Jesus the Galilean. But he denied before them all saying : I know not what thou sayest. And as he went out of the gate, another maid saw him and she saith to them that were there : This man also was with Jesus of Nazareth. And again he denied with an oath : That I know not the man. And after a little while they came that stood by, and said to Peter : Surely thou also art one of them ; for even thy speech doth discover thee. Then he began to curse and swear that he knew not the man. And immediately the cock crew. And Peter remembered the word of Jesus which he had said : Before the cock crow, thou wilt deny me thrice. And going forth he wept bitterly. And when morning was come, all the chief priests and ancients of the people took counsel against Jesus, that they might put him to death. And they brought him bound and delivered him to Pontius Pilate, the governor. Then Judas, who betrayed him, seeing that he was condemned, repenting himself, brought back the thirty pieces of silver to the chief priests and ancients, saying : I have sinned in betraying innocent blood. But they said : What is that to us ? look thou to it. And casting down the pieces of silver in the temple, he departed, and went and hanged himself with a halter. But the chief priests having taken the pieces of silver, said : It is not lawful to put them into the corbona, because it is the price of blood. And after they had consulted together, they bought with them the potter's field to be a burying place for strangers. For this cause that field was called Haceldama, that is, the field of blood, even to this day. Then was fulfilled that which was spoken by Jeremias the prophet, saying : "And they took the thirty pieces of silver, the price of him that was prized, whom they prized of the children of Israel. And they gave them unto the potter's field, as the Lord appointed to me." And Jesus stood before the governor, and the

governor asked him saying : Art thou the king of
the Jews ?   Jesus saith to him : Thou sayest it.
And when he was accused by the chief priests and
ancients, he answered nothing.   Then Pilate said
to him : Dost not thou hear how great testimonies
they allege against thee ?   And he answered him
to never a word ; so that the governor wondered
exceedingly.   Now upon the solemn day, the
governor was accustomed to release to the people
one prisoner, whom they would.   And he had then
a notorious prisoner, that was called Barabbas.
They therefore being gathered together, Pilate said :
Whom will you that I release to you—Barabbas, or
Jesus, that is called Christ ?   For he knew that for
envy they had delivered him.   And as he was sitting
in the place of judgment, his wife sent to him,
saying : Have thou nothing to do with that just
man.   For I have suffered many things this day
in a dream because of him.   But the chief priests
and ancients persuaded the people that they should
ask Barabbas, and make Jesus away.   And the
governor answering said to them: Whether will
you of the two to be released unto you ?   But they
said Barabbas.   Pilate saith to them : What shall
I do then with Jesus that is called Christ ?   They
say all : Let him be crucified.   The governor said to
them : Why, what evil hath he done ?   But they
cried out the more, saying : Let him be crucified.
And Pilate seeing that he prevailed nothing, but
that rather a tumult was made ; taking water,
washed his hands before the people saying : I am
innocent of the blood of this just man : look you
to it.   And the whole people answering, said :
His blood be upon us, and upon our children.   Then
he released to them Barabbas : and having scourged
Jesus, delivered him unto them to be crucified.
Then the soldiers of the governor, taking Jesus into
the hall, gathered together unto him the whole
band ; and stripping him, they put a scarlet cloak

about him. And platting a crown of thorns, they put it upon his head, and a reed in his right hand. And bowing the knee before him, they mocked him, saying: Hail, King of the Jews. And spitting upon him, they took the reed and struck his head. And after they had mocked him, they took off the cloak from him, and put on him his own garments, and led him away to crucify him. And going out they found a man of Cyrene, named Simon: him they forced to take up his cross. And they came to the place that is called Golgotha, which is the place of Calvary. And they gave him wine to drink mingled with gall. And when he had tasted he would not drink. And after they had crucified him, they divided his garments, casting lots: that it might be fulfilled which was spoken by the prophet, saying: " They divided my garments among them; and upon my vesture they cast lots ": and they sat and watched him. And they put over his head his cause written: THIS IS JESUS THE KING OF THE JEWS. Then were crucified with him two thieves, one on the right hand, and one on the left. And they that passed by blasphemed him, wagging their heads and saying: Vah, thou that destroyest the temple of God, and in three days dost rebuild it, save thy own self: if thou be the Son of God, come down from the cross. In like manner, also, the chief priests with the scribes and ancients, mocking, said: He saved others; himself he cannot save; if he be the king of Israel, let him now come down from the cross, and we will believe him. He trusted in God, let him now deliver him, if he will have him: for he said: I am the Son of God. And the self-same thing, the thieves also that were crucified with him reproached him with. Now from the sixth hour there was darkness over the whole earth until the ninth hour. And about the ninth hour Jesus cried with a loud voice, saying: Eli, Eli, lama sabacthani? that is, " My God, my God, why hast

thou forsaken me ? '' And some that stood there
and heard, said : This man calleth Elias. And
immediately one of them running, took a sponge,
and filled it with vinegar and put it on a reed, and
gave him to drink. And the others said : Let be, let
us see whether Elias will come to deliver him.
And Jesus again crying with a loud voice, yielded
up the ghost.* And behold the veil of the temple
was rent in two from the top even to the bottom,
and the earth quaked, and the rocks were rent.
And the graves were opened : and many bodies of
the saints that had slept arose, and coming out of
the tombs after his resurrection, came into the holy
city and appeared to many. Now the centurion,
and they that were with him watching Jesus,
having seen the earthquake and the things that were
done, were sore afraid, saying : Indeed this was the
Son of God. And there were many women afar off,
who had followed Jesus from Galilee, ministering
unto him, among whom was Mary Magdalene, and
Mary the mother of James and Joseph, and the
mother of the sons of Zebedee. And when it was
evening there came a certain rich man of Arimathea
named Joseph, who also himself was a disciple of
Jesus. He went to Pilate and asked the body of
Jesus. Then Pilate commanded that the body
should be delivered. And Joseph taking the body,
wrapped it up in a clean linen cloth, and laid it
in his own new monument, which he had hewed
out in a rock. And he rolled a great stone to the
door of the monument, and went his way. And
there was there Mary Magdalene and the other
Mary sitting over against the sepulchre. And the
next day, which followed the day of preparation,
the chief priests and the Pharisees came together
to Pilate, saying : Sir, we have rememberd that that
seducer said, while he was yet alive : After three
days I will rise again. Command, therefore, the

* Here all kneel and pause.

sepulchre to be guarded until the third day ; lest perhaps his disciples come and steal him away, and say to the people : He is risen from the dead ; and the last error shall be worse than the first. Pilate said to them : You have a guard ; go, guard it as you know. And they, departing, made the sepulchre sure, sealing the stone and setting guards.

EASTER SUNDAY.

EPISTLE. 1 *Cor.* v. 7, 8. *Brethren :* Purge out the old leaven, that you may be a new paste, as you are unleavened. For Christ our pasch is sacrificed. Therefore, let us feast, not with the old leaven, nor with the leaven of malice and wickedness, but with the unleavened bread of sincerity and truth.

GOSPEL. *Mark* xvi. 1-7. *At that time :* Mary Magdalene, and Mary the mother of James and Salome, bought sweet spices, that coming they might anoint Jesus. And very early in the morning, the first day of the week, they came to the sepulchre, the sun being now risen. And they said one to another : Who shall roll us back the stone from the door of the sepulchre ? And looking, they saw the stone rolled back. For it was very great. And entering into the sepulchre, they saw a young man sitting on the right side, clothed with a white robe : and they were astonished. Who saith to them : Be not affrighted : you seek Jesus of Nazareth, who was crucified : he is risen, he is not here, behold the place where they laid him. But go, tell his disciples and Peter, that he goeth before you into Galilee : there you shall see him, as he told you. CREDO.

QUASIMODO, OR LOW SUNDAY.

EPISTLE. 1 *John* v. 4-10. *Dearly beloved :* For whatsoever is born of God overcometh the world ; and this is the victory which overcometh the world, our faith. Who is he that overcometh the world, but he that believeth that Jesus is the Son of God ? This is he that came by water and blood, Jesus Christ : not by water only, but by water and blood. And it is the spirit which testifieth that Christ is the truth. And there are three who give testimony in heaven, the Father, the Word, and the Holy Ghost. And these three are one. And there are three that give testimony on earth : the Spirit, and the water, and the blood : and these three are one. If we receive the testimony of men, the testimony of God is greater. For this is the testimony of God which is greater, because he hath testified of his son. He that believeth in the Son of God, hath the testimony of God in himself.

GOSPEL. *John* xx. 19-31. *At that time :* When it was late that same day, the first of the week, and the doors were shut where the disciples were gathered together for fear of the Jews, Jesus came and stood in the midst and said to them : Peace be to you. And when he had said this, he showed them his hands and his side. The disciples therefore were glad when they saw the Lord. He said therefore to them again : Peace be to you. As the Father hath sent me, I also send you. When he had said this, he breathed on them ; and he said to them : Receive ye the Holy Ghost : whose sins you shall forgive, they are forgiven them : and whose sins you shall retain, they are retained. Now, Thomas, one of the twelve, who is called Didymus, was not with them when Jesus came. The other disciples therefore said to him : We have seen the Lord. But he said to them : Except I shall see in his hands the print of the nails, and put my finger into the place of the nails, and put my hand into his side, I will not believe. And after eight days, again his disciples were within, and Thomas with them.

Jesus cometh, the doors being shut, and stood in the midst and said : Peace be to you. Then he said to Thomas : Put in thy finger hither, and see my hands, and bring hither thy hand, and put it into my side ; and be not faithless, but believing. Thomas answered and said to him : My Lord and my God ! Jesus saith to him : Because thou hast seen me, Thomas, thou hast believed : blessed are they that have not seen and have believed. Many other signs also did Jesus in the sight of his disciples, which are not written in this book. But these are written that you may believe that Jesus is the Christ, the Son of God : and that believing you may have life in his name. CREDO.

SECOND SUNDAY AFTER EASTER.

EPISTLE. 1 *Peter* ii. 21-25. *Dearly beloved :* Christ also suffered for us, leaving you an example that you should follow his steps. *Who did no sin, neither was guile found in his mouth.* Who when he was reviled, did not revile : when he suffered, he threatened not, but delivered himself to him that judged him unjustly : who his own self bore our sins in his body upon the tree ; that we being dead to sins, should live to justice : by whose stripes you were healed. For you were as sheep going astray ; but you are now converted to the shepherd and bishop of your souls.

GOSPEL. *John.* x. 11-16. *At that time :* Jesus said to the Pharisees : I am the good shepherd. The good shepherd giveth his life for his sheep. But the hireling, and he that is not the shepherd, whose own the sheep are not, seeth the wolf coming and leaveth the sheep, and flieth, and the wolf catcheth and scattereth the sheep : and the hireling flieth, because he is a hireling : and he hath no care for the sheep. I am the good shepherd : and I know mine and mine know me. As the Father knoweth me, and I know the Father : and I lay down my life for my sheep. And other sheep I have that are not of this fold : them also I must bring, and they shall hear my voice, and there shall be one fold and one shepherd. CREDO.

THIRD SUNDAY AFTER EASTER.

EPISTLE. 1 *Peter* ii. 11-19. *Dearly beloved :* I beseech you as strangers and pilgrims to refrain yourselves from carnal desires, which war against the soul, having your conversation good among the Gentiles ; that whereas they speak against you as evil doers, they may, by the good works which they shall behold in you, glorify God in the day of visitation. Be ye subject therefore to every human creature for God's sake ; whether it be to the king as excelling ; or to governors as sent by him for the punishment of evil doers, and for the praise of the good : for so is the will of God, that by doing well you may put to silence the ignorance of foolish men ; as free, and not making liberty a cloak for malice, but as the servants of God. Honour all men : love the brotherhood : fear God : honour the king. Servants, be subject to your masters with all fear, not only to the good and gentle, but also to the froward. For this is thanks-worthy *in Christ Jesus our Lord.*

GOSPEL. *John* xvi. 16-22, *At that time :* Jesus said to his disciples : A little while, and now you shall not see me ; and again a little while, and you shall see me ; because I go to the Father. Then some of his disciples said one to another : What is this that he saith to us : A little while, and you shall not see me ; and again a little while, and you shall see me, and, because I go to the Father ? They said therefore : What is this that he saith, A little while ? We know not what he speaketh. And Jesus knew that they had a mind to ask him : and he said to them : Of this do you inquire among yourselves, because I said : A little while, and you shall not see me ; and again a little while, and you shall see me ? Amen, amen, I say to you, that you shall lament and weep, but the world shall rejoice ; and you shall be made sorrowful, but your sorrow shall be turned into joy. A woman when she is in labour hath sorrow, because her hour has come ; but when she hath brought forth the child, she remembereth no more the anguish, for joy that a man is born into the world. So also you now indeed have sorrow, but I will see you again, and your heart shall rejoice : and your joy no man shall take from you. CREDO.

FOURTH SUNDAY AFTER EASTER.

EPISTLE. *James* i. 17-21. *Dearly beloved :* Every best gift and every perfect gift is from above, coming down from the Father of lights, with whom there is no change nor shadow of alteration. For of his own will hath he begotten us by the word of truth, that we might be some beginning of his creature. You know, my dearest brethren. And let every man be swift to hear, but slow to speak and slow to anger. For the anger of man worketh not the justice of God. Wherefore casting away all uncleanness and abundance of naughtiness, with meekness receive the ingrafted word, which is able to save your souls.

GOSPEL. *John* xvi. 5-14. *At that time :* Jesus said to his disciples : I go to him that sent me, and none of you asketh me : Whither goest thou ? But because I have spoken these things to you, sorrow hath filled your heart. But I tell you the truth. It is expedient to you that I go : for if I go not, the Paraclete will not come to you ; but if I go, I will send him to you. And when he is come, he will convince the world of sin, and of justice, and of

judgment.   Of sin : because they believed not in
me.   And of justice : because I go to the Father
and you shall see me no longer.   And of judgment :
because the prince of this world is already judged.
I have yet many things to say to you : but you
cannot bear them now.   But when he, the Spirit
of Truth, is come, he will teach you all truth.
For he shall not speak of himself ; but what things
soever he shall hear, he shall speak ; and the things
that are to come he shall show you.   He shall
glorify me : because he shall receive of mine, and
shall show IT to you.   CREDO.

FIFTH SUNDAY AFTER EASTER.

EPISTLE.   *James* i. 22-27.   *Dearly beloved :*
Be ye doers of the word, and not hearers only,
deceiving your own selves.   For if a man be a hearer
of the word and not a doer, he shall be compared
to a man beholding his own countenance in a glass.
For he beheld himself and went his way, and presently forgot what manner of man he was.   But he
that hath looked into the perfect law of liberty,
and hath continued therein, not becoming a forgetful
hearer, but a doer of the work : this man shall be
blessed in his deed.   And if any man think himself
to be religious, not bridling his tongue, but deceiving
his own heart, this man's religion is vain.   *Religion*
clean and undefiled before God and the Father, is
this : to visit the fatherless and the widows in their
tribulation ; and to keep one's self unspotted from
this world.

GOSPEL.   *John* xvi. 23-30.   *At that time :* Jesus
said to his disciples : Amen, amen, I say to you,
if you ask the Father anything in my name, he
will give it you.   Hitherto you have not asked anything in my name.   Ask and you shall receive, that
your joy may be full.   These things I have spoken
to you in proverbs.   The hour cometh when I will

no more speak to you in proverbs, but will show you plainly of the Father. In that day you shall ask in my name ; and I say not to you, that I will ask the Father for you. For the Father himself loveth you, because you have loved me, and have believed that I came out from God. I came forth from the Father, and am come into the world ; again I leave the world, and I go to the Father. His disciples say to him : Behold, now thou speakest plainly, and speakest no proverb. Now we know that thou knowest all things, and thou needest not that any man should ask thee. By this we believe that thou camest forth from God. CREDO.

ASCENSION DAY.

LESSON. *Acts* i. 1-11. The former treatise I made, O Theophilus, of all things which Jesus began to do and to teach, until the day on which, giving commandments by the Holy Ghost to the Apostles whom he had chosen, he was taken up. To whom also he showed himself alive after his passion, by many proofs, for forty days appearing to them and speaking of the kingdom of God. And eating together with them, he commanded them that they should not depart from Jerusalem, but should wait for the promise of the Father, which you have heard (saith he) by my mouth ; for John indeed baptized with water, but you shall be baptized with the Holy Ghost not many days hence. They therefore who were come together asked him, saying : Lord, wilt thou at this time restore again the kingdom to Israel ? But he said to them : It is not for you to know the times or moments which the Father hath put in his own power ; but you shall receive the power of the Holy Ghost coming upon you, and you shall be witnesses unto me in Jerusalem, and in all Judea and Samaria, and even to the uttermost part of the earth. And when he had said these things, while they looked on, he was raised up, and a cloud received him out of their sight. And while they were beholding him going up to heaven, behold two men stood by them in white garments, who also said : Ye men of Galilee, why stand you looking up to heaven ? This Jesus who is taken up from you into heaven, shall so come as you have seen him going into heaven.

GOSPEL. *Mark* xvi. 14-20. *At that time :* Jesus appeared to the eleven as they were at table, and he upbraided them with their incredulity and hardness of heart, because they did not believe them who had seen him after he was risen again. And he said to them : Go ye into the whole world and preach the gospel to every creature. He that believeth, and is baptized, shall be saved ; but he that believeth not shall be condemned. And these signs shall follow them that believe : In my name they shall cast out devils ; they shall speak with new tongues ; they shall take up serpents, and if they shall drink any deadly thing, it shall not hurt them, they shall lay their hands upon the sick, and they shall recover. And the Lord Jesus, after he had spoken to them, was taken up into heaven, and sitteth on the right hand of God. But they going forth preached everywhere, the Lord working withal, and confirming the word with signs that followed. CREDO.

SUNDAY WITHIN OCTAVE OF ASCENSION.

EPISTLE. 1 *Peter* iv. 7-11. *Most dearly beloved :* Be prudent, and watch in prayers. But before all things, have a constant mutual charity among yourselves, for charity covereth a multitude of sins. Using hospitality one towards another without murmuring. As every man hath received grace ministering the same one to another, as good stewards of the manifold grace of God. If any man speak *let him speak* as the words of God. If any man minister, *let him do it* as of the power which God administereth ; that in all things God may be honoured through Jesus Christ, to whom is glory and empire for ever and ever. *Amen.*

GOSPEL. *John* xv. 26, 27, *and* xvi. 1-4. *At that time :* Jesus said to his disciples : When the Paraclete cometh, whom I will send you from the Father, the Spirit of Truth, who proceedeth from the Father, he shall give testimony of me ; and you shall give testimony, because you are with me from the beginning. [*Chap.* xvi. 1-4.] These things have I spoken to you, that you may not be scandalised. They will put you out of the synagogues ; yea, the hour cometh, that whosoever killeth you will think that he doth a service to God. And these things will they do to you, because they have not known the Father nor me. But these things I have told you, that when the hour shall come, you may remember that I told you of them. CREDO.

WHIT SUNDAY.

LESSON. *Acts* ii. 1-11. When the days of Pentecost were accomplished, they were all together in one place, and suddenly there came a sound from heaven as of a mighty wind coming, and it filled the whole house where they were sitting. And there appeared to them parted tongues as it were of fire, and it sat upon every one of them ; and they were all filled with the Holy Ghost, and they began to speak with divers tongues, according as the Holy Ghost gave them to speak. Now there were dwelling at Jerusalem, Jews, devout men out of every nation under heaven. And when this was noised abroad, the multitude came together, and were confounded in mind, because that every man heard them speak in his own tongue. And

they were all amazed, and wondered, saying :
Behold, are not all these that speak, Galileans ?
and how have we heard every man our own tongue
wherein we were born ?   Parthians, and Medes,
and Elamites, and inhabitants of Mesopotamia,
Judea, and Cappadocia, Pontus and Asia, Phrygia
and Pamphilia, Egypt, and the parts of Lybia
about Cyrene, and strangers of Rome, Jews also,
and proselytes, Cretes, and Arabians ; we have
heard them speak in our own tongues the wonderful
works of God.

GOSPEL. *John* xiv. **23-31.** *At that time :*
Jesus said to his disciples : If any one love me he
will keep my word, and my Father will love him,
and we will come to him, and will make our abode
with him.   He that loveth me not, keepeth not my
words.   And the word which you have heard is not
mine, but the Father's who sent me.   These things
have I spoken to you, abiding with you.   But the
Paraclete, the Holy Ghost, whom the Father will
send in my name, he will teach you all things,
and bring all things to your mind, whatsoever I
shall have said to you.   Peace I leave with you,
my peace I give unto you : not as the world giveth
do I give unto you.   Let not your heart be troubled,
nor let it be afraid.   You have heard that I said to
you : I go away, and I come unto you.   If you
loved me, you would indeed be glad, because I go
to the Father : for the Father is greater than I.
And now I have told you before it come to pass,
that when it shall come to pass you may believe.
I will not now speak many things with you.   For
the prince of this world cometh, and in me he hath
not anything.   But that the world may know that
I love the Father : and as the Father hath given
me commandment, so do I. CREDO.

TRINITY SUNDAY.

EPISTLE. *Rom.* xi. 33-36. O the depth of the riches of the wisdom and of the knowledge of God ! How incomprehensible are his judgments, and how unsearchable his ways ! For who hath known the mind of the Lord ? Or who hath been his counsellor ? Or who hath first given to him, and recompense shall be made him ? For of him, and by him, and in him are all things : to him be glory for ever. *Amen.*

GOSPEL. *Matt.* xxviii. 18-20. *At that time :* Jesus said to his disciples : All power is given to me in heaven and in earth. Going, therefore, teach ye all nations, *baptizing them in the name of the Father, and of the Son, and of the Holy Ghost.* Teaching them to observe all things whatsoever I have commanded you : and behold I am with you all days even to the consummation of the world. CREDO.

GOSPEL *of the First Sunday after Pentecost. Luke* vi. 36-42. *At that time :* Jesus said to his disciples : Be ye merciful, as your Father also is merciful. Judge not, and you shall not be judged. Condemn not, and you shall not be condemned. Forgive, and you shall be forgiven. Give, and it shall be given to you : good measure and pressed down and shaken together and running over shall they give into your bosom. For with the same measure that you shall mete withal, it shall be measured to you again. And he spoke also to them a similitude : Can the blind lead the blind ? do they not both fall into the ditch ? The disciple is not above his master : but everyone shall be perfect, if he be as his master. And why seest thou the mote in thy brother's eye ; but the beam that is in thy own eye thou considerest not ? Or how canst thou say to thy brother : Brother, let me pull the mote out of thy eye, when thou thyself seest not the beam in thy own eye ? Hypocrite, cast first the beam out of thy own eye, and then shalt thou see clearly to take out the mote from thy brother's eye. *Deo Gratias.*

CORPUS CHRISTI.

EPISTLE. 1 *Cor.* xi. 23-29. *Brethren :* I have received of the Lord that which also I delivered unto you that the Lord Jesus, the same night in which he was betrayed, took bread, and giving thanks, broke, and said : Take ye and eat : this is my body which shall be delivered for you ; this do for the commemoration of me. In like manner also the chalice, after he had supped, saying : This chalice is the New Testament in my blood ; this do ye, as often as you shall drink, for the commemoration of me. For as often as you shall eat this bread, and drink the chalice, you shall show the death of the Lord, until he come. Therefore, whosoever shall eat this bread or drink the chalice of the Lord unworthily, shall be guilty of the body and of the blood of the Lord. But let a man prove himself ; and so let him eat of that bread, and drink of the chalice. For he that eateth and drinketh unworthily, eateth and drinketh judgment to himself, not discerning the body of the Lord.

GOSPEL *John* vi. 56-59. *At that time :* Jesus said to the multitude of the Jews : My flesh is meat indeed, and my blood is drink indeed. He that eateth my flesh and drinketh my blood, abideth in me, and I in him. As the living Father hath sent me, and I live by the Father ; so he that eateth me, the same also shall live by me. This is the bread that came down from heaven. Not as your fathers did eat manna, and are dead. He that eateth this bread shall live for ever. CREDO.

SECOND SUNDAY AFTER PENTECOST.

EPISTLE. 1 *John* iii. 13-18. *Dearly beloved :* Wonder not if the world hate you. We know that we have passed from death to life, because we love the brethren. He that loveth not, abideth in death. Whosoever hateth his brother is a murderer. And you know that no murderer hath eternal life abiding in himself. In this we have known the charity of God, because he hath laid down his life for us ; and we ought to lay down our lives for the brethren. He that hath the substance of this world, and shall see his brother in need, and shall shut up his bowels from him, how doth the charity of God abide in him ? My little children, let us not love in word nor in tongue, but in deed and in truth.

GOSPEL. *Luke* xiv. 16-24. *At that time :* Jesus spoke this parable to the Pharisees : A certain man made a great supper and invited many, and he sent his servant at the hour of supper to say to them that were invited, that they should come, for now all things are ready. And they began all at once to make excuse. The first said to him : I have bought a farm, and I must needs go out and see it ; I pray thee hold me excused. And another said : I have bought five yoke of oxen and I go to try them ; I pray thee hold me excused. And another said : I have married a wife, and therefore I cannot come. And the servant returning, told these things to his lord. Then the master of the house being angry said to his servant : Go out quickly into the streets and lanes of the city, and bring in hither the poor, and the feeble, and the blind, and the lame. And the servant said : Lord, it is done as thou hast commanded, and yet there is room. And the lord said to the servant : Go out into the highways and hedges, and compel them to come in, that my house may be filled. But I say unto you, that none of those men that were invited, shall taste of my supper. CREDO.

THIRD SUNDAY AFTER PENTECOST.

EPISTLE. 1 *Peter* v. 6-11. *Dearly beloved :* Be you humbled therefore under the mighty hand of God, that he may exalt you in the time of visitation. Casting all your care upon him, for he hath care of you. Be sober and watch : because your adversary the devil, as a roaring lion, goeth about seeking whom he may devour : whom resist ye, strong in faith ; knowing that the same affliction befalls your brethren who are in the world. But the God of all grace, who hath called us unto his eternal glory in Christ Jesus, after you have suffered a little, will himself perfect you and confirm you and establish you. To him be glory and empire for ever and ever. *Amen.*

GOSPEL. *Luke* xv. 1-10. *At that time :* The publicans and sinners drew near unto him to hear him. And the Pharisees and scribes murmured, saying : This man receiveth sinners and eateth with them. And he spoke to them this parable, saying : What man of you that hath a hundred sheep, and if he shall lose one of them, doth he not leave the ninety-nine in the desert, and go after that which was lost until he find it ? And when he hath found it, lay it upon his shoulders rejoicing : and coming home, call together his friends and neighbours, saying to them : Rejoice with me, because I have found my sheep that was lost ? I say to you, that even so, there shall be joy in heaven upon one sinner that doth penance, more than upon ninety-nine just men who need not penance. Or what woman having ten groats, if she lose one groat, doth not light a candle, and sweep the house, and seek diligently until she find it ? And when she hath found it, call together her friends and neighbours, saying : Rejoice with me, because I have found the groat which I had lost ? So I say to you, there shall be joy before the angels of God upon one sinner doing penance. CREDO.

FOURTH SUNDAY AFTER PENTECOST.

EPISTLE. *Rom.* viii. 18-23. *Brethren :* I reckon that the sufferings of this time are not worthy to be compared with the glory to come, that shall be revealed in us. For the expectation of the creature waiteth for the revelation of the sons of God. For the creature was made subject to vanity, not willingly, but by reason of him that made it subject, in hope : because the creature also itself shall be delivered from the servitude of corruption, into the liberty of the glory of the children of God. For we know that every creature groaneth and travaileth in pain even till now. And not only it, but ourselves also, who have the first fruits of the Spirit, even we ourselves groan within ourselves, waiting for the adoption of the sons of God, the redemption of our body *in Christ Jesus our Lord.*

GOSPEL. *Luke* v. 1-11. *At that time :* It came to pass, that when the multitude pressed upon him to hear the word of God, he stood by the lake of Genesareth, and saw two ships standing by the lake ; but the fishermen were gone out of them, and were washing their nets. And going up into one of the ships that was Simon's, he desired him to draw back a little from the land. And sitting, he taught the multitudes out of the ship. Now when he had ceased to speak, he said to Simon : Launch out into the deep, and let down your nets for a draught. And Simon answering said to him : Master, we have laboured all the night and have

taken nothing ; but at thy word, I will let down the
net. And when they had done this, they enclosed
a very great multitude of fishes, and their net
broke. And they beckoned to their partners that
were in the other ship, that they should come and
help them. And they came, and filled both the
ships, so that they were almost sinking. Which
when Simon Peter saw, he fell down at Jesus' knees,
saying : Depart from me, for I am a sinful man,
O Lord. For he was wholly astonished, and all
that were with him, at the draught of fishes which
they had taken. And so were also James and John,
the sons of Zebedee, who were Simon's partners.
And Jesus saith to Simon : Fear not, from henceforth thou shalt catch men. And having brought
their ships to land, leaving all things, they followed
him. CREDO.

FIFTH SUNDAY AFTER PENTECOST.

EPISTLE. 1 *Peter* iii. 8-15. *Dearly beloved :*
Be ye all of one mind, having compassion one for
another, being lovers of the brotherhood, merciful,
modest, humble ; not rendering evil for evil, nor
railing for railing, but contrariwise, blessing : for
unto this are you called, that you may inherit a
blessing. " For he that will love life, and see good
days, let him refrain his tongue from evil, and his
lips that they speak no guile. Let him decline from
evil, and do good ; let him seek after peace and pursue it : because the eyes of the Lord are upon the
just, and his ears unto their prayers ; but the
countenance of the Lord upon them that do evil
things." And who is he that can hurt you if you
be zealous of good ? But if also you suffer anything
for justice' sake, blessed are ye. And be not afraid
of their fear, and be not troubled. But sanctify
the Lord Christ in your hearts.

GOSPEL. *Matt.* v. 20-24. *At that time : Jesus*

said to his disciples : Unless your justice abound
more than that of the scribes and Pharisees, you
shall not enter into the kingdom of heaven. You
have heard that it was said to them of old : Thou
shalt not kill. And whosoever shall kill shall be
in danger of the judgment. But I say to you, that
whosoever is angry with his brother, shall be in
danger of the judgment. And whosoever shall say
to his brother, *Raca*, shall be in danger of the
council. And whosoever shall say, Thou fool, shall
be in danger of hell fire. If therefore thou offer
thy gift at the altar, and there thou remember that
thy brother hath anything against thee ; leave
there thy offering before the altar, and go first and
be reconciled to thy brother, and then coming thou
shalt offer thy gift. CREDO.

SIXTH SUNDAY AFTER PENTECOST.

EPISTLE. *Rom.* vi. 3-11. *Brethren :* All we
who are baptized in Christ Jesus, are baptized in
his death. For we are buried together with him
by baptism into death : that as Christ is risen from
the dead by the glory of the Father, so we also may
walk in newness of life. For if we have been planted
together in the likeness of his death, we shall be also
in the likeness of his resurrection. Knowing this,
that our old man is crucified with him, that the body
of sin may be destroyed, to the end that we may
serve sin no longer. For he that is dead is justified
from sin. Now if we be dead with Christ, we believe
that we shall live also together with Christ. Knowing that Christ, rising again from the dead, dieth
now no more, death shall no more have dominion
over him. For in that he died to sin, he died once ;
but in that he liveth, he liveth unto God. So do
you also reckon that you are dead to sin, but alive
unto God in Christ Jesus our Lord.

GOSPEL. *Mark* viii. 1-9. *At that time :* When there was a great multitude with Jesus, and had nothing to eat, calling his disciples together, he said to them : I have compassion on the multitude, for behold they have now been with me three days, and have nothing to eat : and if I shall send them away fasting to their home, they will faint in the way : for some of them came from afar off. And his disciples answered him : From whence can anyone fill them here with bread in the wilderness ? And he asked them : How many loaves have ye ? Who said : Seven. And taking the seven loaves, giving thanks, he broke, and gave to his disciples for to set before them ; and they set them before the people. And they had a few little fishes ; and he blessed them, and commanded them to be set before them. And they did eat and were filled. And they took up that which was left of the fragments, seven baskets. And they that had eaten were about four thousand ; and he sent them away. CREDO.

SEVENTH SUNDAY AFTER PENTECOST.

EPISTLE. *Rom.* vi. 19-23. *Brethren :* I speak a human thing, because of the infirmity of your flesh ; for as you have yielded your members to serve uncleanness and iniquity unto iniquity, so now yield your members to serve justice unto sanctification. For when you were the servants of sin you were free men to justice. What fruit therefore had you then in those things of which you are now ashamed ? For the end of them is death. But now being made free from sin, and become servants of God, you have your fruit unto sanctification, and the end life everlasting. For the wages of sin is death ; but the grace of God, life everlasting, in Christ Jesus our Lord.

GOSPEL. *Matt.* vii. 15-21. *At that time : Jesus said to his disciples :* Beware of false prophets, who come to you in the clothing of sheep, but inwardly they are ravening wolves. By their fruits you shall know them. Do men gather grapes of thorns, or figs of thistles ? Even so every good tree bringeth forth good fruit, and the evil tree bringeth forth evil fruit. A good tree cannot bring forth evil fruit, neither can an evil tree bring forth good fruit. Every tree that bringeth not forth good fruit shall be cut down, and shall be cast into the fire. Wherefore, by their fruits you shall know them. Not every one that saith to me : Lord, Lord, shall enter into the kingdom of heaven ; but he that doth the will of my Father who is in heaven, he shall enter into the kingdom of heaven. CREDO.

EIGHTH SUNDAY AFTER PENTECOST.

EPISTLE. *Rom.* viii. 12-17. *Brethren :* We are debtors, not to the flesh, to live according to the flesh. For if you live according to the flesh, you shall die ; but if by the spirit you mortify the deeds of the flesh, you shall live. For whosoever are led by the Spirit of God, they are the sons of God. For you have not received the spirit of bondage again in fear ; but you have received the spirit of adoption of sons, whereby we cry : Abba (Father). For the Spirit himself giveth testimony to our spirit, that we are the sons of God. And if sons, heirs also ; heirs indeed of God, and joint-heirs with Christ.

GOSPEL. *Luke* xvi. 1-9. *At that time : Jesus spoke to his disciples this parable :* There was a certain rich man who had a steward ; and the same was accused unto him, that he had wasted his goods. And he called him, and said to him : How is it

that I hear this of thee ? give an account of thy
stewardship, for now thou canst be steward no
longer.   And the steward said within himself :
What shall I do, because my lord taketh away
from me the stewardship ?   To dig I am not able ;
to beg I am ashamed.   I know what I will do,
that when I shall be removed from the stewardship,
they may receive me into their houses.   Therefore,
calling together every one of his lord's debtors,
he said to the first : How much dost thou owe my
lord ?   But he said : A hundred barrels of oil.
And he said to him : Take thy bill, and sit down
quickly, and write fifty.   Then he said to another :
And how much dost thou owe ?   Who said : A
hundred quarters of wheat.   He said to him :
Take thy bill, and write eighty.   And the lord
commended the unjust steward, forasmuch as he
had done wisely.   For the children of this world
are wiser in their generation than the children of
light.   And I say to you : Make unto you friends
of the mammon of iniquity, that when you shall
fail, they may receive you into everlasting dwellings.
CREDO.

NINTH SUNDAY AFTER PENTECOST.

EPISTLE.   1 *Cor.* x. 6-13.   *Brethren : Let us*
not covet evil things, as they also coveted.   Neither
become ye idolaters, as some of them ; as it is
written : " The people sat down to eat and drink,
and rose up to play."   Neither let us commit fornication, as some of them committed fornication,
and there fell in one day three-and-twenty thousand.
Neither let us tempt Christ, as some of them tempted,
and perished by the serpents.   Neither do you
murmur, as some of them murmured, and were
destroyed by the destroyer.   Now all these things
happened to them in figure ; and they are written
for our correction, upon whom the ends of the world

are come. Wherefore he that thinketh himself
to stand, let him take heed lest he fall. Let no
temptation take hold on you, but such as is human.
And God is faithful, who will not suffer you to be
tempted above that which you are able, but will
make also with temptation issue, that you may be
able to bear it.

GOSPEL. *Luke* xix. 41-47. *At that time :*
When he drew near to Jerusalem, seeing the city
he wept over it, saying : If thou also hadst known,
and that in this thy day, the things that are to thy
peace ; but now they are hidden from thy eyes.
For the days shall come upon thee, and thy enemies
shall cast a trench about thee, and compass thee
round, and straiten thee on every side, and beat
thee flat to the ground, and thy children who are
in thee ; and they shall not leave in thee a stone
upon a stone : because thou hast not known the
time of thy visitation. And entering into the temple,
he began to cast out them that sold therein, and
them that bought, saying to them : It is written :
" My house is the house of prayer." But you have
made it a den of thieves. And he was teaching daily
in the temple. CREDO.

TENTH SUNDAY AFTER PENTECOST.

EPISTLE. 1 *Cor.* xii. 2-11. *Brethren :* You
know that when you were heathens, you went to
dumb idols, according as you were led. Wherefore
I give you to understand, that no man speaking
by the Spirit of God, saith anathema to Jesus.
And no man can say the Lord Jesus, but by the
Holy Ghost. Now there are diversities of graces,
but the same Spirit. And there are diversities of
ministries, but the same Lord. And there are
diversities of operations, but the same God, who
worketh all in all. And the manifestation of the

Spirit is given to every man unto profit. To one, indeed, by the Spirit, is given the word of wisdom ; and to another, the word of knowledge, according to the same Spirit ; to another, faith in the same Spirit; to another, the grace of healing in one Spirit; to another, the working of miracles; to another, prophecy ; to another, the discerning of spirits ; to another, divers kinds of tongues ; to another, interpretation of speeches. But in all these things, one and the same Spirit worketh, dividing to every one according as he will.

GOSPEL. *Luke* xviii. 9-14. *At that time : Jesus spoke this parable* to some who trusted in themselves as just, and despised others : Two men went up into the temple to pray ; the one a Pharisee and the other a publican. The Pharisee, standing, prayed thus with himself : O God, I give thee thanks that I am not as the rest of men, extortioners, unjust, adulterers, as also is this publican. I fast twice in a week ; I give tithes of all that I possess. And the publican standing afar off, would not so much as lift up his eyes towards heaven ; but struck his breast, saying : O God, be merciful to me a sinner. I say to you, this man went down to his house justified rather than the other ; because every one that exalteth himself shall be humbled ; and he that humbleth himself shall be exalted. CREDO.

ELEVENTH SUNDAY AFTER PENTECOST.

EPISTLE. 1 *Cor.* xv. 1-10. *Brethren :* I make known unto you the gospel which I preached to you, which also you have received, and wherein you stand ; by which also you are saved, if you hold fast after what manner I preached unto you, unless you have believed in vain. For I delivered unto you first of all, which I also received: how that

Christ died for our sins, according to the scriptures, and that he was buried; and that he rose again the third day, according to the scriptures; and that he was seen by Cephas, and after that by the eleven. Then was he seen by more than five hundred brethren at once; of whom many remain unto this present, and some are fallen asleep. After that he was seen by James, then by all the apostles, and last of all, he was seen also by me, as by one born out of due time. For I am the least of the apostles, who am not worthy to be called an apostle, because I persecuted the church of God. But by the grace of God I am what I am; and his grace in me hath not been void.

GOSPEL. *Mark* vii. 31-37. *At that time:* Jesus going out of the coasts of Tyre, he came by Sidon to the sea of Galilee, through the midst of the coasts of Decapolis. And they bring to him one deaf and dumb, and they besought him that he would lay his hand upon him. And taking him from the multitude apart, he put his fingers into his ears, and spitting, he touched his tongue, and looking up to heaven, he groaned and said to him: Ephpheta, which is, Be thou opened. And immediately his ears were opened, and the string of his tongue was loosed, and he spoke right. And he charged them that they should tell no man. But the more he charged them, so much the more a great deal did they publish it. And so much the more did they wonder, saying: He hath done all things well; he hath made both the deaf to hear and the dumb to speak. CREDO.

TWELFTH SUNDAY AFTER PENTECOST.

EPISTLE. 2 *Cor.* iii. 4-9. *Brethren:* And such confidence we have through Christ towards God; not that we are sufficient to think anything of our-

selves, as of ourselves ; but our sufficiency is from
God. Who also hath made us fit ministers of the
New Testament, not in the letter, but in the spirit.
For the letter killeth, but the spirit quickeneth.
Now if the ministration of death, engraven with
letters upon stones, was glorious, so that the children
of Israel could not steadfastly behold the face of
Moses, for the glory of his countenance, which is
made void ; how shall not the ministration of the
Spirit be rather in glory ? For if the ministration
of condemnation be glory, much more the ministration of justice aboundeth in glory.

GOSPEL. *Luke* x. 23-37. *At that time :* Jesus
said to his disciples : Blessed are the eyes that see
the things which you see. For I say to you, that
many prophets and kings have desired to see the
things that you see, and have not seen them ;
and to hear the things that you hear, and have
not heard them. And behold, a certain lawyer
stood up, tempting him, and saying : Master,
what must I do to possess eternal life ? But he
said to him : What is written in the law ? how
readest thou ? He answering, said : " Thou shalt
love the Lord thy God with thy whole heart, and
with thy whole soul, and with all thy strength,
and with all thy mind ; and thy neighbour as
thyself." And he said to him : Thou hast answered
right ; this do, and thou shalt live. But he, willing
to justify himself, said to Jesus : And who is my
neighbour ? And Jesus answering, said : A certain
man went down from Jerusalem to Jericho, and
fell among robbers, who also stripped him, and
having wounded him went away, leaving him half
dead. And it chanced that a certain priest went
down the same way, and seeing him passed by.
In like manner also a Levite, when he was near the
place and saw him, passed by. But a certain

Samaritan being on his journey, came near him; and seeing him, was moved with compassion. And going up to him, bound up his wounds, pouring in oil and wine; and setting him upon his own beast, brought him to an inn, and took care of him. And the next day he took out two pence, and gave to the host, and said : Take care of him ; and whatsoever thou shalt spend over and above, I, at my return, will repay thee. Which of these three in thy opinion was neighbour to him that fell among the robbers ? But he said : He that showed mercy to him. And Jesus said to him : Go, and do thou in like manner. CREDO.

THIRTEENTH SUNDAY AFTER PENTECOST.

EPISTLE. *Gal.* iii. 16-22. *Brethren :* To Abraham were the promises made, and to his seed. He saith not : And to his seeds, as of many ; but as of one : And to thy seed, which is Christ. Now this I say, that the testament which was confirmed by God, the law which was made after four hundred and thirty years, doth not disannul to make the promise of no effect. For, if the inheritance be of the law, it is no more of promise. But God gave it to Abraham by promise. Why then was the law ? It was set because of transgressions, until the seed should come, to whom he made the promise, being ordained by angels in the hand of a mediator. Now a mediator is not of one : but God is one. Was the law then against the promises of God ? God forbid. For if there had been a law given which could give life, verily justice should have been by the law. But the scripture hath concluded all under sin, that the promise by the faith of Jesus Christ might be given to them that believe.

GOSPEL. *Luke* xvii. 11-19. *At that time :* As he was going to Jerusalem, he passed through the midst of Samaria and Galilee. And as he entered into a certain town, there met him ten men that were lepers, who stood afar off, and lifted up their voice, saying : Jesus, Master, have mercy on us. Whom when he saw, he said : Go, show yourselves to the priests. And it came to pass, that as they went, they were made clean. And one of them when he saw that he was made clean, went back, with a loud voice glorifying God. And he fell on his face before his feet, giving thanks : and this was a Samaritan. And Jesus answering, said : Were not ten made clean, and where are the nine ? There is no one found to return and give glory to God, but this stranger. And he said to him : Arise, go thy way, for thy faith hath made thee whole. CREDO.

FOURTEENTH SUNDAY AFTER PENTECOST.

EPISTLE. *Gal.* v. 16-24. *Brethren :* Walk in the spirit, and you shall not fulfil the lusts of the flesh. For the flesh lusteth against the spirit : and the spirit against the flesh : for these are contrary one to another, so that you do not the things that you would. But if you are led by the spirit, you are not under the law. Now the works of the flesh are manifest, which are, fornication, uncleanness, immodesty, luxury, idolatry, witchcrafts, enmities, contentions, emulations, **wraths**, quarrels, dissensions, sects, envy, murders, drunkenness, revellings, and such like. Of the which I foretell you, as I have foretold to you, that they who do such things shall not obtain the kingdom of God. But the fruit of the spirit is charity, joy, peace, patience, benignity, goodness, longanimity, mildness, faith, modesty, continency, chastity. Against such there is no law. And they that are Christ's have crucified their flesh with the vices and concupiscences.

GOSPEL. *Matt.* vi. 24-33. *At that time : Jesus said to his disciples :* No man can serve two masters. For either he will hate the one, and love the other ; or he will sustain the one, and despise the other. You cannot serve God and mammon. Therefore I say to you, be not solicitous for your life, what you shall eat, nor for your body, what you shall put on. Is not the life more than the meat, and the body more than the raiment ? Behold the birds of the air, for they neither sow, nor do they reap, nor gather into barns, and your heavenly Father feedeth them. Are not you of much more value than they ? And which of you, by taking thought, can add to his stature one cubit ? And for raiment why are you solicitous ? Consider the lilies of the field, how they grow ; they labour not, neither do they spin. But I say to you, that not even Solomon in all his glory was arrayed as one of these. And if the grass of the field which is to-day, and to-morrow is cast into the oven, God doth so clothe : how much more you, O ye of little faith. Be not solicitous, therefore, saying : What shall we eat, or what shall we drink, or wherewith shall we be clothed ? For after all these things do the heathens seek. For your Father knoweth that you have need of all these things. Seek ye therefore first the kingdom of God, and his justice, and all these things shall be added unto you. CREDO.

FIFTEENTH SUNDAY AFTER PENTECOST.

EPISTLE. *Gal.* v. 25, 26, *and* vi. 1-10. *Brethren :* If we live in the Spirit, let us also walk in the Spirit. Let us not be made desirous of vain glory, provoking one another, envying one another. [*Chap.* vi. 1-10.] Brethren, and if a man be overtaken in any fault, you, who are spiritual, instruct such a one in the spirit of meekness, considering thyself, lest thou also be tempted. Bear ye one

another's burdens ; and so you shall fulfil the law
of Christ. For if any man think himself to be
something, whereas he is nothing, he deceiveth
himself. But let every one prove his own work,
and so he shall have glory in himself only, and
not in another. For every one shall bear his own
burden. And let him that is instructed in the word
communicate to him that instructeth him, in all
good things. Be not deceived, God is not mocked.
For what things a man shall sow, those also shall
he reap. For he that soweth in his flesh, of the
flesh also shall reap corruption. But he that
soweth in the spirit, of the spirit shall reap life
everlasting. And in doing good let us not fail.
For in due time we shall reap, not failing. Therefore,
whilst we have time, let us work good to all men,
but especially to those who are of the household
of faith.

GOSPEL. *Luke* vii. 11-16. *At that time :* Jesus
went into a city called Naim ; and there went with
him his disciples, and a great multitude. And
when he came nigh to the gate of the city, behold
a dead man was carried out, the only son of his
mother, and she was a widow, and a great multitude
of the city was with her. Whom when the Lord had
seen, being moved with mercy towards her, he said
to her : Weep not. And he came near and touched
the bier. And they that carried it, stood still.
And he said : Young man, I say to thee, arise.
And he that was dead sat up, and began to speak.
And he gave him to his mother. And there came a
fear on them all ; and they glorified God, saying :
A great prophet is risen up among us, and God
hath visited his people.

SIXTEENTH SUNDAY AFTER PENTECOST.
EPISTLE. *Ephes.* iii. 13-21. *Brethren :* I
pray you not to faint at my tribulations for you,

which is your glory.　For this cause I bow my knees
to the Father of our Lord Jesus Christ, of whom
all paternity in heaven and earth is named, that
he would grant you according to the riches of his
glory, to be strengthened by his spirit with might
unto the inward man.　That Christ may dwell by
faith in your hearts, that being rooted and found
in charity, you may be able to comprehend,
with all the saints, what is the breadth, and length,
and height, and depth : to know also the charity
of Christ, which surpasseth all knowledge, that
you may be filled unto all the fulness of God.　Now
to him who is able to do all things more abundantly
than we desire or understand, according to the
power that worketh in us, to him be glory in the
church, and in Christ Jesus, unto all generations,
world without end.　Amen.

GOSPEL.　*Luke* xiv. 1-11.　*At that time :* When
Jesus went into the house of one of the chief of
the Pharisees on the Sabbath-day to eat bread
they watched him.　And behold there was a
certain man before him that had the dropsy.　And
Jesus answering, spoke to the lawyers and Pharisees,
saying : Is it lawful to heal on the Sabbath day ?
But they held their peace.　But he, taking him,
healed him, and sent him away.　And answering
them, he said : Which of you shall have an ass or
an ox fall into a pit, and will not immediately draw
him out on the Sabbath day ?　And they could not
answer him as to these things.　And he spoke a
parable also to them that were invited, marking
how they chose the first seats at the table, saying
to them : When thou art invited to a wedding,
sit not down in the first place, lest, perhaps, one
more honourable than thou be invited by him, and
he that invited thee and him come and say to thee :
Give this man place, and then thou begin with shame

to take the lowest place. But when thou art invited,
go, sit down in the lowest place, that when he who
invited thee cometh, he may say to thee : Friend,
go up higher. Then shalt thou have glory before
them that sit at table with thee, because every one
that exalted himself shall be humbled, and he
that humbleth himself shall be exalted. CREDO.

SEVENTEENTH SUNDAY AFTER PENTECOST.

EPISTLE. *Ephes. iv. 1-6. Brethren :* I, therefore, a prisoner in the Lord, beseech you that you
walk worthy of the vocation in which you are called
With all humility and mildness, with patience,
supporting one another in charity. Careful to keep
the unity of the Spirit in the bond of peace. One
body and one spirit, as you are called in one hope
of your calling. One Lord. one faith, one baptism.
One God and Father of all, who is above all, and
through all, and in us all, *who is blessed for evermore.*

GOSPEL. *Matt. xxii. 35-46. At that time :*
The Pharisees came to Jesus : And one of them,
a doctor of the law, asked him, tempting him :
Master, which is the great commandment of the
law ? Jesus said to him : *Thou shalt love the Lord*
thy God with thy whole heart, and with thy whole
soul, and with thy whole mind. This is the greatest
and the first commandment. And the second is
like to this : *Thou shalt love thy neighbour as thyself.*
On these two commandments dependeth the whole
law and the prophets. And the Pharisees being
gathered together, Jesus asked them saying :
What think you of Christ ? Whose son is he ?
They say to him : David's. He saith to them :
How then doth David in spirit call him Lord,
saying : *The Lord said to my Lord, Sit on my right*
hand until I make thy enemies thy footstool ? If
David then call him Lord, how is he his son ?

And no man was able to answer him a word ; neither durst any man from that day forth ask him any more questions. CREDO.

EIGHTEENTH SUNDAY AFTER PENTECOST.

EPISTLE. 1 *Cor.* i. 4-8. *Brethren :* I give thanks to my God always for you, for the grace of God that is given you in Christ Jesus ; that in all things you are made rich in him, in all utterance, and in all knowledge as the testimony of Christ was confirmed in you. So that nothing is wanting to you in any grace, waiting for the manifestation of our Lord Jesus Christ. Who also will confirm you unto the end without crime in the day of the coming of our Lord Jesus Christ.

GOSPEL. *Matt.* ix. 1-8 *At that time : Jesus* entering into a boat, he passed over the water and came into his own city. And behold they brought to him one sick of the palsy, lying in a bed. And Jesus seeing their faith, said to the man sick of the palsy : Be of good heart, son, thy sins are forgiven thee. And, behold some of the scribes said within themselves : He blasphemeth. And Jesus seeing their thoughts, said : Why do you think evil in your hearts ? Whether is it easier to say : Thy sins are forgiven thee ; or to say : Arise and walk ? But that you may know that the Son of Man hath power on earth to forgive sins (then said he to the man sick of the palsy), Arise, take up thy bed, and go into thy house. And he arose and went into his house. And the multitude seeing it, feared and glorified God that gave such power to men. CREDO.

NINETEENTH SUNDAY AFTER PENTECOST.

EPISTLE. *Ephes.* iv. 23-28. *Brethren :* Be renewed in the spirit of your mind ; and put on the new man, who, according to God, is created in

justice, and holiness of truth. Wherefore putting
away lying, speak ye the truth every man with
his neighbour, for we are members one of another.
Be angry and sin not. Let not the sun go down
upon your anger. Give not place to the devil.
He that stole, let him now steal no more ; but
rather let him labour, working with his hands the
thing which is good, that he may have something
to give to him that suffereth need.

GOSPEL. *Matt.* xxii. 1-14. *At that time :* Jesus
answering, spoke again in parables to them, saying :
The kingdom of heaven is likened to a king, who made
a marriage for his son. And he sent his servants
to call them that were invited to the marriage :
and they would not come. Again he sent other
servants, saying : Tell them that were invited :
Behold, I have prepared my dinner ; my beeves
and fatlings are killed, and all things are ready :
come ye to the marriage. But they neglected and
went their ways, one to his farm, and another to
his merchandise. And the rest laid hands on his
servants, and having treated them contumeliously,
put them to death. But when the king had heard
of it, he was angry, and sending his armies, he
destroyed those murderers, and burnt their city.
Then he said to his servants : The marriage indeed
is ready, but they that were invited, were not
worthy. Go ye therefore into the highways, and
as many as you shall find, call to the marriage.
And his servants going forth into the ways, gathered
together all they found, both bad and good ; and
the marriage was filled with guests. And the king
went in to see the guests, and he saw there a man
who had not on a wedding garment. And he
saith to him : Friend, how camest thou in hither,
not having on a wedding garment ? But he was
silent. Then the king said to the waiters : Bind his

hands and feet, and cast him into the exterior darkness : there shall be weeping and gnashing of teeth. For many are called, but few are chosen. CREDO.

TWENTIETH SUNDAY AFTER PENTECOST.

EPISTLE. *Ephes.* v. 15-21. *Brethren :* See, therefore, how you walk circumspectly, not as unwise, but as wise ; redeeming the time, because the days are evil. Wherefore become not unwise ; but understanding what is the will of God. And be not drunk with wine, wherein is luxury, but be ye filled with the Holy Spirit, speaking to yourselves in psalms and hymns and spiritual canticles, singing and making melody in your hearts to the Lord ; giving thanks always for all things in the name of our Lord Jesus Christ, to God, and the Father. Being subject one to another in the fear of Christ.

GOSPEL. *John.* iv. 46-53. *At that time :* There was a certain ruler whose son was sick at Capharnaum. He having heard that Jesus was come from Judea into Galilee, went to him and prayed him to come down and heal his son, for he was at the point of death. Jesus, therefore, said to him : Unless you see signs and wonders, you believe not. The ruler saith to him : Lord, come down before that my son die. Jesus saith to him : Go thy way, thy son liveth. The man believed the word which Jesus said to him, and went his way. And as he was going down, his servants met him : and they brought word, saying that his son lived. He asked, therefore, of them the hour wherein he grew better. And they said to him : Yesterday at the seventh hour the fever left him. The father, therefore, knew that it was at the same hour that Jesus said to him : Thy son liveth ; and himself believed and his whole house. CREDO.

TWENTY-FIRST SUNDAY AFTER PENTECOST.

EPISTLE. *Ephes.* vi. 10-17. *Brethren :* Be strengthened in the Lord and in the might of his power. Put you on the armour of God, that you may be able to stand against the deceits of the devil, for our wrestling is not against flesh and blood but against principalities and powers, against the rulers of the world of this darkness, against the spirits of wickedness in the high places. Therefore take unto you the armour of God, that you may be able to resist in the evil day, and to stand in all things perfect. Stand, therefore, having your loins girt about with truth, and having on the breast-plate of justice, and your feet shod with the preparation of the gospel of peace ; in all things taking the shield of faith, wherewith you may be able to extinguish all the fiery darts of the most wicked one. And take unto you the helmet of salvation, and the sword of the Spirit, which is the word of God.

GOSPEL. *Matt.* xviii. 23-35. *At that time :* *Jesus spoke to his disciples this parable :* The kingdom of heaven is likened to a king who would take an account of his servants. And when he had begun to take the account, one was brought to him that owed him ten thousand talents. And as he had not wherewith to pay it, his lord commanded that he should be sold, and his wife and children, and all that he had, and payment to be made. But that servant falling down, besought him, saying : Have patience with me, and I will pay thee all. And the lord of that servant being moved with pity, let him go, and forgave him the debt. But when that servant was gone out, he found one of his fellow-servants that owed him a hundred pence ; and laying hold of him, he throttled him, saying : Pay what thou owest. And his

fellow-servant falling down, besought him, saying :
Have patience with me, and I will pay thee all.
And he would not; but went and cast him into prison
till he paid the debt. Now his fellow-servants
seeing what was done, were very much grieved,
and they came and told their lord all that was done.
Then his lord called him, and said to him : Thou
wicked servant, I forgave thee all the debt because
thou besoughtest me ; shouldst not thou then have
had compassion also on thy fellow-servant, even
as I had compassion on thee ? And his lord being
angry, delivered him to the torturers, until he paid
all the debt. So also shall my heavenly Father do
to you, if you forgive not every one his brother
from your hearts. CREDO.

TWENTY-SECOND SUNDAY AFTER PENTECOST.

EPISTLE. *Philip.* i. 6-11. *Brethren :* Being
confident of this very thing, that he who hath begun
a good work in you will perfect it unto the day of
Christ Jesus. As it is meet for me to think this
for you all : for that I have you in my heart :
and that in my bands, and in the defence and cor-
firmation of the gospel, you are all partakers of
my joy. For God is my witness, how I long after
you all in the bowels of Jesus Christ. And this I
pray, that your charity may more and more abound
in knowledge and in all understanding ; that you
may approve the better things ; that you may be
sincere and without offence unto the day of Christ.
Filled with the fruit of justice, through Jesus Christ,
unto the glory and praise of God.

GOSPEL. *Matt.* xxii. 15-21. *At that time :* The
Pharisees going, consulted among themselves how
to ensnare *Jesus* in his speech. And they sent to
him their disciples, with the Herodians, saying :
Master, we know that thou art a true speaker,

and teachest the way of God in truth, neither carest
thou for any man, for thou dost not regard the person
of men. Tell us, therefore, what dost thou think ?
Is it lawful to give tribute to Cæsar, or not ? But
Jesus, knowing their wickedness, said : Why do ye
tempt me, ye hypocrites ? Show me the coin of the
tribute. And they offered him a penny. And
Jesus saith to them : Whose image and inscription
is this ? They say to him : Cæsar's. Then he saith
to them : Render therefore to Cæsar the things
that are Cæsar's, and to God the things that are
God's. CREDO.

TWENTY-THIRD SUNDAY AFTER PENTECOST.

Should there be but twenty-three Sundays after
Pentecost, the Mass of the twenty-fourth is said to-day,
and this on the preceding Saturday (if it be neither a
double nor a semi-double), in which case it is said on
some vacant day before it.

EPISTLE. *Philip.* iii. 17-21, *and* iv. 1-3. *Brethren:*
Be followers of me, and observe them who walk
so as you have our model. For many walk, of whom
I have told you often (and now tell you weeping),
that they are enemies of the cross of Christ, whose
end is destruction, whose God is their belly, and
whose glory is in their shame ; who mind earthly
things. But our conversation is in heaven : from
whence also we look for the Saviour, our Lord Jesus
Christ, who will reform the body of our lowness,
made like to the body of his glory, according to the
operation whereby also he is able to subdue all things
unto himself. [*Chap.* iv. 1-3.] Therefore, my dearly
beloved brethren, and most desired, my joy, and
my crown ; so stand fast in the Lord, my dearly
beloved. I beg of Evodia, and I beseech Syntyche,
to be of one mind in the Lord. And I entreat thee
also, my sincere companion, help those women,
who have laboured with me in the gospel, with

Clement and the rest of my fellow-labourers, whose names are in the book of life.

GOSPEL. *Matt.* ix. 18-26. *At that time :* As *Jesus* was speaking these things unto them, behold, a certain ruler came up and adored him, saying : Lord, my daughter is even now dead ; but come, lay thy hand upon her, and she shall live. And Jesus rising up, followed him, with his disciples. And, behold, a woman who was troubled with an issue of blood twelve years, came behind him and touched the hem of his garment. For she said within herself : If I shall touch only his garment, I shall be healed. But Jesus turning and seeing her, said : Be of good heart, daughter, thy faith hath made thee whole. And the woman was made whole from that hour. And when Jesus was come into the house of the ruler, and saw the minstrels and the multitude making a rout, he said : Give place ; for the girl is not dead, but sleepeth. And they laughed him to scorn. And when the multitude was put forth, he went in, and took her by the hand. And the maid arose. And the fame hereof went abroad into all that country. CREDO.

As there cannot be less than twenty-three, nor more than twenty-eight Sundays after Pentecost, it is to be observed that the Mass of the twenty-fourth is always said on that Sunday which immediately precedes Advent When, therefore, it happens that there are any intervening Sundays between the twenty-third and the last, the Epistles and Gospels are taken from the Sundays which were omitted after Epiphany ; for instance, if but one Sunday, the Mass is of the sixth after Epiphany ; if two, of the fifth and sixth : if three, of the fourth, fifth, and sixth ; and if four, of the third, fourth, fifth, and sixth.

TWENTY-FOURTH, OR LAST SUNDAY AFTER PENTECOST.

EPISTLE. *Coloss.* i. 9-14. *Brethren :* We cease not to pray for you, and to beg that you may be filled with the knowledge of his will, in all wisdom and spiritual understanding ; that you may walk worthy of God, in all things pleasing, being fruitful in every good work. and increasing in the knowledge of God ; strengthened with all might, according to the power of his glory, in all patience and long-suffering with joy. Giving thanks to God the Father, who hath made us worthy to be partakers of the lot of saints in light ; who hath delivered us from the power of darkness, and hath translated us into the kingdom of the Son of his love, in whom we have redemption through his blood, the remission of sins.

GOSPEL. *Matt.* xxiv. 15-35. *At that time : Jesus said to his disciples :* When, therefore, you shall see the *abomination of desolation*, which was spoken of by Daniel the prophet, standing in the holy place, he that readeth let him understand. Then they that are in Judea, let them flee to the mountains ; and he that is on the house-top, let him not come down to take anything out of his house ; and he that is in the field, let him not go back to take his coat. And woe to them that are with child and that give suck in those days. But pray that your flight be not in the winter or on the Sabbath. For there shall be then great tribulation, such as hath not been from the beginning of the world until now, neither shall be. And unless those days had been shortened, no flesh should be saved ; but for the sake of the elect, those days shall be shortened. Then if any man shall say to you : Lo, here is Christ, or there, do not believe him. For there shall arise false Christs and false prophets, and shall show great signs and wonders, insomuch as to deceive (if possible) even the elect. Behold, I have told it to you beforehand ; if there-fore, they shall say to you: Behold, he is in the desert, go ye not out : Behold, he is in the closets, believe it not. For as lightning cometh out of the east and appeareth even into the west, so shall also the coming of the Son of Man be. Wheresoever the body shall be, there shall the eagles also be gathered together. And immediately after the tribulation of those days, the sun shall be darkened, and the moon shall not give her light, and the stars shall fall from heaven, and the powers of heaven shall be moved : and then shall appear the sign of the Son of Man in heaven ; and then shall all tribes of the earth mourn ; and they shall see the Son of Man coming in the clouds of heaven with much power and majesty. And he shall send his angels, with a trumpet and a great voice ; and they shall gather together his elect from the four winds, from the farthest parts of the heavens to the utmost bounds of them. And from the fig-tree learn a parable ; when the branch thereof is now tender, and the leaves come forth, you know that summer is nigh. So you also, when you shall see all these things, know ye that it is nigh, *even* at the door. Amen I say to you, that this generation shall not pass, till all these things be done. Heaven and earth shall pass, but my words shall not pass. CREDO.

The Proper of Saints.

IMMACULATE CONCEPTION OF THE BLESSED VIRGIN MARY.

December 8.

LESSON. *Prov.* viii. 22-35. The Lord possessed me in the beginning of his ways, before he made anything, from the beginning. I was set up from eternity, and of old, before the earth was made. The depths were not as yet, and I was already conceived, neither had the fountains of waters as yet

sprung out ; the mountains with their huge bulk
had not as yet been established : before the hills I
was brought forth : he had not yet made the earth,
nor the rivers, nor the poles of the world. When
he prepared the heavens, I was present : when,
with a certain law and compass, he enclosed the
depths : when he established the sky above, and
poised the fountains of waters : when he compassed
the sea with its bounds and set a law to the waters,
that they should not pass their limits : when he
balanced the foundations of the earth, I was with
him, forming all things, and was delighted every day,
playing before him at all times, playing in the world :
and my delights were to be with the children of men.
Now, therefore, ye children, hear me : blessed are
they that keep my ways. Hear instruction and be
wise, and refuse it not. Blessed is the man that
heareth me, and that watcheth daily at my gates
and waiteth at the posts of my doors. He that
shall find me shall find life, and shall have salvation
from the Lord.

GOSPEL. *Matt.* i. 1-16. The book of the genera-
tion of Jesus Christ, the son of David, the son of
Abraham. Abraham begot Isaac. And Isaac
begot Jacob. And Jacob begot Judas and his
brethren. And Judas begot Phares and Zara of
Thamar. And Phares begot Esron. And Esron
begot Aram. And Aram begot Aminadab. And
Aminadab begot Naasson. And Naasson begot
Salmon. And Salmon begot Booz of Rahab. And
Booz begot Obed of Ruth. And Obed begot Jesse.
And Jesse begot David the king. And David the
King begot Solomon, of her that had been *the wife of*
Urias. And Solomon begot Roboam. And Roboam
begot Abia. And Abia begot Asa. And Asa begot
Josaphat. And Josaphat begot Joram. And
Joram begot Ozias. And Ozias begot Joatham.
And Joatham begot Achaz. And Achaz begot

Ezechias. And Ezechias begot Manasses. And Manasses begot Amon. And Amon begot Josias. And Josias begot Jechonias and his brethren in the transmigration of Babylon. And after the transmigration of Babylon, Jechonias begot Salathiel. And Salathiel begot Zorobabel. And Zorobabel begot Abiud. And Abiud begot Eliacim. And Eliacim begot Azor. And Azor begot Sadoc. And Sadoc begot Achim. And Achim begot Eliud. And Eliud begot Eleazar. And Eleazar begot Mathan. And Mathan begot Jacob. And Jacob begot Joseph, the husband of Mary, of whom was born Jesus, who is called Christ.

St. Patrick, Patron of Ireland.
March 17.

LESSON. *Ecclus.* xliv., xlv. Behold a great priest, who in his time pleased God, and was found just ; and in the time of wrath became an atonement. There were none found like him in observing the law of the Most High. Therefore by an oath did the Lord make him great amongst his people. He gave him the blessing of all nations, and established his covenant on his head. He acknowledged him in his blessing, he stored up his mercy for him, and he found favour in the eyes of the Lord. [*Chap.* xlv.] He exalted him in the sight of kings, and gave him a crown of glory. He made with him an eternal covenant, and bestowed on him a great priesthood, and rendered him blessed in glory. To perform the priestly office, to sing praises to the name of God, and offer him precious incense for an odour of sweetness.

GOSPEL. *Matt.* xxv. 14-23. *At that time : Jesus spoke this parable to his disciples :* A man, going into a far country, called his servants, and delivered to them his goods. And to one he gave

five talents, and to another two, and to another one,
to everyone according to his proper ability ; and
immediately he took his journey. And he that
had received the five talents went his way, and
traded with the same, and gained other five. And
in like manner he that had received the two, gained
other two. But he that had received the one, going
his way, digged into the earth and hid his lord's
money. But after a long time the lord of those
servants came, and reckoned with them. And he
that had received the five talents, coming, brought
other five talents, saying : Lord, thou didst deliver
to me five talents ; behold I have gained other five
over and above. His lord said to him : Well done,
good and faithful servant ; because thou hast been
faithful over a few things, I will place thee over many
things ; enter thou into the joy of thy lord. And
he also that had received the two talents came and
said : Lord, thou deliveredst two talents to me ;
behold I have gained other two. His lord said to
him : Well done, good and faithful servant ;
because thou hast been faithful over a few things,
I will place thee over many things ; enter thou into
the joy of thy lord.

ANNUNCIATION OF THE BLESSED VIRGIN MARY.

March 25.

LESSON. *Isaias* vii. 10-15. *In those days :*
The Lord spoke unto Achaz, saying : Ask thee a
sign of the Lord thy God, either unto the depth of
hell, or unto the height above. And Achaz said :
I will not ask, and I will not tempt the Lord. And
he said : Hear ye, therefore, O house of David :
Is it a small thing for you to be grievous to men,
that you are grievous to my God also ? Therefore
the Lord himself shall give you a sign. Behold
a virgin shall conceive and bear a son, and his name
shall be called.Emmanuel. He shall eat butter and

honey, that he may know to refuse the evil, and to choose the good.

GOSPEL. *Luke* i. 26-38. *At that time* : The Angel Gabriel was sent from God unto a city of Galilee called Nazareth, to a virgin espoused to a man whose name was Joseph, of the house of David ; and the virgin's name was Mary. And the angel being come in, said unto her : Hail Mary, full of grace, the Lord is with thee ; blessed art thou among women. Who having heard was troubled at his saying, and thought with herself what manner of salutation this should be. And the angel said to her : Fear not, Mary, for thou hast found grace with God. Behold, thou shalt conceive in thy womb, and shalt bring forth a son, and thou shalt call his name *Jesus.* He shall be great, and shall be called the Son of the Most High, and the Lord God shall give unto him the throne of David his father. And he shall reign in the house of Jacob for ever, and of his kingdom there shall be no end. And Mary said to the angel : How shall this be done, because I know not man ? And the angel answering, said to her : The Holy Ghost shall come upon thee, and the power of the Most High shall overshadow thee. And therefore also the Holy which shall be born of thee shall be called the Son of God. And behold thy cousin Elizabeth, she also hath conceived a son in her old age, and this is the sixth month with her that is called barren ; because no word shall be impossible with God. And Mary said : Behold the handmaid of the Lord ; be it done to me according to thy word.

SS. PETER AND PAUL.

June 29.

LESSON. *Acts.* xii. 1-11. *In those days :* Herod the king stretched forth his hands to afflict some of the church. And he killed James the brother of John with the sword. And seeing that it pleased the Jews, he proceeded to take up Peter also. Now it was in the days of azymes. And when he had apprehended him, he cast him into prison, delivering him to four files of soldiers to be kept, intending after the pasch to bring him forth to the people. Peter therefore was kept in prison. But prayer was made without ceasing by the church unto God for him. And when Herod would have brought him forth, the same night Peter was sleeping between two soldiers, bound with two chains, and the keepers before the door kept the prison. And, behold, an angel of the Lord stood by him, and a light shined in the room ; and he, striking Peter on the side, raised him up, saying : Arise quickly. And the chains fell off from his hands. And the angel said to him : Gird thyself, and put on thy sandals. And he did so. And he said to him : Cast thy garment about thee, and follow me. And going out, he followed him, and he knew not that it was true which was done by the angel, but thought he saw a vision. And passing through the first and second ward, they came to the iron gate that leadeth to the city, which of itself opened to them. And, going out, they passed on through one street, and immediately the angel departed from him. And Peter, coming to himself, said: Now I know in very deed that the Lord hath sent his angel, and hath delivered me out of the hand of Herod, and from all the expectation of the people of the Jews.

GOSPEL. *Matt.* xvi. 13-19. *At that time* : Jesus came into the quarters of Cesarea Philippi, and he asked his disciples saying : Whom do men say that the Son of Man is ? But they said : Some, John the Baptist, and other some, Elias, and others, Jeremias, or one of the prophets. Jesus saith to them : But whom do you say that I am : Simon

Peter answered and said : Thou art Christ, the Son of the living God. And Jesus answering, said to him : Blessed art thou, Simon Bar-Jona, because flesh and blood hath not revealed it to thee, but my Father who is in heaven. And I say to thee : That thou art Peter, and upon this rock I will build my church, and the gates of hell shall not prevail against it. And I will give to thee the keys of the kingdom of heaven. And whatsoever thou shalt bind upon earth, it shall be bound also in heaven ; and whatsoever thou shalt loose on earth it shall be loosed also in heaven. CREDO.

ASSUMPTION OF THE BLESSED VIRGIN MARY.

August 15.

LESSON. *Ecclus*. xxiv. 11-20. I sought rest *everywhere*, and I shall abide in the inheritance of the Lord. Then the Creator of all things commanded and said to me : and he that made me rested in my tabernacle, and he said to me : Let thy dwelling be in Jacob, and thy inheritance in Israel, and take root in my elect. From the beginning, and before the world, was I created, and unto the world to come I shall not cease to be, and in the holy dwelling-place, I have ministered before him. And so was I established in Sion, and in the holy city likewise I rested, and my power was in Jerusalem. And I took root in an honourable people, and in the portion of my God his inheritance, and my abode is in the full assembly of saints. I was exalted like a cedar in Libanus, and as a cypress-tree on Mount Sion. I was exalted like a palm-tree in Cades, and as a rose-plant in Jericho ; as a fair olive-tree in the plains, and as a plane-tree by the water in the streets, was I exalted. I gave a sweet smell like cinnamon and aromatical balm. I yielded a sweet odour like the best myrrh.

GOSPEL. *Luke* x. 38-42. *At that time : Jesus*
entered into a certain town, and a certain woman
named Martha received him into her house. And
she had a sister called Mary, who, sitting also at
the Lord's feet, heard his word. But Martha was
busy about much serving. Who stood and said :
Lord, hast thou no care that my sister hath left
me alone to serve ? Speak to her, therefore, that
she help me. And the Lord answering, said to her,
Martha, Martha, thou art careful and art troubled
about many things. But one thing is necessary.
Mary hath chosen the best part, which shall not be
taken away from her. CREDO.

FEAST OF ALL SAINTS.

November 1.

LESSON. *Apoc.* vii. 2-12. *In those days :*
Behold I, John, saw another angel ascending from
the rising of the sun, having the sign of the living
God ; and he cried with a loud voice to the four
angels, to whom it was given to hurt the earth
and the sea, saying : Hurt not the earth, nor the
sea, nor the trees, till we sign the servants of our
God in their foreheads. And I heard the number of
them that were signed, an hundred forty-four
thousand were signed of every tribe of the children
of Israel. Of the tribe of Judah, *were* twelve thousand
signed ; of the tribe of Reuben, twelve thousand
signed ; of the tribe of Gad, twelve thousand signed :
of the tribe of Aser, twelve thousand signed ; of the
tribe of Nephthali, twelve thousand signed ; of
the tribe of Manasses, twelve thousand signed ;
of the tribe of Simeon, twelve thousand signed ;
of the tribe of Levi, twelve thousand signed ; of the
tribe of Issachar, twelve thousand signed ; of the
tribe of Zabulon, twelve thousand signed ; of the
tribe of Joseph, twelve thousand signed ; of the
tribe of Benjamin, twelve thousand signed. After

this I saw a great multitude which no man could
number, of all nations and tribes, and peoples and
tongues, standing before the throne and in sight
of the Lamb, clothed with white robes, and palms
in their hands : and they cried with a loud voice,
saying : Salvation to our God who sitteth upon
the throne, and to the Lamb.   And all the angels
stood round about the throne, and the ancients
and the four living creatures : and they fell down
before the throne upon their faces, and adored God,
saying :   Amen :   Benediction,   and   glory,   and
wisdom, and thanksgiving, honour, and power, and
strength to our God for ever and ever.   Amen.

GOSPEL. *Matt.* v. 1-12.   *At that time : Jesus*
seeing the multitudes, went up into a mountain,
and when he was set down, his disciples came unto
him.   And opening his mouth he taught them,
saying : Blessed are the poor in spirit ; for theirs
is the kingdom of heaven.   Blessed are the meek ;
for they shall possess the land.   Blessed are they
that mourn ; for they shall be comforted.   Blessed
are they that hunger and thirst after justice ; for
they shall have their fill.   Blessed are the merciful ;
for they shall obtain mercy.   Blessed are the clean of
heart : for they shall see God.   Blessed are the peace-
makers ; for they shall be called the children of God.
Blessed are they that suffer persecution for justice'
sake ; for theirs is the kingdom of heaven.   Blessed
are ye when they shall revile you, and persecute
you, and speak all that is evil against you untruly,
for my sake : be glad and rejoice, for your reward
is very great in heaven.   CREDO.

COMMEMORATION OF THE FAITHFUL DEPARTED.
November 2.

EPISTLE. 1 *Cor.* xv. 51-57.   *Brethren :* Behold
I tell you a mystery : We shall all indeed rise again ;

but we shall not all be changed. In a moment, in the twinkling of an eye, at the last trumpet : for the trumpet shall sound, and the dead shall rise again incorruptible : and we shall be changed. For this corruptible must put on incorruption : and this mortal must put on immortality. And when this mortal hath put on immortality then shall come to pass the saying that is written : Death is swallowed up in victory. O grave, where is thy victory ? O death, where is thy sting ? Now the sting of death is sin, and the strength of sin is the law. But thanks be to God, who hath given us the victory through our Lord Jesus Christ.

GOSPEL. *John* v. 25-29. *At that time : Jesus said to the multitude of the Jews :* Amen, amen, I say unto you, that the hour cometh, and now is, when the dead shall hear the voice of the Son of God, and they that hear shall live. For as the Father hath life in himself ; so he hath given to the Son also to have life in himself ; and he hath given him power to do judgment, because he is the Son of Man. Wonder not at this, for the hour cometh wherein all that are in the grave shall hear the voice of the Son of God. And they that have done good things shall come forth unto the resurrection of life ; but they that have done evil, unto the resurrection of judgment.

Common of Saints.

FOR THE VIGIL OF AN APOSTLE.

Which may be read on the festival day.

LESSON. *Ecclus.* xliv. *and* xlv. The blessing of the Lord is on the head of the righteous man. Therefore did the Lord give him an inheritance, and assign him a part among the twelve tribes ;

and he found grace in the sight of all flesh. And he made him great to the terror of his enemies, and by his words he tamed monsters. He rendered him glorious in the presence of kings, and gave him his commandment in the sight of his people, and showed him his glory. For his faith and meekness he sanctified him, and made choice of him among all flesh ; and publicly gave him his precepts, and the law of life and discipline, and highly exalted him. He settled with him an eternal covenant, and encompassed him with the girdle of righteousness ; and the Lord hath put on him a crown of glory.

GOSPEL. *John* xv. 12-16. *At that time : Jesus said to his disciples :* This is my commandment, that you love one another as I have loved you. Greater love than this no man hath, that a man lay down his life for his friends. You are my friends, if you do the things that I command you. I will not now call you servants, for the servant knoweth not what his lord doth. But I have called you friends, because all things whatsoever I have heard of my Father, I have made known to you. You have not chosen me, but I have chosen you and have appointed you, that you should go, and should bring forth fruit, and your fruit should remain ; that whatsoever you shall ask of the Father in my name, he may give it you.

OF A MARTYR AND BISHOP.

EPISTLE. *James* i. 12-18. *Dearly beloved :* Blessed is the man that endureth temptation ; for when he hath been proved, he shall receive the crown of life which God hath promised to them that love him. Let no man, when he is tempted, say that he is tempted by God. For God is not a tempter of evils, and he tempteth no man. But every man is tempted by his own concupiscence, being drawn

away and allured. Then when concupiscence hath
conceived, it bringeth forth sin. But sin, when
it is completed, begetteth death. Do not err,
therefore, my dearest brethren. Every best gift
and every perfect gift is from above, coming down
from the Father of lights, with whom there is no
change nor shadow of alteration. For of his own
will, hath he begotten us by the word of truth,
that we might be some beginning of his creatures.

GOSPEL. *Luke* xiv. 26-33. *At that time : Jesus
said to his disciples :* If any man come to me and
hate not his father, and mother, and wife, and children, and brethren, and sisters, yea, and his own life
also, he cannot be my disciple. And whosoever
doth not carry his cross and come after me, cannot
be my disciple. For which of you having a mind
to build a tower, doth not first sit down and reckon
the charges that are necessary, whether he have
wherewithal to finish it ; lest, after he had laid the
foundation, and is not able to finish it, all that see
it begin to mock him, saying : This man began
to build, and was not able to finish. Or what king
about to go and make war against another king,
doth not first sit down and think whether he be
able with ten thousand, to meet him that with
twenty thousand cometh against him. Or else,
whilst the other is yet afar off, sending an embassy,
he desireth conditions of peace. So likewise every
one of you that doth not renounce all that he
possesseth, cannot be my disciple.

Of a Martyr who was not a Bishop.

LESSON. *Wisdom* x. 10-14 *Wisdom conducted
the just man* through the right ways, and showed
him the kingdom of God, and gave him the knowledge of the holy things : made him honourable in
his labours, and accomplished his labours. In the

deceit of them that overreached him, she stood by him and made him honourable. She kept him safe from his enemies, and she defended him from seducers, and gave him a strong conflict that he might overcome, and know that wisdom is mightier than all. She forsook not the just when he was sold, but delivered him from sinners; she went down with him into the pit, and in bands she left him not, till she brought him the sceptre of the kingdom, and power against those that oppressed him: and showed them to be liars that had accused him, and gave him everlasting glory.

GOSPEL. *Matt.* x. 34-42. *At that time: Jesus said to his disciples:* Do not think that I came to send peace upon earth; I came not to send peace, but the sword. For I came to set a man at variance against his father, and the daughter against her mother, and the daughter-in-law against her mother-in-law. And a man's enemies shall be they of his own household. He that loveth father or mother more than me is not worthy of me: and he that loveth son or daughter more than me is not worthy of me. And he that taketh not up his cross and followeth me, is not worthy of me. He that findeth his life shall lose it: and he that shall lose his life for me shall find it. He that receiveth you receiveth me; and he that receiveth me receiveth him that sent me. He that receiveth a prophet in the name of a prophet, shall receive the reward of a prophet: and he that receiveth a just man in the name of a just man, shall receive the reward of a just man. And whosoever shall give to drink, to one of these little ones, a cup of cold water only in the name of a disciple, amen I say to you, he shall not lose his reward.

OF MANY MARTYRS.

EPISTLE. 1 *Peter* i. 3-7. Blessed be the God

and Father of our Lord Jesus Christ, who, according to his great mercy hath regenerated us unto a lively hope, by the resurrection of Jesus Christ from the dead, unto an inheritance incorruptible and undefiled, and that cannot fade, reserved in heaven for you, who, by the power of God, are kept by faith unto salvation, ready to be revealed in the last time. Wherein you shall greatly rejoice, if now you must be for a little time made sorrowful in divers temptations ; that the trial of your faith (much more precious than gold which is tried by the fire) may be found unto praise, and glory, and honour, at the appearing of Jesus Christ *our Lord.*

GOSPEL. *John* xv. 5-11. *At that time : Jesus said to his disciples :* I am the vine, you the branches. He that abideth in me, and I in him, the same bareth much fruit ; for without me you can do nothing. If any one abide not in me, he shall be cast forth as a branch, and shall wither, and they shall gather him up, and cast him into the fire, and he burneth. If you abide in me, and my words abide in you, you shall ask whatever you will, and it shall be done unto you. In this is my Father glorified, that you bring forth very much fruit, and become my disciples. As the Father hath loved me, I also have loved you. Abide in my love. If you keep my commandments, you shall abide in my love, as I also have kept my Father's commandments, and do abide in his love. These things have I spoken to you, that my joy may be in you, and your joy may be filled.

Of a Confessor (not a Bishop).

LESSON. *Ecclus.* xxxi. 8-11. Blessed is the rich man that is found without blemish, and that hath not gone after gold, nor put his trust in money nor in treasures. Who is he, and we will praise him ? for he hath done wonderful things in his life. Who hath been tried thereby and made perfect, he shall have glory everlasting. He that could have transgressed, and hath not transgressed ; and could do evil things, and hath not done them. Therefore are his goods established in the Lord, and all the church of the saints shall declare his alms.

GOSPEL. *Luke* xii. 35-40. *At that time : Jesus said to his disciples :* Let your loins be girt, and lamps burning in your hands, and you yourselves like to men who wait for their Lord, when he shall return from the wedding, that when he cometh and knocketh, they may open to him immediately. Blessed are those servants whom the Lord, when he cometh, shall find watching. Amen I say to you, that he will gird himself, and make them sit down to meat, and passing will minister unto them. And if he shall come in the second watch or come in the third watch, and find them so, blessed are those servants. But this know ye, that if the householder did know at what hour the thief would come, he would surely watch, and would not suffer his house to be broken open. Be you then also ready : for at what hour thou think not, the Son of Man will come.

Printed by BROWNE & NOLAN, LTD., *Dublin.*

Milton Keynes UK
Ingram Content Group UK Ltd.
UKHW021309210923
429120UK00013B/165